D0886832

Psychiatry and the Humanities, Volume 3

Psychoanalysis and Language

Assistant Editor
Gloria H. Parloff

Editorial Aide
Katherine S. Henry

Published under the auspices of the
Forum on Psychiatry and the Humanities
The Washington School of Psychiatry

Psychiatry and the Humanities

VOLUME 3

Psychoanalysis and Language

Editor
Joseph H. Smith, M.D.

New Haven and London   Yale University Press

1978

Published with assistance from
the Louis Stern Memorial Fund.

Designed by John O. C. McCrillis
and set in Baskerville type.
Printed in the United States of America by
The Vail-Ballou Press, Inc., Binghamton, N.Y.

Published in Great Britain, Europe, Africa, and
Asia (except Japan) by Yale University Press,
Ltd., London. Distributed in Australia and
New Zealand by Book & Film Services, Artarmon,
N.S.W., Australia; and in Japan by Harper & Row,
Publishers, Tokyo Office.

Library of Congress Cataloging in Publication Data
Main entry under title:

Psychoanalysis and language.

(Psychiatry and the humanities; v. 3)
Includes index.
1. Psycholinguistics—Addresses, essays, lectures.
2. Psychoanalysis—Addresses, essays, lectures.
I. Smith, Joseph H., 1927–   II. Series. [DNLM:
1. Language. 2. Psychoanalysis. W1 PS354T v. 3 /
WM460. 5.L2 P974]
RC321.P943 vol. 3 [BF455] 616.8'9'008s
ISBN 0-300-02249-2   [150'.19'5]   78-9156

Contributors

Noam Chomsky, Ph.D. Institute Professor, Department of Linguistics and Philosophy, Massachusetts Institute of Technology

Arthur C. Danto, Ph.D. Johnsonian Professor of Philosophy, Columbia University

Henry Edelheit, M.D. Training and Supervising Analyst, New York Psychoanalytic Institute

Marshall Edelson, M.D., Ph.D. Professor of Psychiatry, Yale University School of Medicine; Member, Western New England Institute for Psychoanalysis

Norman N. Holland, Ph.D. Director, Center for the Psychological Study of the Arts, State University of New York, Amherst, N.Y.

Stanley A. Leavy, M.D. Clinical Professor of Psychiatry, Yale University School of Medicine

Bonnie E. Litowitz, Ph.D. Assistant Professor, Department of Communicative Disorders, Northwestern University

Hans W. Loewald, M.D. Training Analyst and Faculty Member, Western New England Institute for Psychoanalysis; Clinical Professor of Psychiatry Emeritus, Yale University

Karl H. Pribram, M.D. Professor, Departments of Psychiatry and Psychology; Head, The Neuropsychology Laboratories, Stanford University

Paul Ricoeur, Ph.D. Professor, Divinity School, University of Chicago; Professor, Université de Nanterre (Paris)

Contents

Introduction

JOSEPH H. SMITH

In the final sentences of his introduction to chapter 7 of *The Interpretation of Dreams,* Freud wrote:

No conclusions upon the construction and working methods of the mental instrument can be arrived at or at least fully proved from even the most painstaking investigation of dreams or of any other mental function taken *in isolation.* To achieve this result, it will be necessary to correlate all the established implications derived from a comparative study of a whole series of such functions. Thus the psychological hypotheses to which we are led by an analysis of the processes of dreaming must be left, as it were, in suspense, until they can be related to the findings of other enquiries which seek to approach the kernel of the same problem from another angle. [1900, p. 511; Freud's italics]

In his article herein, "Language and Unconscious Knowledge," Noam Chomsky writes:

To gain further understanding of the general nature of the human mind, we should ask in what domains humans seek to develop complex intellectual structures in a more or less uniform way on the basis of restricted data. . . . Language is an obvious area. It might be argued that the major intellectual interest in the study of language lies in the fact that it is a complex domain, particularly amenable to study, distinctively human, and associated in the most intimate way with every aspect of human life. [pp. 35–36]

The contributions in this volume focus on the place of language in the development and general nature of the human mind, ranging from the purely linguistic perspective of Chomsky's paper, through comparative studies from various vantage points, to the purely psychoanalytic perspective of Hans Loewald's "Primary Process, Secondary Process, and Language." Both Chomsky and Loewald, probably the foremost theoreticians in their respective fields, disclaim systematic knowledge of the other's discipline. All other contributors have undertaken careful studies in both language and Freud's work. They offer here studies of Freud's thought as interpreted by Lacan— the latter a major source of current psychoanalytic interest in language (see Stanley Leavy's and Paul Ricoeur's contributions)—or of Freud's thought as correlative with their own or Chomsky's linguistic studies (Henry Edelheit, Karl Pribram, Marshall Edelson, Bonnie Litowitz, Paul Ricoeur) or of Freud's thought in the context of philosophical perspectives on language (Norman Holland, Arthur Danto). The essays also vary in their concepts of how best to approach the study of mind, and in their ideas of possible limitations on such study.

Rather than commenting on each of these studies, I shall focus on a question raised by Chomsky regarding the accessibility of unconscious mental processes. In so doing, I hope to underline some connections between the linguistic perspective epitomized by Chomsky and the psychoanalytic one epitomized by Loewald.

In tracing out Freud's position on the accessibility of unconscious psychic processes, the guiding point is that the repressed and the unconscious do not coincide.

Everything that is repressed must remain unconscious; but let us state at the very outset that the repressed does not cover everything that is unconscious.
The unconscious has a wider compass: the repressed
is a part of the unconscious. [1915, p. 166]

Freud wrote of three senses in which psychic processes
could be unconscious. Preconscious thought is merely latent—not at present conscious but easily available to consciousness. The dynamically repressed refers to ideational
representatives of instincts and their derivatives that are
barred from consciousness because any beginning of
entry signals danger. Entry into consciousness is possible,
but with difficulty. The third sense of *unconscious* refers to
aspects of psychic process that are in principle inaccessible to conscious perception. The latter would include
both Piaget's (1973) cognitive unconscious and unconscious knowledge as herein described by Chomsky. Since
most of the indexed references to unconscious thought in
the Standard Edition of Freud are to discussions of the
repressed (sense 2) rather than to discussions of processes
that are unconscious in principle (sense 3), the latter will
be outlined in some detail as a basis for an interpretation
other than that given by Chomsky (see his n. 9).
    Freud made no attempt to characterize the basic nature
or essence of the psychical. He did deny the equation between what is psychical and what is conscious.

No; being conscious cannot be the essence of what is
psychical. It is only a *quality* of what is psychical, and
an inconstant quality at that—one that is far oftener
absent than present. The psychical, whatever its nature may be, is in itself unconscious and probably
similar in kind to all the other natural processes of

which we have obtained knowledge. [1940b, p. 283; Freud's italics]

He also wrote:

The data of conscious self-perception . . . have proved in every respect inadequate to fathom the profusion and complexity of the processes of the mind, to reveal their interconnections and so to recognize the determinants of their disturbances.

The hypothesis we have adopted of a psychical apparatus extended in space . . . which gives rise to the phenomena of consciousness only at one particular point and under certain conditions—this hypothesis has put us in a position to establish psychology on foundations similar to those of any other science, such, for instance, as physics. In our science as in the others the problem is the same: behind the attributes (qualities) of the object under examination which are presented directly to our perception, we have to discover something else which is more independent of the particular receptive capacity of our sense organs and which approximates more closely to what may be supposed to be the real state of affairs. We have no hope of being able to reach the latter itself, since it is evident that everything new that we have inferred must nevertheless be translated back into the language of our perceptions, from which it is simply impossible for us to free ourselves. But herein lies the very nature and limitation of our science. It is as though we were to say in physics: 'If we could see clearly enough we should find that what appears to be a solid body is made up of particles of such and such a shape and size and occupying such and such relative positions.' In the meantime we try to increase the efficiency of our sense organs to the furthest pos-

sible extent by artificial aids; but it may be expected
that all such efforts will fail to affect the ultimate outcome. Reality will always remain 'unknowable'. The
yield brought to light by scientific work from our
primary sense perceptions will consist in an insight
into connections and dependent relations which are
present in the external world, which can somehow be
reliably reproduced or reflected in the internal world
of our thought and a knowledge of which enables us
to 'understand' something in the external world, to
foresee it and possibly to alter it. Our procedure in
psycho-analysis is quite similar. We have discovered
technical methods of filling up the gaps in the phenomena of our consciousness, and we make use of
those methods just as a physicist makes use of experiment. In this manner we infer a number of processes
which are in themselves 'unknowable' and interpolate
them in those that are conscious to us. And if, for instance, we say: 'At this point an unconscious memory
intervened', what that means is: 'At this point something occurred of which we are totally unable to
form a conception, but which, if it had entered our
consciousness, could only have been described in
such and such a way.' [1940a, pp. 196–97]

This is the broadest assertion of inaccessibility. It is the
Kantian point, repeated in a number of passages (for example, 1900, p. 613; 1915, p. 171; 1940a, pp. 158,
282–83), regarding the unknowability of the object in itself. Even with preconscious thought, which can be easily
brought into awareness, its unconscious persistence is inferred on good evidence but without proof and without
any conception of the form in which it persists while out
of awareness. It is assumed, that is, that some kind of
"transformation or translation" (1915, p. 166) occurs in

connection with a censorship at the point of transition, not only from unconsciousness to preconsciousness, but also from preconsciousness to consciousness (1915, pp. 193–94). Thus, no aspect of unconscious process, including no aspect of transformational process, is directly accessible to conscious perception. One only knows of such processes by inference and from their effects on consciousness. Freud wrote:

> It is true that the physician cannot learn of these unconscious processes until they have produced some effect upon consciousness which can be communicated or observed. But this conscious effect may exhibit a psychical character quite different from that of the unconscious process, so that internal perception cannot possibly regard the one as a substitute for the other. The physician must feel at liberty to proceed by *inference* from the conscious effect to the unconscious psychical process. He thus learns that the conscious effect is only a remote psychical result of the unconscious process and that the latter has not become conscious as such; and moreover that the latter was present and operative even without betraying its existence in any way to consciousness. [1900, p. 612; Freud's italics; see also 1915, p. 166]

On the principle of giving a reading that maintains consistency, the question, in reading Freud or Chomsky, is that of degrees and kinds of indirect accessibility. Unconscious processes of any class are, as such, inaccessible in principle to direct conscious perception. However, the inference—on good and sufficient reasons—of different classes of unconscious processes has led to the understandable but inaccurate phraseology of easy accessibility (preconscious thought), accessibility with difficulty (the dynamically repressed), and inaccessible in principle (unconscious processes other than preconscious or repressed ideation or thought). Chomsky suggests that the Freudian concept of unconscious processes does not include the latter. Freud asserted that his concept of the unconscious had assumed so many meanings—so profound an ambiguity—that

> we must admit that the characteristic of being unconscious begins to lose significance for us. It becomes a quality which can have many meanings, a quality which we are unable to make, as we should have hoped to do, the basis of far-reaching and inevitable conclusions. Nevertheless we must beware of ignoring this characteristic, for the property of being conscious or not is in the last resort our one beacon-light in the darkness of depth-psychology. [1923, p. 18]

In "The Unconscious" he wrote:

> Hence consciousness stands in no simple relation either to the different systems or to repression. The truth is that it is not only the psychically repressed that remains alien to consciousness, but also some of the impulses which dominate our ego—something, therefore, that forms the strongest functional antithesis to the repressed. The more we seek to win our way to a metapsychological view of mental life, the more we must learn to emancipate ourselves from the importance of the symptom of 'being conscious'. [1915, pp. 192–93]

In *The Ego and the Id,* he wrote:

> From the point of view of analytic practice, the consequence of this discovery is that we land in endless obscurities and difficulties if we keep to our habitual forms of expression and try, for instance, to derive

neuroses from a conflict between the conscious and unconscious. We shall have to substitute for this antithesis another, taken from our insight into the structural conditions of the mind—the antithesis between the coherent ego and the repressed which is split off from it. [1923, p. 17]

The citations above condense the reasons for and the fact of a major revision in Freud's theory of mind. In the first topography, the unconscious, the preconscious, and the conscious were conceived as systems, to be designated in that sense by the abbreviations *Ucs., Pcs.,* and *Cs.* The *Ucs.* as a system, later to be conceptualized as the id, referred to a drive-organized (Rapaport, 1951, pp. 696–97, 708), unconscious class of mental phenomena with freely mobile psychic energy and pleasure-principle regulation. The major role of what later would be conceptualized as the ego was vested in the *Pcs./Cs.* To the *Pcs.* were attributed conceptual organization (ibid.), easy access to consciousness, bound energy, and reality-principle regulation. *Cs.* was conceived of as "a sense organ for the apprehension of psychical qualities" (1900, pp. 574, 615). In *Pcs./Cs.*, attention/perception had the role that instinct had in the *Ucs.* (compare 1923, p. 25). The main conflict was joined at the border of *Ucs.* and *Pcs.* and was roughly characterized as being between unconscious impulsion and the dominant conscious organization.

The whole conceptual organization became unwieldy and finally unworkable. It was unwieldy, for instance, in that *unconscious* now had three meanings—the systematic (*Ucs.*), the dynamic (the repressed), and the descriptive (the quality of unconsciousness regardless of class—that is, preconscious, repressed, or otherwise unconscious). It was unworkable, as outlined above, in that psychic conflict did not fall between unconscious and conscious but between the dynamically repressed and what came to be conceptualized as the coherent ego.

Aspects of the ego as repressing agent (for example, the mechanisms of repression itself) and certain superego motives for repression (for example, unconscious reasons for guilt) were as unconscious as that which was repressed. Furthermore, conceptually organized (secondary-process) material (for example, fantasies [1915, pp. 190–91], but also "All the complicated processes of selection, rejection and decision" [1940b, p. 284] involved in difficult intellectual problems) could occur outside of conscious awareness, and drive-organized (primary-process) material could erupt into awareness.

For all these reasons, the second topography—the structural view of the mind as composed of id, ego, and superego—was introduced. Notwithstanding the fact that Freud in *Moses and Monotheism* (1939, p. 95) wrote *"Ucs."* (sometimes even incorrectly; 1923, p. 7), the second topography, in effect, removed the "the" from "the unconscious." There would no longer be "the unconscious" as one locale or one system or one grouping of mental phenomena to be given one systematic meaning by a consistent reading of the text, as Chomsky suggests; *unconscious* would henceforth be merely a quality that could pertain to aspects of id, ego, or superego phenomena.

The revision in *The Ego and the Id,* along with the not unrelated reversal in the theory of anxiety in *Inhibitions, Systems and Anxiety* (that is, reversing the theory that repression causes anxiety to the theory that the anxiety signal institutes repression), was a major move away from the early id psychology toward an ego psychology, and it lends itself to greater compatibility with the studies in cognitive psychology by both Piaget and Chomsky. Although the two hold different concepts of innatism (Smith, 1976a, pp. 152–53), the work of both is centered in what psychoanalytic theory conceptualizes as innate aspects of ego endowment (Freud, 1940a, p. 163)—"the inheritance of an intellectual disposition similar to the ordinary inheritance of an instinctual disposition" (Freud, 1939, p. 99).

I have attempted in the above discussion to show that Freud's position was that psychical processes are in themselves unconscious and thus are not accessible to direct conscious perception. The processes referred to are instinct, remembering, and thinking, as such, and the principles and structures that determine their representation and organization; perceptions and feelings are directly conscious. However, there are different kinds and degrees of indirect accessibility. Instincts as such are inaccessible (1915, p. 177). Instincts that have achieved representation are accessible via those representations; they are not purely inferred. Id contents that have not achieved representation, if there be such (1940a, p. 163; 1937, pp. 242–43; Loewald, 1972, pp. 236–37), are inaccessible, although whether in fact or in principle remains moot. Regulatory, representational, and organizational principles and structures are without quality (1900, p. 574) and are purely inferred—inaccessible in principle. There is access to memories and thought, but not to the processes of remembering (1950 [1895], p. 308) and thinking.

Rapaport's summary of the essential components of the general Freudian theory of consciousness is pertinent here:

> It is known to everyone who is familiar with psychoanalysis that Freud (1900) distinguished between *consciousness as a subjective experience* and the concept of the *system Conscious-Preconscious (Cs.-Pcs.)*. The latter was the predecessor of the *ego* concept of his

later, so-called structural theory. It is less well known that he also postulated an *apparatus of consciousness,* which he distinguished from both the subjective experience of consciousness and the system *Cs.-Pcs.* [see Gill, 1963]. The function of this apparatus was to account for the phenomenon of *subjective conscious experience.*

It is worth while, I believe, to stop here for a moment to remind ourselves that some psychologists have eschewed all reference to consciousness, i.e., to introspective reports, while others have made a more or less deliberate use of introspective reports in trying to discover the laws governing behavior. But it seems that Freud was the only one who proposed a psychological theory to explain the phenomenon of the subjective conscious experience. I would like to point out that whether the specific theory proposed by Freud is valid or not, the very program it implies, namely, the exploration of the processes underlying the phenomenon of subjective conscious experience by psychological methods, is one of his most significant and most overlooked contributions to psychological theory. It should be stressed that what he proposed in this theory was neither an explanation of the *contents* of consciousness, nor a physiological explanation of the phenomenon of consciousness, but a psychological explanation of the phenomenon of consciousness. . . . [Rapaport, 1960, p. 897; Rapaport's italics]

In the figurative terms of chapter 7 of *The Interpretation of Dreams,* the aspects of mentation that Freud pictured as accessible to consciousness in his model of mind were those which he described as the "virtual" product of, in themselves, inaccessible mental structures and processes. This interpretation can be defended in spite of—and partly because of—a passage that contradicts it.

> ideas, thoughts and psychical structures in general must never be regarded as localized in organic elements of the nervous system but rather, as one might say, *between* them, where resistances and facilitations [*Bahnungen*] provide the corresponding correlates. Everything that can be an object of our internal perception is *virtual,* like the image produced in a telescope by the passage of light-rays. But we are justified in assuming the existence of the systems (which are not in any way psychical entities themselves and can never be accessible to our psychical perception) like the lenses of the telescope, which cast the image. [1900, p. 611; Freud's italics]

The parentheses in the passage cited enclose either a misstatement—untrue to Freud's own text—or an unmarked condensation. In accord with the first possibility, he should have written "which, though psychic entities themselves, can never be accessible to our psychical perception." Obviously, the neurophysiological structures would not be accessible, but he had committed himself here to the concept of a *"psychical locality.* I shall entirely disregard the fact that the mental apparatus with which we are here concerned is also known to us in the form of an anatomical preparation, and I shall carefully avoid the temptation to determine psychical locality in any anatomical fashion. I shall remain upon psychological ground, and I propose simply to follow the suggestion that we should picture the instrument which carries out our mental functions as resembling a compound microscope or a photographic apparatus, or something of the kind" (1900, p. 536; Freud's italics).

At best, the passage on page 611 is an unmarked condensation of what might be a valid figurative portrayal at both neurophysiological and psychical levels. The entirety of what is psychical could be seen as located "between" elements of the nervous system in the sense he pictures it here, but only a part of what is psychical would have psychic quality such as to be an object of internal perception.

If by "virtual" he meant to portray the entirety of what is psychical, he should have written, "Everything that can be an object of our internal perception or our endopsychic perception," which would have been to say; "everything that could be the object of our conscious and unconscious knowledge." Internal perception refers to conscious perception of, first of all, inner sensations and feelings—for example, those belonging to the pleasure-unpleasure series—and, with the interposition of word-presentations, of internal thought-processes (1923, pp. 21–23). Endopsychic perception refers not to direct conscious perception at all, but to the indirect effects of unconscious knowledge. It is "the obscure recognition"—"a recognition which, of course, has nothing in the character of a [true] recognition"—"of psychical factors and relations in the unconscious" (1901, p. 258, and 258 n.). It is "conscious ignorance and unconscious knowledge" (1901, p. 258) of motivations, of repression (1907, p. 51), of what is repressed (1909, p. 164), and even of the "structural conditions" of mind (1913, p. 91). (It would not be the only instance of an inconsistency in the use of "internal perception." See the 1900, p. 612, passage cited on p. xiv.)

If the page 611 passage could be interpreted to mean that the whole of what is mental is, in principle, accessible to internal perception, it would amount to a throwback to the position of the *Project* (1950 [1895]), where the need for postulating any unconscious mental processes was entirely avoided in favor of attempting to construct a purely physical chain of neural events that would cover all the facts of observation. That position, discussed in Strachey's introduction to "The Unconscious" (pp. 161–65), was again mentioned by Freud in the *Outline* in a way that provides the corrective, emphasized by my italics, for what I have questioned as a misstatement in the chapter 7 passage.

> Many people, both inside and outside [psychological] science, are satisfied with the assumption that consciousness alone is psychical; in that case nothing remains for psychology but to discriminate among psychical phenomena between perceptions, feelings, thought-processes and volitions. It is generally agreed, however, that these conscious processes do not form unbroken sequences which are complete in themselves; there would thus be no alternative left to assuming that there are physical or somatic processes which are concomitant with the psychical ones and which we should necessarily have to recognize as more complete than the psychical sequences, since some of them would have conscious processes parallel to them but others would not. If so, it of course becomes plausible to lay the stress in psychology on these somatic processes, to see in *them* the true essence of what is psychical and to look for some other assessment of the conscious processes. The majority of philosophers, however, as well as many other people, dispute this and declare that the idea of something psychical being unconscious is self-contradictory.
>
> But that is precisely what psycho-analysis is obliged to assert. . . . *It explains the supposedly somatic concomi-*

tant phenomena as being what is truly psychical, and thus
in the first instance disregards the quality of consciousness. [1940a, pp. 157–58; my italics in second
paragraph; see also 1940b, p. 286]

I have felt it necessary to review these passages from
Freud—which to theoreticians are largely commonplace
psychoanalytic knowledge—because in other passages the
question of unconscious processes inaccessible in principle is stated much more ambiguously. The issue arose in
a discussion between Chomsky and members of a seminar
on psychoanalysis and language sponsored by the Forum
on Psychiatry and the Humanities. In response to
Chomsky's position in this seminar, I subsequently assembled illustrative references that I had judged were
clear indications of Freud's acknowledgment of a class of
unconscious processes inaccessible in principle. However,
a rereading revealed that in virtually every case, Freud
proceeds from a statement of inaccessibility to asserting
evidence for the validity of inferring a psychic unconscious not only on grounds of logical necessity but also by
way of illustrating forms of spontaneous return of the repressed and by marshaling evidence for how psychoanalytic intervention can, even though with difficulty, make
the unconscious conscious. Without an overall grasp of
the development of Freud's theory—especially without an
understanding of his reasons for introducing the second
topography—the nearly inevitable impression is that his
concept of unconscious processes refers to unconscious in
fact and does not include a class of phenomena unconscious in principle. If such an impression could be sustained in a careful reading, it would mean that the Freudian text could be the basis for only a theory of therapy
and not also an approach toward a theory of mind.
Of course, so far as a theory of mind is concerned,

what is missing in the work of Chomsky and Piaget—and quite rightly so, in view of their projects—is any adequate theory of motivation or of affect. Even with the development from an id to an ego psychology, the hallmark of the Freudian theory is the theory of instinct, and much of Freud's work was in explicating how unconscious motivations are made manifest in human thought, feeling, and action. Notwithstanding shorthand usage about making the unconscious conscious, I believe Freud's specific disclaimers cited above are sufficient to show that his meaning is not different from the idea that the deep structure of a sentence, though not itself directly accessible, is still made manifest in its surface structure.

Differences emerge, of course, in connection with the broader scope of psychoanalysis, and particularly in the actual practice, one might say, of psychoanalysis and linguistics. If the claims of psychoanalysis to be a general psychology are valid, the findings of cognitive psychology would relate to it as a branch, with linguistics as a branch of the latter, and studies in grammatical competence but one branch of linguistics. To the complexity and intricacy of Chomsky's theory of grammatical competence, it is thus necessary to add the complexity of any adequate theory of pragmatic competence that "places language in the institutional setting of its use, relating intentions and purposes to the linguistic means at hand" (Chomsky, this volume, p. 11).

Regarding practice, psychoanalysis is unique in that its mode of investigation is, simultaneously, a mode of therapy. Studies in grammatical competence can be undertaken in what Freud termed a "cool scientific interest" (1940a, p. 197) and the knowledge gained is relatively neutral. The same is true for psychoanalytic studies of all those phenomena that are unconscious in principle. But what is central to psychoanalysis as a therapy pertains to what is unconscious in fact—the dynamically repressed. If one engages in this study as an analysand, he (and his analyst) soon encounters the fact that he has a highly charged, sometimes life-or-death, personal stake in the study. But I am suggesting that even this highly charged class of unconscious phenomena can be considered purely from the point of view of cognitive psychology. There is a sense in which the overcoming of resistance that allows access to a previously repressed memory involves the same processes as those in any instance where an unconscious phenomenon—in fact or in principle—is made manifest in a surface representation, whether by transformative and interpretive processes or by inference to unobservables.

But in the therapeutic situation this is radically irrelevant. From the point of view of cognitive psychology and also of a general psychology, it is of importance in its own right that a person has unconscious knowledge of intricate methods for storing memory; that this knowledge is unconscious in principle—that is, that the shape of memory as stored is unconscious in principle; and that the means of recalling certain memories and also the means of averting the recall of certain memories are unconscious in principle. But what is relevant in the therapeutic situation is that the analysand knows—also unconsciously—that he is motivated to avoid the recall of certain memories—no matter the means of storage, recall, or avoidance of recall. The focus is on what would appear, and the danger involved, if recall were permitted, and this is how the struggle comes to be experienced, by analysand and analyst, as one of making the unconscious conscious, as though the memory had the same shape in repressed form as in overt appearance. The point is that at least some aspect of the dynamically repressed has, at some prior time, been manifest in conscious awareness. Freud put this in its extreme form when he wrote, "only something which has once been a *Cs.* perception can become conscious" (1923, p. 20).

Psychoanalytic theory assumes that the forerunner of the word is an image of the absent object (Smith, 1976a, b) and that this image, no matter what its initial coenesthetic shape, may be said to also represent, along with its associated affect, a need; it is in this way that drive or instinct achieves representation. Need and absence of the object constitute a danger situation. The image is at once a memory of and an anticipation of the presence of the object in a way that did and will allow for need resolution. In the human being this primary-process mode of thinking in images evolves into the capacity for secondary-process, language-based thought.

These assumptions run in no way counter to Chomsky's theory of language or the innatism concept of that theory. They are not directed toward explaining language, but toward locating language in the broader spectrum of phenomena that psychoanalytic theory is required to address. Language, as heir of the image of the absent object, represents both instinct and object. This is how Freud could write both that "only something which has once been a *Cs.* perception can become conscious" (1923, p. 20) and that "Everything conscious has an unconscious preliminary stage" (1900, p. 612). But locating language in this way highlights not only the cognitive role in relation to conscious and unconscious knowledge and conscious and unconscious error, but also the motivational and affective aspects of its role in differentiation and integration, alienation and reconciliation.

Freud wrote:

> Conscious processes on the periphery of the ego and everything else in the ego unconscious—such would

be the simplest state of affairs that we might picture. And such may in fact be the state that prevails in animals. But in men there is an added complication through which internal processes in the ego may also acquire the quality of consciousness. This is the work of the function of speech, which brings material in the ego into a firm connection with mnemic residues of visual, but more particularly of auditory, perceptions. Thenceforward the perceptual periphery of the cortical layer can be excited to a much greater extent from inside as well, internal events such as passages of ideas and thought-processes can become conscious, and a special device is called for in order to distinguish between the two possibilities—a device known as *reality-testing*. The equation 'perception = reality (external world)' no longer holds. Errors, which can now easily arise and do so regularly in dreams, are called *hallucinations*. [1940a, p. 162; Freud's italics]

This passage can be interpreted purely at the level of cognitive psychology. But in an interpretation that attempts to highlight the motivational and affective aspects of subjectivity, of differentiation and integration, of alienation and reconciliation, it is possible and even necessary to think in different terms.

Let us put it this way: It is not because of Babel that humans are vulnerable to confusion and torment. To be dispersed among a multiplicity of tongues is but a small complication. The fundamental problem is already there in a single tongue. The hubris, Chomsky says, is innate. Astonishingly, the human animal speaks. A gift, yes, to be owned and celebrated as such, before us, in the beginning there, but at the same time our own self-originating act.

As a gift for naming animals and things in the nursery

or Eden, language is innocent enough. But there is this added complication. Every naming, every instance of differentiating an aspect of the world, also names and differentiates the namer. For the most part the latter knowledge is tacitly organized while conscious attention remains focused on the objects of need, interest, or danger out there in the world. The fact that rupture of a prior unity has occurred is but dimly felt. The fact that a world and a self are being mutually constituted only occasionally flashes forth—as when, in recognizing water, Helen Keller recognized, became in some new way, Helen Keller. The word not only marks a point of differentiation; it also mediates reconciliation at a higher level. Both are aspects of the evocative power of language that Loewald discusses.

From the first to the last of his published volumes, Freud tied consciousness of thought with speech (for example, 1950 [1895], p. 365; 1900, p. 574; 1915, p. 202; 1923, pp. 19–21; 1939, p. 97; 1940a, p. 162). Many of his assertions about consciousness and word-representation might seem to imply a simple naming concept of language. His initial formulations in this regard were also related to efforts toward systematic characterization of mind in terms of *Ucs.*, *Pcs.*, and *Cs.* Both the latter systematization and the exclusive role of speech as the basis of access to preconscious organization had to be abandoned.

In the *Outline* he wrote:

> It would not be correct, however, to think that connection with mnemic residues of speech is a necessary precondition of the preconscious state. On the contrary, that state is independent of a connection with them, though the presence of that connection makes it safe to infer the preconscious nature of the process. [1940a, p. 162]

This modification of Freud's earlier statements on language is compatible with the shift from a pre-Saussurian naming concept of language to the idea of language as an organized system, itself largely unconscious. However, it should be noted that even the early statements about word-representation were almost invariably associated with the idea of hypercathexis in the sense of a higher level of organization (1915, p. 194). In any event, the overall gist of his thinking was that knowledge, beyond the simplest level, was knowledge of relationships (1900, pp. 530–31; 1915, p. 202; see also Gill, pp. 28–29), and that it is through language that at least a certain class of higher-level relationships are revealed. The question of whether all higher-level relationships are language-based depends on whether language is understood exclusively as the grammar of discursive thought, or whether one can properly think also of a grammar of art, music, poetry, myth, ritual, or religion. For now and for this volume, it is enough that new linguistic and psychoanalytic perspectives on language be comparatively considered—that implications in common be recognized and points of difference defined.

REFERENCES

Freud, S. *Standard Edition of the Complete Psychological Works.*
    London: Hogarth, 1953–74:
        Project for a Scientific Psychology (1950 [1895]), vol. 1.
        The Interpretation of Dreams (1900), vol. 5.
        The Psychopathology of Everyday Life (1901), vol. 6.
        "Delusions and Dreams in Jensen's *Gradiva* (1907)," vol. 9.
        "Notes upon a Case of Obsessional Neurosis (1909)," vol.
            10.
        Totem and Taboo (1913), vol. 13.
        "The Unconscious (1915)," vol. 14.
        The Ego and the Id (1923), vol. 19.
        Inhibitions, Symptoms and Anxiety (1926), vol. 20.

Moses and Monotheism (1939), vol. 23.

"Analysis Terminable and Interminable (1937)," vol. 23.

An Outline of Psycho-analysis (1940), vol. 23. (a)

"Some Elementary Lessons in Psycho-analysis (1940)," vol. 23. (b)

Gill, M. M. "Topography and Systems in Psychoanalytic Theory." *Psychological Issues,* vol. 3, no. 2, Monograph 10 (1963).

Loewald, H. "Freud's Conception of the Negative Therapeutic Reaction, with Comments on Instinct Theory." *Journal of the American Psychoanalytic Association* 20 (1972) : 235–45.

Piaget, J. "The Affective Unconscious and the Cognitive Unconscious." *Journal of the American Psychoanalytic Association* 21 (1973) : 249–61.

Rapaport, D. *Organization and Pathology of Thought.* New York: Columbia University Press, 1951.

———. "On the Psychoanalytic Theory of Motivation" (1960). In *The Collected Papers of David Rapaport.* Edited by M. M. Gill. New York: Basic Books, 1967.

Smith, J. "Language and the Genealogy of the Absent Object." In *Psychiatry and the Humanities,* vol. 1. Edited by J. H. Smith. New Haven: Yale University Press, 1976. (a)

———. Review of E. Bär, *Semiotic Approaches to Psychotherapy,* and M. Edelson, *Language and Interpretation in Psychoanalysis. Psychiatry* 39 (1976) : 404–09. (b)

Psychiatry and the Humanities, Volume 3

Psychoanalysis and Language

1

Language and Unconscious Knowledge

Noam Chomsky

If the study of human language is to be pursued in a
serious way, it is necessary to undertake a series of abstractions and idealizations. Consider the concept "language" itself. The term is hardly clear; "language" is no
well-defined concept of linguistic science. In colloquial
usage we say that German is one language and Dutch
another, but some dialects of German are more similar to
Dutch dialects than to other, more remote dialects of
German. We say that Chinese is a language with many
dialects and that French, Italian, and Spanish are different languages. But the diversity of the Chinese "dialects" is roughly comparable to that of the Romance languages. A linguist knowing nothing of political
boundaries or institutions would not distinguish "language" and "dialect" as we do in normal discourse. Nor
would he have clear alternative concepts to propose, with
anything like the same function.

Furthermore, even within the more restricted "languages" there may be considerable diversity. Two dialects
of what we call a single language may be mutually incomprehensible. A single individual will generally com-
mand diverse modes of speech in part associated with
varying social conditions of discourse. No clear principles

The Edith Weigert Lecture, sponsored by the Forum on Psychiatry and the
Humanities, Washington School of Psychiatry, Nov. 19, 1976.

are known that determine the range and character of possible variation for a particular individual. Indeed, there is little reason to believe that such principles exist.

In the natural sciences, it is common to adopt what has sometimes been called "the Galilean style"—that is, to construct "abstract mathematical models of the universe to which at least the physicists give a higher degree of reality than they accord the ordinary world of sensations" (Weinberg, 1976, p. 28). A comparable approach is particularly appropriate in the study of an organism whose behavior, we have every reason to believe, is determined by the interaction of numerous internal systems operating under conditions of great variety and complexity. Progress in such an inquiry is unlikely unless we are willing to entertain radical idealization, to construct abstract systems and to study their special properties, hoping to account for observed phenomena indirectly in terms of properties of the systems postulated and their interaction.

Even when we speak of "an organism," we are engaged in idealization and abstraction. One might, after all, study an organism in the world from a very different point of view. Suppose we were to study the flow of nutrients or the oxygen–carbon dioxide cycle. Then the organism would disappear in a flux of chemical processes, losing its integrity as an individual placed in an environment. The "furniture of the world" does not come prepackaged in the form of individuals with properties, apart from human intervention: either the analysis provided by the cognitive systems that we might call "common sense," or the more self-conscious idealizations of the scientist seeking to comprehend some aspect of physical or mental reality. Similarly, if we go on to study particular physical organs such as the eye or the heart, we abstract away from an intricate web of interconnections and adopt a point of view that is by no means a logically necessary one. Any serious study will, furthermore, abstract away from variation tentatively regarded as insignificant and from external interference dismissed as irrelevant at a given stage of inquiry. Such steps may eventually prove to have been misguided, but the only alternative is a form of natural history, tabulation and arrangement of facts, hardly a very serious pursuit however engaging the data.

There is no reason to abandon the general approach of the natural sciences when we turn to the study of human beings and society. Any serious approach to such topics will attempt, with whatever success, to adopt "the Galilean style." Political economy, with its far-reaching abstractions, is an obvious classic example, as, in the Marxian version, "individuals are dealt with only in so far as they are the personifications of economic categories, embodiments of particular class-relations and class interests" (Marx, vol. 1, p. 10), and capital is considered "not a thing, but rather a definite social production relation, belonging to a definite historical formation of society, which is manifested in a thing and lends this thing a specific social character" (Marx, vol. 3, p. 814); and in general, economics is regarded in the final analysis as a study of class relations.

It should come as no surprise, then, that a significant notion of "language" as an object of rational inquiry can be developed only on the basis of rather far-reaching abstraction. How to proceed is a matter of controversy. My own view is this. We may imagine an ideal homogeneous speech community in which there is no variation in style or dialect. We may suppose further that knowledge of the language of this speech community is uniformly represented in the mind of each of its members, as one element in a system of cognitive structures. Let us refer to this representation of the knowledge of these ideal speaker-hearers as the grammar of the language. We must be careful to distinguish the grammar, regarded as a structure postulated in the mind, from the linguist's grammar, which is an explicit articulated theory that attempts to express precisely the rules and principles of the grammar in the mind of the ideal speaker-hearer. The linguist's grammar is a scientific theory, correct insofar as it corresponds to the internally represented grammar. (Exactly what is meant by the notion "corresponds" in the case of the abstract study of a physical system is a complex question, not unique to this enterprise.) It is common to use the term "grammar" with systematic ambiguity, letting the context determine whether it refers to the internalized grammar or to the linguist's theory. The practice is unobjectionable but may lead to confusion unless care is taken.

The grammar of the language determines the properties of each of the sentences of the language. For each sentence, the grammar determines aspects of its phonetic form, its meaning, and perhaps more. The language is the set of sentences that are described by the grammar. To introduce a technical term, we say that the grammar "generates" the sentences it describes and their structural descriptions; the grammar is said to "weakly generate" the sentences of the language and to "strongly generate" the structural descriptions of these sentences. When we speak of the linguist's grammar as a "generative grammar," we mean only that it is sufficiently explicit to determine how sentences of the language are in fact characterized by the grammar.[1]

The language generated by the grammar is infinite. Putting aside irrelevant limitations of time, patience, and memory, people can in principle understand and use sentences of arbitrary length and complexity. Correspondingly, as these limitations are relaxed in practice,

---

1. For discussion, see my *Aspects of the Theory of Syntax* (1965).

our ability to use language increases in scope—in principle, without bound. A sentence that is incomprehensible in speech may be intelligible if repeated several times or presented on the printed page, where memory limitations are less severe. But we do not have to extend our knowledge of language to be able to deal with repeated or written sentences that are far more complex than those of normal spoken discourse. Rather, the same knowledge can be applied with fewer extrinsic constraints.

To illustrate with a simple analogy, consider a person who knows arithmetic, who has mastered the concept of number. In principle, he is now capable of carrying out or determining the accuracy of any computation. Some computations he may not be able to carry out in his head. Paper and pencil are required to extend his memory. But the person does not have to learn something new to carry out a more complex computation, using paper and pencil. Rather, he uses the knowledge already represented in his mind, with access to more computing space than his short-term memory provides. Some computations may be too complex even for paper and pencil, but these limitations are independent of knowledge of arithmetic. They hold for other domains as well. Therefore a scientist interested in determining "arithmetical competence" would quite properly disregard these limitations, attributing them to independent components of the mind.

Although the language generated is infinite, the grammar itself is finite, represented in a finite brain. Thus, the rules of grammar must iterate in some manner to generate an infinite number of sentences, each with its specific sound, structure, and meaning. We make use of this "recursive" property of grammar constantly in ordinary life. We construct new sentences freely and use them on appropriate occasions, just as we comprehend the new sentences that we hear in novel circumstances, generally bringing much more than our knowledge of language to the performance of these creative acts. Though our language use is appropriate to situations, it is not controlled by stimulus conditions. Language serves as an instrument for free expression of thought, unbounded in scope, uncontrolled by stimulus conditions though appropriate to situations, available for use in whatever contingencies our thought processes can comprehend. This "creative aspect of language use" is a characteristic species property of humans. Descartes appealed to this property of language use as a criterion for the existence of "other minds."

It is important to bear in mind the fundamental conceptual distinction between generation of sentences by the grammar, on the one hand, and production and interpretation of sentences by the speaker, making use of the resources of the grammar and much else, on the other. The grammar, in whatever form its principles are represented in the mind and brain, simply characterizes the properties of sentences, much as the principles of arithmetic determine the properties of numbers. We have some understanding of the principles of grammar, but there is no promising approach to the normal creative use of language, or to other rule-governed human acts that are freely undertaken. The study of grammar raises problems that we have some hope of solving; the creative use of language is a mystery that eludes our intellectual grasp.

Proposals do exist with regard to the autonomy of normal behavior, but they do not seem to me to be very fruitful. Consider, for example, a formulation by David Rapaport (1957).[2] In his view, the "ultimate nutriments" of the

2. I am indebted to Dr. Joseph Smith for calling my attention to this interesting study. Rapaport contrasts a "Berkeleian view of man," in which "the outside world is the creation of man's imagination," with the "Cartesian-Humian world view," which, "admitting no guarantees of man's autonomy from his environ-

ego structures are drive stimuli, on the one hand, which
"are the ultimate guarantee against stimulus slavery,"
and, on the other, external stimuli that "are the ultimate
guarantees against drive slavery." "The balance of these
mutually controlling factors does not depend on the outcome of their chance interactions, but is controlled by
laws of the epigenetic sequence, termed autonomous ego
development" (pp. 726–27). Ego structures and the motivations arising from them provide intrinsic nutriments
apart from those arising from the evolutionary givens: (1)
drives and (2) "apparatuses which prepare [the organism]
for contact with its environment" (pp. 740–41). What is
the status of the "nutriments" provided by autonomous
ego structures? If autonomous ego development were
taken to be determined by the "ultimate nutriments" provided by biologically given drives and external stimuli, we
would have an unsatisfactory deterministic theory; if not,
the homunculus still resides within, its choices unex-
plained.

The fact is that we simply have no reasonable grasp of
the general problem of autonomy, as far as I can see. I
mention this to distinguish the mystery posed by the creative aspect of language use from the difficult but still intelligible problems that arise in the investigation of the
unbounded scope of grammar and human knowledge
quite generally.

The grammar of a language, conceived as a system of
rules that weakly generates the sentences of a language
and strongly generates their structures, has a claim to
that "higher degree of reality" that the physicist ascribes
to his mathematical models of the universe. At an appro-

---

ment, makes him virtually a slave of it" (pp. 722–23, 726). He notes that the
sketch of the opposing positions is oversimplified; but in fact, the actual views
of Descartes and Hume, at least, seem very remote from what Rapaport describes, in my opinion.

priate level of abstraction, we hope to find deep explanatory principles underlying the generation of sentences by
grammars. The discovery of such principles, and that
alone, will justify the idealizations adopted and indicate
that we have captured an important element of the real
structure of the organism. To account for the confused
and disorderly phenomena of the "ordinary world of sensation," we will, in general, have to move from the idealizations to systems of greater complexity, considering
variation of languages and grammars, the interaction of
cognitive systems, and the use of language under specific
conditions of human life.

We suppose, then, that the ideal speaker-hearer has a
finite grammar, internally represented in some manner,
generating a language that consists of an infinite number
of sentences, each with its specific properties. He knows
the language generated by the grammar. This knowledge
of language encompasses a variety of properties of sentences. The grammar must deal with the physical form of
a sentence and its meaning. Furthermore, the person
who knows a language knows the conditions under which
it is appropriate to use a sentence, knows what purposes
can be furthered by appropriate use of a sentence under
given social conditions. For purposes of inquiry and exposition, we may proceed to distinguish "grammatical
competence" from "pragmatic competence," restricting
the first to the knowledge of form and meaning and the
second to knowledge of conditions and manner of appropriate use, in conformity with various purposes. Thus we
may think of language as an instrument that can be put
to use. The grammar of the language characterizes the
instrument, determining intrinsic physical and semantic
properties of every sentence. The grammar thus expresses grammatical competence. A system of rules and
principles constituting pragmatic competence determines

how the tool can effectively be put to use. Pragmatic competence may include what Paul Grice has called a "logic
of conversation." We might say that pragmatic competence places language in the institutional setting of its use,
relating intentions and purposes to the linguistic means at
hand.[3]

Linguistic knowledge, of course, extends beyond the
level of the sentence. We know how to construct and understand discourses of various sorts, and there are no
doubt principles governing discourse structure. Furthermore, knowledge of language is intimately related to
other systems of knowledge and belief. When we identify
and name an object, we tacitly assume that it will obey
natural laws. It will not suddenly disappear, turn into
something else, or behave in some other "unnatural" way;
if it does, we might conclude that we have misidentified
and misnamed it. It is no easy matter to determine how
our beliefs about the world of objects relate to the assign-
ment of meanings to expressions. Indeed, it has often
been argued that no principled distinction can be drawn.

Theories of grammatical and pragmatic competence
must find their place in a theory of performance that
takes into account the structure of memory, our mode of
organizing experience, and so on. Actual investigation of
language necessarily deals with performance, with what
someone does under specific circumstances. We often attempt to devise modes of inquiry that will reduce to a
minimum factors that appear irrelevant to intrinsic competence, so that the data of performance will bear directly
on competence, as the object of our inquiry. To the extent that we have an explicit theory of competence, we
can attempt to devise performance models to show how
this knowledge is put to use. If we know only that lan-

3. For discussion, see Wittgenstein, 1953; Austin, 1962; Searle, 1969.

guage consists of words, our performance models would necessarily be very primitive and of restricted interest; we could study the sequence of linguistic signs and their formal and semantic properties, but nothing else. With a richer theory of competence that incorporates structures of greater depth and intricacy, we can proceed to more interesting performance models. Study of performance relies essentially on advances in understanding of competence. But since a competence theory must be incorporated in a performance model, evidence about the actual organization of behavior may prove crucial to advancing the theory of underlying competence. Study of performance and study of competence are mutually supportive. We must simply try to be clear about what we are doing in attempting to investigate something as complex and hidden as the human faculty of language and its exercise.

Ultimately, the study of language is a part of human biology. In the study of any organism or machine, we may distinguish between the abstract investigation of the principles by which it operates and the study of the physical realization of the processes and components postulated in the abstract investigation. Thus, the study of visual perception might lead to the hypothetical construction of certain abstract components—for example, feature detectors—that enter into this system. A further inquiry might reveal the physical mechanisms that meet the abstract conditions postulated. In studying some automaton, we might attempt to determine its program at an abstract level, then proceed to inquire into the circuitry or mechanical principles by which this abstract program is realized. We may say that the same program is represented in devices of very different design and constitution. In the study of humans, direct experimental inquiry into physical mechanisms is generally impossible because of the ethics of experimentation or simply the time span of feasible study. Therefore, the abstract level of inquiry must bear an inordinate burden. It is important to realize that there is no issue of principle here, no philosophical problem unique to this inquiry as a result of the limitations of feasible experiment. Similar problems would arise in the study of an inorganic device that for some reason we could not take apart.

We may speak of the abstract study of human intellectual capacities and their functioning as the study of mind, without thereby implying that there is a *res cogitans* as a "second substance" apart from body. We may also attempt to investigate the physical basis of mind insofar as this is possible.

How can we proceed to investigate the properties of language? To clarify the issue, we might think about the less controversial task of studying the physical structure of the body. A rational approach would be to select some reasonably self-contained physical system of the body— some bodily organ—and to try to determine its nature. Having done this in a number of cases, we might proceed to a higher level of analysis and ask how organs interact, how they grow and develop, how they function in the life of the organism.

Consider the kinds of questions we might ask about an organ of the body—say the eye, or more broadly, the visual system regarded as an organ. We might organize our inquiry along the following lines:

1. *a.* function
   b. structure
   c. physical basis
   d. development in the individual
   e. evolutionary development

Thus we might ask (*a*) what the visual system does, what purpose it serves in human life. We seek further to determine (b) the principles in accordance with which it is organized and operates. Given some characterization of the structure of the visual system at this abstract level, we might try to establish (c) the physical mechanisms that meet the conditions of (b), asking how the structural principles and postulated elements are actually realized in the physical system of the brain. We want to know (d) how the system comes to assume its mature form, how nature and nurture interact in the growth of the organ—a question that can be raised at the abstract level of study of mind or with respect to the physical study of the brain. And finally, we might try to discover (e) how the genetically determined aspects of the organ, as established under (d), came to be as they are, for the species.

Pursuing these fundamental questions with regard to the visual system, we note that the organism begins in some genetically determined initial state common to the species with variations that we may ignore at the outset. It passes through a sequence of states until it attains a mature final state which then undergoes only marginal further change. This "steady state" is, it seems, attained at some relatively early stage in life. But though the organ of vision is essentially fixed in structure at that time, we may still "learn to see" in new ways throughout our lives, for example, by applying knowledge gained later in life or through exposure to some new form of visual representation in the arts, say, cubism. As the seventeenth-century British Platonist Ralph Cudworth expressed it:

> a skillful and expert limner will observe many elegancies and curiosities of art, and be highly pleased with several strokes and shadows in a picture, where a common eye can discern nothing at all; and a musical artist hearing a consort of exact musicians playing some excellent composure of many

parts, will be exceedingly ravished with many har-
monical airs and touches, that a vulgar ear will be utterly insensible of. [p. 446][4]

Classical rational psychology assumed that it was the
mind, not the physical eye or ear, that was responsible for
these more subtle accomplishments. Today, few would
deny that some kind of physical change underlies, for example, the ability of the skilled and expert limner to perceive much that escapes the common eye, but it is reasonable to regard these achievements as based on an
interaction of the organ of sight—the eye and visual
cortex—with other components of the full cognitive system.

In recent years there has been exciting work on the nature and growth of the organ of vision, work that is
highly suggestive for the study of cognitive structures
such as language as well. Studies of the mammalian visual
system have made some progress in determining the general structural principles of organization (1*b*) as well as
their physical basis (1*c*), and in sorting out the genetically
determined properties of the initial state (1*d*). A further
task is to determine how the genetically determined initial
state developed through evolution (1*e*), but this is evidently a problem of a very different order. It is here that
questions of function (1*a*) arise in a significant way. No
one supposes that children learn to have an eye capable
of sight because it would be useful for this function to be
fulfilled; the function of the eye is to see, but that observation is not a very interesting contribution to the study
of ontogeny. Rather, it is in the context of (1*e*) that functional questions have their real interest, it would seem.

4. For some discussion of Cudworth's perceptive comments on cognitive psychology as related to questions under discussion here, see my *Cartesian Linguistics* (1966) and *Reflections on Language* (1975).

Suppose that we attempt to study language on the model of a bodily organ, raising the questions (1a)–(1e). Let us briefly consider these questions in turn.

What is the function of language? It is frequently alleged that the function of language is communication, that its "essential purpose" is to enable people to communicate with one another. It is further alleged that only by attending to this essential purpose can we make any sense of the nature of language.

It is not easy to evaluate this contention. What does it mean to say that language has an "essential purpose"? Suppose that in the quiet of my study I think about a problem, using language, and even write down what I think. Suppose that someone speaks honestly, merely out of a sense of integrity, fully aware that his audience will refuse to comprehend or even consider what he is saying. Consider informal conversation conducted for the sole purpose of maintaining casual friendly relations, with no particular concern as to its content. Are these examples of "communication"? If so, what do we mean by "communication" in the absence of an audience, or with an audience assumed to be completely unresponsive, or with no intention to convey information or modify belief or attitude?

It seems that either we must deprive the notion "communication" of all significance, or else we must reject the view that the purpose of language is communication. While it is quite commonly argued that the purpose of language is communication and that it is pointless to study language apart from its communicative function, there is no formulation of this belief, to my knowledge, from which any substantive proposals follow. The same may be said of the idea that the essential purpose of language is to achieve certain instrumental ends, to satisfy needs, and so on. Surely language can be used for such purposes—or for others. It is difficult to say what "the purpose" of language is, except, perhaps, the expression of thought, a rather empty formulation. The functions of language are various. It is unclear what might be meant by the statement that some of them are "central" or "essential."

A more productive suggestion is that functional considerations determine the character of linguistic rules. Suppose it can be shown, for example, that some rule of English grammar facilitates a perceptual strategy for sentence analysis. Then we have the basis for a functional explanation for the linguistic rule. But several questions arise, quite apart from the matter of the source of the perceptual strategy. Is the linguistic rule a true universal? If so, then the functional analysis is relevant only on the evolutionary level; human languages *must* have this rule or one like it, by virtue of a species property. Suppose, on the contrary, that the linguistic rule is learned. We may still maintain the functional explanation, but it will now have to do with the evolution of English. That is, English developed in such a way as to accord with this principle. In either case, the functional explanation applies on the evolutionary level—either the evolution of the organism or of the language. The child does not acquire the rule by virtue of its function any more than he learns to have an eye because of the advantages of sight.

The second basic question (1*b*) is the one that deserves the most extensive discussion, but I will have little to say about it here. I cannot attempt to outline the answers that have been proposed to the question, What is the abstract structure of language?, or the problems that arise along the way.[5] If work of recent years is anywhere near the mark, then a language is generated by a system of rules

5. For my own views on this subject, see *Reflections on Language* and *Essays on Form and Interpretation* (1977).

and principles that enter into complex mental computations to determine the form and meaning of sentences. These rules and principles are in large measure unconscious and beyond the reach of potential consciousness. Our perfect knowledge of the language we speak gives us no privileged access to these principles; we cannot hope to determine them by introspection or reflection, "from within," as it were. Correspondingly, there is no basis whatsoever for dogmatic stipulations as to the degree or quality of the complexity or abstractness that is "permitted" in a theory of language structure, just as such a priori doctrine would be out of place in the study of the visual system or any bodily organ.

The most intriguing of the studies of language structure are those that bear on linguistic universals, that is, principles that hold of language quite generally as a matter of biological (not logical) necessity. Given the richness and complexity of the system of grammar for a human language and the uniformity of its acquisition on the basis of limited and often degenerate evidence, there can be little doubt that highly restrictive universal principles must exist determining the general framework of each human language and perhaps much of its specific structure as well. To determine these principles is the deepest problem of contemporary linguistic study.

Let us consider again the model of the visual system. Recent work has led to the conclusion that "the development of the nervous system is a process sharply constrained by a genetic program. . . . the genetic program permits a range of possible realizations, and individual experience acts only to specify the outcome within this range" (Grobstein and Chow, 1975, p. 356). For example, an individual neuron has a fixed orientation specificity, but the genetic program determines the range within which it can be fixed by experience. Similarly, the general properties of binocular vision are genetically determined but the precise control of matching inputs from the two eyes is fixed on the basis of visual experience. Comparable conclusions seem to hold in the case of human language. Here, too, it seems that biological endowment sharply constrains the course of language growth, or what is called, with somewhat misleading connotations, "language learning."

To account for the rapid transition to a uniform steady state on the basis of the limited experience available, we must postulate a genetically determined initial state that "permits a range of possible realizations," and furthermore, a fairly narrow range, with individual experience acting "only to specify the outcome within this range." There is good reason to suppose that across the human species the ability to acquire language is invariant within narrow limits, apart from pathology. We may assume that a fixed and highly restrictive initial state is a common human possession.

The child's initial state, it seems, must lay down the general principles of language structure in fair detail, providing a rich and intricate schematism that determines (1) the content of linguistic experience and (2) the specific language that develops under the boundary conditions given by this experience. If the initial restriction is sufficiently severe, it will be possible for the child to attain a system of great intricacy on the basis of limited data, data sufficient to rule out all possibilities but one or a few. Then he will know the language compatible with his limited experience, though there will be no relation of generalization, abstraction, induction, habit formation, or the like that relates the system attained at the final state to the data of experience. The relation between experience and knowledge will be quite abstract. The principles of language structure incorporated in the initial state express this relationship. Qualitative considerations suggest that this may be a reasonable approach to the fundamental question of development in the individual (1d). If so, the human language faculty is much like other organs known to biology.

We need not content ourselves with vague and metaphoric discussions of this sort. Rather, we can proceed to spell out in specific detail a schematism that characterizes the initial state. Call this schematism "universal grammar." We may think of universal grammar as, in effect, the genetic program, the schematism that permits the range of possible realizations that are the possible human languages. Each such possible realization is a possible final steady state, the grammar of a specific language. Universal grammar is a system that is genetically determined at the initial state, and is specified, sharpened, articulated, and refined under the conditions set by experience, to yield the particular grammars that are represented in the steady states attained. Looking at the question of growth of language ("language learning") in this way, we can see how it is possible for a person to know vastly more than he has experienced.

Once the steady state is attained; knowledge of language and skill in using language may still be refined, as in the case of learning to see. Wilhelm von Humboldt argued that the resources of a language can be enriched by a great thinker or writer, without any change in the grammar. An individual can expand his facility or the subtlety of his comprehension of the devices of language through his own creative activities or immersion in the cultural wealth of his society. But as in the case of the visual system, it seems quite appropriate to set this matter aside in abstracting the linguistic system as a separate object of study.

An approach of this sort contrasts with a familiar learning model, in accordance with which it is assumed that language is a system of habits and skills, acquired gradually through generalization, conditioning, induction, and abstraction. Linguistic knowledge, in this view, is a system of learned categories and patterns. This approach, too, can be made explicit in various ways, and in fact has been, in behavioral psychology and certain branches of structural linguistics.

Under either of these contrasting approaches, we assume a fixed, genetically determined state. The approaches differ in their conception of the nature of this initial state. One approach takes the initial state to be a rich system of principles, a restrictive schematism that specifies the range of possible grammars. The other takes it to be a system of procedures of segmentation, classification, generalization, and induction to be applied to the data of experience to yield a grammar. I have argued elsewhere that these two approaches can properly be described as rationalist and empiricist, respectively. One can, of course, consider mixed approaches of various sorts, but I think it is very useful to keep in mind these two general models, each with its possible variants, as points of reference.

One might ask whether there are not quite different models to explore in investigating the growth of language. Thus, it has been suggested by Piaget and his colleagues that an "interactionist" or "constructivist" theory is superior to either the empiricist or rationalist model.[6] In this theory, it is proposed that through interaction with the environment the child develops sensorimotor constructions which provide the basis for language, and

6. See Jean Piaget, *Structuralism* (1970). Also, Piaget's contributions to the *Proceedings of the Royaumont Conference on Phylogenetic and Ontogenetic Models of Development, 1975* (forthcoming). Also, Inhelder, Sinclair, and Bovet, *Learning and the Development of Cognition* (1974).

as understanding and knowledge grow, new constructions are developed in some more or less uniform way.
Thus, it is claimed, language at any stage merely reflects
independent mental constructions that arise in the course
of dealing with the environment, and at each stage the
child develops new systems that reorganize his experience. "The basic hypothesis of developmental construc-
tivism . . . postulates that no human knowledge, with the
obvious exception of the very elementary hereditary
forms, is preformed in the structures of either the subject
or the object" (Inhelder et al., p. 8).

The studies conducted by the Geneva school have been
extremely illuminating, but the interactionist-construc-
tivist model itself is difficult to assess, because it remains
at the level of metaphor. Allegedly, the child progresses
through a fairly regular sequence of cognitive stages, but
no mechanism or principle is proposed to explain why
the child moves from a given stage to the next rather
than to some quite different stage. It is difficult to imagine what answer could be provided, apart from recourse
to some assumption concerning maturation to a genetically determined target stage, at each point. And when
such an assumption is made precise, it seems that it will
express genetically determined aspects of human belief
and knowledge that are far more intricate than the "elementary hereditary forms" that the Geneva school is willing to contemplate. Furthermore, no suggestion has been
offered as to how the specific principles of language
structure that have been proposed might relate to constructions of sensorimotor intelligence. On consideration
of the relevant principles, the prospects for any such association seem rather dim. Therefore, the Piagetian models do not seem to be a genuine alternative to those
sketched above. The crucial questions remain unanswered, and no hint of an answer is offered. I know of no

general principles advanced within developmental psychology that shed any real light on these questions.

The empiricist models are in accord with our normal way of discussing the development of language. Thus, we say that the child "learns language," not that language grows or matures. But we do not say that the embryo or the child learns to have arms rather than legs, or a visual system of a particular kind, or, say, mature sexual organs, to take a case of development that we assume to be genetically determined in essentials though it takes place well after birth. Furthermore, we are naturally impressed with the diversity among attested languages.

All of this is true but not very important. We say that the sun rises, but the fact—easy enough to explain in terms of commonsense experience—is of no interest to the physicist. It is entirely natural that in our normal lives we should be impressed with the diversity of language and the influence of experience on language acquisition. In normal life, there is no reason for us to pay attention to the uniformities among individuals and across cultures; these we can take for granted. What concerns us are the differences. For example, when we learn a foreign language, we concentrate on the respects in which this language differs from our own. A good teaching grammar or a standard traditional grammar will say little about general properties of language. Intended for the use of the intelligent reader, such grammars do not provide an analysis of the qualities of intelligence that the reader brings to bear on the information presented. The grammars discuss irregularities, but not deeper principles of universal grammar. These very general conditions on the form of language constitute part of the intelligence of the language learner; they form part of the schematism that is brought to bear in acquiring language, and therefore need receive no particular attention in our normal lives. In fact, we are quite unconscious of these elements of our knowledge of language, and cannot gain awareness of them through introspection.

For the scientist interested in the nature of language, it is the general principles that are of primary importance; the special properties of particular languages are of much less interest. For the normal person dealing with language in his daily life, precisely the opposite is true. The deeper principles, which are in any event far beyond the level of consciousness, are of no consequence, while the unpredictable irregularities must receive careful attention. It is no surprise that the commonsense view, focusing on irregularities and diversity, regards language as a learned and arbitrary phenomenon. Every frog, no doubt, considers his fellows to be a remarkably diverse and interesting crew; insofar as their behavior conforms to his own, it is only that this is the natural and obvious way to act, requiring no special attention.

In short, we can easily understand why empiricist models should seem compelling to a commonsense view, and why we should think of language as being "learned" rather than as growing in accordance with a fixed, genetically determined program, modified and filled out with specific detail through experience. The irregularities, which alone concern us in normal life, *are* learned. Similarly, the distribution of vertical and horizontal receptors in the visual system is fixed (learned) through experience, we learn how to do the high jump, and so forth. But we do not learn to have arms rather than wings, to walk or run rather than fly, to have binocular vision with analysis of stimuli in terms of linear contours, or to adhere to the principle that linguistic rules meet the various conditions of universal grammar. These requirements are elements of the genetically determined initial state, though of course they may only come into operation at a particular stage of maturation, much as sexual maturation—or, for that matter, death—though genetically determined, takes place only at a specific stage of life. And as in the case of physical structures of the body, the timing and precise character of the maturational development may themselves be influenced by environmental factors.

As the stages of development of other cognitive capacities come to be better understood, we may discover that quite generally the transition from one stage to the next is a matter of growth and maturation within bounds set by the genetic program, with some variation depending on nutritional level, social environment, accidental experience, and so on.

I have said nothing so far about the questions (1c) and (1e)—namely, the physical realization of the abstract structures of language and their evolutionary history. In fact, little is known about these questions, though the first, at least, may be open to serious investigation.

Can we expect to find, in other organisms, faculties closely analogous to the human language capacity? It is conceivable, but not very likely. That would constitute a kind of biological miracle, rather analogous to the discovery, on some unexplored island, of a species of bird that had never thought to fly until instructed to do so through human intervention. Language must surely confer enormous selectional advantage. It is difficult to imagine that some other species, say the chimpanzee, has the capacity for language but has never thought to put it to use. Nor is there any evidence that this biological miracle has occurred. On the contrary, the interesting investigations of the capacity of the higher apes to acquire symbolic systems seem to me to support the traditional belief that even the most rudimentary properties of language lie well beyond the capacities of an otherwise intelligent ape.

The fundamental differences between human language and the systems taught to apes are clear at the most elementary level. Consider the five basic dimensions of inquiry suggested earlier, (1a)–(1e). From a functional point of view, human language is a system for free expression of thought, essentially independent of stimulus control, need-satisfaction, or instrumental purpose, hence qualitatively different from the symbolic systems taught to apes. Structurally, human language is a system with recursive structure-dependent rules, operating on sequences organized in a hierarchy of phrases to generate a countable infinity of sentences. These basic properties are, so far as we know, unique to human language, and the same is true, a fortiori, of the more complex principles of universal grammar that characterize human language.

As far as the physical basis of human language is concerned, the very little that is known indicates that a crucial role is played by specific language centers in the dominant hemisphere that seem to have no direct analogue in other mammals. There is also evidence that humans with severe injury to the language centers of the brain and consequent irremediable language loss can readily acquire the systems designed for apes, supporting the natural assumption that these systems have only the most superficial resemblance to human language. As for development, language grows in the child through mere exposure to an unorganized linguistic environment, without training or even any particular language-specific care. Turning finally to the evolutionary level, though little is known, it seems clear that language is a fairly ancient human possession that developed long after the separation of humans from other primates.

Hence, along each dimension of inquiry, even the most superficial examination reveals fundamental properties that radically distinguish human language from other systems. This is not to suggest that studies of the intellectual capacities of apes are without interest. On the contrary, they are of considerable interest in themselves. One would assume that apes in the wild are capable of intellectual achievements specific to their lives and world that go well beyond the ability to acquire the symbolic systems artificially induced under laboratory conditions. Experiments in training apes to use symbolic systems are sure to further understanding of ape intelligence, and thus, indirectly, to teach us something more about the apparently quite different specific qualities of intelligence that underlie the use of language and other human achievements. We might discover that the unique human achievements in the linguistic domain result in part from organization of capacities that are individually present in some form in other organisms, though it is not unlikely that more than this is involved in the evolutionary development of a species capable of human language.

I have been suggesting that we pursue the study of mind—that is, the principles that underlie our thoughts and beliefs, perception and imagination, the organization of our actions, and the like—much as we investigate the body. We may conceive of the mind as a system of "mental organs," the language faculty being one. Each of these organs has its specific structure and function, determined in general outline by our genetic endowment, interacting in ways that are also biologically determined in large measure to provide the basis for our mental life. Interaction with the physical and social environment refines and articulates these systems as the mind matures in childhood and, in less fundamental respects, throughout life.

In considering such an approach to the structure of mind, we depart, as already noted, from beliefs that are deeply established in our intellectual tradition. I think it is fair to say that this tradition has been marked by a belief in the accessibility, uniformity, and simplicity of the mind, in a sense that I would now like to discuss.

In referring to "accessibility" of the structures of mind, I am thinking of the belief that its contents are in principle open to reflection and careful thought if only the barriers of dogma, superstition, or psychic disorder are removed. Classical rationalism held that the "natural light" of common sense suffices to lay bare the basic elements of our reasoning, thought, and understanding, though not necessarily the explanatory hypotheses of physical science.[7] Empiricist speculation shared much of this doctrine, and sought to show, by careful analysis, how our ideas could be resolved into their simple constituents by introspection. Vico's defense of the *Geisteswissenschaften* against the claims of scientific naturalism relied essentially on the principle that inner access to the products of our minds and our acts yields a degree of certainty unattainable in the natural sciences: the principles of what has "been made by men . . . are . . . to be found within the modifications of our own human mind" (1948, para. 331),[8] though how we determine these modifications of mind, in his view, is not very clear. Even Freud's evocation of the unconscious was not, I believe, accompanied by far-reaching questioning of the accessibility in principle of the products of mind.[9]

7. For a discussion of often overlooked complexities in Descartes's views, see Gerd Buchdahl, *Metaphysics and the Philosophy of Science* (1969).

8. See Isaiah Berlin, *Vico and Herder* (1976), for a very illuminating study.

9. Freud's complex views on accessibility of the unconscious require a far more serious examination than I can attempt here. At some points, he seems to deny accessibility. The clearest example I have found is in the final section of *The Interpretation of Dreams*, where he distinguishes the *Ucs.* (unconscious), which is *"inadmissible to consciousness,"* from the *Pcs.* (preconscious), with excitations that "are able to reach consciousness" (pp. 614–15; his italics). Thus there are systems that "can never be accessible to our psychical perception" (p. 611). But the question is whether by "accessible" (or "inadmissible") Freud has in mind accessibility in principle or accessibility in fact, given other contingencies. My impression is that only the latter interpretation is consistent with his general

I do not mean to suggest that the principle of accessibility was articulated without qualification (cf. n. 9), but rather that it may be regarded as a kind of limit toward which much traditional thinking tended. Qualifications can be found, and in some cases they are severe. Thus, to Vico, "the clear and distinct idea of the mind, i.e., the

---

view. Thus in the same work (p. 541), he emphasizes that the *Ucs.* "has no access to consciousness *except via the preconscious,* in passing through which its excitatory process is obliged to submit to modifications" (his italics), which implies accessibility in principle. Elsewhere, Freud discusses ways "in which something that is in itself unconscious becomes preconscious" (*The Ego and the Id,* p. 21), implying again accessibility in principle. In *Moses and Monotheism* he again defines *Pcs.* as what is "capable of being conscious" (p. 96), so that *Ucs.* is incapable of being conscious; but it is evident from the context that "capable" must mean "capable in fact" or "easy of access," since he goes on at once to argue that "unconscious processes in the id are raised to the level of the preconscious" and that "Thought-processes, and whatever may be analogous to them in the id, are in themselves unconscious and obtain access to consciousness . . ." (pp. 96–97).

The same interpretation seems to me appropriate for the discussion in *An Outline of Psycho-Analysis.* Here, *Pcs.* is "preferably described as 'capable of becoming conscious,' " that is, as "Everything unconscious . . . that can thus *easily* exchange the unconscious state for the conscious one" (pp. 159–60; my italics). He reserves "the name of the unconscious proper" for "psychical processes and psychical material which have no such *easy access* to becoming conscious . . ." (p. 160; my italics). His basic principle is this: "What is preconscious becomes conscious . . . without any assistance from us; *what is unconscious can, through our efforts, be made conscious,*" with effort that "varies in magnitude" as "resistance" varies (p. 160; my italics). "The inside of the ego, which comprises above all the thought-processes, has the quality of being preconscious," that is, "having access to consciousness" (p. 162). As for the "contents of the id," a portion thereof can be "raised to the preconscious state" and thus "incorporated into the ego" (*Moses and Monotheism,* pp. 96–97). And more generally, "The core of our being, then, is formed by the obscure *id,* which has no direct communication with the external world and is accessible even to our own knowledge only through the medium of another agency" (*Outline of Psycho-Analysis,* p. 197). That is, it too is accessible in principle, though generally inaccessible.

It seems to me, then, that a consistent interpretation requires that we take Freud's observations on inaccessibility to be denying "easy access" but not access in principle.

I am again indebted to Joseph Smith for bringing many relevant passages to my attention, but I do not want to imply that he agrees with this interpretation. [*Editor's note:* The differences in interpretation are discussed at length in the Introduction to this volume.]

Cartesian criterion, not only cannot be the criterion of other truths, but it cannot be the criterion of the mind itself; for while the mind apprehends itself, it does not make itself, and because it does not make itself, it is ignorant of the former mode by which it apprehends itself."[10] Or consider the notion of "mental chemistry" that developed within associationist psychology. Joseph Priestley, in the eighteenth century, wrote that "from the combination of ideas, and especially very dissimilar ones, there may result ideas which, to appearance, shall be so different from the parts of which they really consist, that they shall no more be capable of being analyzed by mental reflection than the idea of white."[11] John Stuart Mill developed a similar view:

> The laws of the phenomena of mind are sometimes analogous to mechanical, but sometimes also to chemical laws. When many impressions or ideas are operating in the mind together, there sometimes takes place a process of a similar kind to chemical combination. When impressions have been so often experienced in conjunction that each of them calls up readily and instantaneously the ideas of the whole group, these ideas sometimes *melt and coalesce* into one another, and appear not several ideas but one. [Cited by Warren, pp. 54–55]

We cannot, then, discover the "elementary ideas" in which our complex notions originate. "These, therefore, are cases of *mental chemistry,* in which it is proper to say that the simple ideas generate, rather than that they compose the complex ones" (ibid.). Where ideas are generated

10. Cited by Berlin, p. 20, from *De Antiquissima.*
11. Cited by Howard C. Warren, *A History of the Association Psychology from Hartley to Lewes* (1921, p. 23).

by mental chemistry, as distinct from association on a mechanical model, it is presumably impossible to resolve them into their constituents by introspection.

More explicit rejection of accessibility appears in remarks by C. G. Jung. He writes that "there is little hope of our ever being able to reach even approximate consciousness of the self, since however much we may make conscious there will always exist an indeterminate and indeterminable amount of unconscious material which belongs to the totality of the self." Jung's archetypes are "empty and purely formal" structures; each is "a possibility of representation which is given *a priori*," "an irrepresentable, unconscious, pre-existent form that seems to be part of the inherited structure of the psyche." It seems to him "probable that the real nature of the archetype is not capable of being made conscious."[12] With regard to consciousness, he holds that it is "a secondary phenomenon" both phylogenetically and ontogenetically: "the psyche of the child in its preconscious state is anything but a *tabula rasa;* it is already preformed in a recognizably individual way, and is moreover equipped with all specifically human instincts, as well as with the a priori foundations of the higher functions" (Jung, 1965, p. 348). I take this to be an insistence on the inaccessibility to introspection of basic principles of the psyche, at least those that form part of its inherited structure, which, it should be stressed, is taken to comprise the a priori foundations of the higher mental functions, a conception that can be traced to Kant and his rationalist predecessors. It is worth noting, however, that Kant takes a clear contrary position on accessibility. Thus, in the *Critique of Pure Reason* he holds the following position: "All representations have a necessary relation to a *possible* empirical conscious-

12. Cited in glossary, C. J. Jung, *Memories, Dreams and Reflections* (1965).

ness. For if they did not have this, and if it were altogether impossible to become conscious of them, this
would practically amount to the admission of their non-
existence" (Kant, p. 142 n.).

Despite such observations, which can no doubt be considerably extended, it still seems to me generally accurate
to say that accessibility of the contents of the mind in
principle is a fairly well-established doctrine that appears,
in various forms, in diverse currents of our intellectual
tradition. The study of language seems to me to suggest
that it should be abandoned, even as a point of depar-
ture. There is no reason to suppose that we have any
privileged access to the principles that enter into our
knowledge and use of language, that determine the form
and meaning of sentences or the conditions of their use,
or that relate the "mental organ" of language to other
cognitive systems.

The second doctrine I mentioned is the belief in the
"uniformity" of the mind. Of course, it was traditionally
assumed that the mind consists of separate faculties:
"memory, imagination or fancy, understanding, affection, and will."[13] What I intend to signify in referring to
the doctrine of uniformity of mind is the belief that the
various cognitive structures develop in a uniform way—
that is, that there are general principles of learning that
underlie all of these systems, accounting for their development: "multipurpose learning strategies," as they are
sometimes called, that apply "across the board." In contrast, it might be proposed that various "mental organs"
develop in specific ways, each in accordance with the genetic program, much as bodily organs develop; and that
multipurpose learning strategies are no more likely to
exist than general principles of "growth of organs" that

13. David Hartley, cited by Warren, p. 8.

account for the shape, structure, and function of the kid-
ney, the liver, the heart, the visual system, and so forth.
Such principles may exist at the level of cellular biology,
but there is no reason to anticipate a "higher level" theory
of general organ growth. Rather, specific subcomponents
of the genetic program, coming into operation as the organism matures, determine the specific properties of
these systems. The same may well be true of the basic
structures involved in our mental life.

The belief in uniformity, in this sense, is common to
approaches as distinct as those of Piaget and Skinner,
within psychology, and has been expressed by many contemporary philosophers in various forms. In Piaget's system, the early growth of language is modeled on prior
"sensorimotor constructions," while later development is
determined by general principles of "assimilation," "accommodation," and the like, that underlie other aspects
of cognitive development as well. As already noted, these
proposals seem to me too vague to be properly discussed.
There seems little reason to suppose that the principles of
grammar or universal grammar have any close analogue
in other cognitive systems, though naturally one must
keep an open mind about the matter. Furthermore, it
would be in no way surprising if this were to prove to be
the case, just as we do not expect the fundamental properties of the visual system to be reflected in language.
Confident assertions to the contrary, which are prevalent
in recent literature, seem to me rather dogmatic as well as
without empirical support or plausible argument.

The belief in the "simplicity" of mental structures is
related to the doctrine of uniformity. In the case of language, it is commonly argued by linguists and others that
the principles of grammar cannot be "too complex" or
"too abstract" but must reflect properties of sound and
meaning, or must be directly determined in some manner

by "functional considerations," aspects of language use. Evidently, there can be no a priori argument to this effect. To me, it seems that recent work tends to support a rather different view: that rules of syntax and phonology, at least, are organized in terms of "autonomous" principles of mental computation and do not reflect in any simple way the properties of the phonetic or semantic "substance" or contingencies of language use.

There are classical debates that bear on these questions. Consider, for example, the controversy over principles of geometry and the organization of perceptual space in early modern philosophy. Descartes and Cudworth believed the mind to be endowed with the principles of Euclidean geometry as an a priori property. We see a presented irregular figure as a (possibly distorted) triangle, straight line, circle, and so forth, because our minds produce these figures as "exemplars," just as "the intelligible essences of things" are produced by "the innate cognoscitive power." In Kant's phrase, objects conform to our "modes of cognition." To Hume, in contrast, nothing could be more certain than that we have no concept of "a perfect geometrical figure" (p. 156) beyond what the senses convey:

> As the ultimate standard of these figures is derived from nothing but the senses and imagination, it is absurd to talk of any perfection beyond what these faculties can judge of; since the true perfection of anything consists in its conformity to its standard. [Hume, pp. 13–14]

Thus, the first principles of geometry "are founded on the imagination and senses" and are far from certain; and our notions of regular figures are derived through experience. More generally, *all our simple ideas in their first appearance, are derived from simple impressions, which are correspondent to them, and which they exactly represent"* (p. 65), and our complex ideas are formed by union of these simple ideas on the basis of resemblance, contiguity, and causation (with unimportant exceptions, such as the missing colors). In these early debates, the questions of uniformity and simplicity arise in an interesting way, though as I have remarked, the principle of accessibility seems generally to be accepted, with some qualification.

Finally, let us consider briefly how language fits into the general system of cognitive structures. Surely the normal use of language requires access to other systems of knowledge and belief. We have already noted how difficult it is—if indeed it is possible in principle—to distinguish between semantic properties that are simply language-dependent and others that relate to our beliefs about the natural world. We use language against a background of shared beliefs about things and within the framework of a system of social institutions. The study of language use must be concerned with the place of language in a system of cognitive structures embodying pragmatic competence, as well as structures that relate to matters of fact and belief.

To gain further understanding of the general nature of the human mind, we should ask in what domains humans seem to develop complex intellectual structures in a more or less uniform way on the basis of restricted data. Wherever this is the case, we can reasonably suppose that a highly structured genetic program is responsible for the achievement, and we can thus hope to learn something significant about human nature by studying the systems attained. Language is an obvious area. It might be argued that the major intellectual interest of the study of language lies in the fact that it is a complex domain, particularly amenable to study, distinctively human, and associated in the most intimate way with every aspect of human life.

There are other topics that might be studied in a similar way. For example, humans have remarkable perceptual abilities in certain domains. Consider recognition of faces. A person can recognize an enormous number of human faces and can identify a presentation of a single face with various orientations. This is a remarkable feat that cannot be duplicated with other figures of comparable complexity. It might therefore be interesting to try to develop a "grammar of faces," or even a "universal grammar of faces," to explain these abilities. Perhaps, at some stage of maturation, some part of the brain develops an abstract theory of faces and a system of projection that allows it to determine how an arbitrary human face will appear in a given presentation. There is some evidence that face recognition is neurally represented in the right hemisphere and that this neural representation is delayed until past the time when language is fixed in the left hemisphere. Currently, these questions are being investigated. They might be profitably pursued along the general lines outlined above, much in the manner of the language faculty.

Are there other systems, more distinctively human in character, more enlightening as regards deeper and more fundamental characteristics of the human species? Perhaps so. Thus, one curious property of the human mind is our ability to develop certain forms of mathematical understanding—specifically, concerning the number system, abstract geometrical space, continuity, and related notions. It is hard to imagine that these capacities can be explained directly in terms of natural selection. It does not seem very likely that ability to solve problems in number theory was a factor in differential reproduction.

Presumably, these capacities developed as a concomitant of others that did confer selectional advantage. However this may be, it is certainly possible to inquire into the nature of these abilities and to try to discover the initial state of the mind that enables these abilities to develop as they do. Surely, these capacities lie at the core of the remarkable human ability to develop scientific knowledge in certain domains. The work of Piaget and his colleagues has been particularly suggestive in this regard.

These speculations raise further questions. Where complex intellectual structures are developed in an essentially uniform way on the basis of limited evidence, we have hopes of finding something significant about human nature, since it is natural to account for the fact on the basis of assumptions about the initial state of the mind; indeed, it is difficult to imagine an alternative, apart from sheer accident. In some cases, the empirical contingencies of human life may suffice to account for the general lines of development, but the extent to which it is necessary to postulate fixed capacities for organizing experience is often not fully appreciated.

The history of science suggests examples that might possibly be illuminating. Time after time, people have been able to construct remarkable explanatory theories on the basis of very limited evidence, often rejecting much of the available evidence on obscure intuitive grounds as they sought to construct theories that are deep and intelligible. Furthermore, although the creation of new theory is an achievement of the gifted few, it has been possible through most of the history of science for others, less talented, to comprehend and appreciate what has been accomplished. The theories that have been constructed, regarded as intelligible, and generally accepted as science has progressed have been vastly underdetermined by evidence. Intellectual structures of vast scope have been developed on the basis of limited and (until recently) fairly degenerate evidence. Applying the paradigm suggested earlier, we are led to inquire into the innate structures of mind that make this achievement possible.

What is the "science-forming capacity" that enables us to recognize certain proposed explanatory theories as intelligible and natural, while rejecting or simply not considering a vast array of others that are no less compatible with evidence? I do not speak here of the creative achievement, but rather of the appreciation of the achievement, a common human ability; the ability to recognize, with understanding and pleasure, that an intelligible explanatory theory has been produced. Some such science-forming capacity must be an innate property of mind. That is not to say that all potential scientific knowledge is "preformed" at birth. Rather, the human mind is endowed with some set of principles that can be put to work when certain questions are posed, a certain level of understanding has been achieved, and certain evidence is available, to select a narrow class of possible theories. Perhaps these principles, too, might fruitfully be regarded as a general schematism that characterizes the class of intelligible theories, thus permitting us to develop systems of belief and knowledge of great scope and power on limited evidence.

Evidently the scope and limits of knowledge are intimately related. Thus, if there are principles that make possible the acquisition of rich systems of knowledge and belief, then these very principles limit the class of accessible theories. Analogously, a rich set of principles of universal grammar permits us to attain our extensive knowledge of language on limited evidence, and by the same token, these principles exclude languages that violate the principles as inaccessible to the language faculty (some might be learned, with effort, application, and explicit formulation and testing of hypotheses, by means of other faculties of mind).

It is conceivable that we might discover the principles that underlie the construction of intelligible theories, thus arriving at a kind of "universal grammar" of scientific theories. And by analyzing these principles, we might determine certain properties of the class of accessible theories. We might then raise the following question: What is the relation between the class of humanly accessible theories and the class of true theories? It is possible that the intersection of these classes is quite small, that few true theories are accessible. There is no evolutionary argument to the contrary. Nor is there any reason to accept the traditional doctrine, as expressed by Descartes, that human reason is a "universal instrument which can serve for all contingencies." Rather, it is a specific biological system, with its potentialities and associated limitations. It may turn out to have been a lucky accident that the intersection is not null. There is no particular reason to suppose that the science-forming capacities of humans or their mathematical abilities permit them to conceive of theories approximating the truth in every (or any) domain, or to gain insight into the laws of nature. It might turn out, for example, that inquiry into what humans do and why lies beyond human competence, though a science of human nature can in principle be constructed by a biological organism with different qualities of mind. A pessimistic conclusion, but not necessarily false.

Similar questions can be raised with regard to the arts. Certain conditions on the choice and arrangement of linguistic expressions characterize literary genres intelligible to humans, with aesthetic value for humans; others do not. Not every way of organizing sounds is a humanly accessible system of music. In these and many other do-

mains, a certain range of possibilities has been explored
to create structures of marvelous intricacy, while others
are never considered, or if explored, lead to the production of work that does not conform to normal human
capacities. Just why this should be so, we do not really
know. Perhaps these questions are, nevertheless, amenable to inquiry modeled on the study of those few cognitive systems that have yielded at least a few of their secrets.

As Marshall Edelson has recently pointed out in some
extremely interesting studies, Freud raised similar questions in his classic work. Edelson suggests that in making
"explicit the operations by which a dream—a symptom, a
joke, a myth, a work of art—is constructed," Freud made
"one of his greatest contributions to psychoanalysis as a
science of semiology" (1972, p. 249). A dream, in Freud's
view, is "nothing other than a particular *form* of thinking"
created by principles that he calls "the dreamwork,"
which constitute "the essence of dreaming—the explanation of its particular nature." He posed the task "of investigating the relations between the manifest content of
dreams and the latent dream-thoughts, and of tracing out
the processes by which the latter have been changed into
the former. . . . the dream-content seems like a tran-
script of the dream-thoughts into another mode of expression, whose characters and syntactic laws it is our
business to discover by comparing the original and the
translation."[14] It is tempting to draw an analogy here to
rules of grammar, which relate various levels of linguistic
representation. One would not expect to find the same
representations and the same principles of "transcription" in such different "forms of thinking" as dreams and
normal use of language, but it is not at all unreasonable, I

14. Cited by Edelson (1972, pp. 244, 252), from *The Interpretation of Dreams*
(1900).

think, to search for a more abstract relationship between the two systems, as Edelson does in pursuing Freud's intriguing suggestions. I think he is quite right to suggest this as a proper approach to "a science of semiology for understanding works of the mind of man as apparently disparate as poetry, music, metaphor, and the psychoanalyst's interpretation" (1972, p. 206).[15]

Such a "science of semiology" may not lie very far beyond the horizons of current inquiry. There has, of course, been very distinguished and suggestive work in several of the domains that might fall within a general theory of symbolic function, some of it consciously related to ideas on the structure of human language,[16] and some attempts at a general synthesis.[17] One might hope to relate this work to somewhat comparable studies on visual processing—for example, on the analytic systems involved in identification of three-dimensional objects under various conditions.[18] Perhaps it may be possible to sketch the bare outlines of a general cognitive psychology that will attempt to determine the structural properties of specific "mental organs" and their modes of integration, and to propose biological universals governing these systems, thus laying the foundations for a significant theory of human learning in various domains. Conceivably, the full range of questions on the nature of function, struc-

15. Cf. Edelson's further development of these themes in his *Language and Interpretation in Psychoanalysis* (1975).

16. For example, Leonard Bernstein, *The Unanswered Question* (1976); Ray Jackendoff and Fred Lerdahl, *The Formal Theory of Tonal Music* (forthcoming). See also Nelson Goodman, *Languages of Art* (1968).

17. Cf. Dan Sperber, *Rethinking Symbolism* (1975); Thomas A. Sebeok, "Semiotics: A Survey of the State of the Art" (1974), and "The Semiotic Web: A Chronicle of Prejudices" (1975). Also, Umberto Eco, *A Theory of Semiotics* (1976).

18. For a report on very promising recent research, see David Marr and T. Poggio, "From Understanding Computation to Understanding Neural Circuitry" (1976).

ture, physical basis, and development in the individual and the species may be open to investigation in coming years, for various components of the human mind. With the dramatic successes of the biological sciences in the past generation, it is perhaps not too much to hope that the classical questions concerning the nature of the human mind and its products may also be assimilated to the general body of natural science in the years that lie ahead.

REFERENCES

Austin, J. *How to Do Things with Words.* Oxford: Oxford University Press, 1962.
Berlin, I. *Vico and Herder.* New York: Viking, 1976.
Bernstein, L. *The Unanswered Question.* Cambridge, Mass.: Harvard University Press, 1976.
Buchdahl, G. *Metaphysics and the Philosophy of Science.* Cambridge, Mass.: MIT Press, 1969.
Chomsky, N. *Aspects of the Theory of Syntax.* Cambridge, Mass.: MIT Press, 1965.
———. *Cartesian Linguistics.* New York: Harper & Row, 1966.
———. *Reflections on Language.* New York: Pantheon, 1975.
———. *Essays on Form and Interpretation.* Amsterdam: Elsevier, 1977.
Cudworth, R. "Treatise Concerning Eternal and Immutable Morality." In *Works,* vol. 2. Edited by T. Birch. [U.S.], 1838.
Eco, U. *A Theory of Semiotics.* Bloomington, Ind.: Indiana University Press, 1976.
Edelson, M. "Language and Dreams: *The Interpretation of Dreams* Revisited." *Psychoanalytic Study of the Child* 27 (1972) : 203–82.
———. *Language and Interpretation in Psychoanalysis.* New Haven: Yale University Press, 1975.
Freud, S. *Standard Edition of the Complete Psychological Works.* London: Hogarth, 1953–64:
    The Interpretation of Dreams, vol. 5.

The Ego and the Id, vol. 19.

Moses and Monotheism, vol. 23.

An Outline of Psycho-Analysis, vol. 23.

Goodman, N. *Languages of Art.* Indianapolis: Bobbs-Merrill, 1968.

Grobstein, P., and Chow, K. L. "Receptive Field Development and Individual Experience." *Science,* October 24, 1975.

Hume, D. *A Treatise of Human Nature* (1738), vol. 1. New York: E. P. Dutton, 1961.

Inhelder, B.; Sinclair, H.; and Bovet, M. *Learning and the Development of Cognition.* Cambridge, Mass.: Harvard University Press, 1974.

Jackendoff, R., and Lerdahl, F. *The Formal Theory of Tonal Music.* (Forthcoming.)

Jung, C. G. *Memories, Dreams and Reflections.* Recorded and edited by A. Jaffé. New York: Vintage, 1965.

Kant, I. *Critique of Pure Reason.* Translated by N. K. Smith. London: Macmillan, 1963.

Marr, D., and Poggio, T. "From Understanding Computation to Understanding Neural Circuitry." Artificial Intelligence Laboratory, Memo 357, MIT, May 1976.

Marx, K. *Capital,* vols. 1, 3. New York: International Publishers, 1967.

Piaget, J. *Structuralism.* New York: Basic Books, 1970.

———. Contributions to *Proceedings of the Royaumont Conference on Phylogenetic and Ontogenetic Models of Development, 1975.* Paris: Seuil (forthcoming).

Rapaport, D. "The Theory of Ego Autonomy" (1957). In *The Collected Papers of David Rapaport.* Edited by M. M. Gill. New York: Basic Books, 1967.

Searle, J. *Speech Acts.* Cambridge: Cambridge University Press, 1969.

Sebeok, T. A. "Semiotics: A Survey of the State of the Art." In T. A. Sebeok, ed., *Current Trends in Linguistics,* vol. 12. The Hague: Mouton, 1974.

———. "The Semiotic Web: A Chronicle of Prejudices." Mimeographed. Bloomington, Ind.: Indiana University Press, 1975.

Sperber, D. *Rethinking Symbolism.* Cambridge: Cambridge University Press, 1975.

Vico, G. B. *The New Science.* Translated by T. G. Bergin and M. H. Fisch. Ithaca, N.Y.: Cornell University Press, 1948.

Warren, H. C. *A History of the Association Psychology from Hartley to Lewes.* Ph.D. dissertation, Johns Hopkins University, 1917. New York: Scribner's, 1921.

Weinberg, S. "The Forces of Nature." *Bulletin of the American Academy of Arts and Sciences,* January 1976.

Wittgenstein, L. *Philosophical Investigations.* London: Blackwell, 1953.

2

On the Biology of Language: Darwinian/Lamarckian Homology in Human Inheritance (with some thoughts about the Lamarckism of Freud)

HENRY EDELHEIT

> Symmetry establishes a ridiculous and wonderful cousin-ship between objects, phenomena and theories outwardly unrelated.
>
> —J. R. Newman (1956, p. 670)

Freud's work on aphasia (1891) had already focused his attention on language. It also brought him into admiring contact with the writings of Hughlings Jackson, whose Doctrine of Dependent Concomitance (discriminating mental events from events in the brain) set the method-ological terms for Freud's later development of psycho-analysis as a discipline separate from neurophysiology.[1] Freud hoped, nevertheless, to establish roots for a science of mind in physiology and ultimately in physics and chemistry. It may be, however, that if psychoanalysis is to find a firm basis in biological science, the path will lead through language.

The human language capacity is genetically given. More than that, I hope to demonstrate that language and

1. I have developed this idea in my paper on Complementarity (1976).

45

the genetic code form a complementary pair. Together they encompass human heredity. If we assign to language a place at the core of culture, we shall uncover an unsuspected symmetry between cultural transmission and genetic inheritance. For language and the genetic code share a structural feature that has enormous generative power. In language that feature has sometimes been called duality of patterning (Hockett, 1960), sometimes duality of structure (Lyons, 1970), and sometimes double articulation (Martinet, 1962). It applies also to the genetic code. That is, in both language and the genetic code, information is conveyed by a pattern of message-*carrying* units superimposed upon a pattern of message-*distinguishing* units—morpheme patterns on phoneme patterns in language, codon sequences on codons in the genetic code. These paired mechanisms are homologous in the general sense of sameness of relation: the organized components of each correspond in position, structure, and function to the organized components of the other.

1 Language and Evolution

On February 2, 1786, Sir William Jones, the founder of comparative linguistics, delivered to the Asiatic Society an address which contains the following passage:

> The *Sanskrit* language, whatever be its antiquity, is of a wonderful structure; more perfect than the *Greek,* more copious than the *Latin,* and more exquisitely refined than either, yet bearing to both of them a stronger affinity, both in the roots of verbs and in the forms of grammar, than could possibly have been produced by accident; so strong indeed, that no philologer could examine them all three, without believing them to have sprung from some common source. . . . [Quoted by Edgerton, 1946, pp. 5–6]

"That languages often resemble each other is obvious enough," observes Edgerton. "Even the specific fact that Sanskrit resembles Greek and Latin had been seen before. But no one before Jones had drawn the inference that these resemblances must be explained by the assumption of common descent" (ibid.).

A. L. Kroeber (1960) lists Jones's achievement among the precursors of evolutionary biology and marks it as the only one which went beyond the search for "regularity within process" to a genuine historicity. Jones's grouping of species of idioms into genera, and genera into a family, resulted, Kroeber observes, in "a genuine phylogeny, perhaps the first in any field of knowledge" (p. 8).

Thus Darwin's theory of the evolution of species by natural selection arose in a context of evolutionary concepts that had already long included the evolution of diverse languages from a common root form. The many similarities between the evolution of languages and the biological evolution of species had often been noted—by Darwin himself, and by Lyell and Schleicher, among others (Critchley, 1960). This interesting development in the history of ideas enforces a clear distinction, however, between the evolution of *languages* and the evolution of *human capacity for language*. From this point forward, it is the latter process that will occupy me here, especially in its relation to the evolution of the brain.

Loren Eiseley (1957) first brought my attention to the remarkable fact that the human brain triples in volume after birth, the largest part of the increment occurring in the first year of life. This extraordinary rate of postnatal growth is unique and not even approached by other species.[2] The threefold postnatal growth of the human brain is associated with a most significant and problematic

2. See graphs comparing brain and body growth in man and chimpanzee in Lenneberg, 1967, pp. 172–73.

aspect of human evolution—the "sudden" appearance of a large and complex brain constituting a "totally new factor in the history of life" (Eiseley, 1958, p. 306). It was this "explosive" appearance of the human brain on the evolutionary scene that brought Darwin into conflict with Wallace, the man who shared his discovery of natural selection.

Darwin, intent on establishing the affinity of man with the lower animals, seems to have posed his argument in such a way as to minimize the difference, making an effort to obliterate the gulf between the mental powers of human beings and those of the most highly developed "lower" mammals (for example, anthropoids, dolphins, dogs). Wallace confronted the fact of the enormous gulf and steadfastly refused to explain it away. He felt that the principle of natural selection (as it was then understood) could not account for the extraordinary properties of the human brain. Wallace, lacking the paleontological data and the theoretical instruments for understanding the enigma of the human brain, instruments which are still today incompletely developed, was inclined to the belief that "some higher intelligence may have directed the process by which the human race was developed" (Wallace, quoted by Eiseley, 1958, p. 312). Eiseley notes that "Wallace observed [correctly] what he was not able to understand." He adds that, from our present vantage point, Wallace's views do not mean that we have to abandon natural selection as a principle, "but it is obvious that we must seek selective factors of a sort that Darwin never envisaged and which may be bound up with speech and social factors difficult to investigate paleontologically" (1958, p. 320). Trager (1956) makes the point concisely: "In the fossil records of various manlike creatures, there is obviously no indication of the noises they made."

Wallace's views on special intervention displeased Darwin, though his responses to Wallace were remarkably temperate:

> Altogether I look at your article as appearing in the "Quarterly" as an immense triumph for our cause. I presume that your remarks on Man are those to which you alluded in your note. If you had not told me I should have thought that they had been added by someone else. As you expected, I differ grievously from you, and I am very sorry for it. I can see no necessity for calling in an additional and proximate cause in regard to Man. [Quoted in F. Darwin, 1959, p. 297]

Actually, Wallace's early insight (Eiseley, 1958, pp. 304, 307), that the explosively rapid evolution of the human brain was related to environmental factors which had already been crucially altered by the expanding brain itself, is a view now widely shared (see Washburn, 1960; Dobzhansky, 1964; Monod, 1971, p. 133). The critical alteration of selection pressures by "speech forming man" (Wallace, quoted by Eiseley, 1958, p. 307) deserves to be regarded as a prime factor in the effect of culture on human biological evolution. As Dobzhansky has put it:

> Since the environment in which man lives is in the first place his sociocultural environment, the genetic changes induced by culture must affect man's fitness for culture. The process thus becomes self-sustaining. Biological changes increase the fitness for, and the dependence of, their carriers on culture, and stimulate cultural developments. Cultural developments in turn instigate further genetic changes. This amounts to a positive feedback relationship between the cultural and the biological evolutions. Positive

feedback explains the great evolutionary change, so great that it creates the illusion of an unbridgeable gap, that transformed our animal ancestors into man. [p. 7]

Thus, a more sophisticated understanding of natural selection, coupled with the major paleontological discoveries of the past three decades (Dart, Broom, Leakey, and others), has fully vindicated Wallace's views while at the same time bringing them back into the Darwinian fold.

The following six interrelated factors (derived from various authors, including Washburn, 1960; Krantz, 1961; and Eiseley, 1957, 1958), seem to have been of major importance in the extremely complex process of human evolution:

1. The human pelvis (making possible upright posture, true bipedal gait, and liberation of the hands)

2. Manipulative hand with opposed thumb (facilitating the use of tools)

3. Increased cranial capacity (*phylogenetic;* volume increases by 50% from man-ape to modern man) [Eiseley, 1957, p. 94]

4. Threefold growth of the brain after birth (*ontogenetic*) [Eiseley, 1957, pp. 109–10]

5. Prolonged period of obligatory dependency of the human infant

6. Capacity for language.

Washburn (1960) summarizes the interplay of several of these factors as follows:

Some very limited bipedalism left the hands sufficiently free from locomotor functions so that stones or sticks could be carried, played with and used. The advantage that these objects gave to their users led both to more bipedalism and to more efficient tool use. . . . Selection is based on successful behavior, and in the man-apes the beginnings of the human way of life depended both on inherited locomotor capacity and on the learned skills of tool-using. The success of the new way of life based on the use of tools changed the selection pressure on many parts of the body, notably the teeth, hands and brain, as well as on the pelvis. But it must be remembered that selection was for the whole way of life. [p. 69]

An interesting and important point, because it bears on the prolonged period of dependency of the human infant, is that the enormous postnatal growth of the brain is, among other things, a necessary concomitant of the relatively narrow and rigid birth canal of the human pelvis (too narrow and too rigid to accommodate a fully developed brain), and it is this architecture of the pelvis that makes possible the upright posture, true bipedal gait, and freeing of the hands. Central to these interrelated processes is the dialectical relationship between the emerging capacity for language and the evolution of an ever larger and more complex brain.

The centrality of the language function in human evolution is underscored by Krantz (1961), who in an ingenious hypothesis attempts to explain the paucity of cultural innovation over a very long period of the Lower Paleolithic as against the Mousterian (a Middle Paleolithic culture). Krantz proposed that "the small-brained Paleolithic people *as adults* were mentally as well endowed as their modern descendants, but that as *young children* they were incapable of the use of symbolic language. This shortened the time available for acculturation and thus limited the culture content." The brain of the present-day human child crosses the 750 cc. level (empirically, the minimum compatible with communication by means of arbitrary symbols) toward the end of the first year of life.

A projected growth curve for the brain of Pithe-
canthropus (Krantz's Paleolithic population) indicates
that the 750 cc. threshold was not passed until after the
sixth year (or the fourth at the earliest). Since the life
span was also very short, this made for a limited period of
cultural experience and a reduced quantity and complexity of culture content transmitted to each generation.

Krantz's hypothesis provides an independent argument
(from the relation of minimal skull capacity to speech) for
the coexistence of speech with the manufacture of tools,
for progressively more elaborated artifacts begin to appear only with fossil human skulls of greater than 750 cc.
capacity.

The genetically given character of the *language capacity*
is revealed not only in the size and structure of the *brain*
but also in the structure of *language*. Human language is
both critically different from other animal communication systems and characterized by traits that hold
for all known human languages. Lenneberg (1960) takes
the universal presence of such traits as *phonemic behavior*
(all languages are organized on the basis of invariant
sound categories) and *grammatization* (all languages are
structured according to grammatical rules) as evidence
for genetic inheritance of the language capacity. It has
been observed that the areas of the human cerebral cortex associated with vocalization are proportionately very
large and that the control of the flow of speech is situated
in various areas of the dominant hemisphere. The brains
of apes (Vallois, 1955) are essentially symmetrical, while
that of man is larger on the dominant side. In a survey of
evolution and culture, Washburn and Howell (1960) observe that "a person can learn any language, but only a
human being is capable of learning language" (p. 52).

As for recent intensive efforts to teach human language to chimpanzees,[3] a proper evaluation of the results calls for an understanding of the precise difference between the structure of human speech and the structure of communication systems used by other species (see also Chomsky, 1972, pp. 69–70, p. 102; and chap. 1 of the present volume). Ingenious though they may be, the successful efforts to teach verbal or other language signs to chimpanzees are only superficially analogous to the teaching of human language to a child.

The discussion in some of the recent literature (for example, Lieberman et al., 1969), arguing that the chimpanzee is not endowed with the proper oral or thoracic configuration for the production of speech sounds, is ultimately irrelevant. The language-important anatomical difference between chimpanzee and human is not in the mouth or the shape of the pharynx but in the size and organization of the brain.[4] The widespread opinion that associates the large size and rapid postnatal growth of the human brain with *intelligence* rather than with *language capacity* may be a prejudice, for high intelligence is clearly an attribute of many infrahuman species and exists independent of language. On the other hand, much of the characteristic architecture of the human brain (Vallois and others) has to do with the language function, and it is this special language-connected organization that sharply differentiates the human brain from that of the ape.

As I have already suggested, this anatomical difference is reflected in the specific and universal structure of human languages as compared with the communication systems of other animals, including the higher primates.

3. Kellogg and Kellogg, 1933; Kellogg, 1968; Gardner and Gardner, 1969; D. Premack, 1971; Premack and Premack, 1972; A. J. Premack, 1975.
4. See Lenneberg, Eiseley, Krantz, Washburn and Howell, and others previously cited.

Apes organize sounds or semantic counters (Premack and Premack, 1972) on a single level only. Even though they generalize some signs or make a few novel sign combinations, each sign corresponds more or less to one meaning. Human languages, on the other hand, are uniquely characterized by the *duality of patterning* already referred to above (Hockett, 1960; Martinet, 1962).

Duality of patterning refers to the simultaneous patterning of a language on two levels—a level of smallest phonological elements (*phonemes*) serving to signalize differences in meaning but in themselves meaningless; and a level of smallest meaningful units (*morphemes*), each consisting of a limited arrangement of phonemes. Duality of patterning makes possible the propagation of an unlimited lexicon from a small and limited set of phonemic signs. The order of magnitude, therefore, of the human vocabulary is incomparably greater than that of the ape, whose inventory of thirty or forty signs (whether in the wild or in the laboratory) is limited to a comparably small number of meanings. Pushing the natural "vocabulary" of the ape from thirty or forty units to one hundred or several hundred units does not significantly increase the order of magnitude in relation to human language. Moreover, the laboratory-trained chimpanzee cannot transmit its acquired (*human-created*) vocabulary to its own offspring, for it is another universal of human language that the language capacity is passed from generation to generation; it is *genetically determined.*

I will show in part 3 how duality of patterning bears a special relationship to biological inheritance. For the present, I will anticipate the contents of part 2 (Language and Empathy) with the observation that the growth of language in each individual is intimately related to the very long period of obligatory biological dependency of the human child. Language plays a part in intrapsychic differentiation and at the same time in the separation of self from the image of the mothering person. Successful separation/individuation is a kind of weaning process epigenetically linked to the development of speech and alternative language forms. These are stimulated by the need to restore and in some ways to improve upon the surrendered maternal connection. With maturation the maternal bond, reconstituted as language, is refined to form a social instrument of great adaptive power. The growth of empathy belongs to the same maturational process.

2   Language and Empathy: Learning How to Talk

Empathy, according to a popular view, is a quasi-mystical intuitive modality whereby one person experiences, without mediation, the emotional state of another, primarily that other person's pain or suffering.

Such a view was dramatized in a 1968 television program in the science-fiction series *Star Trek*. On the second planet of the Minarian star-system, the crew of the starship *Enterprise* encounter a perfectly empathic creature—humanoid but not human. According to the television shooting-script (Muskat, 1968), the creature has a female form, is endowed with large, expressive eyes, and has no vocal cords. "Without speech . . . how's she able to understand us?" asks Captain Kirk, skipper of the *Enterprise*. The answer may be telepathy, but closer examination reveals that the creature is in fact an "empath." She understands by recreating the other person's experience in her own body. Furthermore, her empathic power (we learn as the story develops) not only makes it possible for her to *experience* the suffering of others but gives her the power to relieve this suffering by appropriating the pain to herself. Her perfect empathy expresses a perfect altruism. She is able to suffer *as* another, *for* another, in her own body and entirely without linguistic mediation.

In this appealing fable we recognize the elements of a universal fantasy. Captain Kirk has focused on the essential question: "Without speech, how is she able to understand us?" That is, to what extent is it possible to experience the subjective state of another and how can this be accomplished without words? It is tempting to think of empathy as a totally preverbal faculty developing independently from language and providing a channel for a magical kind of nonmediated communication. We have reason to believe that such fantasies derive from the universal experience of human infants.

A number of psychoanalytic authors have invoked the infantile mother/child unity as a model for the empathic process (see Ferreira, 1961; Olden, 1958). According to this model, empathy is understood as a merging, a reconstitution of the undifferentiated mother/child matrix, albeit in a controlled and segregated way, reminiscent of the concept of regression in the service of the ego (Kris, 1952; Schafer, 1959; Shapiro, 1974).

Freud, who introduced the term "empathy" into psychoanalytic discourse, described it as "a process . . . which plays the largest part in our understanding of what is inherently foreign to our ego in other people" (Freud, 1921, p. 108). Beyond that he had very little to say about it. Kohut (1966, p. 262) claims that "the capacity for empathy belongs . . . to the innate equipment of the human psyche and remains to some extent associated with the primary process." He shares a frequently expressed view that secondary-process modalities, more articulated and more efficient, if not always more effective, get superimposed on empathy in the course of development and impede its operation. He even adds that "The persistence of empathic forms of observation *outside of psychology* is, indeed, archaic and leads to a faulty pre-rational, animistic conception of reality" (p. 262 ff.; my italics). In support of his view, he cites Freud's evocation of an "original, archaic method of communication" which "in the course of phylogenetic evolution . . . has been replaced by the better method of giving information with the help of signals."

In an earlier paper (1959), however, Kohut had observed that "our psychological understanding is most easily achieved when we observe people of our own cultural background. Their movements, verbal behavior, desires and sensitivities are similar to our own, and we are able to empathize with them on the basis of clues that may seem insignificant to people from a different background" (p. 463). "The reliability of empathy declines," he concludes, "the more dissimilar the observed is from the observer" (p. 467). In other words, empathy, like language, is an innate capacity which can be actualized only within an existing culture. It is *from the culture* that it derives its specificity.

Ferreira (1961) deplores and also tries to account for "the quasi-mystic halo" that envelops empathy, which he defines as "an ability correctly to perceive non-verbalized feelings and moods" (p. 91). Such concepts as Ferenczi's "dialogues of the unconscious" or Reik's "third ear" are, Ferreira observes, "merely impressionistic descriptions of a phenomenon for which we continue to lack an appropriate theoretical anchorage."

Citing two articles by Olden (1953, 1958), Ferreira states: "There seems to be general agreement in considering empathy as a process of the ego." Thus, taking due account also of the archaic and autonomous roots of the ego, we begin to see empathy not so much as a primitive vestige but as an evolving function of that increasingly

differentiated structure, the ego, which has been described (Hartmann, 1949, pp. 81 ff.) as the specifically
human organ of adaptation. From a primitive, quasi-mystical phenomenon mediated by "hunches," "guesses," and
"intuition," empathy gradually comes to be viewed as a
highly differentiated and sensitive modality, which, like
musical ability, has the widest distribution and is to
various degrees educable. In these characteristics it bears
a strong similarity (I am inclined to say an *affinity*) to language.

While Ferreira points out that not all ego functions are
acquired, he holds that some of the nonacquired (innate)
functions may be "remnants" of archaic processes, ves-
tigial in normal adults. Ferreira does not, however, adequately account for the fact that such "remnants" may be
highly developed in healthy individuals, or that the language capacity itself (Chomsky, 1976; Lenneberg, 1967)
is paradoxically one of these archaic modalities. I do not
refer, of course, to the *realization* of this capacity in the
acquisition of specific languages. Chomsky conceptualizes
these as "boundary phenomena" resulting from the im-
pingement of a specific linguistic community on an individual with an innate linguistic endowment.

The *Star Trek* vignette is not altogether trivial, for it
focuses on the traditional view that divides empathy from
language. Thus Ferreira sees "highly developed" ego
functions as superimposed on empathy, an "archaic modality" that atrophies in the face of these "more advanced" processes (that is, language). Ferreira regards the
umbilical cord as a precursor of empathy, a primitive
bridge to the maternal environment that is the anatomical
analogue of empathy as a "bridge function" of the ego.

I prefer to place empathy in a linguistic context in
which both language and empathy serve biological adaptation via the most complex cultural elaborations. I have

argued elsewhere (1969) that the vocal-auditory pathway
has unique properties that confer upon it a specific role
in ego formation. In extension of that idea I here propose a model for empathy that relates it to the language
function itself. Such a view would be in harmony with
Ferreira's formulation when he says: "Empathy is rooted
in a primary unity with mother, and its fate and course
relate to the development of the ego" (p. 103). One has
only to understand the fate of that primary unity in the
course of development and its relation to the ontogenesis
of speech.

"We learn to speak the language of other people,"
Freud wrote in his monograph *On Aphasia,* "by en-
deavouring to make the sound-image produced by ourselves as like as possible to the [sound image coming from
the other person]" (1891, *S.E.* 14 : 211). At the same
time, the sounds we ourselves produce, together with the
proprioceptive messages from the organs of speech
(Freud calls these the "motor speech presentations") exert
a constant corrective force on our own vocalizations. In
relation to the emergence of empathy, it is important to
note that the *striving for vocal congruence* is a *preconscious*
process, subject to very delicate *preconscious* control by the
normal auditory feedback of one's own voice. The close
fitting of one's own voice to that of another, the *striving
for vocal congruence in the ontogenesis of speech,* constitutes
a special case of the striving to encompass the *experience,*
and not merely the *articulations,* of another person. As
early as the Project (1895), Freud had suggested that
there is a reciprocity (that is, a dialectic relationship) between the development of speech and the development
of object relationships (p. 366). His early interest in
aphasia focused his attention on language in such a way
that his ideas about language (often in covert form)
permeate his later psychological theories. His descrip-

tion of the speech apparatus in the aphasia monograph, after undergoing partial transformation and further elaboration in the Project, emerges ultimately in his structural theory as a description of the ego itself (Edelheit, 1969, pp. 390–92).

The *close fitting* of one's own voice to that of another, *the striving for vocal congruence in the ontogenesis of speech, provides, I believe, a meaningful model for empathy, potentially more productive than the model of regressive merger alone.*

We must also keep in mind that when the child is learning to speak, it is met "halfway" in its efforts by the mothering person, who "automatically" adapts her own utterances, bringing them closer to the phase-specific articulatory and syntactic competence of the child. From the fully conscious point of view of science, the phase-specific structure of child language, with characteristics quite different from those of adult speech, has only recently begun to be elucidated (Weir, 1962; Bellugi, 1964; C. Chomsky, 1969; Menyuk, 1969; and others).

We designate as especially empathic those mothers who are most successful in fostering age-appropriate speech development in their children. Rosen (1961) notes that "the mother who constantly anticipates the child's needs with inadequate insistence upon their being made explicit may discourage the development of precision in formal verbalization, while [the mother who] makes premature demands upon such a development might promote a formalism that submerges the full capacity for individuality of expression" (p. 456). In a later paper (1967) Rosen showed how a partially deaf mother's empathic failure was reflected in a compensatory obsessional emphasis in the thinking and speech of her child. Speech development is not an isolated phenomenon. It is concurrent with and functionally related to psychic organization and to the separation and individuation of the child.

In the concept of *distancing,* Werner and Kaplan (1963) have posited a similar mechanism for *symbol formation.* Out of an undifferentiated matrix of mother and child, a four-way polarization takes place. There is a distancing of mother and child and concurrently a distancing between thing (referent) and word (symbolic vehicle). As this happens, the word becomes less concrete in its reference and achieves relative autonomy, as mother and child achieve relative autonomy from one another. At first mother, baby, and thing are all tightly bunched. With the passage of time, an increasing distance in both time and place occur, the word as symbol for the thing meanwhile taking on independence. Mother and child come to talk about the thing meaningfully from across the room, even when the thing is no longer actually present.

What has been said about empathy in the ontogenesis of speech has implications also for therapeutic psychoanalysis, which might be characterized as another language-learning situation (relearning corresponding to restructuring). I would regard therapeutic empathy, too, as *postlinguistic* rather than *preverbal,* since it exploits ego-functions in which language development is crucial.

I have argued that empathy is characterized by a genetically determined and developmentally fostered congruence of inner experience with the experience of another—an overlapping that appears to be an expectable consequence of an integrated evolutionary process. From this point of view, the capacity for empathy is organically inherent in both the observer and the observed. It arises at the critical boundary where, as we shall see, Darwinian and Lamarckian mechanisms meet—in the ontogenesis of speech. Empathy, an innate capacity, is potentiated by the process of learning how to talk, and like language, it depends for its elaboration on the stimuli that arise within a given culture.

3   Structural Linguistics, Molecular Biology

Speech is the least deceptive mirror of the mind.
                                    —Erasmus, *Praise of Folly* [5]

When Ernest Jones begged Freud to omit from *Moses and Monotheism* a passage promulgating the Lamarckian view of inheritance (the inheritance of acquired characteristics), Freud simply refused. Jones argued that no responsible biologist any longer regarded Lamarckian theory as tenable. Freud replied that they were all wrong and that the passage must stay.

Freud's relation to Darwinism was, to say the least, equivocal. He appears to have ignored natural selection entirely. Although Jones (1957, p. 310) rejects the thought that Freud could have been unfamiliar with that concept, the evidence does not support Jones's argument. The term *natural selection* does not appear in Freud's writings. More than that, whenever he took a stand on evolutionary theory (and in spite of his many obeisances to Darwin), his position was Lamarckian (see Jones, pp. 306–14). A single exception, passed over without any apparent awareness of contradiction with his usual views, appears in *Beyond the Pleasure Principle* (1920), where Freud summarizes Weismann's concept of the isolation of the germ plasm (pp. 45 ff.).

In fairness it must be said that Freud's Lamarckism was perhaps unique only in its survival far into the twentieth century. Darwin himself, under pressure from Thomson's [6] attack on the geological time scale, retreated into a partial acceptance of the Lamarckian view. [7] Thomson, ar-

5. Trans. B. Radice (Baltimore: Penguin Classics, 1971), p. 67.
6. Later Lord Kelvin.
7. Ritvo (1965, 1972, 1974), in a series of scholarly papers on Freud's Lamarckism, has dealt extensively with its relationship to Darwin's own Lamarckian views. She points out also that though the principle of natural selection was firmly entrenched among biologists by the time of World War I, neo-

guing from a position that did not yet take into account
the phenomenon of radioactivity and the transformation
of mass into energy, calculated that the rate of energy
dissipation from the sun and the related residual heat of
the earth did not permit of such long time spans as the
geologists were postulating. By implication, the time span
that Darwin required for the operation of natural selection was also threatened. "I take the sun very much to
heart," he complained to Lyell, and to Wallace he wrote
(in the letter already quoted in part 1): "Thomson's views
of the recent age of the world have been for some time
one of my sorest troubles" (F. Darwin, 1959, p. 296).

Nineteenth-century condensations of evolutionary time
made it appear logical to look for living survivals of earlier stages of humanity. The search for the "missing link"
even became assimilated to the idea of a hierarchy among
existing races. Such distortions (Freud's evolutionary
views also came out of this context) were based, not only
on the uncertain status of the geological time scale in the
light of Thomson's researches, but also on the long-per-
sistent paucity of paleontological evidence of human evolution and on the nebulous views that enveloped the concept of heredity before the founding, early in this
century, of a scientific genetics based on the work of
Gregor Mendel. Freud's Lamarckism was related to a
general foreshortening of the evolutionary time scale in
the nineteenth century and also to a failure to appreciate
the catalytic function of speech in the evolutionary process. In both regards, as we have seen, he was not alone,
and to some extent he shared these problematic views
with Darwin himself.

Freud's philosophical and scientific roots were not limited to the biological ferment of the nineteenth century.

Lamarckian flickerings occasionally appeared in the serious biological literature
up to the last decade of Freud's life.

Jones (1957) remarks that Freud seems to have followed his ancestral traditions in feeling aloof from the animal world. Jones illustrates this with the folk-saying, "If a Jew says he enjoys fox hunting he is lying," and adds, "It was only at the end of his life that he got on to speaking terms with a dog" (p. 306). Perhaps these same ancestral traditions, which included veneration for the written word, played an unsuspected part in the persistence of his Lamarckism.

Freud's personal compression of evolutionary time (which found expression also in his view of pharaonic Egyptian as a "primal" language [Freud, 1910]) suggests that his implicit time scale was in fact biblical. He would appear to have condensed evolution with history, geology with archaeology, and the evolution of the human capacity for language with the invention and "evolution" of writing. Thus, paradoxically and on an unconscious level, he would seem to have shared a biblical time scale with the anti-Darwinian religious fundamentalists of the second half of the nineteenth century. These unconscious remnants of a biblical perspective seemed to grow more pronounced as Freud grew older and are most clearly represented in *Moses and Monotheism,* precisely the work where, in relation to oedipal guilt and the fear of castration, he most explicitly and stubbornly took a Lamarckian position on the inheritance of acquired characteristics.

We must also take another factor into account in our consideration of Freud's Lamarckism, and that is that *human* evolution does in fact have a Lamarckian component. Though we now know that other species (for example, Japanese macaques) develop rudimentary cultures that in a limited way are transmitted by teaching and learning, or by imitation, the extent to which human experience is fixed in language and is in this form transmitted from one generation to the next is unique and, in recent evolutionary time, has been exponentially facilitated by the invention of writing.

Cultural inheritance is Lamarckian, as Peter Medawar has pointed out (1960). Human beings do adapt to their environments by means of transmitting from generation to generation an acquired "record" of the experience of the group. For untold eons this information passed by oral tradition and through the persistence of manufactured objects. For a few thousand years culturally preserved experience has accumulated at an accelerated rate through written history and the records of science, technology, and the arts. And yet the written word bears the imprint of speech, of which it is an artifact.

Human inheritance is indeed a dual inheritance: Darwinian via the genes, Lamarckian via language and culture. Just as the Darwinian mechanism is embodied in the genetic substance, DNA, so the Lamarckian mechanism is embodied in language; and, as I noted at the beginning of this essay, both language and the genetic code are characterized by *duality of patterning*. Furthermore, *only* language and the genetic code are so characterized (more precisely—only language and its *derivatives; only* the genetic code and its *products*). In both systems, information is conveyed by superimposing a pattern of "full" or message-*carrying* units on a pattern of "empty" or message-*distinguishing* units. To repeat, this arrangement of a few simple invariants in two simultaneous patterns makes possible the generation of a corpus having unlimited scope and variability. I quote Hockett's own definition:

> Any utterance in a language consists of an arrangement of the phonemes of that language; at the same time, any utterance in a language consists of an

arrangement of the morphemes of that language, each morpheme being represented by some small arrangement of phonemes. [1958, pp. 574–75]

It is an obligatory characteristic of this system of dual patterning that the units of the first level are contained as constituents in the units of the second level and that the units of the first level are functionally different from the units of the second level. As I have already pointed out in part 1, the function of the first-level units (*phonemes*) is to signalize differences in the meaning (semantic content) carried by the second-level units (*morphemes*). The first-level units are called *cenematic* (meaning *empty*). The second-level units carry the message and are therefore called *plerematic* (meaning *full*).

These elegant and resonant terms (*cenematic* and *plerematic*) were suggested by Hjelmslev (Hockett, 1963, p. 12). They are of particular value here because they serve precisely to extract the concept of *duality of patterning* from its rootedness in speech, to free it from exclusive association with the vocal-auditory pathway, and to extend it to other modalities. Beyond that, Hjelmslev's terms underscore the homology between duality of *morphophonemic* patterning of languages and duality of *stereochemical* patterning in the genetic code. I have hinted at this homology elsewhere (1969) and have also there discussed the ways in which language functions intrapsychically, to create structure, as well as intersubjectively, to communicate. (Similarly, the genetic code, which in the first instance determines biological structure, may be said to have a kind of teleonomic communicative function [see Monod, 1971], conveying adaptive "information" from one generation to the next.) More important, however, language (anchored in duality of patterning) provides an armature for an unlimited plurality of cultures, just as the genetic code determines the differential structure of a multiplicity of species.

By sequential arrangement of a limited number of phonemes (there are approximately thirty-six segmental phonemes in English)[8] it becomes possible to construct an unlimited number of meaningful elements (morphemes, the plerematic units of speech). A plurality of cultures results in the multiplication of linguistic species (lexicons). Each lexicon is composed of a catalog of morphemes and serves to communicate about *an unlimited universe of subjects.*

In the same way, through the sequential arrangement of only sixty-four codons (constituting all the possible combinations of four nucleotides taken three at a time [see Monod, 1971, pp. 189 ff.]), it becomes possible to specify the sequence of only twenty amino acids and in this incredibly parsimonious way to reproduce *an unlimited universe of biological forms.*

Each phoneme can be further analyzed in terms of an even smaller number of *distinctive features* (Jakobson and Halle, 1956). In the genetic substance—DNA—the nucleotides which constitute the codons correspond to this smaller number of distinctive features.

Just as the phonemes are not in themselves the bearers of meaning (this is a function of the morphemes), the codons are not in themselves the carriers of genetic information (that is, the codons are the cenematic or empty elements of the genetic code). It is the *sequential arrangements* of the codons within the DNA molecule that form the plerematic (or full) units of the genetic code. Thus, the *codon sequences* in the DNA molecule correspond to

8. Since apes can produce thirty or forty different kinds of sounds, their *sound* inventory would be sufficient for true language production. But they lack the crucial capacity to organize those sound categories in simultaneous patterns of cenematic and plerematic units.

morphemes in language. Insofar as the codon sequences (set off between specific individual codons that serve as markers for "start" and "finish") are known to be coterminous with *genes,*[9] we can reduce our equations to read simply: phonemes ≅ codons, and morphemes ≅ genes (that is, phonemes in language correspond structurally to codons in the genetic substance, and morphemes correspond structurally to genes). Ultimately, as I have indicated above, the codon sequences specify amino acid sequences in the structure of protein.

What is remarkable is that the complementary mechanisms of human inheritance—Darwinian and Lamarckian, biological and cultural—are homologous (that is, exactly parallel) in structure.[10]

Medawar observed that the Lamarckian character of cultural transmission may account, in general, for a persistent psychological pressure to ascribe Lamarckian mechanisms (erroneously) to genetic evolution. I am suggesting, more specifically, that the crucial role of *lan-*

9. Not all discrete codon sequences code for a gene product. Some serve other functions in the transcription process (personal communication, Dr. William Konigsberg, Yale University School of Medicine). See also McKusick and Ruddle (1977, p. 390).

10. That such an astonishing homology could arise as a result of random variation might be accounted for as follows: (1) Natural selection favors those design features (configurations) that are most successful in conferring optimal adaptation in competition with other organisms. (2) Duality of patterning is preeminently such a configuration, manifesting both a constancy of core structure and a variability that allows for both maximal persistence of the trait and maximal operation of the selection principle. (3) Such a design feature, having once appeared, has an extremely high probability of survival. This one has, *by chance,* occurred twice in the course of evolution; first, as a design feature of the germ plasm; again, as a design feature of speech (a behavioral capacity conferred by the germ plasm). (4) Each of these occurrences has had such great adaptive potential as to guarantee survival of the trait through positive feedback.

Duality of patterning is not just a winning hand—it is a royal flush. By chance this royal flush has occurred twice in the very long history of evolution, and each time has profoundly altered its course.

guage in cultural transmission (a Lamarckian mechanism dependent upon a capacity achieved through a Darwinian evolutionary process) may have been a factor in Freud's Lamarckism, for Freud's stubborn insistence on the heritability of acquired characteristics in the human species derives a measure of justification from the homology of the two mechanisms and the functional evolutionary relationship that exists between them.

It is, in the end, not surprising that the first true phylogeny was the linguistic one formulated by Sir William Jones, and it is touching to learn that he was also mindful of the more general beauty and order of nature. His intellectual interests expanded broadly beyond language. He wrote on Indian music, chess, Indian chronology, the solar zodiac and the Hindu lunar year (Edgerton, 1946). According to his successor and biographer, Lord Teignmouth:

> His last and favorite pursuit was the study of botany. It constituted the principal amusement of his leisure hours. In the arrangement[s] of Linnaeus, he discovered system, truth, and science, which never failed to captivate and engage his attention; and, from the proofs he exhibited of his progress in botany, we may conclude, if he had lived, that he would have extended the discoveries in that science. [Quoted by Edgerton, p. 9]

Jones responded intuitively to a kinship between language and botany that he could not himself have formulated. He could not have known to what extent language would turn out to be a part of nature. We can now see that language may provide the most striking manifestation of human dual inheritance: Darwinian insofar as its fundamental characteristics are genetically determined, Lamarckian in that its specific forms are acquired and passed via the culture from generation to generation. The resulting superimposition of one duality upon another is a unique feature of human language, and it may be that this compounding of dualities is reflected in the remarkably fluid adaptation of the human species and in its power over the rest of the natural world.

REFERENCES

Bellugi, U., and Brown, R., eds. *The Acquisition of Language*. Monographs of the Society for Research in Child Development, No. 29, 1964.

Chomsky, C. *The Acquisition of Syntax in Children from 5 to 10*. Cambridge, Mass.: MIT, Research Monograph Series, No. 57, 1969.

Chomsky, N. *Language and Mind*. New York: Harcourt, Brace, Jovanovich, 1972.

———. *The Language Faculty as a Mental Organ*. Fourth annual Bychowski lecture. Mount Sinai School of Medicine of the City University of New York, May 3, 1976.

Critchley, M. "The Evolution of Man's Capacity for Language." In S. Tax, ed., *Evolution After Darwin*, vol. 2 of *The Evolution of Man*. Chicago: University of Chicago Press, 1960.

Darwin, F., ed. *The Life and Letters of Charles Darwin*, vol. 2. New York: Basic Books, 1959.

Dobzhansky, T. "Evolution—Organic and Superorganic." *Bulletin of Atomic Scientists*, May 1964, pp. 4–8.

Edelheit, H. "Speech and Psychic Structure." *Journal of the American Psychoanalytic Association* 17 (1969) : 381–412.

———. "Complementarity as a Rule in Psychological Research." *International Journal of Psycho-Analysis* 57 (1976) : 23–29.

Edgerton, F. "Sir William Jones" (1946). In T. A. Sebeok, ed., *Portraits of Linguists*, vol. 1. Bloomington: Indiana University Press, 1966.

Eiseley, L. *The Immense Journey* (1957). New York: Random House, Vintage Edition (paper), 1959.

———. *Darwin's Century*. Garden City, N.Y.: Doubleday, 1958.

Ferreira, A. J. "Empathy and the Bridge Function of the Ego." *Journal of the American Psychoanalytic Association* 9 (1961) : 91–105.

Freud, S. *On Aphasia* (1891). Translated by E. Stengel. New York: International Universities Press, 1953. Also extracted in *Standard Edition* 14 : 209–15.

———. *Standard Edition of the Complete Psychological Works*. London: Hogarth, 1953–74.

Project for a Scientific Psychology (1895), vol. 1.

"The Antithetical Meaning of Primal Words" (1910), vol. 11.

Beyond the Pleasure Principle (1920), vol. 18.

Group Psychology and the Analysis of the Ego (1921), vol. 18.

Moses and Monotheism (1939), vol. 23.

Gardner, R. A., and Gardner, B. T. "Teaching Sign Language to a Chimpanzee." *Science* 165 (1969) : 664–72 (August 15, 1969).

Hartmann, H. "Comments on the Psychoanalytic Theory of the Instinctual Drives" (1949). *Essays on Ego Psychology*. New York: International Universities Press, 1964.

Hockett, C. F. *A Course in Modern Linguistics*. New York: Macmillan, 1958.

———. "The Origin of Speech." *Scientific American* 203, no. 3 (September 1960) : 88–96.

———. "The Problem of Universals in Language." In J. H. Greenberg, ed., *Universals of Language,* 2d ed. Cambridge, Mass.: MIT Press, 1963.

Jakobson, R., and Halle, M. *Fundamentals of Language*. The Hague: Mouton, 1956.

Jones, E. *The Life and Work of Sigmund Freud,* vol. 3. New York: Basic Books, 1957.

Kellogg, W. N., and Kellogg, L. A. *The Ape and the Child*. New York: McGraw Hill, 1933. Reprinted, New York: Hafner, 1967.

Kellogg, W. N. "Communication and Language in the Home-

Raised Chimpanzee." *Science* 162 (1968) : 423–27 (October 25, 1968).

Kohut, H. "Introspection, Empathy, and Psychoanalysis." *Journal of the American Psychoanalytic Association* 7 (1959) : 459–83.

———. "Forms and Transformations of Narcissism." *Journal of the American Psychoanalytic Association* 14 (1966) : 243–72.

Krantz, G. S. "Pithecanthropine Brain Size and Its Cultural Consequences." *Man* (May 1961), pp. 85–87.

Kris, E. *Psychoanalytic Explorations in Art.* New York: International Universities Press, 1952.

Kroeber, A. L. "Evolution, History and Culture." In S. Tax, ed., *Evolution After Darwin,* vol. 2 of *The Evolution of Man.* Chicago: University of Chicago Press, 1960.

Lenneberg, E. H. "Language, Evolution and Purposive Behavior." In S. Diamond, ed., *Culture in History: Essays in Honor of Paul Radin.* New York: Columbia University Press, 1960.

———. *Biological Foundations of Language.* New York: Wiley, 1967.

Lieberman, P. H., Klatt, D. H., and Wilson, W. H. "Vocal Tract Limitations on the Vowel Repertoires of Rhesus Monkey and Other Nonhuman Primates." *Science* 164 (1969) : 1185–87 (June 6, 1969).

Lyons, J. *Chomsky.* Fontana Modern Masters, edited by F. Kermode. London: Fontana/Collins, 1970.

McKusick, V. A., and Ruddle, F. H. "The Status of the Gene Map of the Human Chromosomes." *Science* 196 (1977) : 390–405.

Martinet, A. *A Functional View of Language.* Oxford: Clarendon Press, 1962.

Medawar, P. B. *The Future of Man.* New York: Basic Books, 1960.

Menyuk, P. *Sentences Children Use.* Cambridge, Mass.: MIT, Research Monograph Series, no. 52 (1969).

Monod, J. *Chance and Necessity.* Translated by A. Wainhouse. New York: Knopf, 1971.

Muskat, J. *The Empath.* In J. Blish, adapter, *Star Trek 10.* New York: Bantam Books, 1974.

Newman, J. R. *The World of Mathematics*. New York: Simon & Schuster, 1956.

Olden, C. "On Adult Empathy with Children." *Psychoanalytic Study of the Child* 8 (1953) : 111–26.

———. "Notes on the Development of Empathy." *Psychoanalytic Study of the Child* 13 (1958) : 508–18.

Premack, D. "Language in Chimpanzee?" *Science* 172 (1971) : 808–22 (May 21, 1971).

Premack, A. J., and Premack, D. "Teaching Language to an Ape." *Scientific American* 227, no. 4 (October 1972) : 92–99.

Premack, A. J. *Why Chimps Can Read*. New York; Harper & Row, 1975.

Ritvo, L. B. "Darwin as the Source of Freud's Neo-Lamarckianism." *Journal of the American Psychoanalytic Association* 13 (1965) : 499–517.

———. "Carl Claus as Freud's Professor of the New Darwinian Biology." *International Journal of Psycho-Analysis* 53 (1972) : 277–83.

———. "The Impact of Darwin on Freud." *Psychoanalytic Quarterly* 43 (1974) : 177–92.

Rosen, V. H. "The Relevance of 'Style' to Certain Aspects of Defence and the Synthetic Function of the Ego." *International Journal of Psycho-Analysis* 42 (1961) : 447–57.

———. "Disorders of Communication in Psychoanalysis." *Journal of the American Psychoanalytic Association* 15 (1967) : 467–90.

Schafer, R. "Generative Empathy in the Treatment Situation." *Psychoanalytic Quarterly* 28 (1959) : 342–73.

Shapiro, T. "The Development and Distortions of Empathy." *Psychoanalytic Quarterly* 43 (1974) : 4–25.

Trager, H. "Language and Evolution." *Encyclopaedia Britannica*, 1956.

Vallois, H. V. "Ordre des primates." In *Traité de Zoologie, Anatomie, Systématique, Biologie*, 17 : 1854–2206. Paris: Masson, 1955. (Cited in Washburn and Howell, 1960, p. 51.)

Washburn, S. L. "Tools and Human Evolution." *Scientific American* 203, no. 3 (September 1960) : 63–75.

Washburn, S. L., and Howell, F. C. "Human Evolution and Culture." In S. Tax, ed., *Evolution after Darwin,* vol. 2 of *The Evolution of Man.* Chicago: University of Chicago Press, 1960.

Weir, R. H. *Language in the Crib.* The Hague: Mouton, 1962.

Werner, H., and Kaplan, B. *Symbol Formation.* New York: Wiley, 1963.

3

The Linguistic Act

KARL H. PRIBRAM

Noam Chomsky suggests in his essay in this volume that inquiry into language should proceed as it would for any body organ or system. This suggestion should meet a receptive audience in psychoanalytically trained psychiatrists and psychologists who daily use language as a self-contained system of communication. After all, psychotherapy is for all practical purposes a linguistic discipline and so has much to gain from a deepened understanding of what language is all about.

As a biologist steeped (Pribram and Gill, 1976) in Freud's *Project for a Scientific Psychology* (1895), I feel at home with both Chomsky's and Freud's approaches to language. Freud's experience and insights (*On Aphasia,* 1953) into the disturbances of language produced by brain injury were the cornerstone of the portions of the Project devoted to thought, speech, and language (Forrester, 1975). Chomsky treats the brain as the locus of origin of the organ of language, and most of my life has been devoted to studying brain function. I want, therefore, to anchor the discussion of the relationship between language and psychoanalysis by reviewing the relevant facts about brain function, and will do this according to the outline for inquiry provided by Chomsky: function, structure, physical basis, development in the individual, evolutionary development.

Language and Cognition

First, let us inquire whether it is appropriate to treat language as a separate functional system. Might it not be preferable to think of language as the ultimate development in cognitive ability? Freud, in the Project, does in fact treat speech in this fashion:

> The biological development of this extremely important . . . [kind of] association also deserves consideration. Speech-innervation is originally a path of discharge for ψ, operating like a safety-valve, . . . it is a portion of the path to *internal change,* which represents the only discharge till the *specific action* has been found. This path acquires a secondary function from the fact that it draws the attention of the helpful person (usually the wished-for object itself) to the child's longing and distressful state; and thereafter it serves for *communication* and is thus drawn into the specific action. At the start of the function of judgement, when the perceptions, on account of their possible connection with their wished-for object, are arousing interest, and their complexes (as has already been shown) are dissected into an unassimilable component (the thing) and one known to the ego from its own experience (attribute, activity)—what we call *understanding*—[at this point] two links emerge in relation to utterance by speech. In the first place, there are objects—perceptions—that make one *scream,* because they arouse pain; and it turns out as an immensely important fact that this association of a sound (which arouses motor images of one's own as well) with a perceptual [image], which is composite apart from this, emphasizes that object as a hostile one and serves to direct attention to the perceptual

[image]. When otherwise, owing to pain, one has received no good indication of the quality of the object,
the information of one's own scream serves to characterize the object. Thus this association is a means of
making memories that arouse *unpleasure* conscious
and objects of attention: the first class of *conscious
memories* has been created. Not much is now needed
in order to invent speech. There are other objects,
which constantly produce certain sounds—in whose
perceptual complex, that is, a sound plays a part. In
virtue of the trend towards *imitation,* which emerges
during judging, it is possible to find the information
of movement attaching to this sound-image. This
class of memories, too, can now become conscious. It
now still remains to associate intentional sounds with
the perceptions; after that, the memories when the
indications of sound-discharge are observed become
conscious like perceptions and can be cathected from
ψ.
    Thus we have found that it is characteristic of the
process of *cognitive* thought that during it attention is
from the first directed to the indications of thought-
discharge, to the indications of speech. [*S.E.,*
1 : 366–67; Freud's italics, translator's brackets]

And again: *"Thus thought accompanied by a cathexis of the
indications of thought-reality or of the indications of speech is the
highest, securest form of cognitive thought-process"* (*S.E.,*
1 : 374; Freud's italics). This treatment of language in the
Project is consistent with Freud's analysis in his book *On
Aphasia.* The book was written in protest to the naïve
localization of psychological functions in the brain so
popular in the latter part of the nineteenth century.
Freud emphasized the relationship between cortical areas
in the construction of functional systems, a view later es-

poused by Liepman and currently by Geschwind (1965).

Thus, if we accept the psychoanalytic metapsychology uncritically, we cannot proceed with the inquiry as Chomsky has proposed. If language is simply the tip of the cognitive iceberg, we had better look to cognitive processes as a whole—to the development of intelligence rather than of language—as the subject matter of our analysis.

Two facts argue against identifying language with cognitive ability. First, although Freud correctly argued against naïve localizationism, it is untrue that brain damage, cognitive deficit, and language disturbance occur indiscriminately and pari passu with one another. Freud was, in fact, responsible for naming the agnosias (cognitive deficits—disabilities in "gnosis" or knowing) and distinguishing them from aphasias, disabilities in speaking. Every neurologist, including Freud, knows that the agnosias come in a variety of sensory-related modes (stereognosis, visual agnosia, and so forth) and that the brain loci for injury to one or another gnostic system are different from the loci that result in language disturbances. I believe Freud took these distinctions for granted and emphasized the development of the audiovocal process and its disruption because he had already made the distinction between audiovocal agnosia—that is, aphasia— and other forms of agnosia. But I may be mistaken in this belief, and Freud may well have considered the audioverbal, visuoverbal, tactiverbal functions—and thus the aphasias, alexias, and agraphias—as part and parcel of the brain's cognitive mechanism. Such a view would not, in itself, be contrary to the data on the localization of language functions in the brain. (For review, see Pribram, 1971, chap. 19.)

There is a second piece of evidence, however, in support of Chomsky's approach, and this one is less ambiguous. Anyone who has visited an institution that houses the mentally retarded cannot but be impressed by the verbal fluency of so many of the retardates. Despite severe cognitive limitations, these patients are able to speak and communicate readily. There are some, in fact, whose mathematical language ability is so well developed that they are known as "idiot savants"—they can often outperform simple computers in speed and accuracy of computation. Whatever the brain mechanisms for cognition and language, they are separately affected in these patients—language fluency often remains intact despite severe cognitive retardation. Thus, language cannot be just the tip of the cognitive iceberg, the ultimate expression of cognitive ability.

Language and Communication

Having disposed of this initial problem concerning the separateness of the human linguistic system, we are now ready to proceed seriously with Chomsky's suggestions for analysis. What is the function, structure, and physical basis for language? I have elsewhere presented my views on these topics (Pribram 1971, 1973, 1975, 1977) and the reasons for them, but they bear reviewing in the context of the psychoanalytic frame. Further, linguists, neurolinguists, and psycholinguists continue to be active in exploring these questions, so new relevant data are continuously being brought to bear on the hypotheses put forward.

Human language appears to be used for two purposes: communication between individuals and communication within an individual (that is, thinking). However, interindividual communication can take place without the use of language (as by eye contact, simple gesture, distancing, and the like); and thinking can use imagery, be devoid of the rules that define ordinary language, or, for that mat-

ter, be devoid of any other discernible structure. Interpersonal communication and thought thus do not define
human language; they only describe its functions. The
situation is a familiar one in physiology: the main function of breathing is respiration, but respiration encompasses oxygen and carbon dioxide transport by red blood
cells, membrane properties, and so forth, as well as
breathing. The definition of a process is ordinarily given
in terms of its structure, that is, its components and their
arrangement. The function of a process relates it to a
larger domain (much as relativity relates mechanistic laws
to larger universes).

Language and Information

In short, the function of language is communication—
inter- and intrapersonal. The next question to be answered, therefore, is how is the function accomplished—
how does language communicate? The contemporary answer to this question given by behavioral and neuroscien-
tists is in terms of information-processing. This answer
can easily mislead one, however, if the definitions of "information" and "processing" are not clearly delineated.

The term *information* is used by scientists in three distinct ways. One way is akin to the common definition that
information conveys meaning. This is the "semantic" definition. Second, communication scientists speak of information as the amount of uncertainty reduced when a
message is transmitted. This measure on information has
been related to its novelty and to the reciprocal of entropy, a thermodynamic concept that defines the efficiency with which energy is organized (Brillouin, 1962).
This second definition of information is its "transmission"
definition. Third, control engineers use the term *information* to denote the amount of match or mismatch between
a setpoint and the input/output to that setpoint in a feed-

back loop. Here "information" becomes synonymous with "error." This, then, is the "control" definition of information.

The distinction between information as "novelty" and as "error" was initially recognized by Shannon and Weaver (1949), who labeled them "good" and "bad" information. Ashby (1960) also recognized the distinction, pointing out that error reduction was in fact different from uncertainty reduction—error reduction enhances redundancy rather than providing novelty.

During the nineteen-fifties and early sixties, information scientists failed to perceive the distinction between error-processing by closed feedback loops and the processing of messages conveying novelty—that is, instructions—by computer programs which are hierarchical open-loop (helical) constructions. This failure in part accounted for difficulties in applying information concepts to problems in the behavioral sciences, including psycholinguistics.

However, once the distinction between the two types of processes is achieved, information concepts become extremely helpful. For instance, it is clear that the psychoanalytic concepts of primary and secondary process are based in large part on such a distinction. Primary processes are defined by Freud in the Project as those in which neuronal discharge takes place. Such discharge can lead to muscular contraction, chemical secretion, or neural association—all primary processes which are subject to feedback regulation via the environment, neural sensitivities to the chemicals secreted (or others stimulated by the secretions), and reciprocal innervation. Freud clearly distinguishes such primary from secondary or cognitive processes, which are hierarchically organized by a variety of carefully described neural mechanisms. (See Pribram and Gill, 1976, for review.)

As noted, Freud places speech at the top of the secondary-process, cognitive hierarchy, whereas Chomsky considers language as a separate system. Are these two views incompatible? The answer to this question cannot be given in functional terms. We must, therefore, now turn to linguistic structure and its physical embodiment to pursue the question posed by this difference between Freud and Chomsky.

Language, Sign, and Symbol

Note that Freud discusses speech, while we have been discussing language. Perhaps herein lies the key not only to any possible differences between Freud's approach to language and Chomsky's, but to the larger problem of what makes human language human.

We have already encountered the fact that interpersonal communication can occur nonverbally through gestures and the like. Communication is also established by artifacts, and it is only by way of such artifacts that prehistoric man communicates with us. Whether such cultural artifacts are to be considered a "language" is a moot point. Certainly they are representations, and their communicative use is specified by rules. If we agree that communication by gestural signs can constitute a language (as claimed by those using American Sign Language to communicate with apes—for example, Gardner and Gardner, 1975), then why not communication by cultural artifacts?

Artifacts as language have an advantage over gestures and speech not only in that they are palpable, but in that they allow us to view in slow motion, as it were, the biological processes involved in their construction. These processes, as we shall see, are the same as those that characterize gestural and verbal languages; but because artifacts are less temporary, their construction and communicative impact can be analyzed at leisure.

Artifacts are of two sorts—both representations of occurrences, that is, of objects and events. One type of artifact attempts to portray the object or event as faithfully as possible, recording it for subsequent use. The other type of artifact is an arbitrary token whose meaning is locked in the rules of usage. The record type of artifact depends on the stability of the physical universe for its interpretation; the arbitrary token demands social stability for decoding.

Different brain mechanisms are responsible for the two types of representations. Records are constructed by way of the posterior convexity of the cortex, while arbitrary tokens involve the functioning of the fronto-limbic forebrain (Pribram, 1971, chaps. 17 and 18).

The distinction between record and token has also been used to analyze verbal communication (Peirce, 1934), where the term *sign* is often used to indicate a record while *symbol* stands for a token. Thus, the letters *a*, *c*, and *t* are signs that invariably denote letters of the alphabet in many languages, while "act" and "cat" place these letters in symbolic combinations, "words," whose meaning (that is, usefulness) depends on the particular language and the sentences of that language in which the "words" are found.

Computer scientists also distinguish between constructions that are sensitive only to the local context—a figure-ground relationship—and those that depend on more general contextual structure for meaning. The figure-ground type of record is ordinarily called context-free to contrast it with more generally context-dependent constructions. The organization of context-free constructions is by way of categorization and is therefore hierarchical. The organization of context-dependent constructions is by way of interweaving graph structures, more weblike than treelike.

There is every reason to believe that the brain organization involved in the construction of context-free signs is categorical and hierarchical, while that of context-dependent symbolic representations is weblike and often paradoxical. I have elsewhere (Pribram, 1971, 1974a, 1974b, 1974c, 1976) detailed the evidence for these two types of neural mechanisms, proposed some mathematical tools by which to describe them, and delineated the problems they raise for understanding human verbal propositional language. Before reviewing some of these facets of the issues, however, let us return to artifacts as communicative representations and discuss the more general problem of human action as a representational process.

Language and Action

The analysis of what constitutes an "act" must take into account the difference between the structure of a process and its function, discussed earlier. There are three levels to be considered: The anatomical (structure), the physiological (process—which maps structure into function), and the behavioral (function). The anatomical substrate of action is the neural motor mechanism with its muscle effectors. The physiological process of that mechanism concerns movements, that is, patterned muscle contractions and relaxations. The behavioral function engaged by the neuromuscular system is an environmental consequence of those movements. The levels are distinct and what is known about each poses problems for the others to explain.

Thus, anatomically, the motor system displays a precise topographical relationship between muscle and brain cortex. Functionally, however, this topographical relationship becomes organized into patterns centered on joints. The question arises as to how this is accomplished. Further, at the behavioral level equivalences become manifest—the same act can be performed by a variety of movements (one can write with one's left hand, toes, or teeth if one has to—and experience with these uncommonly used effectors is not essential).

I have suggested that the mapping of topographical precision into movement and movement into action occurs by virtue of the inhibitory interactions among the topographically distinct pathways; that mathematically, the frequency domain best describes these inhibitory interactions; and that equivalences are accounted for by the sensitivities of the frequency domain to the environmental consequences of movements rather than to the pattern of movements or the singular muscle contractions (or relaxations) per se. Thus, the reactivity of cortical motor neurons reflects the force exerted on or by the muscles rather than the extent of their isotonic or isometric contraction. The evidence for these suggestions has been reviewed in some detail (Pribram, 1971, chaps. 12 and 13; 1974c).

The important point here is that an explanation is possible and that it involves making the distinction between the structure of a physical organ or substrate, and the process by which that substrate is mapped into a behavioral function. It is most important not to confuse the process with the behavioral function engaged by the process. The organization of the neuromuscular mechanism is not the same as the pattern of movements it produces. Nor are patterns of movements the same as the acts (such as cultural artifacts) that are organized by them. Freud in the Project carefully makes these distinctions and adheres to them subsequently, and though most psychologists refer to responses as acts (Skinner once pointed out that behavior is the set of responses recorded on a cumulative chart to be taken home and studied), they do so implicitly rather than explicitly. By contrast, ethologists and other more biologically oriented behaviorists identify responses with the patterns of movements elicited from the organism by environmental stimuli. Is it any wonder, therefore, that psychologist and biologist fail to understand one another, despite the fact that both are studying "the behavior of organisms"?

When we extend this analysis to communicative acts, to the construction of signs and symbols (and to combining them into statements—see below), we attain a new perspective. Motor *acts* (as contrasted to movements) involve environmental consequences and can thus be sensed as such. In fact, the entire motor mechanism operates in large part by regulating the sensitivities of muscle receptors (through the γ efferent neurons). The thermostat, with its feedback organization, becomes the model for action, rather than a stimulus-response arc. George Miller, Eugene Galanter, and I (1960) proposed the Test-Operate-Test-Exist (TOTE) as the elementary representation of this process. Powers (1973) has developed our proposal into a theory which emphasizes that *all behavior* is undertaken to satisfy some *perceptual* requirement. And George Miller and Philip Johnson-Laird (1976) have applied the same principle to the study of language—especially the meaning of words. So let us take a look at the relationship between perception and language as it pertains to the construction of signs, symbols, and statements.

Language and Perception

Artifacts as records and tokens can be processed at leisure. By contrast, gestures and voiced articulations are fleeting, and their sense must be processed rapidly for communication to occur. Still, the neural mechanism for *generating* gestures and voiced articulations cannot differ in kind from the motor mechanism described in the previous section. The generative process must be built by control over receptor processes that sense *consequences,* not the muscular contractions in fingers or in the vocal apparatus.

Again, let us take an intermediate step to see how this might be accomplished. Consider first a musical instrument interpolated into the communication between fingers and audience. According to the principles outlined above, the guiding representation in the brain of the musician would be that of the consequences of fingering the instrument (keyboard, strings, or stops), rather than that of the contractions of the finger muscles.

Now consider a voiced articulation. Here the vocal apparatus becomes the instrument, and the representation must consist of the effective *use* of that apparatus, not of the individual contractions of vocal cords, palate, tongue muscles, and so forth. In this instance, as in the case of the musical instrument, use is registered via hearing—but other modalities may become involved as well. Use, therefore, constructs a multimodal representation in the motor mechanisms of the brain, a representation of the effect muscular contractions have on altering a variety of *sensory* inputs. Communication occurs when a match is established between these sensorimotor representations in the communicants.

The point of this analysis is that though we perceive acts, including communicative acts, the communication is a form of action, *not* perception. Action is different from perception. Perceptions generate brain representations of occurrences, that is, of objects and events in the perceiver. Communications can also be said to involve "perception," but this broad use of the term obscures the fact that an entirely different process is described. Occasionally, the term *perception* is used in this broad sense to also denote feelings—in which instance brain biochemical states are "perceived" and labeled. In its more restricted sense, the term *perception* refers only to the process of imaging and categorizing objects and events—while the term *feeling* is used to refer to our awareness of internal states. In the same manner, actions describe yet another process, distinct from perceptions and feelings. Actions denote the generation of environmental representations. When the act is communicative, the environment in which the representation is generated is another brain. Thus, a communication occurs when act and percept fuse in both actor and perceiver.

Language and Feelings

Language thus derives from action but *generates* perceptions and feelings. When language generates perceptions, signs are constructed. When language describes feelings, symbols result (Langer, 1972, p. 400).

By what process, then, does language generate perceptions and feelings? Return once again to artifacts. Artifacts are external, environmental representations of the internal, neural, sensorimotor representations that generate the artifacts. The artifacts can be *made* to resemble some object or event. However, as a representation it resembles the object or event, it does not reproduce it (*we* paint a picture of an orange; only orange *trees* reproduce oranges). On the other hand, the artifact can be made to generate a feeling—a feeling of familiarity or novelty, of comfort or effort, of feasibility or infeasibility, and so forth. The artifact as token is so constructed that its use reevokes a feeling rather than an occurrence per se. (A religious symbol is a token of shared feelings.) Of course, an artifact can be both record and token, a duality that enhances its communicative power.

When communication is less stable, as by gesture and speech, the duality of record (sign) and token (symbol) becomes processed in a variety of ways. In human language, making significant and symbolic representations is called making statements. Ordinarily, statements symbolize *feelings* about the significance of objects and events. "The boy is running away." The statement is one about a belief regarding "boy," "running," and "away." "Boy," "running," and "away" record (signify) occurrences; "is" serves as a token (symbol) for the belief (feeling of familiarity and feasibility) that the statement is representative.

Several levels of sign and symbol construction can be identified in human language. Two have already been used as examples: (1) *a, c, t* as signs vs. *act* and *cat* as symbols, and (2) the just-completed analysis of the statement "The boy is running away." How did human language develop such an intricate and involved organization of statements composed from the same two always distinct brain processes, those generating signs and those generating symbols, processes that are repeatedly fused in level upon level?

As both Freud and Chomsky suggest, the answers to this question must come from looking at the development of the human organism, both in history and as an individual.

Language and Thought

An important discovery has recently (Marshack, 1975) emerged from the study of prehistoric human art and artifact: Beyond any reasonable doubt, some such artifacts are symbols depicting feelings, not just signifying occurrences, and symbolic art and artifact can be found whenever and wherever the genus *Homo* existed. Early man thus molded sign into symbol in order to communicate his feelings. It is, of course, equally clear that the beginning of the historic period is characterized by the significant use of symbols—arbitrary tokens representing the

familiar are combined *according to shared rules* (feasibilities) into *words* that signify occurrences.

It is unlikely that words were first generated in man's
haptic-visual (written) competences; in fact, there is evidence in the body of prehistoric legend that "in the
beginning was the word"—that is, that the significant use
of symbols was initiated by the vocal-auditory apparatus,
perhaps as early as the making of symbolic artifacts. But
the evidence is not conclusive. Two distinct stages in the
development of human communication—and thus culture—may well have occurred. During the first stage, artifacts and gestures predominated. The competencies
that developed during this period were primarily haptic
and visual. Gestures were used to denote occurrences,
while other nonverbal, though not necessarily nonvocal,
means were used to express and communicate feelings.
Only in artifacts were the two processes combined—environmental representations could signify both an occurrence and its symbolic evocation of feelings.

The second stage of development of human communication appears to have centered on the use of the
vocal-auditory apparatus. Either the dramatically increased vocal-auditory competence occurred early but remained latent, or because of the environmental imper-
manence of the representations it generates, there is no
early record of the exercise of this competence. In any
case, by the time of the legendary period of prehistory,
vocal-auditory communication had been honed to a high
level of sophistication. By the end of this period, the
vocal-auditory competence had become sufficiently well
developed so that expressions of feelings—symbols—
could be used to denote occurrences; shared rules had
been developed—that is, logical thinking had taken place.
However, in order that such rules could be formulated
and formally transmitted, a new cultural tool (artifact)

was invented that gave permanence to the vocal-auditory achievements. This tool combined the vocal-auditory and haptic-visual competencies in the act of writing and ushered in the historic period.

The significant use of symbols—best exemplified by mathematics—manipulates tokens according to shared rules that allow the symbols to be used as signs, provided the frame of rules remains inviolate. Logic thus depends on establishing axioms, frames, or contexts—symbolic constructions representing familiarities and feasibilities. Within the context of these frames, symbols can be used as signs; ordered manipulation of the content of the representation can take place. In short, the organism can think logically.

The vocal-auditory competence and the haptic-visual competence thus differ in emphasis. When art and artifact are generated, significance, that is, record, is essential to the representation. The sign can then be used as a token to represent a feeling—but this becomes a secondary use. Vocalization, by contrast, is used by all primates to express feelings; thus the vocal-auditory competence is primarily and initially a symbolic competence. How that competence came to be used to signify occurrences remains the main question to be answered regarding the evolution of man.

Language and Learning

A few tentative answers to this question are beginning to emerge from studies of the relationship of the development of the brain and the development of language in individual human beings. In most of us vocal-auditory competence—speech—is located in the left hemisphere. Its cortical representation, as might be expected, is centered on the termination of tracts bringing signals from the cochlea and the origin of others that control the vocal apparatus. Phylogenetically the ear developed from the gill slits of fishes; thus, both peripherally and centrally, ear and vocal apparatus are juxtaposed—there is no long route to traverse from throat to ear or from auditory sensory cortex to vocal, sensory, and motor cortex. Our vocalizations directly influence the cochlea, and there is overlap between secondary auditory and secondary sensory areas receiving input from the vocal mechanism.

One of the most pervasive attributes of human existence is the long period of dependency of human infants, children, and juveniles. During this period the normal brain cortex becomes programmed by its input. Thus, in individuals who for one reason or other are born without arms (for example, the thalidomide babies) only a rudimentary cortical representation of arms develops. Or, if animals or humans are deprived of normal patterned visual input (as in squint or congenital cataract) during this developmental period of plasticity, the cells of the visual cortex fail to develop and even deteriorate in their innate competence to resolve patterns (Wiesel and Hubel, 1965; Hirsch and Spinelli, 1970; Westheimer, 1972). And we all know how easily and flawlessly children can learn second languages until puberty, after which much greater difficulty is experienced and "accents" cannot be erased.

This extended period of plasticity of the human brain is perhaps best illustrated by the well-known fact that entire hemispherectomies—even of the hemisphere in which the language representation has been initiated—can be performed before the ages eight to ten with remarkably little permanent damage (Smith, 1966, 1972).

More recently a subtle finding has emerged. When the brain is damaged during childhood in and around the auditory cortex, it is frequently possible for other portions of the same hemisphere to be recruited to take over the language competency. When, however, damage occurs in the sensorimotor representations of the vocal apparatus, the development of language competence invariably shifts to the opposite hemisphere (Milner and Rasmussen, 1976). This suggests that the vocal aspect of the vocal-auditory competency is the more pervasive and primary of the two—that the act of vocalization is the origin of the competence.

Remember once more, however, that an act is constituted by making an *environmental* representation—in the case of vocalization this would mean a representation in the vocal apparatus that produces an invariant input to the auditory portion of the vocal-auditory mechanism.

The process so described calls up an image of a primitive young person—perhaps even an infant—vocalizing for the pure joy of being able to produce recognizable sounds. The babbling stage of modern man, which quickly leads to holophrases, is the contemporary equivalent. Having generated these identifiable sounds by virtue of this characteristically human competence, the primitive person begins to attach these vocal-auditory artifacts to the haptic-visual ones that his humanness has already generated. It is only a step then to use the vocalizations to denote the occurrences that the artifacts were meant (used) to represent. Symbolic expressions of joy (familiarity, effort, feasibility, and comfort) are being used as signs. Thought has occurred. Speech has developed and human communication by statements of symbolic significance become possible.

Conclusion

In concluding, let us return to Freud and Chomsky and the question of a separate linguistic competence—a separate organ of mind for language. As noted, Freud considers speech to be useful in generating representations with a minimal expenditure of energy. In the quotation from the "Project," Freud emphasizes the role of somatic experience in the genesis of thought through judgment. It is perhaps for this reason, as well as for the obvious fact of the written word, that Freud views language as a part of a more pervasive process. Yet, the clinical and psychometric facts do distinguish between linguistic and other cognitive competencies and even between various linguistic competencies—such as composing music or poetry or computer programs or mathematical models. Perhaps herein lies the solution to the puzzle: The human brain is composed of a variety of cognitive organs, *each* of which is graced with linguistic competence. Freud is right—language is the highest development of the cognitive mechanism.

But Chomsky is also right—there are a variety of cognitive processes, each with its own form and structure. The transformational aspects of only some of these cognitive structures are recognized as a form of human "language"; musical composition, poetry, mathematics, logic, and ordinary communicative language are among these. Gestural communications, musical melody and harmony, geometry and topology, the know-how of motor skills (for example, skiing, auto repairing, sculpture), we may be less inclined to call "language"—and the reader may have had his doubts about admitting the cultural artifacts that were used as examples in this essay as instances of the expression of any linguisticlike competence. But I hope that the analysis will not be scuttled because we are not yet agreed as to just which type of structure we shall admit to the category "linguistic." Such a definition should arise out of understanding, not be imposed on it.

In short, sociobiological and neuropsychological evidence and analysis suggest that in a sense both Freud and Chomsky are correct. Certain identifiable systems have developed in man's brain that make cognitive processing possible to an extent not found in other primate brains. The enhanced cognitive processing of several of these systems—not just one, as Chomsky suggests—partakes of characteristics that we may comfortably identify as linguistic. They thus form the tips of cognitive icebergs, as Freud suggests; but contrary to Freud, we might not be comfortable in identifying all cognitive tips as linguistic. Currently, a great deal of attention is being centered on hemispheric specialization of brain systems. The left hemisphere in ordinary right-handed persons is specialized for processes that we commonly call linguistic. The right hemisphere is also specialized, for other cognitive processes, also peculiarly human—musical and manipultive abilities, for example—but not commonly called linguistic.

The problem remains, therefore, to distinguish the commonality among processes that we are willing to label "linguistic" and to determine whether one brain mechanism is responsible for them.

Sequentiality and stimultaneity are good candidates as the critical dimensions involved. Analysis of sequences is necessitated by the evanescence of the representations formed by vocal-auditory acts, while simultaneity is fostered by the structure of the gestural-visual mechanism. Thus, in the end we may well want to subscribe to Chomsky's suggestion and opt for a linguistic organ (or group of organs)—an organ derived from the operation of the vocal-auditory apparatus. As noted, Freud and all subsequent neurologists have defined vocal-auditory agnosias as aphasias—disturbances of language.

I, for one, am willing at this time to leave open the question of what constitutes a language. Written forms of the vocal-auditory act—with its phonemes, and so forth—constitute the prototype of linguistic communication today. But perhaps with the advent of television, the gestural enactment of drama and the visualization of occurrence will become organized into a cultural communicative process that derives its structure more from gestural-visual generation of artifacts than from the vocal-auditory apparatus. Whether in the long run we shall call this structure "linguistic" remains to be seen. We are already concerned with "body language"; perhaps other "languages" based on tonicity and mime are in the offing.

REFERENCES

Ashby, W. R. *Design for a Brain.* 2d ed. New York: Wiley, 1960.

Brillouin, L. *Science and Information Theory.* 2d ed. New York: Academic Press, 1962.

Forrester, J. "The Function of Language in Freud's Psycho-Analysis." Fellowship dissertation, King's College, Cambridge, November 1975.

Freud, S. *On Aphasia.* New York: International Universities Press, 1953.

———. *Project for a Scientific Psychology* (1895). *Standard Edition of the Complete Psychological Works,* vol. 1. London: Hogarth, 1966.

Gardner, R. A., and Gardner, B. T. "Early Signs of Language in Child and Chimpanzee." *Science* 187 (1975) : 752–53.

Geschwind, N. "Disconnexion Syndromes in Animals and Man: Part I." *Brain* 88 (1965) : 237–94.

Hirsch, H., and Spinelli, D. N. "Visual Experience Modifies Distribution of Horizontally and Vertically Oriented Receptive Fields in Cats." *Science* 168 (1970) : 869–71.

Langer, S. K. *Mind: An Essay on Human Feeling.* Vol. 2. Baltimore: Johns Hopkins University Press, 1972.

Liepman, H. "Anatomische Befunde bei Aphasischen und Apraktischen." *Neurologisches Zentralblatt* 31 (1912) : 1524–30.

Marshack, A. *Origins and Evolution of Language and Speech.* New York: New York Academy of Sciences, 1975.

Miller, G. A.; Galanter, E.; and Pribram, K. H. *Plans and Structure of Behavior.* New York: Henry Holt, 1960.

Miller, G. A., and Johnson-Laird, P. *Language and Perception.* Cambridge, Mass.: Harvard University Press, 1976.

Milner, B., and Rasmussen, T. *The Role of Early Brain Injury in Determining Lateralizations of Cerebral Speech Functions.* New York: New York Academy of Sciences, 1976.

Peirce, C. S. *Collected Papers.* Vols. 1–6. Cambridge, Mass.: Harvard University Press, 1934.

Powers, W. T. *Behavior: The Control of Perception.* Chicago: Aldine, 1973.

Pribram, K. H. *Languages of the Brain: Experimental Paradoxes and Principles in Neuropsychology.* Englewood Cliffs, N.J.: Prentice-Hall, 1971.

————. "The Comparative Psychology of Communication: The Issue of Grammar and Meaning." *Annals of the New York Academy of Sciences* 223 (1973) : 135–43.

————. How Is It That Sensing So Much We Can Do So Little?" In F. O. Schmitt and F. G. Worden, eds., *The Neurosciences Study Program, III, 1974.* Cambridge, Mass.: MIT Press, 1974. (a)

————. "The Isocortex." In D. A. Hamburg and H. K. H. Brodie, eds., *American Handbook of Psychiatry,* vol. 6. New York: Basic Books, 1974. (b)

————. "Toward a Holonomic Theory of Perception." In S. Ertel, L. Kemmler, and M. Stadler, *Gestalttheorie in der modern Psychologie.* Cologne: Erich Wengenroth, 1974. (c)

————. "Neurolinguistics: The Study of Brain Organization in Grammar and Meaning." *TOTUS HOMO* [Milan] 6 (1975) : 20–30.

————. "Self-consciousness and Intentionality: A Model Based on an Experimental Analysis of the Brain Mechanisms Involved in the Jamesian Theory of Motivation and Emotion." In G. E. Schwartz and D. Shapiro, eds., *Consciousness and Self-Regulation, Advances in Research,* vol. 1. New York: Plenum Press, 1976.

————. "Modes of Central Processing in Human Learning." In T. Teyler, ed., *Brain and Learning.* Stamford, Conn.: Greylock, 1977. In press.

Pribram, K. H., and Gill, M. M. *Freud's 'Project' Re-assessed.* New York: Basic Books, 1976.

Shannon, C. E., and Weaver, W. *The Mathematical Theory of Communication*. Urbana, Ill.: University of Illinois Press, 1949.

Smith, A. "Speech and Other Functions After Left (Dominant) Hemispherectomy." *Journal of Neurology, Neurosurgery, and Psychiatry* 29 (1966) : 467–71.

———. "Dominant and Non-dominant Hemispherectomy." In W. L. Smith, ed., *Drugs, Development, and Cerebral Function*. Springfield, Ill.: Thomas, 1972.

Westheimer, G. "Mapping the Visual Sensory on to the Visual Motor System." *Investigative Ophthalmology* 11 (1972) : 490–96.

Wiesel, T., and Hubel, D. "Comparison of the Effects of Unilateral and Bilateral Eye Closure on Cortical Unit Responses in Kittens." *Journal of Neurophysiology* 28 (1965) : 1029–40.

4

What Is the Psychoanalyst
Talking About?

Marshall Edelson

. . . the whole question of adapting language to psychology, after all the ages during which it has been adapted to
bad logic, is so difficult that I can hardly do more than indicate some of its problems.

Bertrand Russell

The psychoanalyst as a scientist expresses in theoretical
sentences propositions about the mind. This paper considers some ways we might answer the question: What do
the sentences making up the scientific theory of psychoanalysis mean?

The analysand also formulates expressions. The psychoanalyst tries to understand what these expressions
mean. The psychoanalyst also tries to understand what
the analysand means by these expressions. These two
uses of 'mean' are not synonymous. The latter use of
'mean' implies such questions as: What does the analy-

Professor Ruth Marcus, Yale University Department of Philosophy, with
whom I have studied philosophical issues in logic, did not discuss this paper or
its contents with me throughout the writing of it. She is therefore in no way
responsible for any errors; for my exposition or application of symbolic logic;
or for any of my formulations or conclusions. However, any clarity in the paper
regarding logic and philosophical issues in logic should be attributed to her. I
owe a great debt to her for the stimulus and example of her thinking, which
manages to be at the same time rigorous and precise, elegant, truth-seeking,
and completely lucid.

sand signal, indicate, or perhaps unwittingly betray by these expressions? What does the analysand intend to effect or achieve by using these expressions? The former use of 'mean' implies the following group of questions: What is the analysand talking about? What is the analysand saying about whatever-it-is-the-analysand-is-talking-about? The psychoanalyst in his clinical work formulates in various expressions interpretations which purport to answer, however tentatively, *both* kinds of questions. When we ask, 'What do these expressions—these interpretations—of the psychoanalyst mean?' we may want as answer a scientific theory of psychoanalytic interpretation. This paper seeks to make a contribution toward the formulation of such a theory.[1]

To answer the question 'What is the psychoanalyst talking about?' requires a theory of language and meaning. Such a theory calls upon the resources of a number of disciplines. Linguistics is one of these disciplines. Linguistics in turn—even if its domain is limited to the phonological, syntactic, and semantic properties of sentences in natural languages—contributes to and depends upon the philosophy of language, symbolic logic, and cognitive psychology. Poetics is a second such discipline. What might be considered a branch of both biology and psychology—the biology and psychology of symbolic functioning—is a third. Also, we should add the discipline of sociology, especially insofar as it studies symbolic media in interactional systems (Edelson, 1971b), and the discipline of anthropology, which studies culture, systems of cultural objects or the symbolic world which is the milieu of distinctively human life. In fact, it is difficult to think of any human science or any branch of the humanities

---

1. For previous discussions of the questions 'What is the subject matter of psychoanalysis as a science and what conceptual apparatus does such a science require?' and 'What is a theory of interpretation in psychoanalysis?' see Edelson (1971a, 1971b, 1972, 1975, 1977).

that may safely be omitted from such a catalogue. This difficulty is enough to suggest that the very existence of the question posed by the title of this paper, and the requirements listed for answering it, imply the existence of conceptual bridges between science and the humanities.

A theory of sign-processes or symbolic functioning will have many branches. One might focus on the formal properties of sign systems. Another might focus on individual works or types of works, which are artifacts of culture constructed of signs. Still another might focus on the acquisition or development of the capacity for symbolic functioning; or instead study the use of signs in particular and various circumstances in personality and interactional systems to conceive and to achieve ends. A branch of such a theory might focus on the actual (as opposed to the intended) effects of signs in particular circumstances; or upon the conditions (neurophysiological, psychological, social) which are necessary for, and which constrain, the use of signs. Another branch might concern itself with the pathologies of symbolic functioning.

It is possible that an adequate logic of signs and theory of sign-processes might help to account for the fact that many statements made by the various sciences of man as well as by disciplines within the humanities are logically homologous. Certainly such a logic of signs and theory of sign-processes will prove indispensable in addressing definitively the questions raised in this paper about a scientific psychoanalytic theory of the mind in general and about a scientific theory of psychoanalytic interpretation in particular.

Psychoanalysis as Science

Is psychoanalysis a science of tropes? At the beginning of a recent series of brilliant lectures on Wallace Stevens,[2]

2. Yale University, January–April, 1976.

Harold Bloom turned my attention to a passage in Lionel Trilling's essay, "Freud and Literature." Trilling's review of Freud's influence on literature begins on a somewhat deprecatory note. Here, Trilling emphasizes Freud's "positivistic rationalism"; his "simple materialism"; his "simple determinism"; his "limited sort of epistemology"; his denial of validity to myth or religion; his contempt for art as "substitute gratification," a "narcotic," "a sort of inner dishonesty." an illusion (albeit harmless and beneficent) in contrast to reality.

Trilling attributes these positions and attitudes to Freud's therapeutic work. Psychoanalytic therapy treats patients who suffer from illusions—what is *not there*. It enables the patient to discover the cause of his illusions, free himself from its effects, and thus cope with reality practically and effectively rather than fictively.[3] This naïve opposition of what is *there* and what is *not there* conflicts with Freud's view that "the mind, for good as well as bad, helps create its reality by selection and evaluation . . . the reality of social life and of value, conceived and maintained by the human mind and will" (Trilling, 1950, p. 44).

According to Trilling, Freud's conception of art, for all these reasons, is inadequate; and the application of psychoanalytic methods in attempts to understand the hidden meanings of specific works or to explain the artist as man pretends to more than it can accomplish. Nevertheless, Freud's great contribution outweighs these deficiencies. This contribution "lies in no specific statement that he makes about art but is, rather, implicit in his whole conception of the mind." It is in the following passage that psychoanalysis is asserted to be a science of tropes.

> For, of all mental systems, the Freudian psychology is the one which makes poetry indigenous to the

---

3. Trilling's formulation.

very constitution of the mind. Indeed, the mind, as Freud sees it, is in the greater part of its tendency exactly a poetry-making organ. This puts the case too strongly, no doubt, for it seems to make the working of the unconscious mind equivalent to poetry itself, forgetting that between the unconscious mind and the finished poem there supervene the social intention and the formal control of the conscious mind. Yet the statement has at least the virtue of counterbalancing the belief . . . that poetry is a kind of beneficent aberration of the mind's right course.

Freud has not merely naturalized poetry; he has discovered its status as a pioneer settler, and he sees it as a method of thought. Often enough he tries to show how, as a method of thought, it is unreliable and ineffective for conquering reality; yet he himself is forced to use it in the very shaping of his own science, as when he speaks of the topography of the mind and tells us with a kind of defiant apology that the metaphors of space relationship which he is using are really most inexact since the mind is not a thing of space at all, but that there is no other way of conceiving the difficult idea except by metaphor. . . . [It] was left to Freud to discover how, in a scientific age, we still feel and think in figurative formations, and to create, *what psychoanalysis is, a science of tropes,* of metaphor and its variants, synecdoche and metonymy. [Italics mine, pp. 52–53]

No scientist, regardless of what discipline, needs to be convinced today of the importance of tropes. Metaphor, for example, is not only a figure or trope in rhetoric or poetics. Metaphor can be defined in the terminology of logic as an expression of identity or similarity in the form of relations among entities in different domains.

A formal system is a set of abstract statements about

the kind of relations (unnamed) among entities (un-named) in a domain (unspecified). An interpretation of a formal system specifies a domain, identifies the entities in the domain, and names the relations among them. One interpretation is a model of another interpretation of the same formal system (Suppes, 1957). Metaphors may be considered to be models in this sense. A metaphor is a different interpretation of the underlying abstract system of relations of which we already have an interpretation. Metaphors as models are important in the natural sciences (for example, the isomorphism between the universe of discourse called mathematics constituted by numbers and their relations, and the universe of discourse constituted by physical spatiotemporal entities in the object-world and their relations). Metaphors as models are important in the social sciences (for example, the isomorphism—documented by Levi-Strauss—between the universe of discourse constituted by mythical entities and their relations, and the universe of discourse constituted by persons, physical objects, cultural objects, and social institutions, and their relations). Metaphors as models are important in psychoanalysis (for example, the isomorphism, called "transference," between the analysand's conception of events in the psychoanalytic situation and conception of events in his past personal history). Freud's use of analogies should not be regarded as mere literary device. By the use of analogies, he develops in *The Interpretation of Dreams* a model of dream-construction in particular and a model of the workings of the mind in general (Edelson, 1977, p. 18).

However, Harold Bloom tells me he is skeptical that *any* linguistic expression is other than tropological or figurative; there is, he believes, no such thing as a literal statement. I am inclined to dissent, because I cannot conceive of "figurative" without recourse to "literal." The disagreement here is minor. Bloom is interested in particular expressions occurring in texts and contexts. Indeed, his sensitivity to the contribution of an extended context (the full range of which he has internalized) to the meaning of an expression is paralleled in my experience only by what is required of the psychoanalyst attempting to interpret what the analysand is talking about. On the other hand, insofar as I am committed to scientific work I am committed to the study of the properties of idealized objects. 'Tropes' and 'literal statements' are such idealizations. 'Figurative' and 'literal' are abstract aspects of actual expressions—that is, they are semantic properties which have been abstracted from actual linguistic entities. Noam Chomsky has demonstrated by his own achievement to what degree scientific advance in a particular field depends upon appropriate idealization. Such idealization is exemplified in linguistics by the study of: sentences rather than actual utterances; syntax (or phonology or semantics) as a separate component of language; linguistic competence abstracted from linguistic performance; and linguistic competence abstracted from other cognitive capacities.[4]

How, then, distinguish 'figurative' from 'literal'? Trilling comments, "The unconscious mind works without the syntactical conjunctions which are logic's essence" (Trilling, 1950, p. 53). He includes not only "because," "therefore," and "but," under logic, but the "general" in opposition to the "concrete" and the "large abstraction" in opposition to the "tangible trifle."

Of course, this is an inadequate conception of the scope and essence of logic as it is understood today. It seems to me as well (and perhaps I read unfairly too much of some tone into his phrases in these paragraphs) that here Trilling comes perilously close to falling prey to the same

4. See, for example, Chomsky (1972, 1975a).

kind of simplistic view that, at the beginning of his essay, he attributes to Freud. For he seems to imply that logic in contrast to poetics is lifeless and unimaginative.

Many who work in other branches of the humanities and many psychoanalysts particularly concerned with the relationship of psychoanalysis and the humanities seem to have a distaste for logic. They feel antipathy for its technical vocabulary and forbidding notation. They conceive of it as machinelike or automatic, and therefore having little to offer—compared to poetics, history, and metaphysics—to those who investigate and daily remind us, as no others do, of the mysteries, complexities, and wonders of the mind.

Chomsky, whose work, of course, has its roots in symbolic logic, has instructed us in his discussions of science. The way in which insight or theory is achieved is rarely automatic, even in mathematical logic or metalogic, but usually requires unpredictable intuitions and inventiveness. It is misguided to seek to discover automatic procedures to generate some one-and-only true theory (that is, a theory, unlike any scientific theory, which is completely determined by the data). However, it is still necessary to be rigorously explicit in stating alternative theoretical formulations, in deriving their consequences, and in stating the criteria for choosing among them.[5] Chomsky's discussion of the problems of theory-construction, the goals of theory, and the evaluation of alternative theories is particularly apposite to psychoanalysis, because of both the rigor of his thought and the relation of his discipline (and the particular problems posed by its subject matter) to psychoanalysis.[6]

In fact, the achievements of symbolic logic in the past

5. See, for example, Chomsky (1957, 1965, 1975b).
6. For a consideration of this relation, see Edelson (1972, 1975, 1977). For Chomsky's discussion of theory, see Chomsky (1957, 1959, 1964, 1965, 1966, 1972, 1975a, 1975b). Apposite are his discussion of "the Galilean style" in the

one hundred and twenty-five years, for sheer audacity, imaginative insight, and the capacity to integrate knowledge in disparate realms and to demonstrate the power of symbolism, are matched only by those of psychoanalysis. Freud's *The Interpretation of Dreams* and Whitehead and Russell's *Principia Mathematica,* with all their progeny, continue to dominate the intellectual life of the twentieth century.[7] It is a crude conception of the attribute "imaginative" that bestows it upon theatricals and poems and withholds it from mathematics and symbolic logic. The contributions of such gifted investigators as Chomsky and Piaget have depended upon their appreciation of this point, just as that appreciation has separated them from many of their colleagues.

To make the distinction between 'literal' and 'figurative' needed to answer the question 'Is psychoanalysis a science of tropes?' it is necessary (rather than opposing logic and poetics) to have recourse to some notions of symbolic logic and some logical apparatus; to abstract from actual expressions that sense which they possess independent of any context; and to find some way to discuss truth and illusion, and practical reality and fictive reality, that is adequate to the complexities of expressions and their interpretation in the psychoanalytic situation.[8]

---

natural sciences at the beginning of his paper in this volume and his conclusion, in the same paper, that "it is perhaps not too much to hope that the classical questions concerning the nature of the human mind and its products may also be assimilated to the general body of natural science in the years that lie ahead."

7. Susanne Langer describes, in her fine *An Introduction to Symbolic Logic* (1967), the great structure of ideas in *Principia Mathematica.* In her work *Philosophy in a New Key* (1942), she calls attention to the importance of psychoanalysis and symbolic logic in focusing intellectual query in our time upon the power of symbolism. Strangely enough, after such a percipient beginning, she makes little direct use of either psychoanalysis or symbolic logic in her subsequent philosophical writings on art and feeling.

8. A beginning attempt to base an analysis of "kinds of reality" on Freud's still startling discovery of psychic reality and his efforts to cope with this discovery may be found in Edelson (1971b).

A literal language is a regimented, formalized language. In such a language, one and only one object from a specified domain of unequivocally distinguishable objects is assigned to each name or definite description which denotes that object. A name or definite description is used to refer only to the object it denotes. The sense of a sentence is a function of the sense of its parts. In such a language, no name or description that does not denote is meaningful. A sentence in a literal language is either true or false, and it is possible by logical operations or the empirical procedures of science to decide its truth-value.

Such a regimented, formalized language may suffice for most—perhaps, some believe, for all—scientific purposes; but, even if the psychoanalyst aspires to such a language in formulating his theory (Edelson, 1977), it is surely not the language he studies—the figurative, allusive language of the analysand. Certainly, when the analysand contructs a fantasy, a dream, or a neurotic symptom, names or descriptions are often used to refer or allude to other than what they customarily denote, and often it would be difficult indeed to find or point to an object named or described. It is part of the competence of the psychoanalyst, which enables him to make clinical interpretations, that he understands the ways in which figurative language departs from literal language. The explication of that interpretative competence is a task for an adequate theory of psychoanalytic interpretation.

We may conclude from all this that a precise, rigorous description of the relation between figurative and literal language is important for both a psychoanalytic theory of the mind and a theory of psychoanalytic interpretation. The tension between the language of psychoanalysis as science and the language it studies is a tension we owe in part to the differences between literal language or language that aspires to be literal, which as scientists is the language we try to use, and a figurative language whose aspirations lie in a very different direction, which belongs to the object world which we as scientists try to describe. I have discussed elsewhere (Edelson, 1977) how this tension, which has inspired great discoveries (principally, those found in *The Interpretation of Dreams*), is also responsible for much confusion and futile polemic around pseudo-issues in contemporary psychoanalytic thought.

Is psychoanalysis a science of illusions? Wallace Stevens, in his essay "Imagination as Value" (1949), writes, "We live in the mind." He writes of the imagination: "When one's aunt in California writes that the geraniums are up to her second-story window, we soon have them running over the roof." The imagination is a capacity—"the power of the mind over the possibilities of things." It is the "liberty of the mind," which is not constrained by what *is* and what is *immediate*. Upon imagination depend our conceptions of past or future, our expectations, our social forms.

Imagination "creates images that are independent of their originals." Imagination "produces an image of the world," and is the power to invent objects, each one of which is "an instance of a real object that is at the same time an imaginative object." Imagination is "the extent of artifice within us" and "the extent of artifice in the external world" which by its power we help to create. The "extreme of its achievement lies in abstraction."

Imagination and reason "are engaged in a struggle for reality" that will go on; there will never be an outcome. Yet, ultimately, these are not antagonists.

> It is not possible to say, as between the two, which is paramount. For that matter it is not always possible to say that they are two. When does a building stop being a product of the reason and become a product of the imagination? If we raise a building to an imag-

inative height, then the building becomes an imaginative building since height in itself is imaginative.
[p. 150]

. . . [Reason] is simply the methodizer of the
imagination. It may be that the imagination is a miracle of logic and that its exquisite divinations are calculations beyond analysis, as the conclusions of the
reason are calculations wholly within analysis. [p.
154]

Logical positivism in its opposition to metaphysics rejects, and the merely romantic belittles, imagination. The
merely romantic is incapable of abstraction and is a failure to use the liberty of the mind; its achievement "lies in
minor wish-fulfillments." It is "a failure of the imagination precisely as sentimentality is a failure of feeling."

If we escape destruction at the hands of the logical
positivists and if we cleanse the imagination of the
taint of the romantic, we still face Freud. What would
he have said of the imagination as the clue to reality
and of a culture based on the imagination? Before
jumping to the conclusion that at last there is no escape, is it not possible that he might have said that in
a civilization based on science there could be *a science
of illusions?* [Italics mine, p. 139]

Imagination is the capacity or power to entertain or
contemplate not only what is, but what may be—to entertain, contemplate, or construct symbolic forms designating states of affairs that are neither necessarily existent
nor immediate.[9]

9. C. S. S. Peirce was the pioneer in the development of a logic of signs. He
saw the need for it and began its formulation. His work is original and seminal,
although—partly because it is inconsistent, unorganized, and wedded to meta-
physical preoccupations—neglected. He was the first to write that propositions
could be contemplated or entertained (the latter term is Russell's) as well as as-

An expression in some object language (for example, a sentence, which designates a property of, or relation among, objects in a world of objects) may itself as an entity have the property "conceivable" or "inconceivable," "possible" or "impossible," "necessary" or "non-necessary," as well as "true" or "false." These predicates which describe sentences in the object language are terms in another language, a metalanguage. Other predicates may be used to describe the physical-utterance tokens of sentences in the object language (for example, "similar in sound to"). Metalogic is a metalanguage. Linguistic theory is a metalanguage. At least some psychoanalytic interpretations use terms in a metalanguage, which describe the sentences or physical-utterance tokens of sentences produced by the analysand. If the analysand describes his own expressions, he speaks in a metalanguage. In describing these descriptions, the psychoanalyst uses a metametalanguage.[10]

When Stevens writes of psychoanalysis as a science of illusions, clearly he does not propose a science of deceptive appearances. (The sun appears to rise and set. This appearance is deceptive relative to a theory of it. The theory explains it, referring to an actual or underlying reality. The explanation cannot dispel this deceptive appearance, which continues to belong to the phenomenal world.) Rather, a science of illusions studies: (1) a set of possible or conceivable worlds and how these are related to each other; (2) a man's knowledge of and beliefs about the actual world; and (3) how members of the set of those

serted to be true; the first to consider a multivalued logic; and the first to develop a logic of signs—and one in which propositions may be expressed by nonlinguistic as well as linguistic signs. See, for example, Hartshorne and Weiss (1932); Buchler (1955); Weiss and Burks (1945); Feibleman (1950); Goudge (1969); Wiener (1966); Moore (1972); and Greenlee (1973).

10. For the difference between an object language and a metalanguage or metametalanguage, see, for example, Carnap (1956, 1958) and Hunter (1971).

possible worlds he conceives affect how he acts in and upon this actual world.

In other words, man's actions and works are governed by possibilities as well as actualities. Man does not merely react to the world as it is, but rather acts and invents objects in response to his conceptions of alternative worlds. He makes choices among these alternatives. He exerts imaginative effort to actualize in various ways one rather than another conceivable or possible world. He finds ways to create an appearance that seems at least to actualize simultaneously more than one possible world (for example, condensation in dream-construction and the construction of neurotic symptoms). Psychoanalysis as a science of illusions seeks to answer such questions as: How does a human being create the illusion, through his works and acts, that a logically possible (although not necessarily physically possible) world is part of the actual world, the illusion that what is true in some logically possible world is true in the actual world?

Imagination is a capacity or power to invent the artifice within us, and to make objects of artifice and by placing these in the external world to transform it. Its analysis requires a logic not only of argument and conclusion but of invention—the invention of symbolic expressions or forms, including linguistic expressions. What are the ways in which what is imagined is presented and represented? What are the methods of imagination's methodizer, reason? What are the rules, operations, and principles that are used in constructing the real object that is also an imagined object—a cultural artifact; an object possessing value, that symbolizes? Chomsky's theory of the logical structure of language is part of the analysis of imagination.[11]

11. These questions are explored in Edelson (1972, 1975). For a discussion of the difference between presentation and representation, see Edelson (1975, pp. 78–85).

Freud's *The Interpretation of Dreams* (1900) is an exemplification of a science of illusions. He argues that all dreams are wish-fulfillments (chap. 3). There are unequivocal, uncomplicated dreams (children's dreams, dreams instigated by physical deprivations), for which everyone would agree this generalization holds. Counterexamples do not falsify the generalization, if a clear distinction is made between manifest dream-content and latent dream-thoughts. The properties of one must be distinguished from the properties of the other; once this is done, supposed counterexamples lose their force as counterexamples (chap. 4).

In making this distinction, Freud has made a logical analysis of the terms 'dream' and 'wish-fulfillment' in his original generalization: 'All dreams are wish-fulfillments.' The results of the analysis follow. 'The wish-that-such-and-such' is a member of the set of latent dream-thoughts. 'The-wish-that-such-and-such is fulfilled' is a description of (or a summary of descriptions of) the imagery of the manifest dream—to the extent that there is no objection to the wish or interference with the direct representation in imagery of its fulfillment. If there is and to the extent there is such objection or interference, then the manifest dream is a disguised, distorted, or indirect representation of 'the-wish-that-such-and-such is fulfilled.' The disguise or distortion is a result of the dream-work.

'The-wish-that-such-and-such is fulfilled' is, then, a description of (or a summary of descriptions of) the imagery of the manifest dream only by interpretation, an interpretation achieved by following the procedure Freud explicates (chap. 2). This interpretation depends upon reconstructing from associations the steps by which 'the-wish-that-such-and-such' and 'the-wish-that-such-and-such is fulfilled' have been transformed to become the descriptions of the imagery of the (disguised or distorted) manifest dream. Interpretation involves mapping the set of descriptions of the imagery of the manifest dream or components of these descriptions upon the set of verbal representations of the latent dream-throughts or components of these representations.

Freud develops a model of dream-construction (chap. 5). Stimuli, whatever their type or source, do not as necessary and sufficient conditions "cause" dreams. They instigate dream-construction, or provide an occasion for dream-construction, as an occasion or situation instigates an act of speech, although one cannot predict from the characteristics of the occasion or situation alone what the speech will be or even if any speech will occur. Stimuli are such instigators if they disturb sleep. Otherwise, they may serve merely as material in the construction of the dream. (Instigators may also serve as material.)

To have made the distinction between manifest dream-content and latent dream-thoughts was to raise the questions a science of illusions must answer. What are the constraints upon the construction of a dream, upon the selection of material among all the materials available that might be used, upon the choice of elements making up the manifest dream-content (chap. 6)? Either a wish is an instigator or a wish must be recruited to provide the motive-force, energy, or "capital" needed to construct the dream. The dream must be constructed to create a perception of a wish-as-fulfilled.

If it were not for additional constraints, such a perception would as an image represent without distortion the possible world represented by the internal verbal representations of the latent dream-thoughts. However, the dream-content is an abbreviation. Which of the latent dream-thoughts will be directly represented in the manifest dream? First, those dream-thoughts that have the greatest number of direct connections with other dream-thoughts, that can be represented many times over by each of the relatively few elements in the dream-content, and that serve as dense nodes through which the most dream-thoughts have indirect connections with each other. Second, those dream-thoughts which, because of their relative "indifference" or lack of "psychic significance," can evade the obstacle of censorship. Third, those dream-thoughts that have verbal representations susceptible to translation into images.

In order to satisfy all these constraints, it may be necessary to call upon the resources of language for material in constructing the dream (Edelson, 1972, 1975).[12] Ambiguous or polysemic switch-words or words with similar properties serve as verbal linkages or connections when other more direct connections are blocked (Freud, 1900, p. 530).

"Distortion" in this science of illusions does not refer to a deceptive appearance or to the representation of what is false or only possible rather than what is true. "Distortion" is a property of a work or act which results from the difficulties, obstacles, constraints upon the direct representation of a possible world in a construction (the work or act) designed to create an illusion that this possible world is part of the actual world or that the actual world has been transformed to conform to this possible world.

In general, when considering the difference between dreams, transference, neurosis, social institutions, and art, one may examine the procedures or operations used in creating illusion; what conditions are necessary or sufficient for the use of given procedures or operations;

12. Freud writes: "Indeed, dreams are . . . closely related to linguistic expression" (p. 99 n. 1). ". . . a good part of the intermediate work done during the formation of a dream . . . proceeds along the line of finding appropriate verbal transformations for the individual thoughts" (p. 340). "We have attached . . . importance in interpreting dreams to every shade of the form of words in which they were laid before us" (p. 514).

what materials are available and the stringencies these impose; and what possible worlds collide and compete for resources.

One may speak of the pathology of excessive distortion, in which there is so much interference with invention that construction fails altogether (e.g., waking up instead of constructing a dream) or the attempt to create a particular illusion fails (e.g., anxiety dreams). One may also speak of the pathology that is not a pathology of distortion but of poverty, poverty of imagination. An act or work of illusion may be defective because the possible worlds it represents are barely or vaguely imagined, limited in scope or content, and inadequately related to, or even cut off from, each other and the actual world. In this view, neurosis is not the result of a victory of imagination over reason, but a failure of both, insofar as we can speak at all of imagination and reason as two. Neurosis is not to live in a fictive world, but rather to live in an insufficiently imagined world.

Freud warns in *The Interpretation of Dreams* against confusing the manifest dream-content (the illusion) and the latent dream-thoughts (which include representations of possible, that is, wished-for states of affairs), and in particular against overvaluing the latent dream-thoughts as the essential elements in dreams. He emphasizes that, however nonsensical the manifest dream-content or rebus is (see p. 278), the latent dream-thoughts are, contrary to general conception, correct (see the original German) or rational (pp. 506–07; p. 506, n. 2).

But what can Freud mean by calling the dream-thoughts, which include wishes, correct or rational? (One way to interpret the statement that contradictories exist side by side in the unconscious, in the light of Freud's assertion that the latent dream-thoughts are correct or rational, is to say that a sentence describing one possible or conceivable world may be incompatible with a sentence describing another possible or conceivable world or a sentence describing the actual world.) One cause of all this confusion is the ambiguity and inconsistencies in the usage of words such as 'possible' and 'impossible.'

There are three different ways in which these words are used. First, they may be semantic predicates in a metalanguage describing predicates in an object language. Some examples of predicates in an object language are 'x is a dream,' 'x is a man,' 'x is a unicorn,' or 'x loves y.' Such predicates, propositional forms, or sentence-matrices, in which x and y are variables or placeholders for which any object in a domain of discourse may be substituted, are neither true nor false. If an object is substituted for the variable, the form becomes a sentence and the sentence may be described by 'true' or 'false,' which are also semantic predicates in a metalanguage. On this account 'true' and 'false' are qualities of sentences and 'possible,' 'impossible,' and 'necessary' are qualities of propositional forms (or, as Russell called them, propositional functions). If any object whatsoever in the domain of discourse makes the propositional form a true sentence, the predicate or propositional form is necessary (e.g., x is identical with x). If there is at least one object (or ordered pair or triple or n-tuple of objects) that makes the propositional form a true sentence, the predicate or propositional form is possible (e.g., x is a man, x loves y). If there is no object that makes the propositional form a true sentence, the predicate or propositional form is impossible (e.g., x is a unicorn) (Russell, 1918, p. 231).

It is important to note here that if one does not define a limited domain of discourse, so that one can say such and such is or is not an entity in the domain, but instead one talks about 'everything,' the door is open to endless and probably fruitless discussions about whether or not, for example, '*x* is a unicorn' is really 'impossible' or not. It is also important to note that if the domain is infinite, an object may be a member of it, even though one is not able to find or name it.

When psychoanalysts have talked about something being illogical or impossible, this Russellian usage may have been involved. I do not think it is the most felicitous usage of these words. The ideas are better expressed by using the universal quantifier ('for any object in the domain,' 'it is true that . . .' or 'it is the case that . . .'); the existential quantifier ('for at least one object in the domain,' 'it is true that . . .' or 'it is the case that . . .'); and denial of an existential assertion ('it is not the case that for at least one object in the domain, it is true that . . .'), which defines 'the null set,' or the set in the domain that has no members.

The difficult problem for psychoanalysis is defining its domain in such a way that there are clear procedures for identifying an entity or object as belonging or not belonging to its domain; stating the conditions which distinguish unequivocally one entity in the domain from another; and avoiding defining its domain in such a way that the domain includes 'everything' (Edelson, 1977, especially pp. 22–24).

Second, such words as "possible" may be semantic predicates in a metalanguage describing sentences in an object language.[13] A sentence is necessary if and only if it is logically true. If a sentence is true by virtue of its logical form, then it is logically true. If a sentence is true no mat-

---

13. For what follows, see, for example, Carnap (1956), especially p. 175. Ruth Marcus has presented reasons for regarding the modalities "necessary" and "possible" as operators upon sentences (as are "and," "not," "or," "if . . . then") *that belong to the object language,* rather than as semantic predicates in the metalanguage; but a consideration of this alternative is beyond the scope of this paper.

ter what its extralogical content is, so long as its logical
form remains constant, then it is logically true. If a sentence is true by virtue of the meaning of its logical elements or expressions, then it is logically true. No empirical circumstance can make it false. If, given the logical
operators or connectives that constitute logical form, and
given a logical form that does not change 'under any interpretation,' a particular sentence in a formal language
is true, then that sentence is logically true. If a sentence is
true, no matter what interpretation of its abstract non-
logical symbols is made (that is, no matter what objects
are assigned to its individual symbols; no matter what
qualities, relations, or sets are assigned to its predicate
symbols; no matter what truth-value is assigned to symbols representing component sentences), then that sentence is logically true.

If no matter what interpretation is made ("under any
interpretation") a sentence is false, it is logically false. If a
sentence is logically false, it is impossible. If a sentence is
not logically false—that is, not impossible—it is possible.
If a sentence is neither logically true (if it is not necessary)
nor logically false (if it is possible), then it is factual or
contingent. A factual or contingent sentence may be either (empirically) true or (empirically) false.

A possible world may be (internally) represented by a
set of possible sentences (e.g., the latent dream-thoughts).
Before the dream-work operates upon them, the latent
dream-thoughts are probably given verbal representation
(Freud, 1900, p. 340). Freud's assertion that the latent
dream-thoughts are correct or rational is probably an assertion that the sentences representing them are all possible, not that these sentences are factually or contingently true. That is, these sentences remain within the
framework of logical connectives or operators and quantifiers which give logical form or logical structure to the

sentences representing our everyday thoughts and the latent dream-thoughts.

The corollary to this, which may be hard to accept, is that the dreamer, just like anyone else, does not think in images or without logical form. Insofar as thinking is propositional, logical form is essential. Images are ineluctably ambiguous. They never determine unequivocally one particular proposition. Images can express or mean a definite proposition only "under description" (Fodor, et al., 1974, pp. 1–21). Insofar as thinking is propositional, if it is a process that operates on images at all (and it seems likely that it can do so), it operates on images "under description." The dream-work, however, does not think at all, as Freud pointed out (p. 507). The dream-work only gives form to thoughts which have already been thought. Just as it is important in our scientific discourse to distinguish manifest dream-content from latent dream-thoughts, it is important to distinguish the process of producing the latent dream-thoughts from the dream-work which gives these latent dream-thoughts a distinctive form.

A third use of such words may attribute the predicate "necessary" to a sentence which is true according to physical law. One may have the idea that if something is eternally true in the actual world, because it is an instance of physical law, then it is necessarily and not merely contingently true. An impossible sentence then is a sentence that represents a state of affairs violating physical law. The relevant "property" seems to be in fact a relation between laws and other sentences they explain, such that the latter are "deducible from" the former; "impossible" sentences are the negation of, or contradict, sentences deducible from laws. The predicate "possible" has an uncertain, if any, status here. If one is simply attributing a property to a sentence, it is not clear to what extent one is merely paraphrasing the expressions true-in-the-actual-world and false-in-the-actual-world. Such a frame of reference seems to exclude ways of talking about something it is essential psychoanalysts be able to talk about—that, however things are, it is logically conceivable that they might be otherwise. Human action, clearly, is governed as much by what might conceivably be so as it is by what *is* so (Edelson, 1971a). Psychic reality in psychoanalytic theory is one way of expressing this theorem (Edelson, 1917b).

Psychoanalysis as a science of illusions is likely to receive considerable assistance from developments in so-called modal logic, which is concerned with systems of logic of possible and necessary as well as contingent sentences, and semantic interpretations of such systems in terms of possible worlds and such relations among them as "accessibility of one to another" (Hughes and Cresswell, 1968).

Is psychoanalysis a science of self-deception? In a passage to which I have previously drawn attention,[14] Heinz Hartmann writes of the inherent difficulties in psychoanalysis as science, including "the problem of how knowledge of the mental processes of others can be achieved." He raises a question about the "cognitive value" of self-experience, the indicative value of a given element of self-perception. He adds that, "while self-experience is an important element," psychoanalytic theories "transcend this level of discourse." Nevertheless, "looked at from this angle, analysis can be termed a *systematic study of self-deception* and its motivations. This implies that thinking about our own mental processes can be found to be true or false" (italics mine; Hartmann, 1959, p. 335).

Such a view requires a logic of belief and knowledge. That complicated problems are involved is indicated by

14. Edelson (1975, p. 48).

two examples. If an analysand says, "I am happy," there are two propositions whose truth-value is in question: 'I [the analysand] believe this,' and 'I am happy.' Either one may be judged true or false, and the truth or falsity of the one does not affect the truth or falsity of the other.

Second, if an analysand says, "I am always deceiving you/myself," of "Everything I say is not really true," assuming we can distinguish between hyperbole and literal belief, there are again two propositions whose truth-value is in question. In addition, these propositions involve a version of the Epimenides paradox.[15] If the analysand is deceptive in saying, "I am always deceiving you/myself," this proposition is true. But if the proposition is true, then he is not being deceptive in uttering it. But then the proposition is false. A contradiction—a proposition cannot be both true and false. If the analysand is not deceptive in saying, "I am always deceiving you/myself," the proposition must be false. However, if the proposition is false, then the analysand is being deceptive in uttering it. But then the proposition must be true—again a contradiction.

Bertrand Russell has analyzed this and similar paradoxes and antinomies.[16] The results of his analysis are important to us in our attempt to discover what the psychoanalyst is talking about in his theory and in his interpretations of what the analysand is talking about. First, one must distinguish, when 'always' or 'all' is used, between talking about 'any' member of a collection, no matter which one is selected, and talking about 'all members'—that is, about the totality. Talcott Parsons has made this point repeatedly in his theory construction.[17] A

15. Epimenides the Cretan is supposed to have said, "All Cretans are liars."
16. Perhaps the best—at least the most accessible—account is Russell (1918, especially pp. 259–68). Russell (1908) is a technical discussion.
17. See, for example, Parsons (1937, 1951, 1959, 1964); Parsons and Shils (1951); Edelson (1970a, 1970b).

society, for example, is a totality (as is a family or the psychoanalyst-analysand dyad) which has properties that no individual member of it has. Thus, a society is characterized by a value system that is shared by its members, is supraindividual like language, prior to and independent of any individual member. "Shared" does not make sense as a property of an individual person, any more than "two" can be a property of one of the members of the psychoanalytic dyad or "numerous" can be the property of one member of a collection. What is meant by 'always' or 'everything' in the two sentences in the paradox example is: 'any proposition I utter, no matter which one is selected.' So the analysand is not talking about the property of a totality of propositions, only a property of particular propositions, no matter which such proposition is selected. Not " 'All my utterances' are deceptive" but rather, "If I utter a proposition, it is deceptive," is the proper paraphrase.

A second aspect of Russell's analysis is the following prohibition. One cannot include, as one of the collection from which the selection is made of a specific entity about which something definite is to be said, that proposition (or linguistic expression of that proposition) which says it. The 'which one' in 'no matter which one is selected' or the 'something' in 'something I utter' cannot include the statement predicating something of this 'which one selected' or 'something uttered.'

There is a hierarchy of propositions or linguistic expressions. Any proposition about another proposition must be of a higher type than the one it is about. A proposition about an entity which is an individual, or a proposition about an entity which is a class of individuals or a property or relation determining membership in such a class, cannot be included in a proposition of the same type as that entity about which something is predicated. A proposition which assigns a predicate to any distinguishable individual, which for a particular universe of discourse is to remain unanalyzable, cannot be included as one of the individuals assigned the predicate; the proposition is complex and not itself an unanalyzable individual.

To make sense, one must decide what in a universe of discourse shall be considered elementary in relation to other entities—what shall be considered an individual. Propositions assign predicates to such individuals. Higher-level propositions assign predicates to entities which are classes of such individuals and still higher-level propositions to entities which are classes of classes of such individuals. In each case, the predicate must fit the entity to which it is assigned—must be such as to be predicable of that kind of entity. Parsons, for this reason, states that "persons" are not the elementary entities of a social system, a personality system, or an organism, but rather in each case the elementary entity is what in that frame of reference is an unanalyzable aspect of persons. "Roles" are individual entities in discussing social systems; "needs" are individual entities in discussing personality systems; and physicochemical objects are individual entities in discussing the organism. In this volume, Chomsky, discussing "the Galilean style," alludes to a similar analysis of political economy: "individuals" are personifications of economic categories and "capital" is not a thing but a relation.

In summary, there are complex sentences which involve the relation between analysand and a proposition. These sentences involve what in logic is called a propositional attitude—for example, 'believe,' 'wish,' 'perceive,' 'know,' 'forbid.' Such sentences pose complex problems for psychoanalysis as science, which probably must include them in its explanatory theory; I have discussed some of these problems elsewhere (Edelson, 1977, especially pp. 22–24).

The problems arising from the attempt to understand what such utterances are about, although susceptible to logical analysis, may contribute if unanalyzed to a persistent dichotomy of 'I' or 'ego' and 'self' in clinical studies and practice and in the theoretical literature, and to the persistence of some confusion in thought and language of both psychoanalyst and analysand. Similarly, it is probable that it is expressions such as 'I know that thinking is more enjoyable to me than relating to people is' which seem to call for the distinction between 'ego' ('I know'), 'ego functions' ('thinking,' 'relating to people'), and 'self' ('me'). It is not clear that such concepts reflect the results of a logical analysis of such utterances. The propositions expressed are: 'I know something$_1$,' 'I enjoy something$_2$ more than something$_3$,' 'I think anything,' and 'I relate to people.' In any event, the psychoanalyst in his practice senses the difference when the analysand says, "I hate you" (the relation is between 'I' and 'you') and when the analysand says, "I have figured out that I hate you" (the relation is between 'I' and the proposition expressed by a sentence stating a relation between 'I' and 'you').

I mention in passing another problem for the psychoanalyst. Whether or not self-deception is involved when an analysand utters something depends upon whether the relation between the analysand and the sentence or what it expresses is in fact 'believes.' The psychoanalyst must often infer an unstated attitude. Given the sentence, is the attitude of the analysand 'I believe (that),' 'I wish (that),' 'I perceive (that),' or 'I forbid (that)'? Many interpretations involve in at least one aspect the attribution of such an attitude, when none is made explicit, by inference from properties of the utterance, its context, or other than linguistic signs. What may appear 'belief' is often not. What may appear to be asserted is often contemplated or entertained. In what sense self-deception can be said to be involved, when a state of affairs is contemplated for whatever purpose rather than asserted to be true, is not at all clear.

Psychoanalysis as a science of self-deception requires a logic of propositional attitudes, not simply a logic of elementary propositions, nor a logic in which the substitution of expressions with the same truth-value in the same matrix results in expressions which have the same truth-value. For "John believes 'the woman living in the next apartment loves him' " does not necessarily have the same truth-value as "John believes 'the woman in the street keeps looking at him longingly,' " even when the two propositions John believes have the same truth-value (either both true or both false). Because, of course, it may be the case that John believes one and not the case that he believes the other. Similarly, it may be the case that John believes both the one and the other, although one proposition believed by him may be true and the other false.[18]

Psychoanalysis as a science of self-deception will increasingly need to examine its presuppositions about truth, and will turn to studies in logic for assistance in this task. There are two kinds of cases with which psychoanalysis as a science of self-deception may be concerned. Case 1 is exemplified by the existence of two or more different accounts of the same event, where the question of which account is the true one arises. Case 2 is exemplified by an instance in which an assertion that such-and-such is true is judged to be false because it does not satisfy certain conditions. That is, the minimum requirement is that for

18. See, for example, the entry "Logic, Applied" in the 15th edition of *The Encyclopaedia Britannica* (1974) for a discussion of the logic of belief; the logic of knowing; the logic of questions; the logic of preference or choice; the logic of commands; normative logic or the logic of the permitted, the obligatory, the forbidden, or the meritorious; modal logics of necessity, possibility, and contingency; temporal logic; and the logic of part-whole—as well as for a useful list of references on these topics.

'true' to be applied, an assertion in a language must satisfy certain conditions. An independent question is whether or not procedures exist, and if so what they are, for determining whether these conditions do in fact hold. It is possible, in other words, given this way of regarding truth, that an assertion may be true but there may be no procedure for deciding that it is true. For example, a sentence may be 'true,' but not 'provable' (Tarski, 1969).

With regard to Case 1, it should be noted that the existence of two or more different assertions in a language of the same state of affairs does not necessarily imply that one must be in error or be an instance of self-deception. First, the object world is ambiguous. There is no existent state of affairs which determines one and only one description of it or one and only one statement in a language asserting it. In fact, any existent state of affairs satisfies an infinite number of statements in a language, that is, is the condition that makes any one of these statements true. That the object world is ambiguous in this sense makes it possible for the psychoanalyst to listen to what the analysand says as "one way of looking at things," as a legitimate account of "psychic reality," rather than as false, erroneous, or deceptive. If the analysand makes different assertions of the same state of affairs, the psychoanalyst may regard them as all true and ask what about the analysand leads him to choose to make this assertion at one time and a different assertion at another time, or to combine these assertions rather than some others.

Second, if the analysand gives two or more accounts of the same event, these are not necessarily incompatible. They do not necessarily contradict one another in the sense that if one is true the other must be false. Even if logically they both cannot be true, they may in fact both be false. Here is an instance of error or deception, but it does not necessarily yield what is true. Neither the psychoanalyst nor the analysand should be led to conclude that if it is possible to decide one assertion is false, then some other assertion must be true.

The psychoanalyst studies unconscious motives, affects, resistance and defense, transference—what in the analysand leads to error. Psychoanalysis as a science of self-deception has made a major contribution to our understanding of what may interfere with cognition, what may interfere with the acquisition of error-free knowledge and true beliefs about the object world (including the self), and what may contribute to the development of ignorance, error, false beliefs. It has also made a major contribution to a different problem (Case 2). It has contributed to our understanding of what may interfere with carrying out the procedures that are necessary if we are to be able to decide whether an assertion in a language is true (e.g., "reality testing"). Among such procedures are : (1) proving something true by reasoning or logical argument, according to rules of inference which conserve truth through a sequence of transformations; and (2) the procedures of empirical science.

The cautions here are almost self-evident. Motivation, affect, resistance, defense, and transference are not the only sources of error and ignorance, or of incapacity in carrying out decision procedures. Interests, values, biases, and prejudices are not necessarily unconsciously motivated or the result of conflict and defense. If it can be demonstrated that a belief does have its origin in unconscious motives or arises out of conflict or serves defense or is a manifestation of transference, it does not necessarily follow that the belief is false. Affect in and of itself is not a source of error. Affect may be disciplined or undisciplined. Disciplined affect is not identical with absence of affect. Disciplined affect may be necessary if one is to reason correctly, carry out a proof, or do scientific or professional work. Undisciplined affect, however, is not incompatible with true knowledge and true belief. Undisciplined affect should not be conflated with unconscious determinants of error or false belief; undisciplined affect is neither necessarily unconscious nor necessarily a determinant of error or false belief.

Psychoanalytic interpretation that is concerned with a distorted illusion reconstructs what internal representation has been distorted in an act or work, by what operations, conforming to what constraints. Not truth or falsity, but fidelity, the directness or indirectness of a representation or a performance, are the alternatives to be examined. An illusion in the sense used here cannot be false; it is an object in the object world, just as any image or iconic symbol is an object in the object world. 'True' or 'false' are not properties of objects but of assertions in a language. Psychoanalytic interpretation which is concerned with error, deception, or false belief seeks sources in unconscious motives. Interpretation depends upon knowledge of the conditions to be satisfied to establish the truth of an assertion in a language, and the existence of a procedure making it possible to decide whether or not these conditions are in a particular case satisfied.

Metapsychology. One way to discover what the psychoanalyst is talking about is to look at the psychoanalyst's own answer to this question in metapsychology. In a recent book on language in psychoanalytic theory and practice, I commented on some differences between explanation and interpretation (Edelson, 1975, chaps. 2 and 3). I suggested that linguistics must be a necessary part of the metalanguage of psychoanalytic theory (pp. 19–20). I alluded in passing to disturbances created by the term "metapsychology" in the psychoanalytic community and literature (p. xiii; p. 20 and n. 10).

My allusions to metapsychology in that book were partial and introductory. Even a brief inspection of the pages just mentioned reveals that I used the term "metapsychology" in a number of senses. The incompleteness of my remarks on metapsychology prompted a more systematic presentation (Edelson, 1977).

The impulse to continue or briefly develop further this explication is abetted by the uneasiness I feel as I continue to encounter in meetings and literature references to metapsychology which seem to me to involve not merely multiple but shifting and inconsistent usages of the term, as well as to reflect confusions about various concepts and their implications. When the term "metapsychology" is used, it is not at all clear what the psychoanalyst is talking about. These intradisciplinary difficulties of course do nothing to mitigate the reductiveness, oversimplification, or obfuscation characteristic of approaches to psychoanalysis (either enthusiastic or deprecatory) and the rather odd intellectual uses sometimes made of it by some members of other disciplines (Edelson, 1977).

The following controversies, among others, will serve as examples of these difficulties. With regard to the relation of metapsychology to clinical theory in psychoanalysis, some psychoanalysts elevate metapsychology as an indispensable tool for adequate clinical practice, while others dismiss it as entirely irrelevant to, if not destructive of, clinical practice. With regard to the physicalistic terminology of metapsychology and in particular the uses of the term "psychic energy" and what is subsumed under "the economic point of view," some attack and wish to eliminate such uses; others claim that this terminology exemplifies the proper use of hypothetical entities and processes in theory-building; and still others claim that use of this terminology is necessary to assert the status of psychoanalysis as a biological—as distinct from a merely psychological—discipline and to facilitate its development as such and its ultimate interarticulation with other empirical sciences. With respect to the status of metaphors in Freud's metapsychological writing, some treat these metaphors as Freud's best attempts to formulate admittedly imperfect theoretical models: he said what can be said of things about which it is difficult to say anything, with the expectation that his reader would abstract what in the metaphor makes the point from that which is extraneous to it. Others (including some colleagues in the humanities) focus upon one or another metaphor out of context; often emphasize just those aspects which for them are only apparently extraneous; regard the metaphor as a hint, or a betrayal, of Freud's own rejection of or lack of satisfaction with major ideas in his work, or of his implicit unrealized intentions, interests, and intellectual preferences; and even without regard to Freud's attitudes or intentions use the metaphor to "sabotage" his main "text" (not my terms) or to challenge or radically revise psychoanalytic theory.

What follows is not a contribution to metapsychology. It is not metapsychology. It is a discussion of ways of thinking and talking about metapsychology. I shall distinguish three senses—the generalization-sense, the abstraction-sense, and the metalanguage-sense—of the term *metapsychology*. I shall consider or at least hint at some problems of metapsychology associated with each sense of the term and some implications of each sense.

1. 'Metapsychology' might be used to refer to the results of a progressive generalization of the propositions of psychoanalytic theory. I shall call this usage the generalization-sense of 'metapsychology.'[19] Here the use of uni-

19. The best presentation I know of the distinction between generalization and abstraction has been made by Langer (1967, especially chaps. 4 and 10).

versal and existential quantifiers is what is characteristic (Edelson, 1977, especially p. 9).

2. 'Metapsychology' might be used to refer to an abstract formal system.[20] A formal system consists of a set of primitive elements; rules of formation or operations for combining these elements into formulas, strings, or "sentences" which are acceptable or well-formed in that system; rules of transformation or operations upon well-formed formulas, strings, or "sentences" to form or derive other well-formed formulas, strings, or "sentences." (Chomsky's linguistic theory is an interpretation of such a system.)

A formal system is not committed to a particular semantic interpretation of its elements, rules or operations, or formulas. Any semantic interpretation of a formal system is a model of any other semantic interpretation of that system.[21] The psychoanalytic theory of the mind may be one semantic interpretation of one such formal system. Apparently homologous theories, often presented by Freud as analogies, are then models of psychoanalytic theory (Edelson, 1977, especially pp. 15–18).

Suppose that each of three sets of propositions, one about dreams, one about neuroses, and one about parapraxes, were to be a different semantic interpretation, in other words, a different model, of the same formal system. Then the propositions in each set would differ from the propositions in the other sets only in content, that is, only in the entities about which properties or relations are predicated.[22] Such propositions would not differ

20. For accessible discussions of formal systems, see Copi (1967); Hunter (1971); Langer (1967); Nagel and Newman (1956, 1958). See also Edelson (1977, especially pp. 8–9).

21. For a discussion of models and the various senses in which this term is used, see Suppes (1957, pp. 253–54); also Hunter (1971, pp. 5–6, 201).

22. Entities are not necessarily spatiotemporal. See Quine (1952, pp. 80–82).

from each other in the form of the relations between entities.

That formal system might be considered a representation of the structure of the mind—whose formulation is
the task of metapsychology (in this abstraction-sense of
'metapsychology'). (However, it must also be remembered
that other theories in other empirical domains—that is,
involving other universes of discourse than psychoanalysis or even psychology—may be discovered to be interpretations or exemplifications of that same formal system.)

I shall call the usage in which 'metapsychology' refers
to such a formal system, and to semantic interpretations
of a formal system which are models of each other, the
abstraction-sense of 'metapsychology.'

3. 'Metapsychology' might be used to refer to a
metalanguage (to be distinguished from an object language). Metapsychology would then be a language in
which to talk about psychoanalytic theory, or a set of
propositions whose subject matter is psychoanalytic
theory itself (rather than the subject matter of the propositions of psychoanalytic theory, which are expressed in
statements about the objects, processes, entities, or relations of interest to psychoanalytic theory). In a metalanguage, one makes predications about statements,
rather than composing statements.[23] I shall call this usage
the metalanguage-sense of 'metapsychology.'

Each sense of 'metapsychology' implies different standards for evaluating a metapsychological enterprise and
metapsychological formulations, different questions, and
different strategies for coping with the problems of psychoanalysis as a theory and body of knowledge—and for
attempting to define its relation to other theories and

23. For an illuminating discussion of metalogic as a metalanguage used to
discuss logic, see Hunter (1971). See also Edelson (1977, especially p. 10).

other bodies of knowledge in the realms of science and the humanities (Edelson, 1977, especially pp. 15–21).

Psychoanalytic Interpretation

What is the psychoanalyst talking about in interpreting what the analysand is talking about? In considering psychoanalytic interpretation, the question of the structure of interpretation is logically prior to other questions, which may interest us more. For example: How does the psychoanalyst actually come to understand the meaning of what the analysand is saying? Is the psychoanalyst's interpretation correct?—true?—better than any other? What is the therapeutic effect of an interpretation?

By logically prior, I mean approximately what Chomsky meant in proposing to study the nature of linguistic competence apart from a consideration of how such competence is used in the actual processes of reception and production of utterances or in the use of utterances to achieve a variety of ends. In other words, we ought to understand what a psychoanalytic interpretation is, what its logical structure is—which is another way of defining what competence the psychoanalyst must have to make one—before asking what process is actually involved in coming to a particular interpretation, what its truth-value is, or what the psychoanalyst is able to achieve with it. Here, I am attempting to describe the phenomena—those events classified as 'making an interpretation'—and to consider these as the data to be scientifically explained by a theory of psychoanalytic interpretation.

That there is no possibility for developing an automatic procedure enabling a psychoanalyst, given a particular symbolic entity (e.g., a dream), to discover the right—or even a good—interpretation of it, I take for granted. An interpretation is always underdetermined by the data.

What we might hope for is similar to what Chomsky is

attempting to achieve in linguistics. That is, given at least
two structures or forms, we might be able to state explicitly the relation between them—what transformation
might be said to lead from one to the other. In psychoanalysis we have the data to be interpreted and the psychoanalyst's interpretation and we can try to formulate by
what operations we can get from one to the other. Such
an inquiry is prior to and separate from the question,
Does the psychoanalyst actually carry out such operations? My account, like Chomsky's, is intended to be neutral with regard to performance.

In order to examine the structure of psychoanalytic interpretation, I believe it might be profitable to put aside,
at least temporarily, certain assumptions. For example, it
is assumed that an interpretation is a theory or explanation of phenomena produced or presented by the analysand. The psychoanalyst's associations, then, are a form
of inferential reasoning. Since it is possible that these associations are not bound by and do not proceed according to any known rules of inference, but rather are part
of the "context of discovery," this psychological process
may prove logically refractory in the sense that no truth-
value can be assigned to its conclusion. (That is not to say
that the conclusion is not either true or false.) Such would
not be the case if the conclusion were the final step in a
sequence of steps, each one determined by a rule of inference that conserved truth. If an interpretation is a
theory or an explanation, then even if we do not suffer
the delusion that, given the data, there is a best or only one
true interpretation, an interpretation should still by some
criteria be capable of being evaluated as better than some
other interpretation of the same data. Criteria for making
such an evaluation have proved difficult to explicate.

I must confess that it is almost as difficult for me to
think of a psychoanalytic interpretation as an explanation

as it would be to think of a translation of a poem into another language as an explanation of the poem or a response to someone's utterance as an explanation of that utterance. I realize that at times reports of psychoanalytic interpretations seem to suggest an interest in what internal conditions have caused (are the necessary and sufficient conditions of) or are indicated by (are causally or physically connected to) certain phenomena. However, I suspect that such formulations may be in some way distortions of the interpretation as given. If such explanations do occur in clinical work, they are probably infrequent or insignificant with respect to the aims of the psychoanalytic process. Perhaps they should not even be included in the set we wish to call "psychoanalytic interpretations."

I think it well to emphasize here that in discussing psychoanalytic interpretation I shall, on the whole, confine myself to the idea of understanding what the analysand is talking about and avoid when I can the idea of understanding the analysand. For perhaps similar reasons, although with regard to different investigations, Russell has written:

> I should like to say about understanding, that that phrase is often used mistakenly. People speak of 'understanding the universe' and so on. But, of course, the only thing you can really understand (in the strict sense of the word) is a symbol, and to understand a symbol is to know what it stands for. [1918, pp. 204–05]

I am glad to have his word on this, because I should like to think I have at least some of the sense of what is possible and what is impossible in such matters that is so strong in both Russell and Chomsky.

Another assumption to be questioned is that the psy-

choanalyst interprets the meaning(s) of a dream, a symptom, a parapraxis. I am not sure that a dream, a symptom, or a parapraxis has the kind of meaning a
psychoanalytic interpretation attributes to it, in isolation
from the so-called associations of the analysand. In other
words, the meaning(s), which let us provisionally assume
a psychoanalytic interpretation tries to make explicit, are
the meaning(s) of a-dream-plus-all-the-analysand's-as-
sociations-to-the-dream. A psychoanalytic interpretation
of a dream is an interpretation of the associations to the
dream as well. We may say the same of a symptom or
parapraxis. Those of my readers who know Russell's
theory of descriptions (1905, 1918) will understand when
I say that I believe that it may no more be true that a
dream has meanings apart from the context of associations to it than that a description such as 'the so-and-so,'
according to Russell's analysis of descriptions, can have
meaning divorced from the context provided by the
proposition in which it occurs.

A description is an incomplete symbol; it has only
"meaning in use" and does not have any "meaning in itself" (1918, p. 253). (I do not intend to suggest here that
a dream and a description are necessarily in any other
way—except as incomplete symbols—the same sorts of
things.) If the interpretations of literary works are interpretations of complete symbols, then that is one respect perhaps in which interpretation in the humanities
differs from interpretation in psychoanalysis. Another
way of approaching this problem is to point out that, in
the absence of a verbal description which picks out features, it is impossible to say what among a set of infinite
possibilities an image symbolizes and certainly impossible
to say what proposition is asserted by it on any occasion.
To the extent that thinking is propositional, we cannot
think or represent thoughts in images alone. (The latter

point has been argued in greater detail earlier in this
paper.)

The analysand's associations are primarily utterances.
These utterances may be classified according to: (1) what
the analysand is talking about, that is, the propositions
expressed by the utterance; (2) explicit or implicit attitudes toward these propositions (including the attitude
'remember,' which includes the ordering of each proposition in terms of time or some era in the analysand's life).
The analysand talks about dreams, symptoms, parapraxes, phantasies, feelings; body; parents, siblings, extended family; what kind of person he or she is and
wants to be; play; school; work; friends; wife or husband
and children; social institutions; and psychoanalysis and
the psychoanalyst.

In whatever way these utterances are classified, the psychoanalyst becomes aware of certain disjunctions (a useful word I owe to Harold Bloom's use of it in interpretations of similar phenomena in poetry), disruptions,
disconnectedness, or lack of structure. Sometimes
members of one set or another seem to be entirely absent
for varying periods of time. Even when placed side by
side, the members of one set are apparently unrelated to
those of another set. A relation, even if in some sense
known, goes unnoticed. Even if a relation is apparent to
the psychoanalyst, it is not apparent to the analysand.

The psychoanalyst does not seek to explain so much as
to overcome disjunction. He does not seek only to make
what is unconscious conscious. He seeks to join what is
kept apart, separated, disconnected, dissociated, by whatever means. (Something may have been lost when Freud
largely abandoned the term "dissociation" after using it in
Studies on Hysteria. Ultimately, of course, many defenses
besides repression were discovered, and the concept in
the old term found a new status.) The psychoanalyst is

usually opposed in this endeavor to one degree or another by the analysand, so that the psychoanalyst supposes the analysand has some stake in maintaining the disjunctions. But the psychoanalyst is also usually assisted in this endeavor to one degree or another by the analysand, so that the psychoanalyst supposes the analysand has some stake in overcoming the disjunctions.

To overcome a disjunction is to demonstrate a relation. This aim determines much of the strategy of psychoanalytic interpretation. It is inaccurate to accuse today's psychoanalyst of trying to reduce everything to one privileged set—early childhood experiences, sexual wishes, transference, or what not. The psychoanalyst brings up what is not being talked about. If the sexual wishes of early childhood were all that were being talked about, the psychoanalyst would ask, "What is going on today?"—and vice versa. Similarly, if the psychoanalyst were all that was being talked about, with nothing said of current experience outside the psychoanalytic situation, just as in the converse, the psychoanalyst would ask about what was missing.

The psychoanalyst shows no favoritism. It is not one thing or another, one realm or another, that is important, but the relation between the two. It is the disjunction that is a matter of concern, that is to be overcome. In this view, not explanation, but acts of analysis which recover and present relations for contemplation are required of the psychoanalyst. Analysis is in the service of synthesis. Not that an analysand should come to have free access to all the facts in his or her life, but rather that he or she should come to have free access to the relations between these facts. Russell's emphasis on, and logic of, relations is especially important to psychoanalysis.

This discussion is of course an oversimplification. If I were to try to do justice now all at once in this paper to the complexity of clinical psychoanalysis and psychoanalytic interpretation, I could not get anything written.[24] I have left out here consideration of much of what is most important to psychoanalysis and to the art of psychoanalytic therapy: the transference and transference neurosis; the characteristics of the psychoanalytic situation; and in fact all that has to do with what goes into creating a situation in which psychoanalyst and analysand come to have access to what is ordinarily not expressed and therefore inaccessible to interpretation. I am attempting to write more rigorously about those aspects of psychoanalytic work about which I can at this time write more rigorously. These are not necessarily the most important aspects of psychoanalytic work.

What is especially characteristic of psychoanalytic interpretation is its analysis and exploitation of various kinds of ambiguity in achieving its aims.[25] (There is no reason to assume at this stage that this is its most important characteristic.) Every ambiguity offers possibilities for making unsuspected connections—offers an opening for establishing broken relations. With respect to the importance of ambiguity for a venture such as psychoanalysis, which is wholly devoted to understanding one person's experiences, it is interesting to note that Russell, while deploring the logical defects of natural languages, accepted that an ideal logical language "would of course be wholly useless for daily life" (1924, p. 338).

The whole question of the meaning of words is very full of complexities and ambiguities in ordinary language. When one person uses a word, he does not

24. The interested reader may find a somewhat similar view of interpretation, embedded in much fuller discussions of it, in Loewenstein (1951, especially pp. 6–7; 1957) and Kris (1956a, especially pp. 58, 64, 78–86).

25. See, for example, Edelson (1972, 1975); Isay (1977); Kris (1952, chap. 10).

mean by it the same thing as another person means
by it. I have often heard it said that that is a misfor-
tune. That is a mistake. It would be absolutely fatal if
people meant the same things by their words. It
would make all intercourse impossible, and language
the most hopeless and useless thing imaginable, because the meaning you attach to your words must
depend on the nature of the objects you are ac-
quainted with, and since different people are ac-
quainted with different objects, they would not be
able to talk to each other unless they attached quite
different meanings to their words. We should have
to talk only about logic—a not wholly undesirable
result. . . . If you were to insist on language which
was unambiguous, you would be unable to tell people
at home what you had seen in foreign parts. It would
be altogether incredibly inconvenient to have an unambiguous language, and therefore mercifully we
have not got one. [1918, pp. 195–96].

Returning to an earlier comment (in the section of this
paper *Is psychoanalysis a science of tropes?*), I should say that
it is unambiguous language which is literal language. Or
that language attended to without regard to ambiguity is
language attended to literally. In this sense, psychoanalytic interpretation is entirely tropological in its characteristic attitude to language and strategies of discourse.

Previously, drawing especially on Chomsky's work
(Edelson, 1972, 1975), I have considered the importance
of semantic, syntactic, and phonological ambiguities (e.g.,
polysemy, Chomsky's syntactic or constructional ambiguities, homonyms) for psychoanalysis. Freud (1900, 1901,
1905) has documented fully the role of such ambiguities
in phenomena of interest to psychoanalysis in his work on
the interpretation of dreams, the techniques of jokes, and

the interpretation of parapraxes. I shall not consider such linguistic-proper ambiguities further in this paper.

Neither shall I attempt to deal here with linguistic-expressive ambiguities, for example, ambiguities of tone and intention. How can we tell—and how can we express how we tell when in fact we can tell—in what way someone wants us to take his or her remarks? Are the utterances to be taken as ironic, bitter, reticent, resigned, quietly affirmative? How can we tell—and how can we express how we tell when in fact we can tell—whether someone means what he or she says, whether someone means what his or her words seem to mean? How can we tell—and how can we express how we tell when in fact we can tell—what some utterance presumes about its audience? Harold Bloom on a number of occasions has pointed out, both forcefully and plaintively, that we have almost no language for talking about ambiguities of tone in poetry—nor, I should emphatically add, do we have in psychoanalysis.

In this paper, I shall consider primarily what might be called linguistic-logical ambiguities. Examples include: the ambiguity of a propositional form with respect to truth-value; the ambiguity of a proposition with respect to whether it is presupposed, entertained, or asserted; the ambiguity of such quantifiers as 'any' or 'all' and the ambiguities related to the order and scope of quantifiers; the ambiguity resulting from the vagueness and impreciseness of natural language (the case of the missing variable, the case of the suppressed relation); the ambiguity of an abstract formal system with respect to its possible semantic interpretations; the ambiguity of the level of language of an expression with respect to whether it is used or mentioned, whether it belongs to the object language or metalanguage.

In a first approximation, as a way of examining psychoanalytic interpretation we may use the same triad of concepts that gave us our three senses of metapsychology. (1) A psychoanalytic interpretation makes use of the ambiguity of a propositional form, and shifts, or draws attention to shifts, from one to another specification of the values of one or another variable belonging to such a form. (2) A psychoanalytic interpretation makes use of the ambiguity of an abstract formal system, and shifts, or draws attention to shifts, from one to another semantic interpretation of such a system. (3) A psychoanalytic interpretation makes use of ambiguities in level of language, and shifts, or draws attention to shifts, from one level of language to another.

That such shifts occur in either the analysand's or the psychoanalyst's use of language does not imply that either is being illogical or does not have at least unconscious knowledge of the distinctions involved. Someone who has no capacity, witting or unwitting, to differentiate the various possibilities offered by ambiguity would, by Freud's analysis, be incapable of dreams, humor, and parapraxes—and would be unable to recognize ambiguity (even when it was pointed out), respond to it, or make use of it. Psychoanalysts and analysands are capable of all these things. It may be that for some time in a psychoanalysis the psychoanalyst's use of ambiguity is more witting than the analysand's. The analysand may be constrained to regard utterances warily and literally. However, there is no reason to suppose that every psychoanalyst would or needs to express what is happening in the interpretive process in these terms any more than a competent speaker of English must be able to articulate the grammatical rules that make up his linguistic competence in order for such a speaker to be able to make use of these rules in producing or understanding sentences.

The following statements provide some principles for understanding the transformations by which one so-called association may lead to—may be derived from—

another association, for understanding, that is, the nature of the relations between associations. (1) Disjunctive propositions (*disjunctive* in the sense "unconnected" or "apparently unrelated") may be related by the propositional form of which each is an instantiation or specification. That is, each proposition can be seen to have specified a different value for at least one variable in a single propositional form. (2) Disjunctive sets of propositions may be related by the abstract structure of which each is a different interpretation. That is, each set of propositions can be seen to be a different semantic interpretation of a single abstract system, and therefore the sets are models of each other. (3) Disjunctive propositions may be related by the fact that in one a symbolic expression is used and in the other the same symbolic expression is mentioned. Properties of a symbolic expression or relations between such expressions (expressions mentioned or talked about) may also be properties of an entity or object or relations between entities or objects which such expressions are used to symbolize.

In recovering or presenting lost relations between propositions, it is important to be careful not to elevate one proposition over another as "what the analysand is *really* talking about." It is probably best not to assert, for example, that the analysand in talking about his psychoanalyst is *really* talking about a parent, or that the analysand in talking about a teacher is *really* talking about the psychoanalyst. Ultimately, it is not one or another proposition or "fact" that is not available to the analysand—even if it is, as it not always is, unconscious—but the relations between propositions or "facts." The most important loss is loss of the awareness of these relations. The most important recovery is a recovery of this awareness, supposing it at some previous time existed. The most important change is the development of this awareness, especially when it has never existed. Even the recovery of unconscious memories in and of itself is secondary (Kris, 1956b).

Shifts from one value of a variable to another. The matrix 'x is a dream' is called a sentence-schema or propositional form. In this form, x is a place-holder, like an indefinite pronoun, for all the terms which may occupy its place in the form. Although x is called a variable—an individual variable—its values are not necessarily, like most variables in mathematics, on a continuum. Its values are particular individuals or entities.

The values of x are all the possible objects whose names may be substituted for it so that a meaningful true or false statement results. These values are "the range of significance" of x. For example, any particular individual image or perception may be substituted for x in the above propositional form. With such substitutions, the statement will sometimes be true, sometimes false. Expressions for certain abstract concepts, such as 'abstraction,' may not be substituted for x, since these do not belong to the range of significance of x, and are not logically homogeneous or of the same type as x. Thus, 'Abstraction is a dream' is a sentence without a sense or a semantic reading.[26]

In Freud's report of the Irma Dream (1900, chap. 2), there are a group of associations which can be summarized in the following propositional forms.

1a. Someone$_1$ rejects (conceals) something from someone$_2$.

The form (1a) is equivalent to (1b).

1b. It is not the case that someone$_1$ accepts something from, reveals something to, someone$_2$.

The form (2) is contrasted with (1a) and (1b).

2. Someone$_1$ accepts something from, reveals something to, someone$_2$.

26. See Katz (1972) for a discussion of anomalous sentences, which have no semantic reading.

Specification of values for the variables 'someone$_1$,' 'someone$_2$,' and 'something' gives, for example:

1. A governess conceals dental plates from Freud.
2. Patients reveal little secrets to physicians.
3. Irma's intimate friend rejects help from Freud.
4. Freud's wife rejects help from Freud.
5. Irma rejects the solution of her illness offered by Freud.
6. Dr. M. rejects a suggestion of Freud's.
7. Freud's elder brother rejects a suggestion of Freud's.
8. Children reveal their bodies to physicians.
9. Adult females conceal their bodies from physicians.
10. Freud rejects a solution (the bad liqueur) offered by Otto.
11. Dreams conceal their secrets from Freud.
12. Freud conceals information from Freud. ("Further than this I could not see. Frankly, I had no desire to penetrate more deeply at this point"— p. 113.)
13. Freud conceals information from his readers.

If the relation between someone$_1$, someone$_2$, and something is held constant, as it more or less is in these statements (with the exception of the use of the operation of negation),[27] then 'someone$_1$,' 'someone$_2$,' and 'something'

27. How is negation to be regarded? Every positive proposition has a negative form. Is the negative proposition to be regarded as a proposition about a negative state of affairs, so that, as Russell suggested, there are pairs of positive and negative facts, one of which is true and one false? To what, then, does the paradoxical expression 'false fact' refer? 'False' is a property of sentences, not of the object world sentences are about. There is no more reason to suppose that 'falsity' is in the world than to suppose, as Russell argues in criticizing metaphysics, that 'or-ness,' 'and-ness,' or 'is-ness' or 'Being,' are in the world. Negation may simply be regarded as a logical recursive operation (*recursive* means

are expressions for variables the value of which may change from statement to statement. So, for 'someone$_1$' we have the following values: governess, patients, Irma's friend, Freud's wife, Irma, Dr. M., Freud's elder brother, children, adult females, Freud, dreams. For 'someone$_2$' we have the following values: Freud, physicians, Otto, readers. For 'something' we have the following values: dental plates, secrets, help, solution, suggestion, bodies, information.[28]

The associations or statements are related, because they all belong to the set of statements generated by varying the values of the variables 'someone$_1$,' 'someone$_2$,' and 'something' in a propositional form, while holding the semantic interpretation of the relation between these constant. In general, if x, y, and z stand for entities and R is the relation between x, y, and z, then different sets of propositions or statements expressing such propositions may be generated by varying the values of R, x, y, or z, or any combination of these, while holding the value of the

---

"can be repeated over and over") upon a single proposition to yield another new proposition, as 'if . . . then' is a logical operation that combines two propositions to yield another new proposition. Negation, then, does not refer to states of affairs, but rather functions as a logical operation upon elements in a system and is defined by a rule of formation in that system. This question is too complicated to pursue in this paper. See Russell (1919).

28. For the sake of expedient exposition, I am ignoring that many of these expressions do not designate simple unanalyzable entities. They are complex descriptions, rather than simple names, of the objects that are values of the variables. 'Governess' involves the propositional form 'x is a governess'; 'Freud's wife' the propositional form 'x is married to Freud' (and also the propositional form 'x is a woman'), and so on. Since these expressions are descriptions, they can be handled according to Russell's theory of descriptions. Most, if not all, the statements 1–13 express higher-order propositions—that is, propositions in which the entities that have properties or are related include entities that are relations in lower-order propositions. Since 'governess' or 'married to' are monadic and dyadic relations as analyzed, an expression like 'conceals' or 'rejects' is a property of a relation, not a simple individual entity. This complication does not affect the main ideas expressed in this section of the paper.

remaining one(s) constant. An example of a set of propositions generated by varying the constituent relation R in
a propositional form is suggested by the associations to
the Irma dream that include the components:

> Freud wants to see . . .
> Freud wants to (does not want to) penetrate . . .
> Freud wants to unveil . . .
> Freud wants to inject solutions . . .

Psychoanalytic interpretation may construct a set of relations; the set is defined by some property or properties
that all the values of R have. So, we may come to the notion of an instinctual aim defined by all these values, or
rather by the property or properties they all share.

A variable like 'someone' may be represented in an
image by picturing a particular value of the variable (in
this case, Irma), naming the image, and then regarding
the name as the name of only one possible value of a variable in a propositional form. A variable may also be represented by a vague image: 'there was someone, I don't
know who it was . . . .' Different values of this variable
will give many propositions.

The psychoanalyst abstracts the propositional form itself from the set of propositions generated by varying values of a variable. The propositional form is what relates
the various propositions.

Identification is a concept Freud used to define the
relation of the various values of an individual variable in
a particular propositional form. So Irma, Irma's friend,
and governess are said to be related by identification. A
complex pattern of progressive variation of variables
suggests a complex pattern of identifications:

> Various women conceal something from Freud.
> Freud conceals something from Freud.
> Freud conceals something from his readers.

Identification in this sense is a relation between those values in the range of significance of a variable in a propositional form, each one of which yields, when substituted for the variable, a true proposition. Psychoanalytic interpretation, seeking to enrich further an understanding of what it is that constitutes the identification of such entities, may concern itself with the question: In what other propositional forms can these same values be substituted for a variable to yield true propositions? Thus, identification is seen to be overdetermined, in one of the meanings of the term "overdetermination."

Condensation is a concept Freud used to describe allusion or reference to a set of entities by a particular member of the set—for example, allusion or reference to a number of the values of a particular variable in a particular propositional form by one value of that variable. (Another example is a similar allusion or reference to entire sets of true propositions—or at least propositions believed to be true by the analysand—yielded by holding constant one value of a variable and varying the values of other constituents in propositional forms of which that variable is a constituent.) This allusion or reference is possible because a particular proposition, yielded by specifying one value of a variable, is understood to be only one of a number of propositions that satisfies or makes a true proposition of a particular propositional form. The psychoanalyst abstracts the propositional form as these other propositions appear in the analysand's associations. In this sense, any proposition may be regarded as ambiguous by the psychoanalyst—that is, as implying a propositional form satisfied by an undetermined number of propositions. These sets of propositions may be generated by varying the values of different variables in the propositional form.

Freud's concept of composite-condensation (differen-

tiated from identification-condensation) is exemplified by
a set of statements describing an image:

> Dr. M. is pale.
> Dr. M. is clean-shaven.
> Dr. M. limps.

These statements are generated from the same propositional form by holding 'Dr. M.' constant and specifying
different values of the monadic constituent relation or
property. Associations include the judgments that 'Dr. M.
is clean-shaven' and 'Dr. M. limps' are false but that
'Freud's brother is clean-shaven' and 'Freud's brother
limps' are true. The substitution of 'Dr. M.' for 'Freud's
brother' depends on both of these being values for x in:

> x rejects a suggestion of Freud's.

The combination of monadic constituent relations or
properties in the single image is made possible by the fact
that both 'Dr. M.' and 'Freud's brother' are values of the
variable in

> x rejects a suggestion of Freud's.

This complex condensation is discovered from associations, utterances of the analysand, in which: (1) some
members of a set of propositions are rejected as false; (2)
the question 'What would make these propositions true?'
is asked; (3) a second value is substituted for the first in
order to make the propositions true; and (4) an effort is
then made to discover what propositional form would
yield true propositions when both the first and the second
values are values of a variable in that propositional form.

When all the constituents of a proposition are variables,
then the result is a logical form without content. What
one knows from a set of propositions all of which are values of $R(x,y,z)$ is that there are three individual entities in

some relation to each other (that is, there is a relation which requires three individual entities to express).

Is the psychoanalyst ever concerned with such formal abstractions? I think so. Every psychoanalyst I know is sensitive to the pervasiveness of monadic, dyadic, or triadic relations in a stream of associations no matter what the content, and tends to locate the source of such associations in a developmental epoch dominated cognitively and affectively by monadic, dyadic, or triadic relations. Thus, the attributions "oedipal," "preoedipal," and "primary-narcissistic" can be made on the basis of sets of associations without regard to their content.

The defense intellectualization uses abstractions (for example, 'disobedient' instead of 'x disobeys y') to suppress the logical form of a proposition. The propositions expressed by:

Irma is disobedient
The patient is recalcitrant
Freud is reticent

seem to have the form $R(x)$. As we have seen in 1a, 1b, and 2 above, and n. 28, however, the logical form involves at least four components—three individual entities and their relation—and even that analysis is a simplification. The suppression of logical structure tends to interfere with strategies of psychoanalytic interpretation which depend on a recognition of such structures.

Shifts from one model to another. A set of such logical structures related by rules of transformation constitutes a formal system. Here, I shall merely state the hypothesis that the psychoanalytic interpretation of the transference neurosis depends on the recognition that the set of propositions that have to do with the psychoanalyst and aspects of the psychoanalytic situation, and the interrelations of these propositions, and another set of propositions which have to do with the infantile neurosis and childhood memories and phantasy, and the interrelations of these propositions, are different semantic interpretations of the same formal system and models of each other. Since I have discussed models and formal systems in the first part of this paper and in Edelson (1977), and the scope of this paper does not permit the extended presentation of complicated data that bear upon this hypothesis, I shall simply say here that while I do not now substantiate or even illustrate this hypothesis, I can see how, and I hope the reader can see how, this might be done.

Shifts from one level of language to another. Psychoanalytic interpretation may depend on the ability to shift from one level of language to another.

Subtle logical problems have been discovered to have their origin in a failure to distinguish between the *use* of a word, sentence, or any expression of a proposition or part of a proposition, to refer to or designate something other than the word, sentence, or expression—and the *mention* of a word, sentence, or any expression to refer to or designate that word, sentence, or expression. 'John is a boy,' where John is a person, must be distinguished from " 'John' is a name" or " 'John' has four letters." "John has four letters" and " 'John' is a boy" are both false, if not nonsense. Freud, of course, has discussed mixing up a symbol with what it symbolizes—the psychopathology of failing to distinguish word from thing.

However, this 'mixing up' occurs in normal mental processes as well; Freud makes this especially evident in *The Interpretation of Dreams* and his work on parapraxes and jokes. The intermingling of the use and mention of linguistic entities, though it seems to involve an error with respect to some purposes which logic helps to clarify, is nevertheless critical in psychoanalytic interpretation. The psychoanalyst is attentive to the ambiguity in the spoken name: Is it used or is it mentioned? If the psychoanalyst asks, "What comes to your mind about *John?*" the analysand may respond, "He is my best friend," or "It begins with 'J,' " or both.

An analysand in reporting a dream states, "I was watching Alfred." Associations include statements about the man Alfred:

I don't know Alfred well.
He never has paid much attention to me.

Suddenly there is a shift to associations about the name Alfred:

Alfred can be divided into two—Al and Fred.
A.F. . . . A.H. . . . Ass Hole . . .

A and *F* were the initials of the analysand's parents' first names. Every consonant in 'Alfred'—L, F. R. D—was the first initial of a name of one of the siblings of the analysand. The first initial of the analysand's name, *H,* was not part of 'Alfred'—the only name of a member of the family not so represented in 'Alfred' (the analysand had been "left out"). This initial was added almost immediately in association as one of the initials of a deprecatory epithet (therefore, a self-deprecatory epithet).

Associations to the dream also include propositions involving the analysand's relation to her family: concerns about the strains between mother (*A*) and father (*F*) (the name was "divided"); curiosity about their relation ("I was watching . . ."); and feelings of being excluded by them ("never paid much attention to me").

Any proposition among the associations including the expression 'Alfred' is ambiguous, since the expression 'Alfred' may designate the man, the name, or the analysand's family (by virtue of the relation of the name 'Al-

fred' to the names of members of the analysand's family).
If three sets of propositions are generated which are
identical except for the difference between man, name,
and family (therefore, name and entity have similar or
identical properties or relations), then we have an example both of overdetermination of the expression and
of condensation of content brought about by mention as
well as use of the expression.

Condensation viewed in this way is the operation or
operations linking by means of shared properties or relations: (1) an expression; (2) the entity or entities designated by that expression; (3) a second set of expressions;
and (4) the entity or entities designated by that second set
of expressions. Shifts to the level of mentioning from the
level of using expressions made it possible to present,
through attributes of only one name and associations to
only one name, phantasies and feelings about family-
members and their relations. Similarly, one of the analysand's thoughts about a psychoanalyst (whose initials were
T.R.) was presented in a dream about a woman named
Esther. The name Esther became "*T.R.* is an 'es,' "—that
is, 'The psychoanalyst is an ass.'

The reader may think that throughout I have emphasized too much the cognitive aspects of psychoanalytic interpretation. I can see the objection, although I think it
ignores the difference between what is required to make
an effective clinical interpretation and what is required to
make a theory of clinical interpretation. I am impressed
by the sensitivity of most psychoanalysts I know to form
or structure, by their ability to abstract form or structure
from a multitude of variegated particulars. Here, in clinical psychoanalysis as in science, "structure is the main
study." It may be said of change in clinical psychoanalysis,
as it has been said of scientific work: "[Any] change which
does not involve a change of structure does not make

much difference" (Russell, 1924, p. 340). I cannot see
that psychoanalytic work is possible without the psychoanalyst's capacity to shift attention from a variety of contents to an invariant underlying form or structure, and
from the structure to its many realizations. We might be
astonished at how many psychoanalysts disclaim interest
in abstraction, logic, or mathematics, or deprecate the
role of cognitive capacities in psychoanalytic clinical work,
if Chomsky had not taught us how amazingly complicated
and unsuspectedly unique are capacities such as linguistic
competence or knowledge of the rules of language, which
can be possessed and skillfully used without much, if any,
consciousness of their details or fundamental nature.

Symbolic Logic and Psychoanalysis

In conclusion, I intend, as in Edelson (1977), to argue
for the value of at least partially formalizing psychoanalytic theory, including a theory of psychoanalytic interpretation. It is necessary for such formalization for us
to make an effort to translate at least some of our ideas
into the powerful symbolism of symbolic logic in order to
analyze and clarify their form and content. This advantage and the employment of such notation do not require
that these ideas be "mathematical," although symbolic
logic has its major achievement in providing a foundation
in logic for all branches of mathematics (Quine, 1951, pp.
7–8).

In an area where measurement tends to be either pe-
ripheral or misguided, Chomsky's work on the logical
structure of linguistic theory, which has transformed his
field and our thinking about language, may also be
counted among the major edifices raised upon the foundations of symbolic logic. Chomsky's work demonstrates
that symbolic logic is not limited in its utility to mathematics or to sciences in which measurement is essential. That

symbolic logic need not confine itself to reference to existent entities (so-called extensional entities), that it also has
applications where discourse is of intensional entities
(properties and abstract entities), that it may be concerned with the sense of signs as well as with their denotation, has been stressed by Russell from the beginning in
all of his discussions about foundations.[29]

The persistent confusion between the "illogical" nature
of the phenomena studied and the discourse used in that
study should not be allowed to undermine the conviction
that symbolic logic can be useful to psychoanalytic theory
(Edelson, 1977, especially p. 12). The phenomena may be
"illogical," elusive, and complex. The discourse, if it is to
be a theory of the phenomena, must of course be "logical." Those who discourse should eschew any positive
evaluation of obscurantism and ineffability in the name
of doing justice to the complexity of the phenomena, and
should strive instead for coherence, consistency, and precise rigorous expression.

That John prefers *a* over *b* and *b* over *c* would seem to
imply, if the relation 'prefers' is transitive, that John prefers *a* over *c*. (A relation R is transitive if it is true that: if
aRb and bRc, then aRc.) If John does not prefer *a* over *c*,
then that does not mean logic is inapplicable in a discourse about John's preferences. In fact, it is logic that
enables the theorist to explicate precisely the relation
among the members of John's set of preferences. If this
relation is not transitive, we may say, 'John is not ratio-

29. See Whitehead and Russell (1910). See also, Carnap (1956, 1958);
Church (1951a, 1951b, 1956); Katz (1972, 1975); Lewis (1944, 1946, 1951);
Lewis and Langford (1959); Marcus (1960); and Reichenbach (1947). The references by Church (1951), Katz (1972, 1975), and Lewis (1944) are especially
important in emphasizing the value of symbolic logic in developing an adequate semantic theory in linguistics. It is impossible to appreciate or adequately
assess Chomsky's work in linguistics, previously cited, without an appreciation
of its roots in and use of symbolic logic.

nal,' but that, of course, is the phenomenon to be explained.

Similarly, *a* may imply *b* and *b* may imply *c,* but that John believes *a* may not necessarily imply that John believes *c.* Either the phenomena are such that the relation among some beliefs *a, b, c* in John's set of beliefs is not transitive (the relation of John's beliefs to John's wishes may be important to explaining this nontransitivity)—or the logical relation between compounds involving propositional attitudes such as 'John believes *a,*' 'John believes *b,*' and 'John believes *c,*' is not transitive.

If John asserts that 'he (John) hates his own mother' and 'he (John) loves his own mother' are both true, a failure of adequate analysis may result in the conclusion that logical contradiction poisons psychoanalytic discourse and that therefore any inference at all is possible, no inference is excluded, and logical discourse is impossible. First, one proposition is not the negation or denial of the other. They are not, then, logically contradictory. Second, 'hates' and 'loves' may not even logically exclude each other in psychological contexts (those involving propositional attitudes). Whether or not the relation 'hates' excludes the relation 'loves' is in fact not simply a logical or even a semantic question, but requires empirical investigation of the kind carried out by psychoanalysis. Third, any terms expressing "opposites" have a close semantic relation—for example, a maximum number of semantic features in common, with only one differentiating feature (such as "plus/minus") occurring at the lowest level in a hierarchy of such features.[30] There is no reason, then, to be surprised that "opposites" appear in dreams or that unconscious mental processes do not avoid what appears to be logical contradiction or exclusion.

30. See, for example, Clark (1970).

In addition, whether or not the assertions are John's (and therefore part of the phenomena) or the psychoanalyst's (and therefore part of the discourse about the phenomena) needs at all times to be clarified. Finally, such propositions cannot be regarded as independent of the context of discourse in which they are asserted. Any careful formulation will specify for what time period or occasion these two states of affairs are asserted to be true; in response to what action or aspect of the mother (complete generalization of attitudes to or feelings about mother as an unanalyzed object cannot be assumed); and with respect to what plan of John's or outcome desired by him.

What the psychoanalyst is talking about in his theory is indicated by the range of values taken by each of its variables. "To be is to be the value of a variable" (Quine, 1961, pp. 13, 15). When Chomsky remarks that the "furniture of the world" (Russell's phrase?) does not come prepackaged but is provided by cognitive analysis—that of common sense or the self-conscious idealizations of the scientist—he takes essentially the same view. The achievement of the psychoanalyst as a scientist depends upon his talent for choosing significant semantic interpretations of variables and his ability to form generalized propositions in which such variables are quantified.

The propositions of psychoanalytic theory will benefit from logical analysis. It would appear upon casual inspection that the statement "All dreams are hallucinatory wish-fulfillments" expresses a general proposition about an entity 'all dreams' and that it predicates of this entity the property 'are hallucinatory wish-fulfillments.' Logical analysis reveals that there is no entity 'all dreams' in the proposition. Two predicates are explicit: 'is a dream' and 'is a hallucination of the fulfillment of a wish.' The entity to which these two predicates apply is implicit or suppressed. This entity is any value of x in the propositional forms: 'x is a dream' and 'x is a hallucination of the fulfillment of a wish.'

If the psychoanalyst wants to make the generalization

All dreams are hallucinatory wish-fulfillments,

the paraphrase revealing the logical form of the generalization is:

No matter what value of x is chosen, if x is a dream, then x is a hallucination of the fulfillment of a wish.

A more detailed analysis of this generalization reveals that the predicate

is a hallucination of the fulfillment of a wish

is itself complex, and requires the following explication. If y is some wish, and z is a condition or state of affairs which fulfills or gratifies y, then F is the dyadic relation 'fulfills' which holds between z and y. In other words, z fulfills y, or $F(z,y)$, where F is a so-called first-order or lower-level function or relation 'fulfills,' which requires two individual entities, terms, or arguments, z and y, for its expression. These two individual terms or entities, as well as x, have been suppressed in the original generalization.

Then 'x is a hallucination of the fulfillment of a wish' expresses a so-called second-order or higher-level function or relation G, 'is a hallucination of.' G is a relation between an individual term or entity x and a first-order function or relation F ('fulfills'). In other words, if x is a dream, the relation between x and some state of affairs 'z fulfills y', is: 'is a hallucination of'. We then have as a propositional form: "x is a hallucination of 'z fulfills y'."

A paraphrase revealing the logical structure of the proposition might then read:

Whatever x is chosen, there is at least one y, and there is at least one z, such that: if x is a dream, and if y is a wish, and if z is a condition, and if F is a relation 'fulfills' which holds between a condition z and a wish y, then x is a hallucination of $F(z,y)$—or $G(x,Fzy)$.

In summary, logical analysis reveals that three individual terms or entities, and a relation between an individual term or entity and a dyadic relation, are suppressed or implicit in the original generalization.

Two further examples of logical analysis of theorems in psychoanalytic theory follow.

There is at least one element or aspect x, which is a part P of any psychological structure y, such that x is a derivative or a transformation T of some unconscious wish z.

Since this theorem refers to any psychological structure (for example, dreams, neurotic symptoms, parapraxes), it is part of a theory of mind. As such, it would appear as a theorem in a theory of dreams, a theory of neuroses, and a theory of parapraxes. The theorem asserts that no matter what psychological structure y is chosen, there exists at least one entity x that is in the dyadic relation 'part of' to that structure y, and at least one entity z that is an unconscious wish, and x is in the dyadic relation 'transformation of' or 'derivation of' to z.

The following is a more difficult example. The proposition

All sexual instinctual wishes (each one of which is uniquely specified by the act or aim gratifying it) are freely and without limit displaceable

might be paraphrased:

When anyone wishes to be in a unique relation to something, it does not matter what that 'something' is.

In second-order logic (involving the use of quantifiers with relations as well as individuals) the proposition might be paraphrased (using a and b as constants or specific values of variables):

No matter what x and y are chosen, if x is a person and y is an instinctual wish, and $a = x$ and $b = y$, then the wish b is a state S of the person a—$S(b,a)$—only if, no matter what z is chosen, if z is an inanimate thing, organism, part of an organism, or activity of an organism, there is *at least one and at most one* relation R-of-b, such that the wish b is consummated C only if the person a is in that relation R-of-b to (any) z—$C(b)$ only if R-of-$b(a,z)$.

Logical analysis of the locution in *The Interpretation of Dreams* 'dream-construction' reveals that it involves a relation 'constructs' or 'makes' which requires at least six entities or a sextuple (therefore, a 'sextic' relation): under some circumstance u, such as sleep, something$_1$ or someone v makes or constructs M something$_2$ w, such as a dream, out of something$_3$ x, such as materials, with procedures y, such as the operations of the dream-work, in order to serve some function or purpose z, such as hallucinatory wish-fulfillment. Therefore: $M(u, v, w, x, y, z)$. The 'operations of the dream-work' does not designate an individual of the same type as the others. At the least, it is a set—of procedures, or constraints upon the selection of materials. Neither is 'hallucinatory wish-fulfillment' an unanalyzable individual, as we have seen. So, even this logical analysis is quite a simplification. Certainly, M (u, v, w, x) is a minimal explication of the relation 'makes' or 'constructs.' This logical analysis determines to some extent Freud's organization of the book (chap. 3, z; chap. 4, w; chap. 5, M, x; chap. 6, y; chap. 7, u, v).

I shall assert here, as I have previously (Edelson, 1975, 1977), that the primary data of psychoanalysis are the utterances of the analysand. Of course, I do not mean by primary data physical signals such as might appear on a tape recorder, but rather symbolic entities with semantic, syntactic, phonological, rhetorical, and perhaps other properties. The state of the art in dealing with such data in psychoanalysis so far is similar to that in linguistics prior to Chomsky. A methodology involving the segmentation or categorization of observable data and the discovery of empirical regularities in the relations of such data will not work for psychoanalysis any more than it did for linguistics. What is needed in psychoanalysis is not more data but a degree of sophistication about the nature and goals of theory matching that of Chomsky's, so that we can talk about the plenitude of data we already have.

All this stated, it is nevertheless true that the primary or elementary data of psychoanalysis are linguistic entities, as even a casual inspection of Freud (1900, 1901, 1905) reveals, as I have tried to show in Edelson (1972, 1975, 1977), and as I have illustrated in the part of this paper which deals with psychoanalytic interpretation. For purposes of theory, such entities as the analysand's utterances must be idealized, becoming such entities as declarative, optative, normative, and imperative sentences—expressions of perceptions; beliefs; wishes or desires; values or preferences; ideals; obligations and sanctions. (So, also, linguistic theory is a theory of sentences although many utterances in an empirical corpus are not sentences.)

In passing, I may comment that before expressions of feeling can be included in this list of types of expressions, logical analysis is required. Nonlinguistic indexes of feeling (including vocal indexes such as pitch of voice)—signs but not symbols—need to be distinguished from linguistic expressions. 'John perceives that' may be the context for a proposition about a state of affairs that itself involves a feeling which has been inferred by John from some indexical sign of the feeling. 'John feels that' may be logically equivalent in different contexts to 'John perceives that,' 'John believes that,' 'John wishes that' or 'has a plan to achieve that,' or 'John's evaluation or appraisal of . . . with respect to . . . is that. . . .' An expression designating feeling may also occur as the constituent relation in the state of affairs which John perceives, believes, or wishes: for example, "John believes that 'he (John) loves his mother.' "[31]

A universe of discourse of psychoanalysis includes the propositions perceived, believed, wished, valued, imagined, enjoined, or sanctioned (the list is not exhaustive) by a particular person—that is, classes of perceptions, beliefs, wishes, values, ideals, obligations and sanctions. The constituent relations of this universe of discourse are relations between and among the members of each class (e.g., one belief and another, one wish and another), and between the members of one class and another (e.g., a belief or number of beliefs and a wish). Membership in a particular class depends upon the context in which a proposition occurs. The same entity, then, may be a member of different sets, for the same state of

31. Pribram (1971) presents evidence for the necessity of distinguishing between *values*, which are part of an Image or knowledge of inner or outer reality; *motivations*, which are the executing or "go" part of a Plan; and *emotions*, which are concomitants of "stopping" a Plan (or subplan) upon perceiving that it is not feasible in the face of internal or external obstacles. See, also, Miller, Galanter, and Pribram (1960).

affairs may be, for example, believed, desired, or enjoined. While the psychoanalyst's universe of discourse includes propositions involving states of affairs that do not exist but are possible, and some that are impossible, such propositions may be members of the set of beliefs or wishes of an analysand without necessarily being asserted in psychoanalytic theory.

Theorems belonging to psychoanalytic theory may be based on thousands of instances of relations between and among the utterances of an analysand; between and among members of a set of the perceptions, beliefs, wishes, or valuations and injunctions of an analysand; or between and among one or more members of one such set and one or more members of another such set. These instances are observed and anticipated in the controlled situation and by the disciplined procedures of any psychoanalysis. The theorems of psychoanalytic theory must be adequate to account for the observed relations among the utterances of the analysand.

Psychoanalytic theory may postulate or define hypothetical elements or forms (e.g., unconscious wishes) and a hypothetical sequence of transformations or derivations of such elements or forms (e.g., the so-called mechanisms of defense or the dream-work). The theory will be judged in relation to other theories, when it has achieved a degree of formalization making such judgments possible, by such criteria as economy (variously defined), completeness, consistency, and scope (the realms or the number of different and apparently unrelated kinds of phenomena to which it is applicable), as well as by its adequacy in accounting for characteristics of and relations between and among observable utterances (Edelson, 1977).

Eventually, a psychoanalytic theory of mind will in-

clude a logic of signs or sign-processes.[32] The universe of
discourse of psychoanalysis will include variables whose
values are signs or types of signs and sign-processes, and
relations between and among signs or sign-processes of
the same type and between and among signs or sign-
processes of different types. Dreams, symptoms, and
parapraxes may then be describable along precise dimensions as types of signs or sign-processes, and in that sense
theorems about dreams, neuroses, and parapraxes will be
deducible from a general theory of mind.

REFERENCES

Buchler, J., ed. *Philosophical Writings of Peirce.* New York:
Dover, 1955.
Carnap, R. *Meaning and Necessity.* Enlarged 2d ed. Chicago:
University of Chicago Press, 1956.
———. *Introduction to Symbolic Logic and Its Applications.* New
York: Dover, 1958.
Chomsky, N. *Syntactic Structures.* The Hague: Mouton, 1957.
———. "Review of Skinner's *Verbal Behavior*" (1959). In *The
Structure of Language,* edited by J. Fodor and J. Katz. Engle-
wood Cliffs, N.J.: Prentice-Hall, 1964.
———. "Current Issues in Linguistic Theory." In *The Structure
of Language,* edited by J. Fodor and J. Katz. Englewood
Cliffs, N.J.: Prentice-Hall, 1964.

32. On a logic of signs, see Langer (1942); and my comments on Langer's
work in n. 7, and on Peirce's work, with references, in n. 9 of this paper. C. S.
Morris's work (1938, 1946) is useful, but for me is marred by an insistence on
behavioristic formulations. For discussions of psychoanalytic theory as a theory
of symbolic functioning, see Edelson (1971a, 1971b, 1972, 1975, 1977). I am
here using 'signs' to include both the narrower 'signs' (which refers only to indexes and signals) and 'symbols' (motivated or not), and I am using 'sign-
processes' as equivalent to symbolic functioning, referring to processes involving indexes and signals as well as motivated symbols (symbolic play, psychoanalytic symbols) and unmotivated symbols (language).

———. *Aspects of the Theory of Syntax*. Cambridge, Mass.: MIT Press, 1965.

———. *Topics in the Theory of Generative Grammar*. The Hague: Mouton, 1966.

———. *Language and Mind*. Enlarged ed. New York: Harcourt Brace Jovanovich, 1972.

———. *Reflections on Language*. New York: Pantheon Books, 1975a.

———. *The Logical Structure of Linguistic Theory*. New York: Plenum, 1975b.

Church, A. "A Formulation of the Logic of Sense and Denotation" (1951a). In *Structure, Method and Meaning,* edited by P. Henle et al. New York: Liberal Arts Press, 1951.

———. "The Need for Abstract Entities in Semantic Analysis" (1951b). In *The Structure of Language,* edited by J. Fodor and J. Katz. Englewood Cliffs, N.J.: Prentice-Hall, 1964.

———. "Introduction." In *Introduction to Mathematical Logic,* vol. 1. Princeton: Princeton University Press, 1956.

Clark, H. "Word Associations and Linguistic Theory." In *New Horizons in Linguistics,* edited by J. Lyons. Baltimore: Penguin, 1970.

Copi, I. *Symbolic Logic*. 3d ed. New York: Macmillan, 1967.

Edelson, M. *The Science of Psychology and the Concept of Energy*. Ph.D. dissertation, University of Chicago, 1954.

———. *Sociotherapy and Psychotherapy*. Chicago: University of Chicago Press, 1970a.

———. *The Practice of Sociotherapy: A Case Study*. New Haven: Yale University Press, 1970b.

———. *The Idea of a Mental Illness*. New Haven: Yale University Press, 1971a.

———. "Toward a Study of Interpretation in Psychoanalysis" (1971b). In *Explorations in General Theory in Social Science,* edited by J. Loubser, R. Baum, A. Effrat, and V. Lidz. New York: Free Press, 1976. Vol. 1, pp. 151–81.

———. "Language and Dreams: *The Interpretation of Dreams* Revisited." *Psychoanalytic Study of the Child* 27 (1972) : 203–82.

———. *Language and Interpretation in Psychoanalysis*. New Haven: Yale University Press, 1975.

———. "Psychoanalysis as Science: Its Boundary Problems, Special Status, Relations to Other Sciences, and Formalization." *Journal of Nervous and Mental Disease* 165 (1977) : 1–28.

Encyclopaedia Britannica. 15th ed. "Logic, Applied." Vol. 11, 1974.

Feibleman, J. *An Introduction to the Philosophy of Charles S. Peirce.* Cambridge, Mass.: MIT Press, 1950.

Fodor, J., et al. *The Psychology of Language.* New York: McGraw-Hill, 1974.

Freud, S. *Standard Edition of the Complete Psychological Works.* London: Hogarth, 1953–60.

  The Interpretation of Dreams (1900), vols. 4, 5.

  The Psychopathology of Everyday Life (1901), vol. 6.

  Jokes and Their Relation to the Unconscious (1905), vol. 8.

Goudge, T. *The Thought of C. S. Peirce.* New York: Dover, 1969.

Greenlee, D. *Peirce's Concept of Sign.* The Hague: Mouton, 1973.

Hartmann, H. "Psychoanalysis as a Scientific Theory" (1959). In *Essays on Ego Psychology.* New York: International Universities Press, 1964.

Hartshorne, C., and Weiss, P., eds. *Collected Papers of Charles Sanders Peirce.* Vol. 2: "Elements of Logic." Cambridge, Mass.: Harvard University Press, 1932.

Hughes, G., and Cresswell, M. *An Introduction to Modal Logic.* London: Methuen, 1968.

Hunter, G. *Metalogic.* Berkeley: University of California Press, 1971.

Isay, R. "Ambiguity in Speech." *Journal of the American Psychoanalytic Association* 25 (1977) : 427–52.

Katz, J. *Semantic Theory.* New York: Harper & Row, 1972.

———. "Logic and Language: An Examination of Recent Criticisms of Intensionalism." In *Language, Mind, and Knowledge.* Minnesota Studies in the Philosophy of Science, vol. 7, edited by K. Gunderson. Minneapolis: University of Minnesota Press, 1975.

Kris, E. *Psychoanalytic Explorations in Art.* New York: Schocken Books, 1952.

———. "On Some Vicissitudes of Insight in Psycho-Analysis."

International Journal of Psycho-Analysis 37 (1956a) : 445–55.
———. "The Recovery of Childhood Memories in Psychoanalysis." *Psychoanalytic Study of the Child* 11 (1956b) : 54–88.
Langer, S. *An Introduction to Symbolic Logic.* 3d rev. ed. New York: Dover, 1967.
———. *Philosophy in a New Key.* Cambridge, Mass.: Harvard University Press, 1942.
Lewis, C. "The Modes of Meaning" (1944). In *Semantics and the Philosophy of Language,* edited by L. Linsky. Urbana: University of Illinois Press, 1952.
———. *An Analysis of Knowledge and Valuation.* La Salle, Ill.: Open Court Publishing Co., 1946.
———. "Notes on the Logic of Intension." In *Structure, Method and Meaning,* edited by P. Henle et al. New York: Liberal Arts Press, 1951.
Lewis, C., and Langford, C. *Symbolic Logic.* New York: Dover, 1959.
Loewenstein, R. "The Problem of Interpretation." *Psychoanalytic Quarterly* 20 (1951) : 1–14.
———. "Some Thoughts on Interpretation in the Theory and Practice of Psychoanalysis." *Psychoanalytic Study of the Child* 12 (1957) : 127–50.
Marcus, R. "Extensionality" (1960). In *Reference and Modality,* edited by L. Linsky. London: Oxford University Press, 1971.
Miller, G.; Galanter, E.; and Pribram, K. *Plans and the Structure of Behavior.* New York: Holt, Rinehart, & Winston, 1960.
Moore, E., ed. *Charles S. Peirce: The Essential Writings.* New York: Harper & Row, 1972.
Morris, C. *Foundations of the Theory of Signs.* Chicago: University of Chicago Press, 1938.
———. *Signs, Language, and Behavior.* New York: Braziller, 1946.
Nagel, E., and Newman, J. "Gödel's Proof." *Scientific American,* June 1956.
———. *Gödel's Proof.* New York: New York University Press, 1958.
Parsons, T. *The Structure of Social Action.* New York: Free Press, 1937.

————. *The Social System*. New York: Free Press, 1951.

————. "An Approach to Psychological Theory in Terms of the Theory of Action." In *Psychology: A Study of a Science*, vol. 3, edited by S. Koch. New York: McGraw-Hill, 1959.

————. *Social Structure and Personality*. New York: Free Press, 1964.

Parsons, T., and Shils, E., eds. *Toward a General Theory of Action*. New York: Harper & Row, 1951.

Pribram, K. *Languages of the Brain*. Englewood Cliffs, N.J.: Prentice-Hall, 1971.

Quine, W. *Mathematical Logic*. Cambridge, Mass.: Harvard University Press, 1951.

————. "Notes on Existence and Necessity." In *Semantics and the Philosophy of Language*, edited by L. Linsky. Urbana: University of Illinois Press, 1952.

————. *From a Logical Point of View*. New York: Harper & Row, 1961.

Reichenbach, H. *Elements of Symbolic Logic* (1947). New York: Free Press, paperback, 1966.

Russell, B. *Logic and Knowledge*. New York: G. P. Putnam's, 1956:
    "On Denoting" (1905).
    "Mathematical Logic as Based on the Theory of Types" (1908).
    "The Philosophy of Logical Atomism" (1918).
    "On Propositions" (1919).
    "Logical Atomism" (1924).

Stevens, W. "Imagination as Value" (1949). *The Necessary Angel*. New York: Vintage Books, 1951.

Suppes, P. *Introduction to Logic*. New York: D. Van Nostrand, 1957.

Tarski, A. "Truth and Proof." *Scientific American* 220, no. 6 (1969) : 63–77.

Trilling, L. "Freud and Literature" (1950). *The Liberal Imagination*. New York: Viking Press, 1951.

Weiss, P., and Burks, A. "Peirce's Sixty-Six Signs." *Journal of Philosophy* 42 (1945) : 383–88.

Whitehead, A., and Russell, B. *Principia Mathematica*. 2 vols.

London: Cambridge University Press, 1910. (*Principia Mathematica to *56*. Paperback ed., 1962).

Wiener, P., ed. *Charles S. Peirce: Selected Writings*. New York: Dover, 1966.

5

What Can a Concept of Identity Add to Psycholinguistics?

NORMAN N. HOLLAND

One question before our symposium is: What can psychoanalysts and linguists tell each other? The answer lies sub-
merged in the unmarked channels that separate different
disciplines—that isolate, for example, the psychoanalyst's
"I" from the linguist's "/ay/" from the cognitive psychologist's "eye." To navigate such alien waters, the best I can
offer is a rough, hand-drawn chart and dead reckoning
based on it. Let me start from a point I know and map
the distances and changes I find as we sight places less familiar. New to me are /ay/ and eye.[1] The point I know
and can start from is the psychoanalyst's "I," the person
as a unity.

In my own work on reading, I have found I can understand the wholeness of a person, the way different actions
are all part of one individual, through the idea of identity

1. Precisely because I am rather at sea where linguistics or cognitive psychology is concerned, I am grateful to several people who generously offered criticism, counsel, or encouragement at the beginning of this project: Kenneth
Abrams, Irving Biederman, Noam Chomsky, Marshall Edelson, Morris Halle,
George Lakoff, and Mark Masling. Also, as so often in the past, I am indebted
to my colleagues in the Group for Applied Psychoanalysis (Buffalo branch) for
thoroughly discussing an early draft: Paul Diesing, Claire Kahane, Heinz Lichtenstein, Joseph Masling, Melvin Tucker, and David Willbern. I am particularly
thankful to Murray M. Schwartz for several long conversations, much wisdom,
and searching inquiry into the relations among identity, identity theme, and
primary identity.

as variations on an identity theme. By this concept I can understand how a reader has a particular style of reading plots, characters, events, setting, and the like by generating inner matches to outer texts. I can then see how his or her way of reading represents a style of experiencing such things outside of books as well.

In the rough chart by which I orient myself toward cognitive psychology and psycholinguistics, I see a relation between experiencing as a function of identity and experiencing in those other psychologies. That is, at a more particular level of experiencing language—sentences—I get the impression from current work in psycholinguistics that we understand sentences by generating something within ourselves, which is sentencelike, and comparing it to what we are hearing or reading. At a still more particular level of experiencing—the details of sound, direction, form, or color—I learn a maxim from the psychologists of perception and cognition: "Perception is a constructive act." We perceive by taking in a stimulus, creating an inner schema appropriate to it, and responding to a comparison of the two.

I get the further impression that these different levels interact. That is, my studies of reading and "large" perceptions bring in a whole person while the cognitive psychologist may involve only the retina. Yet at both the "higher" and the "lower" levels, perception seems to take place through a balance of excitations and inhibitions—control at the same level. There also seems to be control and feedback between higher and lower levels, with the higher dominant. Thus, cognitive psychologists call for general theories of personality and motivation to complete their studies of particular perceptions. I believe that identity (thought of as a theme and variations) offers just such a theory of the whole person—a theory, moreover,

that will relate the individual personality to his or her biological and cultural resources.

Thus, I expect to find a likeness in what we think these
days about personality, language, and perception: similar
patterns in the ways we relate the external to the internal
and the control of small units of experience by large
ones. I glimpse a common shape in our joining outside to
inside and top-down to bottom-up at all the levels of our
experience.

That hunch is the rough chart I offer for our naviga-
tion. As for dead reckoning, let us begin with what I
know: the psychoanalysts'

I

for identity. As Aaron Esterson puts it,

> One is not simply a person. One is also this particular
> person. One has an identity. One's identity is es-
> tablished in and through the way one relates to the
> persons and non-persons comprising one's world.
> The way of relating whereby one's identity is es-
> tablished may be called the style of the relation one
> makes. [1970, pp. 214–15]

From a psychoanalytic or perhaps even a commonsense
point of view, a human being constantly changes to enter
new relationships with reality; yet, at the same time, no
matter how much I change, there is a continuing me, an
"I" who is the grammatical and actual subject of every
change. I can stop being a patent lawyer and become a literary critic, yet I bring the same essential style to both activities.

One might well ask, with Heinz Lichtenstein (1961,
1977, pp. 49–122), What keeps a person the same?, for
we do sense both ourselves and one another as continu-

ing beings despite drastic changes. Indeed, it is precisely because there is a continuing "I" with a distinct personal style that you can see that a change in me is in fact a change. We understand difference by means of sameness and sameness by means of difference. I understand someone's right-wing politics as related to but different from his warm personal relations, and both have something, but not everything, in common with his fierce devotion to work. How can I formulate these relations?

Recently, the concept of identity has evolved as the name for these paradoxical minglings of human continuity and change. One way of thinking about that interplay—there may be others, but this I have found the most satisfactory—is to think of identity as a theme and variations. That is, I use identity not with Erikson's meaning (a sense of identity, a sameness felt from inside) but in Lichtenstein's way: identity as a sameness—and difference—observed from outside (1961, 1977, pp. 49–122). I can think of the sameness of someone as whatever theme or style I perceive as persisting in that person through all changes. I can then understand the changes and differences in that person as variations against that theme. Thus, one reader is frightened by Hemingway, approves of Lyndon Johnson and gracious manners, touches his male friends but worries about it, flirts with secretaries, and does housework to relieve tension. I can understand all these different activities as forming part of one lifestyle. I can observe. I can also empathize, participating as much as I can, being a different sort of person, in his sense of his own wholeness. Conversely, I can realize how each of these diverse relations gives him a fresh resource with which to reach out to the world and create anew his original, stable self (Holland, 1975a, "Sam").

Identity in this sense is a way of thinking about personality as living out ever-new transformations of a basic identity theme, much as a musician plays variations on a melody. In a musical theme and variations, the timbres, tones, tempi, or intervals may change—the melody can even turn upside down—but we find something in all those notes that remains constant, and that is what we call the theme. In the same way, I can trace in someone's choices patterns of repetition and contrast, sameness and change, theme and variation.

New experiences challenge our self-continuity and our fit with our surround. They ask that we make new variations. Conversely, all our synthetic acts serve to integrate new experiences (with more or less strain on outer or inner reality) into the cumulating theme and variations that is our identity. In other words, Lichtenstein's concept of identity hypothesizes a rhythm for all human experience like the rhythm of assimilation and accommodation that Piaget has described in cognitive acts.

Identity, then, is a way of conceptualizing the rhythmic succession of a person's choices as a theme and variations.[2] An "identity theme" is what I perceive as constant through all the variations. It is important to distinguish, more sharply than Lichtenstein does, "identity theme" (something inferred from outside) from what Lichten-

2. At the time I write, identity analyses have been published for over a dozen people of different sorts. People living at the time of the study: a prostitute in analysis (Lichtenstein, 1961, 1977, pp. 49–122); five readers reading in an experiment (Holland, 1973a, 1975a); students in a seminar perceiving texts and one another (Holland and Schwartz, 1975). Creative writers offer particularly large amounts of material for formulating identities because each writing records hundreds of choices. Identity studies have been made of Thomas Chatterton (Lichtenstein, 1965, 1977, pp. 245–61); Hilda Doolittle (Holland, 1973a); Robert Frost (Holland, 1973b, 1975c); and F. Scott Fitzgerald (Holland, 1976). I have also interpreted people who exist, so to speak, only as texts: the Nurse in *Romeo and Juliet* (Holland, 1973b) and Freud's "Rat Man" (1975b). Although he does not use a framework of identity theory, Robert Jay Lifton's study of "Dr. Vincent" painfully demonstrates the identity principle—that is, how individuals maintain identity against even such overwhelming forces as brainwashing (1961).

stein terms "primary identity" (something actually "in" the individual): a pervasive personal style created in infancy.

The idea of "primary identity" entails three important hypotheses that the idea of identity inferred from outside does not: first, that we acquire this style in adapting to or "being-for" our first nurturing person; second, that this style persists, in the sense that it is the matrix for all future growth, the innermost core of identity that the individual brings to all later experience; third, that the need to maintain one's primary identity is the deepest of human motivations. To be sure, recent psychoanalytic observations of young children do tend to confirm the idea of an early organization of the self in response to mothering, which becomes the basis for a later, more fully developed personal style (Spitz, 1965; Mahler et al., 1975; Stern, 1974). Again, although in a far more preliminary way, when I look by means of identity at a user of psychotic defenses, a victim of brainwashing, or a beneficiary of psychotherapy, I do see a continuing self that the individual maintains at all costs. Then at a theoretical level, this "identity principle" (prior even to the pleasure principle) provides a more human and satisfying way of understanding the repetitions that make up our character than Freud's biological speculation of a death instinct. Primary identity makes sense.

Finally, however, I can only know what goes on inside myself by psychoanalytic introspection or inside someone else by an empathy or "indwelling" like that of the psychoanalytic relationship—if I can know such things at all. Thus, in a strict sense, one cannot *observe* primary identity. Hypotheses about primary identity must be quite independent of identity *tout court,* which is asking from outside about a person's sameness and differences. Identity from outside justifies itself as a concept by satisfying that inquiry into the relationship between sameness and difference.

To the extent that I find it convincing to look at human lives as identity themes and variations on those themes, to that extent will I find the hypothesis of a primary identity convincing. To that extent, I can believe that the identity theme I infer from outside for someone coincides with some intrinsic unity inside the individual. But my belief that I have found a unity in someone is part of my relation to that person, something between us, neither simply "in" me, nor an identity "out there," "in" him. *Identity, then, as I define it, is a particular relationship: understanding someone as a theme and variations.*

I began to believe in this concept of identity as a fruitful way of looking at people's acts of synthesis because of a question I was asking about reading: How is it that although the text is the same, different readers perceive it differently, varying widely in their interpretations of even a single word? Traditionally, literary critics like me have looked for an answer in the text, but have not discovered it. Letting readers talk freely about what they read, and interpreting what they said, I found, first, that readers' responses varied far more widely than I had expected or than I could account for by ambiguities in the text. Second, each reader had a distinctive personal style of reading and interpreting. Thus, I found that I could relate the differences among several readers reading the same language to the sameness within one reader's reading of different texts by looking for those personal styles—identities. By formulating for each reader an identity theme, I could understand each re-creation of something read as a new variation on a cumulating identity. Further, I could understand how my interpretation of those readers' readings was both similar to and different from someone else's (for both I and that other person become, by our acts of inference, readers reading).

I was simply building on a general principle, that each new relation between self and surround constitutes a further growth in identity. Within that large generalization, however, I could be more precise by teasing out four strands within the relationship of reader to text. These are four modes by which we make the work part of our own psychic economy and by which we make ourselves part of the literary work as we interpret it. Obviously, these four modes of response all go on together, each shaping the others, but I can more easily describe them as a sequence.

Although the four terms I use are traditional to psychoanalysis, they take on new possibilities if we look for them not "in" the individual but in relationships: in the reader's relation to the text and in my own inquiry into that relation (which is itself a relationship).

The most obvious question I can ask about a reader coming to a text is, What are her expectations? Probably they will be a pattern of related wishes and fears, for it seems likely that each of us brings to a literary work a set of expectations like those we bring to any other entity outside ourselves. In another sense, by looking for a reader's expectations, I am exploring her relation of trust or mistrust to what she reads.

To establish trust, we need to be able to re-create from the literary work our characteristic strategies for achieving the pleasure we want and defeating the dangers we fear. That is, it seems useful to assume that the individual can enjoy the literary work only to the extent that he forms from it some match to the defensive or adaptive strategies he uses to meet the world at large. Then, one asks, can he shape the literary text into the form of reality he is adept at dealing with? Such a matching is crucial, for if it is missing or inexact, the individual will feel anxiety rather than pleasure, and he will very likely ward off the whole experience, again, in his characteristic way.[3]

If, however, he succeeds in setting anxiety at a tolerable level, how does the reader then enjoy the work? Presumably, by investing it with things that matter to him—by projection, in other words. If he can shape, change, and delete the literary work so that it matches his own identity considered in terms of defense, then he can confide in the work wishes for his characteristic kind of pleasure: his particular fantasies. Such a projection would be easy indeed, for in wishing, he lets himself go instinctively toward gratification, but in defending or adapting he has to transform, oppose, or redirect his wishes. Hence, the reader has to match his defenses in the text quite exactly, but the wishes he projects can simply express his own drives through the imagery of the literary work.

Thus, a single reader—whatever her character structure—can enjoy a variety of literary works; and many different people from many different cultures can enjoy the same work, if all readers re-create the work in the terms of their own identity themes. Can they make it part of their own characteristic mental processes? Can they use

3. Interestingly, Freud anticipated this point in his remarks on defense mechanisms in "Analysis Terminable and Interminable" (1937): "The adult's ego, with its increased strength . . . finds itself compelled to seek out those situations in reality which can serve as an approximate substitute for the original danger, so as to be able to justify, in relation to them, its maintaining its habitual modes of reaction" (p. 238). Freud's tone is intriguing: he treats the defenses as in themselves pathological, whereas we today would find it difficult to distinguish defense from necessary adaptations except by context. The direction of causality he posits is also striking: the ego seeks dangers so as to justify its usual modes of reaction. Thus, constancy of personality would underlie the compulsion to repeat, not vice versa. He implies a "principle of identity maintenance" prior both to the compulsion to repeat and to the pleasure principle, as posited by Lichtenstein (1961).

characteristic modes of defense to blend into it the particular kind of fantasy they enjoy and remove from it the particular kind of threat they fear?

For example, one reader (Sandra) wanted to deal with her world as a source of nurturing power toward which she could come close, but not too close. A second reader (Sam) created a world in which he sustained his own masculinity by coming close to or fleeing the masculinity of others. Sandra dealt with Bugs, a Hemingway character, by finding him grandly hospitable and reassuring, giving great quantities of food and warmth and attention. Sam, however, thought Bugs a frightening Fu Manchu torturer who might tear off his ears; but then, he reassured himself, the hero gets away from Bugs. Both Sandra and Sam brought characteristic wishes, positive and negative, to Bugs; both defensively shaped him into the kind of person they could cope with; and both projected onto him or the situation their characteristic cluster of wishes (Holland, 1975a).

Expectations aroused, defenses matched, fantasies projected, a fourth principle can come into the inquiry. We can ask how the reader "makes sense" of the work—assuming she has continued to relate to it. In theory, she would make sense of it by using the defenses she has matched from the work to transform the wishes she has projected into it into some esthetic, social, ethical, or intellectual coherence. She might make a unity of the work or compare it to other works, associate to it, imitate it, bring her knowledge or expertise to bear, evaluate it, place it in a tradition, decode it, imitate it—whatever! We can ask, to what extent is she committing one or all of her characteristic strategies for making crude daydreams feel meaningful and respectable? We would be asking at an intellectual level as well as in terms of fantasies and defenses, how this person re-creates her identity through a reading experience.

Thus, with the Hemingway story, Sam decided "to bolster it up," "to infuse in it all the symbolism," and make it "able to stand up more." Sandra dealt with the story by evaluating its style, particularly the descriptions: "kind of short," "kind of straightforward," "fairly blunt," "hitting at the things that'll make something stand out." Both arrived at commentaries that would do for an English class, yet these comments seem to me transformations of their masculinizing of the story at deeper fantasy levels of response.

If we state these four modes of inquiry in traditional psychoanalytic terms, they lead to a convenient mnemonic: a reader reads DEFTly, through some combination of defense, expectation, fantasy, and transformation. The familiar psychoanalytic meanings for these words, however, provide no more than nuclei around which inquiry can take place. Transformation leads into ego synthesis in general, expectation brings in the whole large question of trust, while fantasy and defense both involve the boundaries between inner and outer worlds in the largest sense.

Indeed, these four terms suggest two continua inherent in all experience. One can think of "expectation" as a way of asking, how does this person fit what she is reading into the before-and-after sequence of her experience? "Transformation" enables one to ask, how does she make this reading into a coherent experience in itself, apart from experiences before or after? We are asking, then, about the relation between meaning within a time sequence and meaning independent of time. In the same way, "fantasy" and "defense" form a relation. Fantasy: what does this reader project out into the world? Defense: what does this reader admit in from the world? All four terms are ways to construe aspects of an individual's relationship with a text as part of that person's sameness and difference—that is, identity.

If, however, we were to take these four modalities, each an aspect of identity, as involved only in reading, we would miss why this literary discovery is important for psychoanalysis as a whole. One cannot, after all, draw a sharp line between literature and other kinds of texts. Is the Declaration of Independence "literature"? Is the Communist Manifesto? Are the writings of Sigmund Freud? Reading per se shades off into the perception of any kind of language, indeed of character, event, setting, and the rest, both on and off the page. In short, the small question, Why do different readers read the same novel differently?, leads to a large, psychoanalytic theory of perception.

Each DEFT-perception I can place as one small transaction in the cumulating theme-and-variations that is my idea of the individual's identity. Thus, I can state the relation between DEFT and identity in the language of mathematics. Identity is a function of an identity theme. That is, the way a musician can create ever-new variations on a musical theme corresponds to the way a mathematician can imagine infinitely many functions of a variable like $x^3 + 1$ without ever losing that essential $(x^3 + 1)$ness. Both illustrate the freedom of an individual to make a whole lifeful of choices without ever losing a personal style. Identity is also made up of a great many little DEFT transactions. We could say, then, that a DEFT at any given moment is the derivative of identity with respect to time. Conversely, identity is the integral over time of all those DEFTS, which themselves take place within the limitation that they be functions of the basic variable that is the identity theme.

The language of the poet matches that of the mathematician. As Emily Dickinson said, "Each Life Converges to some Centre," and Yeats mused, "I have often had the fancy that there is some one Myth for every man, which, if we but knew it, would make us understand all he did and thought." A fragment of one of Hopkins's sonnets goes:

> Each mortal does one thing and the same:
> Deals out that being indoors each one dwells;
> Selves—goes itself; *myself* it speaks and spells;
> Crying *Whát I dó is me: for that I came.*

Congreve put the matter more drily, classically, and cosmetically: "Thô our Actions are never so many and different in Form, they are all Splinters of the same Wood, and have Naturally one Complexion, which thô it may be disguised by Art, yet cannot be wholly changed: We may Paint it with other Colours, but we cannot change the Grain."[4]

In short, what began as a theory of reading becomes a general way of relating personality to the imagination or perception of an other. We can understand perception as making the other a part of ourselves by a matching of defense, expectation, fantasy, and transformation. We can understand it, in still a larger sense, as making the event meaningful within and without a time sequence, guardedly taking it into ourselves, and freely projecting ourselves out onto it. More precisely, each of us can understand these polarities in perception as variations on the identity theme of the perceiver (including ourselves).

4. *The Poems of Emily Dickinson*, vol. 2, no. 680, ed. T. Johnson (Cambridge, Mass.: Harvard University Press, 1963), p. 256; W. B. Yeats, "At Stratford-on-Avon," in *Essays* (New York: Macmillan, 1924), p. 131; *Poems of Gerard Manley Hopkins*, 3d ed., ed. W. H. Gardner (New York: Oxford University Press, 1948), p. 95; W. Congreve, "Concerning Humour in Comedy" (1695), in J. E. Spingarn, ed., *Critical Essays of the Seventeenth Century*, vol. 3 (Oxford: Clarendon Press, 1907), pp. 248–49.

Such a theory of perception lets us articulate the relationship between perceiver and perceived in very large terms, yet connect it to highly personal details of perception and expression.

Such a theory asks that we explicitly include ourselves in any account of perceptions by others or by ourselves. Thus, my very statement of identity theory is *my* statement. It expresses the great importance for me of unifying people's seemingly inconsistent behavior, the importance I give to the inside-outside distinction, and my general tendency to see things in polarities. Someone else might state the idea of identity and identity maintenance differently, but such differences do not defeat the theory. Rather, they are precisely the data the theory accounts for. The evidence for the theory is the degree to which it can be used to generalize across the relationships between different perceivers and the same thing perceived and between different things perceived and the same perceiver.

Even such an individualistic theory of perception, however, assumes that people are seeing more or less the same thing at more particular levels than the characters, events, or settings of fiction: we are all seeing the same word or phrase or sentence. This is very much in the tradition of Freud's assumption that a system *Pcpt.* (perception) delivers a faithful copy of the world to a system *Cs.* (conscious), which might then be distorted by unconscious factors. Unfortunately, that may not be a reliable assumption. At least, we need to look closely at it, turning from the level of the whole person, the psychoanalysts' "I," to the level of linguistic particulars, the linguists'

/ay/

I wish I could say that linguists and psycholinguists have arrived at a clear and unanimous account of the way we understand words and sentences; but, of course, they have not. "Almost every aspect of sentence recognition remains unsettled despite the experimental attention the problem has recently received" (Fodor, Bever, and Garrett, 1974, p. 373). "There *is* no theory of language comprehension" (Fillmore, 1974, p. 34). "There is still no satisfactory explanation of how the listener deciphers and assimilates the conceptual relationships that are conveyed by spoken and written language" (Norman et al., 1975, p. 117).

American linguists and psycholinguists do seem to agree on one thing: "There is no simple correspondence between the surface structure of language and meaning" (Smith, 1971, p. 29). On the contrary, a half-century of experimental literature "suggests that what subjects remember about a text is a complicated function of the literal text and their beliefs and values" (Fodor, Bever, and Garrett, 1974, p. 273).[5]

Only by some such complicated function could we explain familiar experiences like the "cocktail party" phenomenon: the way we are able, confronted with a confused babble of speech, to pick out of the crowd one voice and follow it. Clearly, as Bergson suggested in 1896, we are active listeners:

> auditory impressions organize nascent movements, capable of scanning the phrase which is heard and emphasizing its main articulations. These automatic movements of internal accompaniment . . . end by sketching a simplified figure in which the listener

5. Given the large body of experimental evidence to this effect, the recent effort by French and American literary critics to confine theories of structuralism or a semiotics of film or literature to Saussure's nineteenth-century notion of language as an inventory of signs, each a signifier (*signifiant*) and a signified (*signifié*) rigidly linked by the social rules of language, would seem to me misdirected—to say the least.

would find, in their main lines and principal directions, the very movements of the speaker. [p. 136]

Perhaps the most useful term for this scanning process is
Halle and Stevens's "analysis-by-synthesis." They propose
"a recognition model for speech" in which "Patterns are
generated internally in the analyzer according to a flexible or adaptable sequence of instructions until a best
match with the input signal is obtained," in other words,
an analysis "achieved through active internal synthesis of
comparison signals" (1964, p. 604). The same process
applies to reading as to understanding speech: there, too,
we understand by generating hypotheses about the meaning of a string or pattern of symbols (Kolers, 1972).

Thus, we carry on this analysis-by-synthesis at different
levels, depending on our skill and familiarity with the
symbols in question. "The listener can ask himself 'What
sounds are uttered?' or 'What words were spoken?' or
'What was meant?' and proceed to synthesize accordingly" (Neisser, 1967, p. 194). Thus, we hear the /b/ in
"bit" and the /b/ in "bad" both as /b/'s, although they look
like quite different phonemes if we make them visible
electronically.

We construct inner speech at many levels. Analysis-by-
synthesis suggests that we carry around in our heads,
ready for synthesis, not a collection of all possible acoustic
inputs—that would hardly be possible!—but a set of rules
for generating patterns which can be both concrete and
abstract. We make a hypothesis about the original message, apply a rule to determine what the input would be
like if the hypothesis were true, and then check to see if
the input is really like that. At a low level, I can decide
whether the sound denoted /ay/ in the International Phonetic Alphabet represents the person pronoun "I" or the
"eye" that I "C" with. At a much higher level, rapid read-

ing, I attain meaning without ever identifying individual
letters or words. I don't feel engaged in verbal behavior
at all, only a continuing silent stream of thought (Neisser,
1967, pp. 194, 136).

Thus, the idea of analysis-by-synthesis not only presupposes an active hearer or reader, but also means that
he has a complex set of hierarchical rules for generating
language at various levels of abstraction, ranging from
individual letters or phonemes to whole paragraphs.
"Perhaps the most powerful argument for the
analysis-by-synthesis approach is that it provides a coherent account of the way listeners make use of contextual
information" (Neisser, 1967, p. 195).

Listeners listen, in Neisser's summary of the research,
in two stages. The first must, by definition, *not* be a full
analysis-by-synthesis. Rather, the listener must first be
able to choose those parts of what he is hearing that are
worth synthesizing. He must be able to form some kind
of preliminary identification of the parts that matter to
him. This first stage must be relatively passive, something
prior to a full "paying attention," while real "paying attention" must be the analysis-by-synthesis itself.

Thus, at a cocktail party, "irrelevant, unattended
streams of speech are neither 'filtered out' nor 'attenuated.'" They simply are analyzed, not by synthesis, but by
passive processes which do no more than establish place,
form crude segments, and guide response to simple situations. "Their capacity for detail is strictly limited." By
contrast, really listening to someone, particularly against
the background of a cocktail party, requires "a constructive process," "an active . . . analysis-by-synthesis, in
which the listener produces 'inner speech' (at some level
of abstraction) to match the input" (Neisser, 1967, p.
213).

Thus, listeners do two things: they delete and they

supply meanings. "Unimportant information supplied by the speaker passes right through the listener's system, without contributing to processing load, while important information not supplied by the speaker is inferred," for example, the kind of agreements about situation and context that someone like Erving Goffman observes, or simplified, half-stated semantic content—"chunks" that different words will differently contain. For example, "own," "possess," "have," or "hold," all might convey a "chunk,"—possession—for first-stage processing, their differences in nuance mattering only at a later stage (Norman et al., 1975, pp. 276, 246).

One can clearly observe these phases in children's language (although, at this stage, different theorists have different ways of explaining them). Roger Brown, for example, found two levels in the growth of children's speech: first, basic meanings; then, modulations of meaning through plurals, tenses, locatives, and so on (1973 a,b). Brown, McNeill, and others have all found that children learn language or grammar by hypothesizing rules and then modifying them. No one, for example, ever said to my son, "Jane wented to the store." He had formulated a rule, Past→ + -ed, and applied it to a verb of motion, went. Logical—although parents, society, and English teachers would someday ask that he refine that appealingly simple rule (McNeill, 1970a, b).

The notion of a grammar as a system of rules for generating the correct (and only the correct) sentences of a language is, of course, the great achievement of Noam Chomsky. Given such a theory one can ask searching questions with some hope of their being answered—questions like: How is it that I can produce as many new sentences as I please? How can I interpret an infinity of sentences I have never heard before? Indeed, children six years old or so can do that—how did they learn to do it so

NORMAN N. HOLLAND 189

quickly? One cannot possibly answer such questions by a stimulus-response account of language or by a notion of a language as an inventory of completed sentences.

According to Chomsky's "standard theory," every sentence in a natural language has a deep structure and a surface structure.[6] The grammatical relations of each sentence are explicit in its deep structure, although they may be obscured in the surface structure. Chomsky first concerned himself with only the formal syntactic devices of the language, not with meaning, nor with rules that might relate syntactic structures to meaning. Nevertheless, even in the earliest theory, a semantic interpretation of a sentence, including the choice of particular words, is defined over its deep structure, while the sound or writing of a sentence is defined over its surface structure. A finite set of phrase-structure rules will generate the deep structure of every sentence, and a finite set of transformations will rewrite the deep structure sentence into a surface structure sentence.

Other writers besides Chomsky have developed sets of rules (a "semantic component") to relate meanings to syntactic (deep) or phonological (surface) structures (Katz and Fodor, 1963; Katz and Postal, 1964). Since we can compare meanings of sentences from one language to another there must be a universal semantic representation (like the universal phonetic alphabet). Such a semantic representation must be tightly integrated into the cognitive system of the human mind. Innate, presumably: we are born knowing some of the distinctions we need to get along in the world.

6. I am following the succinct statement of principles given by Fodor, Bever, and Garrett (1974, pp. 110–12 and 139). An introduction to the theory that presupposes no prior knowledge is Jacobs and Rosenbaum (1968). A useful survey of psycholinguistic research growing from Chomsky's theories is Greene (1972).

Like Freud, Chomsky has continually revised and refined his theoretical structures around a largely unchanging core of data, sometimes in ways that go beyond his
followers. In the "extended standard theory," he has
given up the semantic relevance of deep structure, defining it simply as a level prior to the application of transformations. He has kept, however, the basic assumption that
sentences can be declared well-formed or ill-formed *by
linguistic criteria alone.*

All these versions of Chomsky's theories thus entail the
same hypothesis: we understand a sentence by assigning
it a phrase structure—that is, giving it a tree diagram with
markers S (= sentence), NP (= noun phrase), V (= verb),
and so on. Obviously, it is unlikely that we do this explicitly, and Neisser has made the ingenious suggestion that
we assign, not a tree diagram or phrase markers, but a
rhythm (1967, pp. 259, 262).

Psycholinguists have tended to confirm the idea that we
synthesize a syntactic structure: "There seems no serious
doubt that structural descriptions are . . psychologically
real; they specify at least some of the descriptions under
which linguistic messages are interpreted and integrated." On the other hand, little evidence suggests that
the "computational processes" specified by transformational grammars are what listeners actually do: there are
"divergences between grammars and recognizers." Also,
researchers have not been able to show that what language learners learn is a transformational grammar
(Fodor, Bever, and Garrett, 1974, pp. 273, 271, 502).
Thus, Chomsky's basic assumption, that linguistic criteria
alone determine whether a sentence is grammatical or
not, cannot at present be extended beyond a strictly formal statement. No one has yet shown that linguistic criteria have a psychological reality.

The strongest antithesis arising from Chomsky's work,

that drawn by the cumbersomely named generative semanticists, drives in at precisely this point. Chomsky, they
say, was wrong to assume that one could talk coherently
about syntax without taking meaning and use into account (Lakoff, 1974). Generative semanticists therefore
generate not just sentences, but quadruples: the sentence;
the logical structure underlying the sentence (which takes
the place of Chomskyan deep structure); context; and the
meaning conveyed.

For example, the sentence, "The policemen were ordered to stop drinking after 2:00 A.M.," is ambiguous; but
the sentence, "The students were ordered to stop drinking after 2:00 A.M.," is not, at least so far as my students
are concerned. The ambiguity rests partly on linguistic
grounds: the sentences can be derived two ways with either reflexive or nonreflexive subjects for *drinking*. But
the ambiguity is *also* a matter of social context. My experience of students is that they drink after 2:00 A.M. and
would not stop others from doing what they themselves
do. My experience of the police is that they might well
drink after 2:00 A.M. themselves but would feel free to
stop someone else from doing so. Consider sentences
like:

1. Helen is Manny's widow.
*2. Manny is Helen's widower.
3. He's a professional.
4. She's a professional.

As Robin Lakoff points out, to understand the unaccept-
ability of (2) and the difference in meaning between (3)
and (4), one needs to bring to bear a knowledge that men
are not usually stereotyped by sex-roles but women are
(1973, pp. 68, 64, 76–77). At a more molecular level, to
know whether the /ay/ of my subheading refers to "I," to
"eye," to both, or to neither, one needs to bring to bear

the logic of this whole essay. "It is impossible to tell where linguistic knowledge leaves off and extralinguistic knowledge takes over" (Jackendoff, 1972, p. 19).

Most recently, George Lakoff and Henry Thompson have suggested beginning with "a direct and intimate relation between grammars and mechanisms for production and recognition," in fact, defining grammar precisely as "collections of strategies for understanding and producing sentences" (1975). "From this point of view, abstract grammars [of the type transformationalists produce] are just convenient fictions for representing certain processing strategies." Lakoff and Thompson then set out the general form of the correspondences among the rules for the recognition grammar, the rules for the production grammar, and the rules for the abstract grammar they both use. Instead of purely transformational grammars that work on whole structures, they prefer a "left-to-right" or "cognitive" grammar, "one which attempts to characterize and explain grammatical phenomena in an incremental, signal-driven fashion." They then find that they can set out the general form of the correspondence between the rules of the recognition grammar and the rules of the abstract grammar and the rules of the production grammar. At the time I am writing, however, these are just beginning to take detailed shape.

Even so, transformationalists themselves acknowledge that their experiments with comprehension show that we map our deep-structure knowledge of the relations into which a given word can enter onto cues from the surface structure as we hear it. We start processing a sentence as soon as it begins—we don't wait for a whole structure in order to untransform it. Both left-to-right and top-to-bottom enter into interpretation (Fodor and Garrett, 1967; Fodor, Garrett, and Bever, 1968).

Thus, despite the diversity of linguistics in 1978, I see a

certain consensus. The precise shape of sentence recognition, particularly the psychological reality of grammatical structures, remains unsettled. There is, however, wide agreement that in order to interpret a sentence, we generate something—maybe a sentence with or without context, maybe part of a sentence or a set of phrase markers or a rhythmical representation of grammatical structure—but we generate something sentencelike in order to understand someone else's sentence. We analyze through synthesis. Moreover, most researchers agree that we do so in two modes. The first is a kind of preliminary, preattentive identification of what merits further analysis. The second is analysis-by-synthesis in the full sense, and that is what we mean by "paying attention" to what we hear or read.

Thus, it was possible for Frank Smith to write a coherent and convincing account of reading at the sentence level on the basis of what was known in 1971. We readers "predict" our way through a text, eliminating alternatives to produce a single interpretation. We eliminate some quickly, in advance as it were, because of what we know from the considerable redundancy of our natural language. As our eyes pass over the page, they acquire just enough visual information to eliminate the remaining alternatives. In such a two-stage process, the brain plays a far greater part than the eye—at least for fluent readers. The eye takes in gulps of information, but to do so, the brain must tell the eye when it has absorbed all the information it can process in short-term memory. Short-term memory can process about five items at a time, but these may be letters, syllables, sounds, words, or ideas, depending on the fluency of the reader; for the capacity of short-term memory depends not on the amount of information but on the number of units into which the brain can group the information (Bever, 1973). Thus, to achieve useful speed in reading, the brain-eye combination must be able to use prior knowledge and skill to shape from what the eye perceives processable units at some level of abstraction: cognitive schemata, structures, or maps. Once short-term memory has reached capacity with four or five units, the brain greatly reduces the eye's seeing and sends it into a saccade (or jump) to the next place on the page where the brain thinks it useful to process information (Smith, pp. 82, 104).

The way we perceive a page—indeed, "the way in which we perceive the world depends on the manner in which we categorize the incoming information, not simply on the characteristics of the incoming information itself" (Smith, p. 74). Conversely, "Much more than the knowledge of words is required to understand a sentence: There must be general knowledge about the world as well." "To understand a sentence, we appear to combine general knowledge about the world with knowledge of the structure of language and the meaning of the parts of the sentence" (for example, that some policemen tipple in the wee hours of the morning—Norman et al., 1975, p. 5).

In general, then, reading involves a dual, active process of analysis-by-synthesis so that "whatever meaning is, it must be defined with respect to a listener or reader" (Smith, 1971, p. 35). In that two-stage process, I can find five places at which the identity of the reader or hearer quite probably affects it. There could be more.

1. The scanning, preattentive mode of being generally open to the stimulus is probably more physiological and less personal than any other part of the process of language interpretation. That preliminary stage, however, ends with decisions that some items are not important. Such decisions correspond to the adaptive or defensive

strategy of denial or disavowal in classical psychoanalytic terms. When and to what we apply the defense is very much a function of personality. This part of the process corresponds (loosely) to the expectation and defense of defense-expectation-fantasy-transformation.

2. The preliminary scan also ends in decisions that some items *are* important, and here, too, personality must enter. We individually define the categories by which four or five units are grouped, stored, and processed in short-term memory. To someone like Sam, masculinity will be an important category; to Sandra, strength; to both of them, closeness and distance; and so on. These categories will correspond to the items the individual can best cope with—hence to the matching of his defensive, adaptive strategies to the linguistic materials provided by the input.

3. To interpret or "process" what has been categorized and taken in, we synthesize a sentence (or part of a sentence, a structural rhythm, some protosentence—sometimes it is called "inner speech"). In inner speech no less than in outer, *le style est l'homme même*. One person will favor one cluster of generatives or transformations, another will favor another. Were this outer speech, we would speak of the individual's style (Holland, 1968). As inner speech, the individual style manifests itself as the individualizing of what is being compared to (or, if you will, subtracted from) the input sentence. The hearer, in this linguistic sense, supplies an EFT for DEFT.

4. The generative semanticists are the most explicit about it, but many writers from many points of view would agree that the interpreter of language has to bring to it categories, concepts, and conventions, including the worldly knowledge of social contexts. Here, too, the individual plays off against the sentence he hears his particu-

lar experiences as he created them through the processes of his identity theme. In interpreting, I introduce, in effect, the history of my identity.

5. Finally, in analysis-by-synthesis, what causes the interpreter to continue his interpreting is a sense of difference between what he has synthesized and what he has taken from out there. For each of us, the sense of what constitutes a difference requiring further processing is itself a personal matter (Frenkel-Brunswik, 1949). How much uncertainty can you tolerate? I cannot tolerate very much, and I resort to intense theorizing. We are dealing in yet another way, with the D (=defense) of the DEFT transformation of identity.

There may well be more points at which personal identity shapes the interpretive process of analysis-by-synthesis. Indeed, it could be that we should speak of identity as something permeating our interpretations of language rather than as a discrete influence at particular points in the transaction.

The mere fact, however, that we can speak of precise influences suggests that, even in the roiling currents of today's linguistics, we can find a channel from the psychoanalytic "I" to the /ay/ of language. Identity is something the psychoanalytic theorist can tell the linguist about. Conversely, the psychoanalyst can learn from the linguist how to turn a knowledge of the way we understand words and sentences into a way of understanding styles of relationship to other people and to things. Now, the next leg of the journey takes us to the psycholinguists' nearest neighbors, the psychologists of perception and cognition and their

"eye"

When we navigate identity theory and psycholinguistics to sensory perception, we enter a region of considerable consensus and—dare I say it in this skeptical age?—certainty. "According to the nineteenth-century conception," writes Henry A. Murray, "the human mind is like an inanimate and impartial motion-picture film which accurately records the succession of physical events. It is a percept-registering or fact-registering organ, with the attributes of a scientific instrument." The twentieth century, however, sees perception very differently. "The introduction of the concept of tendency (animal drive) . . . required that this notion of the mind be modified so as to embrace the function of *selection*. Out of the passing medley of physical patterns the brain picks out those which are pertinent" (1951, p. 446).

Thus, twentieth-century psychologists of perception have arrived, so far as I can tell, at virtual unanimity around the idea of perception as a constructive act. One might call it "unconscious inference," as Helmholtz did in 1925; "probabilistic cue-association," in Brunswik's phrasing; "hypothesis testing," as Bruner said; or simply "trial and check," Solley and Murphy's phrase. Or we might just use again the "analysis-by-synthesis" that Neisser adapted from Halle and Stevens's linguistic hypothesis (Neisser, 1967, p. 193; Norman et al., 1975, p. 280).

In his influential 1967 survey of cognitive psychology, Neisser concluded that seeing, hearing, and remembering are all acts of construction involving the same sort of dual structure that we saw in language processing. "A preliminary analysis, made by a relatively passive, preattentive stage, provides information which guides the more active process of synthesis itself" (p. 199). In vision, for example, "perceiving involves a memory that is not representational but schematic. During a series of fixations, the perceiver synthesizes a model or schema of the scene before him, using information from each successive fixation to add detail or to extend the construction."

Thus, the whole act of perception implies "two kinds of short-term memory for visual information: the iconic replica of a brief and isolated stimulus, and the cumulative schema of the visible world that is constructed in the course of ordinary perception" (Neisser, 1968, p. 255).

Recent experiments with glimpses of jumbled scenes suggest that we see more in that first scan than a sequence of two stages will account for. Even in a glimpse too brief to allow a separate fixation, people identify individual objects along with a characterization of the whole scene. Possibly, then, we perceive in two simultaneous modes, physical positional relations and more semantic relations (Biederman et al., 1974; Biederman, 1975).

Either sequentially or in parallel, however, the basic principle—that perception is constructive—holds. "The reaction of the nervous system to stimulation by light is far from passive. The eye and brain do not act as a camera or a recording instrument. Neither in perceiving nor in remembering is there any enduring copy of the optical input. In perceiving, complex patterns are extracted from that input and fed into the constructive processes of vision" (Neisser, 1968, p. 259). "Memory retains information about mental *acts* rather than copies of experiences" (Neisser, 1967, p. 302). Experiments with the perception of board games (Go and Go-moku) suggest that we do not just list the positions of the pieces statically. We represent them as patterns for actions (Norman et al., 1975, p. 346).

The study of visual illusions, however, provides the most telling evidence in favor of "the new look in perceptual theory." "When perceptual illusions were introduced as a topic of study in the 19th century, the prevailing attitude toward them was that they were . . . minor imperfections or errors in the working of man's perceptual apparatus." Transparent cubes that spontaneously turn inside out, flights of steps that flip from right-side-up to upside-down, lines that seem bigger or smaller according to arrowheads at their ends, parallels that bulge or squeeze in response to their crosshatched backgrounds, the flashing arrows on the movie marquee that seem to move, colors that change because of their surround—all such mysteries were "illusions." "The notion of error . . . implied that there is some 'real world' faithfully reported by the senses. Few contemporary investigators take this view. Instead of thinking of illusions as errors in perceiving they regard them as genuine perceptions that do not stand up when their implications are tested" (Kolers, 1964, p. 316). "It is as though the brain entertains alternative hypotheses of what objects the eye's image may be presenting. When sensory data are inadequate . . . the brain never 'makes up its mind.' " Cubes, colors, and convergences seem to flip back and forth all by themselves, but it is the brain restlessly tossing (Gregory, 1968, p. 241).

When we stop thinking of them as mere errors, the old optical illusions imply a whole change in epistemology. "Illusions are now regarded as putting in question any belief in 'objective' perception." "There is nothing in an experience that testifies to its correspondence with 'reality,' nothing in a perception that guarantees its truth. Judgments of reality and truth must come from sources other than the experience or the perception" (Kolers, 1964, pp. 316, 317). That is, they must come from separate testings, since the perception always contains the hypothesis on which it is based.

For example, when the train next to my train starts up in a station, I have a momentary and startling feeling that my own train is going backwards. Such an illusion illustrates one of the basic hypotheses that people supply to the perception of motion: the surrounding is at rest and

the object surrounded (my train, in this example) is what
is moving (Wallach, 1959). Similarly, as Edwin Land's
famous color slides show, we perceive color by establishing a balance point or fulcrum between the long
and short waves of the incoming colors; then we divide
the waves around that point and compare them to produce the full spectral range (Land, 1959, 1978). In the
same way, we perceive colors by an interaction between
our percepts of the surround and the color surrounded.
"An area of the retina that receives a higher intensity of
stimulation induces a sensation of gray or black in a
neighboring region of lower intensity," causing a color to
appear opaque instead of luminous (Wallach, 1963, p.
284). Cognitive and perceptual psychologists have investigated a host of phenomena from this point of view. The
experiments all lead to the conclusion that seeing, hearing, remembering, and even smelling take place by the
perceiver's comparing his own rule or hypothesis or inner
order with an outer order.

Where, then, do these self-generated hypotheses come
from? Experiments with newly hatched chicks and with
newborn humans show that both come into the world
with some innate, unlearned abilities to perceive forms.[7]
The chicks perceive enough of shape, three-dimen-
sionality, and size so that they can peck at grains of food.
The human infant can pick out faces, providing a basis
for the later recognition of persons, social responsiveness,

7. The psychoanalyst will recognize here an experimental confirmation of
one of Heinz Hartmann's most important ideas: that humans are born into an
"average expectable environment" and are equipped with ego functions of
"primary autonomy" for dealing with that environment—here, the ability to
perceive faces (Hartmann, 1939). Hartmann, however, fitted both primary and
secondary (derived) perception and cognition into the "copying" theories of
nineteenth-century psychology—"immaculate perception" as it has been called.
He thus remained firmly anchored to the traditional Freudian idea of a "reality
principle" to which the well-analyzed psychoanalytic theorist is privy.

and spatial organization. Since the newborn's visual acuity has not fully developed, it seems likely that *what* is perceived enters into the formation of the rules for *how* it will be perceived. That is, the infant's development of visual acuity will go along with the further refinement of rules for selecting the significant faces and other forms in his environment (Fantz, 1961). Thus, a feedback from the environment to these innate or learned procedures guarantees the relevance of these rules. Both natural selection and adaptive growth affect perception.

Thus, infants may register, with their innate equipment, much of the information that adults do, but apparently they can process less of that information than adults can (Bower, 1966). Children move toward adult perceptions and intelligence as they stop immediately responding to stimuli and develop rules for combining new perceptual information with information from memory (Bower, 1974, p. 180). The definitive work here is, of course, Piaget's. He has taught us to think in terms of the cyclic interactions of assimilation (taking in an external object through an internal schema) and accommodation (the adjustment of the schema to the requirements of the object). The first schemata are (evidently) innate, but from them proceeds a cyclic interaction leading through all the stages of childhood to adult intelligence, morality, logic, and the rest.

Piaget's congenital categories of action patterns correspond to Erikson's idea of modes, that is, forms applicable to various organs, like taking in or letting go. Either provides an alternative to associative or learning theories to explain how children learn words, things, and ideas about them (Wolff, 1967). "The roots of logical and mathematical structures are to be found in the coordination of actions, even before the development of language" (Piaget, 1970, p. 21). It may be, moreover, that infants begin to be able to form hypotheses in a truly cognitive sense as early as nine months (Kagan, 1972). "Existing data from many sources and investigators suggest that a special cognitive competence emerges between 7 and 9 months among Western infants and that this competence permits the infant to compare, actively, external events with existing schemata" (Kagan, 1974, p. 247; Rosenblum and Alpert, 1974, p. 170; Fraiberg, 1969).

At whatever age it begins, "Human knowledge is essentially active. To know is to assimilate reality into systems of transformations" (Piaget, 1970, p. 15). For example, images held motionless on the retina, not subjected to the three scanning motions of the eye, break up and disappear (Pritchard, 1961). Speech disintegrates without the normal auditory input from one's own voice (Klein, 1970, p. 352). I do not feel my socks when I am sitting still. Evidently, to speak or see or touch at all, we have to be able to *do* something so as to create a sensory-motor feedback loop (Held, 1965).

The acts and memories that enter into perception will, of course, be quite individual, although they will play into innate, species-specific systems. Thus, the development of vision (in chimpanzees, for example) requires practice working with growth factors that are independent of practice—part of some epigenetic groundplan (Riesen, 1950; Fantz, 1961). Similarly, the stages of child development discovered in the classical phase of psychoanalysis—oral, anal, urethral, phallic, oedipal—must each lead to specially toned perceptions and realities. Sensing or knowing for any of us will combine inherited or developmental patterns common to all humans with personal acts. Evidently, art historian E. H. Gombrich's maxim for realism in the visual arts applies to our mini-perceptions

as well: "making before matching" (1960). What we will
accept as realistic depends on the techniques we have for
imitating reality. Then, in turn, the way we "make" realities is a function, not only of biological and cultural resources, but (I would add) of the identity of the maker,
including unconscious cognitive traits as well as the unconscious processes Freud discovered.

Almost thirty years ago, the late George S. Klein was
stressing the interaction of the formal properties of the
thing perceived and the personality of the perceiver
(Klein and Schlesinger, 1949). Later he would contrast
experiments on perception that involved reaction to a
"unit property" with situations more true to human experience—our being drawn through our own motives to a
"thing quality," its "meaningful aspect" (1970, p. 113).
Thus, the perception of verticality expresses the personality of the perceiver, so much so that one can even use it
to infer his clinical characteristics (Witkin, 1959). Similarly, the eye movements with which people scan objects
and pictures vary widely (Noton and Stark, 1971).

We have some evidence that such perceptions take
place in two modes: a quick, holistic grasp of the object as
a separate entity; a slower, sequential scan of the angles,
vertices, and other high-information parts of the object to
form a feature-ring—a memory of the perceptual acts
that are characteristic for that object, which then constitute a recognition of the object. One can see differences
in this scanning procedure, and they, too, seem to reflect
personality: "Every person has a characteristic way of
looking at an object that is familiar to him" (Noton and
Stark, 1971). Similarly, Klein was able to relate the eye
movements with which people scanned pictures to the
flexibility or constrictedness of control in their total personalities (1970, p. 185).

In general, to take a statement from 1951, we can understand both the optical illusions and the more detailed experiments on normal perceptions in the same way:

> Perception is a functional affair based on action, experience and probability. The thing perceived is an inseparable part of the function of perceiving, which in turn includes all aspects of the total process of living. This view differs from the old rival theories: the thing perceived is neither just a figment of the mind nor an innately determined absolute revelation of a reality postulated to exist apart from the perceiving organism. Object and percept are part and parcel of the same thing.

> All these experiments, and many more that have been made, suggest strongly that perception is never a sure thing, never an absolute revelation of "what is." Rather, what we see is . . . our own personal construction designed to give us the best possible bet for carrying out our purposes in action. [Ittelson and Kirkpatrick, 1951, p. 179]

Three I's Paralleled

We have considered three kinds of transaction. We have gone from one whole person perceiving another whole person or event or situation (on or off the printed page) to the interpretation of particular sentences, to the perception of single colors, details, clicks, letters, and so on. At that most particular level, there is a rich and convincing experimental literature. People have begun to investigate sentence interpretation much more recently, and their conclusions are that much more tentative. Work linking identity to perception has come into being only in the last five years. By contrast, it was in 1960 that Miller,

Galanter, and Pribram pointed out that Chomsky's relationships between deep and surface structure offered psychologists a model for the relation between plans and behavior, thus opening a via media between the extremes of behaviorism and introspection into intention.

Yet, for all the difference in the degree to which we know these three transactions, people who have investigated them, by such varying methods, find that they all have the same shape: analysis-by-synthesis. Be it sentiment, sentence, or sensory detail, we take in the external world as we generate within ourselves a match to it.

Further, it may be (although the evidence is less clear for this point) that each of these analyses-by-synthesis takes place in two modes. (They may be in series or parallel.) In the first, we establish a total, impressionistic relation which provides a base for closer attention. In the second, we generate inner matches to the neuronic data being taken in from without, analysis-by-synthesis proper.[8] We can guess at a table:

Type of Perception	First Mode	Second Mode
Large event	Matching expectation and defense	Projecting fantasy and transforming to significance
Sentence	Establishing meaningful units	Generating phrases or protosentences
Sensory detail	Preliminary identification	Generating a ring of perceptual acts

8. People trying to teach machines to recognize patterns (the numbers in a zip code, say) find that this kind of two-level process works best—indeed, it is precisely this success from the field of artificial intelligence that has made the two-stage, excitatory-inhibitory model so popular in studies of natural cognition and perception (Selfridge and Neisser, 1960).

In the last pages of his 1967 survey, Neisser suggests, citing Kris, that "the secondary process can serve to elaborate primary-process material," identifying the two stages in experimental studies of perceptions with the familiar psychoanalytic division of thought into the dreamlike and the problem-solving. From the larger point of view that joins the theory of personality to the theory of perception, *"All* directed thinking is an elaboration" of the same kind as the psychoanalytic explanation of creativity—the secondary elaboration of primary-process thought (p. 303).

It may be that such a dual process of perception is a part of our biological inheritance. Freud certainly thought so in his "Project" of 1895, for he identified primary-process thought with one system of neurones and secondary-process thought with the result of inhibiting the first process. Within that definition, *"the second system can only cathect an idea if it is in a position to inhibit any development of unpleasure that may proceed from it"* (Freud, 1900–01, p. 601; Freud's italics). "A beginning of [unpleasure] must be allowed, since that is what informs the second system of the nature of the memory concerned and of its possible unsuitability for the purpose which the thought-process has in view" (ibid.; see also Freud, 1950, pp. 382–87; Pribram, 1962). Thus, he anticipated his own discovery of "signal anxiety" twenty-five years later, and also the notion of "matching defenses," which recent identity theory finds essential to perception and to having an experience.

Modern experiments with perception find this pattern elsewhere. We apparently perceive colors through a combination of excited and inhibiting cells (Wallach, 1963). Memory, too, may take place through a holographic process of playing one frequency off against another (Pribram, 1969). Held and Richards suggest that, in general, sensory ganglions work by a combination of excitatory and inhibitory cells (1972, p. 115). Thus, there may be a primary and a secondary process at the cellular level, as in the larger units of perception.

The response of a sense organ would then be a function not only of the properties of the receptor cells themselves but of the ways in which that kind of cell influences its neighbor and then, at a still more general level of inhibition, of the control exerted by other organs. Only by some such larger or higher level of control could the messages from one small group of receptor cells, such as an ear, be made adaptive for the whole organism. Only by a central processing (the Renaissance's sixth or "common" sense, perhaps) could the organism get the inputs from eyes, nose, touch, and taste together so that we endure the ugliness of an oyster in order to savor its delicious nutrient (Miller, Ratliff, and Hartline, 1961).

This central control implies not only that different sense organs interact, but that different levels of perception do. My total needs affect my perception of particulars and, conversely, my perception of details affects the way I structure my needs. I must work "bottom up" from particular to general and "top down" from general to particular. To perceive a face, I bring my schema for "face" into play and check against it the properties of what I perceive through various subschemata for "eye," "nose," or "grin." I then check the results against a superordinate schema, "person," perhaps, or "friend." My "face" schema succeeds in terms of goodness-of-fit. The rate at which I achieve sufficient goodness-of-fit depends on the resources I allocate to this particular perception. What I consider important will in turn depend on my expectations, either from my various cognitive schemata or my hopes and fears in a more global sense. In one sense, the way I allocate my perceptual resources will seem "data driven." In another sense, however, I exhibit intelligence by concentrating on what is likely or relevant in the context. Such a theory leads naturally to a sense of hierarchy: "Those features actually present in the world guide the processing in a bottom-up fashion, whereas the planning process of the subject guides the top-down processing." Perception becomes a search for convergence between these two procedures (Norman et al., 1975, pp. 304–05, 346).

One might phrase it as a hierarchy between "stimulus-bound" or "outer-directed" processes and those more "inner-directed." For "outer-directed" processes of detailed perception and immediate memory, after selection among a few possibilities for synthesis, the constructive act responds closely to stimulus information. "However, the course of thinking or of 'inner-directed' activity is determined at every moment by what the subject is trying to do" (Neisser, 1967, p. 305).

Psychoanalysts talk of a hierarchy of ego functions (Rapaport, 1951, 1952), and brain physiologists speak of a hierarchy of "open systems" (von Bertalanffy, 1952). In a strictly cognitive sense, we have known since the nineteenth century that we are able to perceive or remember between five and seven things at a time. It is, however, only since information theory that we have realized that the amount we can perceive is not limited by the information involved but by the number of units into which we can group the information. We can about equally well remember five digits, five letters, five words, or five phrases, although they contain considerably different amounts of information. "We tend to organize our conscious perception of the world in terms of the highest level of organization" (Bever, 1973).

Something in us does, anyway. Twenty-five years ago, Gardner Murphy suggested this hierarchy: neurones and sensory receptors at the bottom; then the central nervous system and electrical currents in the brain; then perceptual responses dependent on the organism as a whole (involving, therefore, interactions between the central nervous system and its autonomous branches); finally the determination of perception through interactions between the organism and its environment, including social groups—talking things over (Klein and Schlesinger, 1949). Recently, a computer scientist, William T. Powers (1973), brilliantly formalized this hierarchical concept into a testable model of the mind: nine levels of feedback network, each responding to a reference signal from the level immediately above it. As I write, my colleague in linguistics, David Hays (in as yet unpublished work), is refining Powers's model to include a parallel hierarchy of linguistic capabilities.

Even without a final model, however, there is wide agreement from a variety of disciplines and methods that human thought and perception involves a hierarchy of comparisons (analyses through synthesis) ranging from individual cells to whole nations. But there is still something missing in this great chain of being.

The Missing Link

"It has long been known that a person's expectancies play a major role in his perceptual processes" (Norman et al., 1975, p. 155), yet there has been no real way of taking them into account. "Where Is the Perceiver in Perceptual Theory?" was a famous question as far back as 1949, asked by Klein and various coauthors. "A behavior theory should view all behavior within the context of the total organism, and . . . its laws should be organismic principles of control" (Klein and Krech, 1952, p. 13). Often, writes a recent team of cognitive researchers, to interpret the way an organism responds to a stimulus one must know the relation the organism itself senses between that stimulus and its own personal history, knowledge, values, motives, and so on (its "identity," I would say, whether known to the organism or not).

> When this is true, the psychologist who is interested in understanding the mental processes which mediate the relation between stimulus and response has no alternative but to try to learn enough about what the organism knows and values to determine what perceptual analyses it will impose. This is a hard doctrine, for it says that the attempt to short-circuit the organism in specifications of stimulus-response relations will not work. One cannot, in the long run, dispense with the organism's contribution to his own behavior. [Norman et al., 1975, p. 507]

"A stimulus," writes Jerome Kagan, "does not exist independent of a particular context and the individual's expectations. This principle is as valid for baboons as it is for man" (1974, p. 230). Yet, few indeed are the experimenters—on either man or baboons—who have in fact tried to take their contribution into account. As Neisser (1967) sums up the situation:

> The classical procedures of experimental psychology attempt to avoid this problem by brute force. In an ordinary learning experiment, the subject is supposed to have only a single motive: he must get on with the experimental task, learn what he is told to learn, and solve what he is told to solve. If he has any other desires—to outwit the experimenter, to walk out, to ask what the answer is—he must do his best to act as if they did not exist. [p. 305]

Yes, surely there must sometimes be what Masling (1966) has called "The Screw You Effect," the impulse to pay the experimenter back for all the asinine tasks he is imposing. An experimenter working with people is in a social situation. She may take a social role: the all-knowing, impassive scientist, the friendly counselor, the "pal," the tyrant, and so on. The subjects may feel like guinea pigs, like students working for approval and a grade, or like workers confronting a boss. Sex differences between subject and experimenter must enter into their fantasies and expectations. The possibilities are infinite, and have even been experimented on (Masling, 1966; Rosenthal, 1966; Friedman, 1967).

But mostly not, as Neisser (1967) points out:

> Multiplicity of motivation and flexibility of response are characteristic of ordinary life, but they are absent—or are assumed to be absent—from most experiments on the higher mental processes. . . . The simplifications introduced by confining the subject to a single motive and a fixed set of alternative responses can be justified only if motivation and cognition are genuinely distinct. If—as I suppose—they are inseparable where remembering and thinking are concerned the common experimental paradigms may pay too high a price for simplicity.

And Neisser concludes: "A really satisfactory theory of the higher mental processes can only come into being when we also have theories of motivation, personality, and social interaction" (p. 305).

We now have such a theory—at least, the point of this essay is to say we do. *Identity, understanding someone as sameness and difference, as variations on a theme, provides a concept of the whole person that will complete a theory of cognition from its largest to its most detailed forms.* Specifically, we can use DEFT, the derivative of identity, to relate personality to particular perceptions. I can ask how the individual matches expectations and defenses to external reality; then how she projects fantasies into what she has taken in and transforms them into significance for her. Psychological categories cease to be fixed entities in the minds of individuals and become terms by which to articulate relations: both her perception of an event *and* my perception of her perception. I can ask how *each of us* gave our perception meaning within and without the time sequence of our expectations. What does each of us take in and what does each of us project out?

Such inquiries will lead to flat, categorical results only if I choose to limit my inquiry that way. In the nature of the situation, however, my questions should link perception to open systems of identities (of both the person I am studying and myself). Answers to DEFT questions should allow for continuing dialogue and associations in the psychoanalytic manner. In an experimental setting, they should lead to some integration of psychological "laws" with the acknowledged relationship of the investigator and the "subject" to their investigation. "The scientist makes sense of himself in and through making sense of the system, and makes sense of the system in and through making sense of himself" (Esterson, 1970, p. 224). A respect for the necessarily personal quality of our knowledge will be truer to our late twentieth-century ideas of the human sciences and the dynamics of language, cognition, and perception than the ideal of earlier decades, mechanistic or probabilistic "laws" alone. Such an acknowledgment of ourselves in our inquiries is implicit in the very asking posited by the concept of identity. If you can find a sameness and difference in *all* my actions, you must include my experiments as well.

"Everything a person does," wrote Klein, "and the means by which he does it express his individuality," and he went on to speak of "unifying principles" in the individual's modes of delay and control. Yet he never had this holistic concept of identity that would have completed his brilliant syntheses of psychoanalytic and cognitive theory. True, he developed the idea of "cognitive attitudes" to take into account the individually varying standards for a "workable fit" in the feedbacks that guide perceptual, cognitive, and motor actions. The concept "provides for the fact that persons differ in how 'accurate' perception must be in order to be *effective* for the purpose at hand" (Klein, 1970, pp. 119, 220). Such an approach led him to the study of such "variables" as tolerance or intolerance of ambiguity, which would control perception by defining what is adaptive for this particular individual (Frenkel-Brunswik, 1949). But alas, the minute we isolate a "variable" this way, we have lost sight again of the "multiplicity of motivation and flexibility of response" to which Neisser (1967) calls attention. Rather, tolerance of ambiguity should make up one element in a holistic inquiry into an individual's total style of sameness and difference.

That style pervades "everything a person does and the means by which he does it," in Klein's phrase (which might have been Yeats's). As Neisser observes, in his more recent study of cognition (1976), "Every person's possibilities for perceiving and acting are entirely unique, because no one else occupies exactly his position in the world or has had exactly his history." We constantly re-create our sensory and motor resources through sensory-motor feedbacks (Held, 1965); we infer identity as we observe those feedbacks. The original motor actions that go into them, then, and our unique perception of those motor acts, equally admit description by identity, DEFT, and analysis-through-synthesis.

Jerome Kagan suggests that the very creation of perceptual and cognitive schemata is a source of pleasure, and also the matching of schemata to externals (1967, p. 136). If so, then identity controls are at the base of motivation: we are seeing in another way Lichtenstein's "identity principle," his more explanatory alternative to Freud's death instinct. The first, the ultimate motivation, beyond the pleasure principle, is to preserve the essential continuity and sameness of the self. This is deeper, even, than pleasure, or, if we take Kagan's hint, it defines pleasure. The pleasure and reality principles of classical psychoanalysis become corollary not to a death instinct, but to a drive to maintain primary identity.

Our perception of someone's identity is one part of an explanation of her perceptions. Biological inheritance is another. Evidence from paleoneurology suggests that since the "real" world we intuit is a creation of the nervous system, "the 'true' or 'real' world is specific to a species and is dependent on how the brain of the species works." "The work of the brain is to create a model of a possible world rather than to record and transmit to the mind a world that is metaphysically true" (Jerison, 1976, p. 99). Lower vertebrates may be tightly bound to fixed actions in response to particular stimuli, just as, at a higher level, birds go into complex mating dances and nest-building routines in response to particular triggers. That is one kind of world, hard for us to imagine. Mammalian vision, however, involves a considerable processing of visual information. There is much more room for cortical invention.

Compared to other mammals, our human senses are somewhat impoverished, and it may be that language itself evolved to supplement them: a way of building imagery-worlds to enrich the data from eye, ear, nose, and skin (Jerison, 1976). As with bipedal gait, our bodies seem to have physiologically adapted to speech, and we may well have evolved, as Chomsky suggests, innate cognitive matrices for language as well. If so, then we are born adapted to a speech community, and this, too, is important to our sense of reality. Because we can know meaning, we can use projection to create purpose, security, and companionship for ourselves—in short, culture (Novey, 1955).

These evolutionary speculations match recent psychoanalytic efforts to update Freud's "immaculate perception" theory and the reality principle based upon it (Schimek, 1975). If personality, including unconscious defenses and fantasies, determines our ostensibly "objective" sense of reality, that in turn implies that psychic structures like ego and id, heretofore thought of as relatively fixed, must also adapt (Lichtenstein, 1973, 1977, pp. 345–68). Biological inheritance gives rise *both* to human existence within a culture *and* to the acquistition of an individual, noncultural primary identity and psychic structure. Paradoxically, because we are *not* bound to some "objective" reality, either biological or cultural, we are free to create a reality closer to our heart's (or our id's) desire, which will, of course, express both our biology and our culture.

Reality, then, is never simply some fixed something "out there." It may be species-specific for all animals, but for humans reality must include three things: the partnership of our particular bodies with the world, the individual identities we infer, and the community we share through language. Identity (either primary or as we infer it) grows from, is sustained by, and changes culture, while culture in turn is required by human physiology, which is itself the first sameness and variation of self—that is, identity. All our lives we triangulate whatever we know and whoever we are out of biology, culture, and identity.

The Continuum

When I add identity theory to what is known of the way we understand sentences and perceive with our senses, I can see how our relationships to reality link self, species, and society. They also fall into another kind of continuum. That is, at all levels, I relate to reality by comparing something that comes in from outside (a series of electric pulsations, finally) and something that I generate from within (another series of pulses). These comparisons take place at levels ranging from tiny sensory details to whole cultural styles, yet the basic shape of what I do remains the same. I respond to the difference between outer stimulus (from "reality") and inner match (from "self").

At the level of large perceptions—other people, ideas, scenes, whole objects, the things people read—I can understand how we arrive DEFTly at a "reality." I look for the way. in which we both place an event in a time sequence of expectation, wishes, and fears, and transform it into a meaning independent of time and our immediacies. I see us defending: shaping the event as much as we can tolerate to gratify our wishes and defeat our fears. I see us fantasying: projecting still other wishes into the event as we have made it gratifying. And the way I can understand someone's doing all these things is by looking for a characteristic personal style, identity, manifested in individual internalizations.

DEFT describes internalization at a level where the whole human being takes in other people, happenings, or beliefs, in situations involving all of a self. Superordinate to these takings-in are actions outward into the larger physical and cultural surround. Physically, the individual acts out sensorimotor feedbacks that set, hold, and keep his senses accurately adaptive. At a still larger level, she acts into her community so as to receive a confirmation of herself (as in Erikson's sense of "identity") through long cycles of interpersonal, social, or political feedback. She chooses a mate, reproduces, and so embodies that choice in the genetic characteristics of their offspring. In these and myriads of other ways, an individual brings his or her identity to the world and the world confirms it in some ways and denies it in others.

Subordinate to DEFT internalizations, we take in smaller units of language, ranging from individual words, morphemes, and phonemes up to the sentences and paragraphs which shade into the large DEFT transactions. Still more particular are our perceptions of sensory details: color, shape, motion, outline, and the like. Here, too, we analyze by synthesis, but it all takes place in a much more physiological way. Individual identity seems relatively less important. Thus, as we arrange these different internalizings and externalizings of reality into a continuum, they form a hierarchy through which I can trace a number of patterns.

First, these relationships with reality range from the most general to the most particular. To put the matter biologically, they involve different numbers of cells: from a single organ or one area of the brain to the cells of a whole individual to the cells of a whole society.

Second, at every level of our cognitive hierarchy, these relationships involve a four-way interaction: between external and internal; between "top-down, hypothesis-driven searches" and "bottom-up, stimulus-driven searches." Thus, far from a simple stimulus-response pattern, our relationships with reality are activated from within or without, by the general or the particular.

At all levels, however, the more general (i.e., primary identity) controls the more particular. We can turn off even the most insistent of stimuli by some form of avoidance. We can physically get rid of it, or we can psychologically deny it, even if we have to resort to such extreme "adaptations" as psychosis, autism, suicide, or death. It is precisely the power of the mind to resort to such extremes that guarantees an interaction of "top-down" and "bottom-up" matchings at every level and also our ultimate veto from the top down. Paradoxically, it must be our ability to break down primary identity, to destroy our minds or die, that is a precondition for our having a primary identity that permeates and controls our every action—if we have one.

Third, at all levels of our continuum, the processing of information seems to take place in two modes—perhaps in series, perhaps in parallel. One is holistic, immediate, and impressionistic, and provides information for starting the second. The other is sequential, slower, and adjustable for fine or coarse readings. The first seems to be a kind of processing we share with all mammals. The second seems more associated with human abilities for syntax and symbolism. The second may be or presuppose something like the psychoanalyst's ego or the computer scientist's "executive routine." Maybe. The evidence is still scanty.

Fourth, we can find more of identity in our complex relations with reality than in the simpler ones, which are more biological or mechanical, resting finally on the impersonal fire or no-fire of a small number of cells. As the number of cells involved increases, the interactions also increase, and there are more and more places where the play of excitation and inhibition permits the observation of a personal style.

Fifth, at all levels of our continuum of knowing, we apparently combine innate predispositions and a personal style with environmental, community, or cultural feedback. The innate, biological forces outweigh the others at the more particular levels of cognition, where a small number of cells is involved. The environment has more points at which it can influence outcomes where there is more interplay among different cellular groups. Thus, in the triangulation of identity, biology, and culture, biology is stronger the more particular the cognition; identity and culture are stronger the more general it is. Nevertheless, we can assume that all three are involved, in varying degrees, of course, anytime we experience anything. Now, with a way of conceptualizing particular people's identities, we have a theoretical basis for exploring the relationships among the individual, his culture, and his genetic inheritance.

Sixth, at no level in our continuum of cognition is there any way to separate a "subjective" from an "objective." To be sure, we can contrast what is internal with what is external, what is self with what is other, but we are always dealing with some comparison of or differencing between the two. From the point of view of the stimulus, its "effect" comes from the difference between what is put in and what is generated inside. Conversely, what we experience is not just generated within us; it is the difference between what is generated inside and what comes from outside.[9]

If this differencing holds true at the level of simple, immediate perception, then it must also hold true as we add up many different perceptions, as in an experiment—for example, the very experiments that demonstrate the differencing. If we analyze experience by synthesizing it, if

9. Is this the reason for the otherness of the other? Finally, our experience of the world will be the difference between two trains of electrical impulses, one stimulated from without and one generated from within. Suppose that the one from without took the form of 100 pulses and the one from within 91 pulses. Experience, in this crude example, would be 9 impulses, all feeling different from what I had generated in myself, all feeling, in other words, "othered." Conversely, suppose that to those 100 pulses from without, I compared 153 generated from within (being perhaps in a particularly dreamy mood). Then my experience would consist of 53 pulses, all "selved." Most experiences, of course, would combine both feelings. The outer world might stimulate a, b, c, d, and e; and I might generate in response, b, c, d, e, and f. Perhaps. Again, this must remain speculation in 1978.

we perceive by constructing, if we experience by comparing something of self with something from outside, then both the subject's and the experimenter's hypotheses, expectations, defenses, projections, theories, wishes, and fears must permeate experimental perception, just as they do other kinds of perception.

Now, however, with identity theory, we have a way of dealing with the pronoun in sentences like: I tested; I constructed; I sorted; I decided to use a Friedman two-way analysis of variance; in short, I experimented. Identity theory, because it assumes that everything we do replicates our individuality, lets us conceptualize what Rosenthal, Friedman, and other psychological experimenters have demonstrated about psychological experiments. To leave the "I" of the experimenter out would claim for her an exemption from the very psychological principles she is demonstrating. Identity theory suggests that one can *never* subtract out experimenter "bias," for that is, precisely, identity. Trying to get rid of it only shifts it to a different place in the procedure. Rather, identity theory suggests that experiments should acknowledge and respect the personal involvement of the experimenter and his subjects. That is, I realize, a treacherous complexity to find as we near our port of destination. Perhaps I should provide a

Summary

before proceeding further.

However we take them, at the level of sensory detail or as large units of thought and experience or as specifics of language—we can understand consciousness, perception, experience, and even "mind" as a single basic strategy. We analyze by synthesis. In response to a stimulus from outside ourselves, we create an internal schema of that external reality and compare the two. Both what we create and the way we compare it to net an experience of the event are functions of the individual, his species, and his environment. We can think of different "levels" of experience at which these three weigh differently relative to one another, but all three are implicated in all experience. Of the three, however, it is the individual identity that will dominate the other two, in our analyses of perception, cognition, language, and experiencing, although the price of that control may sometimes seem high or its precision low.

Nevertheless—and this is my fundamental point—the concept of identity, understanding a person as a theme and variations, provides a missing link among existing theories of cognition, experience, and the interpretation of experience (including language). Identity connects to a superordinate theory of motivation that recent studies in perception, cognition, and psycholinguistics have shown is needed. It is, to be sure, a troubling concept because it is holistic. It does not offer the logical and causal (and hence predictable) connections for the usual psychological experiment. It offers instead a pattern explanation, one based in meaning, answering to interpretation rather than experimentation, like those used by clinical psychologists, cultural anthropologists, continental geologists, particle physicists, galactic astronomers, molecular biologists, psychoanalysts, and even literary critics.

Identity, however, even as it supplies the missing link, poses the next questions for psychologists of all persuasions (and even literary critics): How can we relate the regularities among groups of people to the individualities that underlie them? How do individual motivations, all different, combine to form categories or lawfulnesses? For example, as a literary theorist, I can explain why this or that reader reacts the way he does to *Hamlet.* I cannot, however, say why a great many readers of different backgrounds, eras, and cultures prefer *Hamlet* to *Timon of Athens*. That, translated into similar questions for the psychoanalyst, the psycholinguist, and the cognitive psychologist, is the methodological issue which the concept of identity opens up. That is the

Heuristic

part of this paper.

If this understanding of the interaction of the personal and the impersonal is correct, experimental strategies follow from it. Psychoanalysis, particularly the theory of identity, can turn the psychological study of language toward a richer methodology. At present, we have two methods, and most people think of them as opposed: the classical experimental procedures in contrast to the search for pattern explanations, variously called case-study, participant-observer, or holistic method.[10]

The experimenter looks for easily comparable or summable results: checking off this or that box in a questionnaire, doing something within a certain time, turning a knob so far, falling into one or another category, and the like. The holistic worker tries for the unique response, often a verbal one. Indeed, if a response is not unique— if, for example, the person interviewed just says, "I dunno"—a holistic worker will try to elicit more and more material; and, of course, these materials are not easily comparable or summable. The holistic researcher deals with the unique information of his single case by tracing variations and converging them to a unifying, thematic center, through verbal meaning. By contrast, the experimenter who has divided her data into categories is in a position to compare them by counting, and she has at her disposal a variety of statistical techniques for assuring

10. I am taking this dichotomy and many of the definitions and assumptions that follow from Diesing (1971).

other workers in the field that her correlations are not happening simply by chance. By and large, the experimenter is *only* interested in correlations, regularities, and repetitions, and she tends to neglect the deviants as unimportant, provided they are few. The holistic researcher, however, insists on looking at all events equally; the deviant interest him as much as the conforming, perhaps even more.

The experimenter assumes she is dealing with processes "out there" to which she is no more than loosely coupled, while the holist (participant-observer) deliberately establishes and acknowledges his relation to the material he is studying. The two methods involve different gains and losses. The holist's work, by and large, cannot be duplicated because of the personal element. The experimenter's work can be duplicated, but it therefore remains locked into particular techniques. Variables involve operational definition so that refinement of the experimenter's knowledge usually means narrowing of technique. "Consequently, widespread use of the experimental method tends to produce a proliferation of variables and laws, many vaguely overlapping, rather than the single clear network of laws originally anticipated" (Diesing, 1971, p. 4). Holistic method, however, leads to the opposite extremes: detailed description in lieu of categories and very high-level generalizations with seductively easy connections between them.

Instead of setting up an opposition between these two methods, it would seem more fruitful to recognize and use their overlap. We can add them. Currently, however, psychologists who investigate language or perception have no way to conceptualize the effects of identity. Indeed, they may be small—but they may not. I have mentioned experiments in which differences in the eye scans of pictures seemed to relate to the personalities of the

perceivers, and the instant we go to something more complicated, such as the perception of scenes, "Large differences in performance on these tasks do occur" (Biederman, 1975, p. 74). Then there is the effect of the
experimenter himself. The investigator who limits himself or his subjects to fixed replies has not controlled for
personality—he has only eliminated the possibility that he
will be able to take it into account at all. "The study of
cognition is only one fraction of psychology, and it cannot
stand alone" (Neisser, 1967, p. 305).

What is needed is a way to let the experimentalist's and
the holist's approaches enrich each other. They can do so
if we understand them as two complementary relations to
the experiment. The problem is *both* to establish the statistical correlation *and* to gather data about deviations
from the statistical norm and relate them to identity—
explicitly.

Consider an actual psycholinguistic experiment, typical
in its assumptions, exemplary in the care with which results were assessed and described. "Forty-five paid Ss
were tested in four groups about equal in size and half
female." The four groups of "Ss" listened to four different sets of prose passages, in which the last and next-
to-last sentences of each passage contained similar content in different grammatical structures, these very carefully constructed and parceled out among the passages.
Then the "E" asked the "Ss" to write down as much of the
end of each passage as they could remember.

Notice that since different listeners were listening to
different passages, the method ruled out any inquiry into
personal similarities or differences in response. Yet it
seems reasonable to suppose that different people might
respond differently to sentences like: "Another bomb
which exploded across the harbor knocked down a radio
tower." "That Castro was threatening his leadership was

understood by the former president." It seems likely that
a listener's personality might well affect his recall of a
sentence involving bombs or presidents. It also seems
possible that different listeners might have different
styles of hearing, storing, and interpreting nominaliza-
tions, embedded relative clauses, and so on. For example,
I myself tend to use a great many sentence modifiers
(such as "for example"); it seems likely that I would be
unusually sensitive to them or their absence in what I
hear or read.

Yet Jarvella and Herman (1972) lavished their care and
counting on grammatical structures alone in an experimental format that made it quite impossible to take the
identity of the listener (or the experimenter) into account. By doing so, they are tacitly assuming that listeners
and experimenters are interchangeable but grammatical
structures are not. In the dynamic relationship of re-creation between listener and sentence, they are looking only
at the sentence and have eliminated the possibility of
looking at the "S." Similarly, by leaving themselves out,
they have no way of assessing their own selectivity in
looking at the results. Within a purely grammatical
frame, they concluded: "Analysis of the recall data indicated that the only variables which had affected performance significantly were the previous [i.e., next-to-last]
sentence vs. the immediate [i.e., last] one and, within the
immediate sentence, clause position (only, initial, final)
and clause function (main, subordinate)." "Variables not
affecting recall of immediate sentences or the member
clauses included: sentence construction type, length of
single-clause sentences, length of two-clause sentences,
order of test items, and quantity of interest material."
And the identities of the listeners? Or the identities of the
investigators who chose and constructed these sentences?

How might Jarvella and Herman have admitted iden-

tity into the experiment? Not by simply handling the recalls statistically. Only if there were a 100 percent pattern
in the recalls could we say (tentatively) that they were independent of listeners' individual DEFTings. Rather, after
an elaborate statistical analysis, Jarvella and Herman concluded, "Sentences with main-subordinate clause order
were actually remembered significantly more poorly than
those with subordinate-main order"—that is, they were
remembered more poorly and there was less than one
chance in twenty that this difference was due to chance or
some other variable *among those they considered.*

Jarvella and Herman could have extended this conclusion (despite its impersonal frame) by taking the identities
of the forty-five listeners into account. To do this, they
would have had to conceptualize those identities (after in-
terviews, presumably) and try to interpret the ways they
related to the various prose passages and sentence structures. Then one could understand the remembering of
main-subordinate vs. subordinate-main clause sentences
as resources by which various listeners established their
individual relations to the content in accordance with
their several identities. Within those relations, the hypothesis of the experiment—that people remember sentences with subordinate-main clause order better than
sentences with main-subordinate order—becomes a possible theme in the total pattern of any one individual's
remembering. In effect, the conclusion describes a rule of
thumb or bias in recall that some listeners will overcome
and some will follow. By looking closely at who does
which in terms of the who as well as the which, one could
find the strength and applicability of that bias. Knowing it
both personally and impersonally, one might be able to
relate different identity-types to different types of clause
recall and so form a typology of recallers involving both
personality and linguistics, hence reflecting more closely

what we suppose to be the inner dynamics of listening to sentences.

Perhaps. Arriving at forty-five identity themes is a prodigious task. One might have to settle for case studies of only a few listeners. Nevertheless, the better understood the case study, the more hypotheses it will yield. The more hypotheses brought to bear on the next case, the better it will be understood. This feedback of methods, each to the other, goes beyond the counting of verbal recalls to the individual processes of recalling. It should give us a fuller, richer picture of the interaction of person and language, which is, I hope, the true aim of psycholinguistics.

And what about the experimenters themselves? The idea of taking one's own identity into account raises many touchy and intriguing questions, yet the advice Know Thyself is as ancient as the oracle at Delphi. Would the psychological experimenter be a better experimenter for knowing why he is curious about the way people work, why he is interested in being "out of" the experiment, why statistical techniques are satisfying, why language or perception interest him? I think so. It encourages me to try new possibilities, when I am applying identity theory to a Sam or a Sandra, to know that I need intensely to feel that people are unified yet tend to perceive the world in dualities, or that I want to master human relationships by understanding them—from the outside. I know enough to try to be more empathic or to read for threes, fours, or no numbers at all. It seems to me that an experimental psychologist could profit from that kind of knowledge at least as much as I do. It can be learned (not taught) in what my colleague Murray Schwartz and I have called a "Delphi" seminar (Holland and Schwartz, 1975).

Finally, then, if we accept the idea that a theory of motivation has a place in cognitive and psycholinguistic research, the idea of identity as a theme and variations and the principle of identity maintenance offer the strongest and most comprehensive theory so far. We can combine a holistic method based on identity with familiar experimental methods by examining both the easy-to-compare and the hard-to-compare, both the summable and the individual, both the correlation and the deviants. We can face the unpredictable human being in ourselves and the people we study; and, as in modern physics and biology, we can frame laws that accommodate that very unpredictability. When we do—if we do—we shall find identity at the core of those laws: the missing link for psychology, psychoanalysis, and psycholinguistics as we know them in 1978.

REFERENCES

Bergson, H. *Matière et mémoire; Matter and Memory* (1896). Translated by N. M. Paul and W. Scott Palmer. New York: Macmillan, 1911.

Bever, T. G. "Language and Perception." In G. A. Miller (1973).

Biederman, I. Research Proposal, National Science Foundation, 1975.

Biederman, I.; Rabinowitz, J. C.; Glass, A. L.; and Stacey, E. W. "On the Information Extracted From a Glance at a Scene." *Journal of Experimental Psychology* 103 (1974) : 597–600.

Bower, T. G. R. "The Visual World of Infants." *Scientific American,* December 1966. Reprinted in Held and Richards (1972).

———. *Development in Infancy.* San Francisco: W. H. Freeman, 1974.

Brown, R. *A First Language: The Early Stages.* Cambridge, Mass.: Harvard University Press, 1973a.

———. "The Development of Language in Children" (1973b). In G. A. Miller (1973).

Bruner, J. S., and Krech, D., eds. *Perception and Personality: A Symposium.* Durham, N.C.: Duke University Press, 1950.

Coopersmith, S., ed. *Frontiers of Psychological Research: Readings from Scientific American.* San Francisco: W. H. Freeman, 1966.

Diesing, P. R. *Patterns of Discovery in the Social Sciences.* Chicago: Aldine-Atherton, 1971.

Esterson, A. *The Leaves of Spring: Schizophrenia, Family, and Sacrifice.* Middlesex, England: Penguin Books, in association with Tavistock Publications, 1970.

Fantz, R. L. "The Origin of Form Perception." *Scientific American,* May 1961. Reprinted in Coopersmith (1966).

Fillmore, C. "The Future of Semantics." In Fillmore, Lakoff, and Lakoff (1974).

Fillmore, C.; Lakoff, G.; and Lakoff, R., eds. *Berkeley Studies in Syntax and Semantics.* Vol. 1. Berkeley: University of California, Department of Linguistics, 1974.

Fodor, J. A.; Bever, T. C.; and Garrett, M. F. *The Psychology of Language: An Introduction to Psycholinguistics and Generative Grammar.* New York: McGraw-Hill, 1974.

Fodor, J. A., and Garrett, M. F. "Some Syntactic Determinants of Sentential Complexity." *Perception and Psychophysics* 2 (1967) : 289–96.

Fodor, J. A.; Garrett, M. F.; and Bever, T. G. "Some Syntactic Determinants of Sentential Complexity, II: Verb-Structure." *Perception and Psychophysics* 3 (1968) : 453–61.

Fodor, J. A., and Katz, J., eds. *The Structure of Language.* Englewood Cliffs, N.J.: Prentice-Hall, 1964.

Fraiberg, S. "Libidinal Object Constancy and Mental Representation." *Psychoanalytic Study of the Child* 24 (1969) : 9–47.

Frenkel-Brunswik, E. "Intolerance of Ambiguity as an Emotional and Perceptual Personality Variable" (1949). In Bruner and Krech (1950).

Freud, S. *Standard Edition of the Complete Psychological Works.* London: Hogarth, 1953–74.
   Project for a Scientific Psychology (1950 [1895]), vol. 1.
   The Interpretation of Dreams (1900–01), vols. 4, 5.
   "Analysis Terminable and Interminable" (1937), vol. 23.

Friedman, N. *The Social Nature of Psychological Research: The Psychological Experiment as a Social Inter-action.* New York: Basic Books, 1967.

Gombrich, E. H. *Art and Illusion.* New York: Pantheon Books, 1960.

Greene, J. *Psycholinguistics: Chomsky and Psychology.* Baltimore: Penguin, 1972.

Gregory, R. L. "Visual Illusions" (1968). In Held and Richards (1972).

Halle, M., and Stevens, K. N. "Speech Recognition: A Model and a Program for Research." In Fodor and Katz (1964).

Hartmann, H. *Ego Psychology and the Problem of Adaptation* (1939). Translated by D. Rapaport. *Journal of the American Psychoanalytic Association,* Monograph Series No. 1. New York: International Universities Press, 1958.

Held, R. "Plasticity in Sensory-Motor Systems" (1965). In Held and Richards (1972).

Held, R., and Richards, W., eds. *Perception: Mechanisms and Models: Readings from* Scientific American. San Francisco: W. H. Freeman, 1972.

Holland, N. N. "Prose and Minds: A Psychoanalytic Approach to Non-Fiction." In G. Levine and W. Madden, eds., *The Art of Victorian Prose.* New York: Oxford University Press, 1968.

―――. *Poems in Persons: An Introduction to the Psychoanalysis of Literature.* New York: Norton, 1973a.

―――. "A Touching of Literary and Psychiatric Education." *Seminars in Psychiatry* 5 (1973b) : 287–99.

―――. *5 Readers Reading.* New Haven: Yale University Press, 1975a.

―――. "An Identity for the Rat Man." *International Review of Psycho-Analysis* 2 (1975b) : 157–69.

―――. "Unity Identity Text Self." *PMLA (Publications of the Modern Language Association)* 90 (1975c) : 813–22.

―――. "Transactive Criticism: Re-Creation Through Identity." *Criticism* 18 (1976) : 334–52.

Holland, N. N., and Schwartz, M. M. "The Delphi Seminar." *College English* 36 (1975) : 789–800.

Ittelson, W. H., and Kilpatrick, F. P. "Experiments in Perception." *Scientific American,* August 1951. Reprinted in Cooper-smith (1966).

Jackendoff, R. S. *Semantic Interpretation in Generative Grammar.* Cambridge, Mass.: MIT Press, 1972.

Jacobs, R. A., and Rosenbaum, P. S. *English Transformational Grammar.* Waltham, Mass.: Blaisdell, 1968.

Jarvella, R. J., and Herman, S. J. "Clause Structure of Sentences and Speech Processing." *Perception and Psychophysics* 11 (1972) : 381–84.

Jerison, H. J. "Paleoneurology and the Evolution of Mind." *Scientific American,* January 1976, pp. 90–101.

Kagan, J. "On the Need for Relativism." *American Psychologist* 22 (1967) : 131–42.

———. "Do Infants Think?" *Scientific American.* March 1972, pp. 74–82.

———. "Discrepancy, Temperament, and Infant Distress." In Lewis and Rosenblum (1974b).

Katz, J. J., and Fodor, J. "The Structure of a Semantic Theory." *Language* 39 (1963) : 170–210. Reprinted in Fodor and Katz (1964).

Katz, J. J., and Postal, P. M. *An Integrated Theory of Linguistic Descriptions.* Cambridge, Mass.: MIT Press, 1964.

Klein, G. S. *Perception, Motives, and Personality.* New York: Knopf, 1970.

Klein, G. S., and Krech, D. "The Problem of Personality and Its Theory." In Krech and Klein (1952).

Klein, G. S., and Schlesinger, H. "Where Is the Perceiver in Perceptual Theory?" (1949). In Bruner and Krech (1950).

Kolers, P. A. "The Illusion of Movement" (1964). In Held and Richards (1972).

———. "Experiments in Reading." *Scientific American,* July 1972, pp. 84–91.

Krech, D., and Klein, G. S., eds. *Theoretical Models and Personality Theory.* Durham, N.C.: Duke University Press, 1952. Reprinted, New York: Greenwood Press, 1968.

Lakoff, G. Interview with Herman Parret. In Fillmore, Lakoff, and Lakoff (1974).

Lakoff, G., and Thompson, H. "Introducing Cognitive Grammar." *Proceedings of the First Annual Meeting of the Berkeley Linguistics Society,* 1975.

Lakoff, R. "Language and Woman's Place. *Language in Society* 2 (1973) : 45–80.

Land, E. H. "Experiments in Color Vision." *Scientific American,* May 1959. Reprinted in Held and Richards (1972).

————. "Our 'Polar Partnership' with the World Around Us." *Harvard Magazine* 80, no. 1 (1978) : 23–26.

Lewis, M., and Rosenblum, L. A., eds. *The Effect of the Infant on Its Caregiver,* vol. 1 of *The Origins of Behavior.* New York: Wiley, 1974a.

————. *The Origins of Fear,* vol. 2 of *The Origins of Behavior.* New York: Wiley, 1974b.

Lichtenstein, H. "Identity and Sexuality: A Study of Their Interrelationship in Man." *Journal of the American Psychoanalytic Association* 9 (1961) : 179–260.

————. Presentation to the Department of Psychiatry, Georgetown University, Washington, D.C., February 26, 1965.

————. "The Challenge to Psychoanalytic Psychotherapy in a World in Crisis." *International Journal of Psychoanalytic Psychotherapy* 2 (1973) : 149–74.

————. *The Dilemma of Human Identity.* New York: Jason Aronson, 1977.

Lifton, R. J. *Thought Reform and the Psychology of Totalism: A Study of 'Brainwashing' in China* (1961). London: Pelican Books, 1967.

McNeill, D. *The Acquisition of Language: The Study of Developmental Psycholinguistics.* New York: Harper & Row, 1970a.

————. "The Development of Language." In P. H. Mussen, ed., *Carmichael's Manual of Child Psychology,* vol. 1. New York: Wiley, 1970b.

Mahler, M.; Pine, F.; and Bergman, A. *The Psychological Birth of the Human Infant: Symbiosis and Individuation.* New York: Basic Books, 1975.

Masling, J. "Role-Related Behavior of the Subject and Psychologist and Its Effects upon Psychological Data." *Nebraska Symposium on Motivation* 4 (1966) : 67–103.

Miller, G. A., ed. *Communication, Language, and Meaning: Psychological Perspectives.* New York: Basic Books, 1973.

Miller, G. A.; Galanter, E.; and Pribram, K. H. *Plans and the Structure of Behavior.* New York: Holt, 1960.

Miller, W. H.; Ratliff, F.; and Hartline, H. K. "How Cells Receive Stimuli." *Scientific American,* September 1961. In Held and Richards (1972).

Murray, H. A. "Toward a Classification of Interactions." In T. Parsons and E. A. Shils, eds., *Toward a General Theory of Action.* Cambridge, Mass.: Harvard University Press, 1951.

Neisser, U. *Cognitive Psychology.* New York: Appleton-Century-Crofts, 1967.

———. "The Processes of Vision" (1968). In Held and Richards (1972).

———. *Cognition and Reality.* San Francisco: Freeman, 1976.

Norman, D. A.; Rummelhart, D. E.; and the LNR Research Group. *Explorations in Cognition.* San Francisco: W. H. Freeman, 1975.

Noton, D., and Stark, L. "Eye Movements and Visual Perception." *Scientific American,* June 1971, pp. 35–43.

Novey, S. "Some Philosophical Speculations About the Concept of the Genital Character." *International Journal of Psycho-Analysis* 36 (1955) : 88–94.

Piaget, J. *Genetic Epistemology.* Translated by E. Duckworth. New York: Norton, 1970.

Powers, W. T. *Behavior: The Control of Perception.* Chicago: Aldine, 1973.

Pribram, K. H. "The Neuropsychology of Sigmund Freud." In A. J. Bachrach, ed., *Experimental Foundations of Clinical Psychology.* New York: Basic Books, 1962.

———. "The Neurophysiology of Remembering." *Scientific American,* January 1969, pp. 73–86.

Pritchard, R. M. "Stabilized Images on the Retina" (1961). In Held and Richards (1972).

Rapaport, D. "The Conceptual Model of Psychoanalysis." *Journal of Personality* 20(1951) : 56–81.

———. "Projective Techniques and the Theory of Thinking." *Journal of Projective Techniques* 16 (1952) : 269–75.

Riesen, A. H. "Arrested Vision" (1950). In Held and Richards (1972).

Rosenblum, L. A., and Alpert, S. "Fear of Strangers and Speci-

ficity of Attachment in Monkeys." In Lewis and Rosenblum
(1974b).
Rosenthal, R. *Experimenter Effects in Behavioral Research.* New
York: Appleton-Century-Crofts, 1966.
Schimek, J. G. "A Critical Re-Examination of Freud's Concept
of Unconscious Mental Representation." *International Review
of Psycho-Analysis* 2 (1975) : 171–87.
Selfridge, O. G., and Neisser, U. "Pattern Recognition by Machine" (1960). In Held and Richards (1972).
Smith, F. *Understanding Reading: A Psycholinguistic Analysis of
Reading and Learning to Read.* New York: Holt, Rinehart and
Winston, 1971.
Spitz, R. *The First Year of Life: A Psychoanalytic Study of Normal
and Deviant Development of Object Relations.* New York: International Universities Press, 1965.
Stern, D. N. "Mother and Infant at Play: The Dyadic Interac-
tion Involving Facial, Vocal, and Gaze Behaviors." In Lewis
and Rosenblum (1974a).
von Bertalanffy, L. "Theoretical Models in Biology and Psy-
chology." In Krech and Klein (1952).
Wallach, H. "The Perception of Motion" (1959). In Held and
Richards (1972).
———. "The Perception of Neutral Colors" (1963). In Held
and Richards (1972).
Witkin, H. A. "The Perception of the Upright." *Scientific American,* February 1959. Reprinted in Coopersmith (1966).
Wolff, P. H. "Cognitive Considerations for a Psychoanalytic
Theory of Language Acquisition." In R. R. Holt, ed., *Motives
and Thought: Psychoanalytic Essays in Honor of David Rapaport.
Psychological Issues,* Monograph 18/19. New York: Interna-
tional Universities Press, 1967.

6

Primary Process, Secondary Process, and Language

HANS W. LOEWALD

The following contribution to the theory of primary process and secondary process and their relation to language is limited to only a few aspects of this vast subject. Primary process and secondary process are generally considered as fundamental, perhaps the most fundamental, concepts in psychoanalytic theory. Having a high degree of abstraction and generality, they subsume in various ways most, if not all, psychoanalytic findings and concepts. Primary process is directly correlated with the concepts *unconscious* and *id,* secondary process with *preconscious* and *ego,* themselves basic conceptualizations in psychoanalytic theory. With language I shall concern myself from a very narrow point of view. Conspicuous by its absence will be, for example, any reference to the important fields of linguistics and psycholinguistics, any consideration of the structure of language. Little will be said about interpretation and the symbolic function. I have set myself merely the task of attempting to throw some addi-

Since circumstances made it impossible for me to contribute to *Psychiatry and the Humanities,* vol. 1 (ed. J. Smith; New Haven: Yale University Press, 1976), dedicated to Edith Weigert, M.D., on the occasion of her eightieth birthday, the article written for this volume is a belated homage to Dr. Weigert.

A shorter version of this article was presented as the 11th Freud Anniversary Lecture, sponsored by The Psychoanalytic Association of New York, May 17, 1976, at the New York Academy of Medicine, New York City.

tional light on the two forms of mental processes that Freud distinguishes, and on the function he attributes to language in the "progression," in mental development, from primary- to secondary-process mentation.

Primary process and secondary process are ideal constructs. Or they may be described as poles between which human mentation moves. I mean this not only in the longitudinal sense of progression from primitive and infantile to civilized and adult mental life and regressions in the opposite direction. Mental activity appears to be characterized by a moving to and fro between, an interweaving of, these modes of mental processes—granted that often one or the other is dominant and more manifestly guiding mentation and that the secondary process assumes an increasingly important role on more advanced levels of mentation. Language itself, considered in terms of these categories, partakes of those two sides of the coin of mentation. The primary-process quality or suggestiveness of language is apparent in certain kinds of schizophrenic speech, in poetry—especially modern poetry—and in modern prose by writers such as Joyce or Faulkner. We see here that what we call dynamically unconscious processes can be compatible with conscious awareness and verbalization, as though there were a direct leap from primary process to conscious awareness, omitting preconscious, secondary-process mediation, despite the fact of expression in words.

In the verbal interventions and interpretations of the analyst in psychoanalysis, the secondary-process aspect of language ordinarily predominates. However, when we encourage the patient to free-associate, we try to move him in the direction of primary process, or in a direction where the influence of primary-process mentation on his verbal productions increases. To the extent to which the patient allows himself free association, his feelings and trains of thought are more influenced by, more embedded in, his global emotional situation of the moment, including the impact the analyst's presence has on it. The injunction to express himself in words, rather than to act or move about, induces the patient to funnel, as it were, his mental activity into the narrow channel of language. Speech thereby tends to gain greater intensity and to resonate more with the total emotional situation. This condition is greatly enhanced by the fact that the analyst is outside the patient's range of vision and his communications are received through auditory channels. Thus language, both spoken and heard by the patient, tends to assume that greater intensity and experiential resonance.

I have emphasized the embeddedness of verbalized thought and feeling in the global emotional situation—that is, in the psychoanalytic situation with its transference significance—because of the bearing this has on the primary-process aspect of language. In the clarifying, reflective, and interpretative interventions of the analyst, on the other hand, secondary-process aspects of language are by and large dominant, insofar as these interventions question, define, highlight, and articulate the hidden connections of what the patient has said. To the extent to which this happens, we may be allowed to speak of a transformation of primary-process aspects of language into secondary-process organization.

The preceding remarks on language in the psychoanalytic situation are merely meant to sketch in vague outline the problem area with which we are dealing.

Two further observations should be mentioned in these introductory comments. One is that language is first conveyed to the child by the parental voice—typically, and in an all-pervasive way, by the mother in the feeding situation and in all her other ministrations to the infant. In these situations her speech and voice are part and parcel of the global mother-child interaction. Secondly, parental voice and speech take on a special significance for the child insofar as they come to convey the parents' closeness at a distance, their presence in absence. When the child is alone, cannot see or touch or smell the parents, hearing their voices tends to render them present in a somewhat remote and less global fashion. The parental voices, responding to the child's crying or other vocal utterance—for example, in the dark—give him a sense of their presence. Thus the child's utterances may conjure up parental presence, even if the parent does not visibly or tangibly appear.

While I have studied only a very small fraction of the vast literature relevant to my subject matter, I am indebted to many authors in the fields of psychoanalysis and developmental psychology who have stimulated and influenced my thinking. I am grateful to the participants—psychoanalytic candidates and graduate analysts—in a seminar on this topic conducted by me under the auspices of the Western New England Institute for Psychoanalysis, for many fruitful discussions. The strongest and most congenial source of stimulation and influence, outside of psychoanalysis itself, has been Werner and Kaplan's book *Symbol Formation: An Organismic-Developmental Approach to Language and the Expression of Thought* (1963).

I

I shall begin with a reconsideration of a crucial passage from Freud's paper "The Unconscious" (1915b):

> The system *Ucs.* contains the thing-cathexes of the objects, the first and true object-cathexes; the system *Pcs.* comes about by this thing-presentation being hypercathected through being linked with the word-

presentations corresponding to it. It is these hypercathexes, we may suppose, that bring about a higher
psychical organization and make possible for the primary process to be succeeded by the secondary process which is dominant in the *Pcs.* [pp. 201–02]

In these sentences Freud sets forth essential relations between the dynamic unconscious, thing-cathexes, thing-
presentation, and primary process, on the one hand, and
the preconscious, word-presentations, and secondary process, on the other.[1] Word-presentations are said to play a
crucial role in the organization of the preconscious, which
is "a higher psychical organization" than the dynamic unconscious. A thing-presentation, according to this account, becomes hypercathected by being linked with the
corresponding word-presentations. The nature of that
correspondence—which seems to be the basis for the linking—remains unspecified. In any case, it is the linking of
thing-presentation with word-presentations by which preconscious or secondary-process mentation becomes established. We note that Freud here equates thing-cathexis
(*Sachbesetzung*) with thing-presentation (*Sachvorstellung*). A
little further on, at the end of the paragraph from which
I quoted, the thing-presentation is called a psychical *act*.
In as much as cathexes and presentations are psychical
acts—no matter how enduring, unchanging, structured,
they appear to be—word-presentations also are psychical
acts, although Freud does not specify this. Nor does he
explicitly state that word-presentations as psychical acts
are themselves cathexes.

Both thing-presentations and word-presentations ultimately derive from sense-perceptions, via "memory-
traces" of the latter. Thing-presentations derive from

1. Freud's postulation of the *systems* Ucs. and Pcs. will not be discussed in this
paper; it is not directly pertinent to the problems considered here.

global, complex perceptions, while word-presentations derive from primarily auditory perceptions (proprioceptive components in the respective memory-traces would play a role in the utterance of words).

It must be stressed that word-presentations per se do not constitute a higher organizational state than thing-presentations: it is the linking of the two by which higher organization comes about. This linking is a hypercathecting act, an act that intensifies and in some way modifies the already existing cathexis of the thing-presentation. But if linking of thing-presentation with corresponding word-presentations establishes hypercathexis[2] in a presentation, then word-presentations no less than thing-presentation would be hypercathected in such linking. It would be more accurate to formulate the state of affairs in the following way: the hypercathecting act, the linking of thing-presentation and word-presentations, brings about a presentation that differs from either in being a novel, more complexly organized psychical act.

At an earlier point in "The Unconscious," Freud explains that having heard something and having experienced it are, in terms of their psychological nature, entirely different psychic acts (pp. 175–76). If the analyst informs the patient in words of the existence of an unconscious presentation (a thing-presentation) in the patient's mind, the patient now will "have" the word-presentations corresponding to the thing-presentation. But the patient will not be able to make adequate use of the information unless the two become linked in his mind, or by his mind, through a hypercathecting act that creates a new form of mental presentation. In less abstract language, we would say that in the joining of words and cor-

2. The term *hypercathexis*, like *presentation, cathexis,* and *perception,* denotes both the act of hypercathecting and the "result" of that act—that is, the organized action-pattern which the act brings into being.

responding experience, the psychic life of the patient is intensified or deepened, has gained a new dimension (as in the so-called *aha Erlebnis*). No longer do unconscious presentation and presentation of the corresponding words exist side by side. There is now a novel present experience or psychical act which, as such, henceforth can become part of the patient's memorial repertoire. This novel mental act, I suggest, is of the nature of a perception. *Hypercathexis* in the sense used here, then, would be something like an actual perceptual act—if we may define a perceptual act as a psychical act in which the continuum of memorial, reproductive activity interacts with novelty in such a way that "a new experience" arises which in turn gives rise to refreshed, modified memorial activity. The two presentations are, in their interaction, lifted out of their status as separate reproductive acts, as it were, and become united in one perceptual act, with the freshness and poignancy characteristic of the latter. (The perceptual act here referred to is, of course, not the patient's perception of the words spoken by the analyst, but an intrapsychic perception, although triggered or induced by the analyst's words.) Such an intrapsychic perceptual act, while often experienced in conscious awareness, in all likelihood may occur outside of awareness.

I have indicated that Freud, when speaking of the linking of thing-presentation with word-presentations corresponding to it, says nothing more about this correspondence. But it is clear that he assumes a correspondence between them that somehow exists prior to the linking and should determine what becomes linked to what in the hypercathecting act.[3]

3. The mechanism of "false (wrong) connection" or link (*falsche Verknüpfung*), adduced by Freud, especially in his earlier writings, in a variety of contexts (transference, compulsion neurosis, obsessions and phobias, screen memories), is related to the issues of linking and correspondence. See Loewald (1960, p. 29).

I have also maintained that in such linking not only the thing-presentation but also the word-presentations would be hypercathected, one by the other. If there is a preexisting correspondence, the linking would reestablish some old bond that had been severed. And indeed, such severance occurs by repression. If presentations are not repressed, presentation of the thing and presentation of the word remain together; they belong together. As Freud puts it, words are the translation of the object and shall remain linked (*verknüpft*) with it. The analyst's interpretation, which translates the patient's unconscious (thing-) presentation into words originally belonging to it, helps to reestablish—once resistances are overcome—a piece of secondary-process mentation, to reestablish the old bond between thing and word.

This clarifies things insofar as the dynamic unconscious and primary process are understood as the results of repression. If secondary-process, preconscious-conscious mentation is our starting point and standard, taking for granted the existence of developed langue, then the phenomena of psychic conflict and defense account for the appearance of primary-process mentation and of its indications, such as condensation and displacement, in dreams, neurosis, and so forth. Merton Gill, in his paper "The Primary Process" (1967), has emphasized a basic ambiguity in that concept: the primary process, on the one hand, is "motivated" (as Gill terms it) by defense, is due to the impact of repression on standard, rational, secondary-process thinking. On the other hand, primary process is assumed to be the original form or mode of mentation according to the pleasure principle, which secondarily becomes changed by the exigencies of life, by "reality," resulting in secondary-process mentation guided by the reality principle. In a way, the ambiguity is resolved by introducing the concept of regression: de-

fense brings about regression from preconscious to unconscious mentation. The primary process is "primary"
because it is the first and more primitive. Defense—
repression—leads to a regression to this old mode of
mental functioning; it does not *create* primary process.

But what about language? What about the old bond between thing-presentation and word-presentations? We
have said that the hypercathecting link between them re-
establishes preconscious organization inasmuch as the old
tie between thing and corresponding words is rewoven.
However, in the passage quoted at the beginning of this
section, Freud speaks not just of the *re*constitution of preconscious presentations, of the *re*establishment of higher
psychical organization by the removal of repression in
analysis through appropriate interpretations. He wishes
to explain the *origin,* the emergence of the preconscious
in the course of mental development, by the linking of
thing-presentation and word-presentations that correspond to it.[4] The correspondence between thing and
word, then, must be older than the preconscious. Where
do word-presentations come from? If the unconscious is
older than the preconscious, if it is true that the unconscious "thing-cathexes of the objects" are "the first and
true object cathexes," then thing-presentations would be
older than word-presentations. Yet, a correspondence between them that precedes the emergence of preconscious
mentation is assumed; that correspondence must be more
ancient than the preconscious.

It is evident that during the first few months of life,
when primary-process mentation is unquestionably dominant, the infant does not have language at his disposal.

4. ". . . the system *Pcs. comes about* by this thing-presentation being hypercathected. . . . ["*das System Vbw entsteht*"] these hypercathexes . . . *bring about* a
higher psychical organization and *make it possible* for the primary process to be
succeeded by the secondary process" (1915b, pp. 201–02; my italics).

He cannot speak; but he is spoken to. He is provided with words, as it were, but he cannot use them. Does he perhaps have word-presentations, but no words to utter them? Or, if not word-presentations, then memory-traces of words he perceived, from which word-presentations eventually derive? Would he then have memory-traces of things and memory-traces of words, contiguous to each other? Would this contiguity constitute the ancient correspondence? We would be thrown back from a correspondence between thing-presentation and word-presentation to an underlying contiguity of the respective memory-traces. This contiguity, in turn, would have come about by "thing" and "words" having been perceived simultaneously or one right after the other.

I believe that such a reconstruction is untenable. It takes for granted the separateness of thing and word and the separate perception of thing and word by the infant. According to modern developmental theory, sensory perception in its initial stages is a global affair; there is no such thing as perception according to distinct sensory modalities in the beginnings of mental life. A thing, event, act, experience, given a word or words by the mother, is one buzzing, blooming confusion (William James) for the infant, and "the word" is part of that confusion. It must be added that during early stages the mother—unless she is out of phase with the infant's developmental stage—does not *name* things for the infant. She speaks with or to the infant, not with the expectation that he will grasp the words, but as if speaking to herself with the infant included. The words of which her speaking is composed form undifferentiated ingredients of the total situation or event experienced by the infant. He does not apprehend separate words—words separate one from the other and separate from the total experience—but he is immersed, embedded in a flow of speech that is part and parcel of a global experience within the mother-child field.

If this is correct, are we entitled to say that the infant's perception of what "in fact" happens represents a condensation of the separate elements and components of a total process? I think not. We can properly speak of condensation, a condensing, only if what is now condensed was at some prior stage separate or differentiated. This fits regression from secondary process to primary process in repression. Speaking of condensation always implies the secondary-process vantage point. In primary-process mentation a primordial density is given, not a condensation achieved.[5]

Our scientific conceptual language—function of a specially developed, highly differentiated form of secondary-process mentation—appears to be particularly inadequate for statements about early mental functioning and about primary-process phenomena in general. For this reason, correctives and qualifications have to be applied almost constantly, in order to make even approximately adequate statements when we wish to describe or formulate in conceptual language primary-process phenomena and processes. The much maligned anthropomorphisms and metaphors, not infrequently used in theoretical psychoanalytic writings, in many instances serve this corrective function. They often are closer to the phenomena in question in having an evocative quality. Just because such language is more influenced by the primary-process aspects of words, by the evocative-magical qualities of language, it often constitutes a more adequate formulation of primary-process phenomena.

Words and things (or objects), in traditional psychoanalytic theory, are treated as separate percepts given to a

5. This statement obviously has implications for the theory of dreams and the dream work, problems that cannot be pursued here.

perceptual system (Pcpt./Cs.). There, sensory data or stimuli are said to be passively received and thence relayed to and further processed in "memory systems" (Freud begins to take a more sophisticated view of perception in the 1925 papers on the "Mystic Writing-Pad" [p. 231] and on "Negation" [p. 238].) In primary-process mentation, however, words and things are not perceptually differentiated entities, the percepts of which would then be laid down in different but contiguous memory-traces.[6]

It is to be noted that "thing" (*Sache*), in "thing-presentation" (*Sachvorstellung*), is not so much or not merely "thing" in the sense of material object or substance, but includes the wider sense of that word: state of affairs, event, circumscribed action, and so forth. The emphasis is on the difference between words as auditory percepts and their correspondence and reference to other perceptual phenomena or experiences, not just to material objects. *Thing*, in this wide sense, and words, in early stages of mentation or primary process—insofar as words come into play—are not separate. Words here are, on the contrary, indistinguishable ingredients of global states of affairs. The mother's flow of words does not convey meaning to or symbolize "things" for the infant—"meaning" as something differentiated from "fact"—but the sounds, tone of voice, rhythm of speech, are fused within the apprehended global event. One might say that while the mother utters words, the infant does not perceive words but is bathed in sound, rhythm, and the like, as accentuating ingredients of a uniform experience. The distinction between sounds and so forth as ingredients of a total occurrence, and what the heard sounds refer to or signify—this is a slowly developing achievement to which we

6. For a discussion on memory and perception, see my paper "Perspectives on Memory" (1976).

apply the term *secondary process*. This is true also for sounds, "words," uttered by the growing child himself.

The linking of thing-presentation and word-presentations is a process that is secondary to an original unity where "word" is embedded in "thing." It is this original unity that constitutes the matrix for a "correspondence" between thing-presentation and word-presentations as they become differentiated from one another. Freud later acknowledged that the connection with word-presentations is not "a necessary precondition of the preconscious state" (1940, p. 162), although language has a special status in the development of what we now may term the symbolic function. Hypercathexis comes about not only in links with word-presentations, but also in links with various other presentations as they differentiate out of global experience.

In sum, the linking between thing-presentation and word-presentations is based on or concomitant with a differentiation of elements out of an original oneness. This differentiation is an unfolding or separating-out of what now are apprehended as different components or aspects of a global experience. Inasmuch as the differentiated elements betray their common origin and respond to each other, a correspondence between them remains as the heir, the reflection, the articulate memory, of the primordial oneness. The linking between thing-presentation and word-presentations in secondary process is a rejoining on a different level, by way of a creative repetition, of elements that had been at one; it is a reconciliation. The differentiating process implied in the differentiation of separate sensory modalities out of "coenesthetic reception" (Spitz, 1965) may be seen as a precursor of secondary process.

Repression, seen from this angle, amounts to a severing or loosening of the connections between thing-presentation and word-presentations. Word-presentations may remain conscious but are no longer or are only loosely linked with corresponding thing-presentations. As I had stated earlier, the hypercathecting link between them constitutes a psychical act of the nature of an internal perception. This internal perception (a "preconscious" mental act), or rather its memorial presentation, in repression becomes disrupted. Thus, repression as an intrapsychic action can be understood as an unlinking. The unconscious thing-presentation that results from repression, however, is not simply a presentation of the "thing" minus the corresponding words. Rather, the words have been reabsorbed into that old memorial formation where thing and words are not yet distinguished as different but corresponding and thus linkable elements of experience. Therefore an interpretation of unconscious presentations, communicated in words by the analyst, is capable of reestablishing differentiation of the thing-presentation in such a way that renewed linking can be achieved. It is as if the analyst's words summon the thing-presentation via the words contained in it, lifting them from the unitary thing as differentiated elements that now can be linked with other thing-elements. The analyst's interpreting words thus redifferentiate the unitary thing-presentation.

I said that word-presentations, unlinked or insufficiently linked with thing-presentations in repression, may remain conscious as such. But they are now void of or deficient in experiential meaning. They have deteriorated to more or less hollow echos of secondary-process presentations. In everyday mental functioning, repression is always more or less at work; there is a relative isolation of word-presentations. Indirect (through "derivatives") or weak links usually remain, sustaining an average[7] level of mental functioning that represents a vi-

---

7. The etymology of the word *average* throws an unexpected light on the use of it in the above context of compromise. A marginal note of this kind may not

able compromise between too intimate and intense closeness to the unconscious, with its threatening creative-des-
tructive potentialities, and deadening insulation from the
unconscious—where human life and language are no
longer vibrant and warmed by its fire. This relative deficiency or weakness of links between verbal thought and
its primordial referents makes it feasible for language to
function as vehicle for everyday rational thought and action, comparatively unaffected by or sheltered from the
powers of the unconscious that tend to consume rationality.

Related, by contrast, to the issue of average mental
functioning are the problems of abstract and of schizophrenic thinking and language. At the end of "The Unconscious," Freud expresses views on them that call for
critical comment. He writes:

> When we think in abstractions there is a danger that
> we may neglect the relations of words to unconscious
> thing-presentations, and it must be confessed that
> the expression and content of our philosophizing
> then begins to acquire an unwelcome resemblance to
> the mode of operation of schizophrenics. We may,
> on the other hand, attempt a characterization of the
> schizophrenic's mode of thought by saying that he

---

be amiss in a paper concerned with words. According to Webster (1958), the
word derives from the Arabic *'awār,* loss or damage in articles of merchandise;
Italian *avaria,* French *avarie,* damage to ship or cargo, port dues. It is used in
marine law. One of Webster's entries runs as follows: "A loss less than total to
cargo or ship, or a charge arising from damage done by sea perils; also, the eq-
uitable and proportionate distribution of such loss or expense among all
chargeable with it." A so-called general average (in marine insurance) "arises
from an intentional sacrifice or expense made for the safety of all the interests
involved in the same adventure under pressure of a common risk." From there
derives the meaning of *average* as "mean value" and eventually as "the usual,
typical or most frequently encountered thing, happening or person of a considerable number," "common run." Thus, the ideas of loss or damage (deficiency)
and proportionate expenses "made for the safety of all the interests involved,"
are hidden in the word *average.*

treats concrete things as though they were abstract. [p. 204]

Earlier in that paper he writes:

> In schizophrenia *words* are subjected to the same process as that which makes the dream-images out of latent dream-thoughts—to what we have called the primary psychical process. They undergo condensation, and by means of displacement transfer their cathexes to one another in their entirety. [p. 199; Freud's italics]

He makes a similar observation in "A Metapsychological Supplement to the Theory of Dreams" (p. 229). But if this is so, abstract thought does not tend to resemble the mode of operation of schizophrenics and the schizophrenic does not treat "concrete things as though they were abstract." Rather, the schizophrenic treats words as concrete things or actions, instead of treating words as being linked with them. This phenomenon is similar to, if not identical with, Freud's observation in "Totem and Taboo" that "savages regard a name as an essential part of a man's personality and as an important possession: they treat words in every sense as things" (p. 56).

It is true that the danger in abstract thinking is to neglect the relations of words to unconscious thing-presentations. But words, in abstract thinking, do not undergo condensation and displacement in the sense in which Freud states it to be the case in schizophrenia. Rather, words tend to acquire a peculiar degree of autonomy. In the neglect of the relations of words to unconscious thing-presentations their links are weakened. Meaning and the links between thing-presentations and word-presentations are thinned out, as it were, to more or less tenuous threads. In excessive abstraction, verbal thought processes give the impression of acquiring a mechanical or automatic activity of their own, like puppets manipulated by invisible hands connected with them only by thin threads attached at certain joints. Verbal thought, then, may have a lifeless nimbleness all its own—very much in contrast to the concretization of verbal thought in schizophrenia. In the latter case there is no link between word and thing, not because the link is cut or too tenuous, but because the distance between thing-presentation and word-presentations vanishes; they are no longer or are insufficiently differentiated. Word stands for thing, not as its symbol or representative, but as being remerged with it, or as magically summoning it into presence. The task of the therapist here is to differentiate or redifferentiate thing-presentation from word-presentations. If that succeeds—unless secondary obsessional defenses come into play—their correspondence, emerging out of identity, is not in question, and the secondary-process linking is no problem; the problem for the patient is to hold on to the differentiation. In neurotic repression, on the other hand, the therapeutic task is to reconstitute weakened or severed links, to narrow the distance between thing-presentation and word-presentation.

Not only differentiation between thing-presentation and word-presentations is absent or underdeveloped in the kind of schizophrenic mentation under consideration. The same is true for the differentiation between thing and thing-presentation, and between word and word-presentation. In schematic outline, we can distinguish four types of differentiation that take place in unison in higher mental development: (1) between thing and word, (2) between thing and thing-presentation, (3) between word and word-presentation, and (4) between thing-presentation and word-presentation. It seems that no one of these four differentiations (or the lack of one of them) takes place without the others being involved as well. The differentiation between thing and thing-presentation and between word and word-presentation, of course, involves subject-object differentiation. Language, considered from the standpoint of secondary-process mentation, develops within the growing differentiation between self and object-world. The concretization of language, as in schizophrenia, whereby the distinction between word and thing collapses, is at the same time concretization in another sense: distinctions between word and word-presentation and between thing and thing-presentation collapse as well. What we call *meaning* comprises both, the differentiating-linking of word and thing (their mutual reference) and that of presentation (memorial act) and percept.

I break off at this point in order to consider some of the metapsychological concepts used so far.

II

I shall begin with a digression that is related to language in a broader sense. While keenly aware of the recent debates in the psychoanalytic literature about some metapsychological concepts that point out their deficiencies, questioning even the relevance or validity of metapsychology itself, I shall proceed here without taking these objections into account in my discussion. But I wish to state my conviction that many—not all—of the objections raised are based on an anxious clinging to an unimaginative comprehension and to rigid and unduly restrictive definitions of certain Freudian concepts and theoretical formulations. If viewed within the overall context of Freud's work and that of his followers, many of them allow for much freer elaboration and development of their content and meaning than has been accorded them by the majority of theoreticians. True, some scientific concepts are so narrowly conceived at the outset, or conversely, so vague and ill-defined, that they have to be dropped along the way. But many Freudian concepts and terms are overdetermined and full of connotations and implications that were not spelled out by him or that he neglected. Others he may have defined more narrowly than necessary because of special theoretical considerations of the moment.

Concepts share the potential of language and words for unfolding new meanings, for changes of meaning, and for returning to earlier meanings. There are, of course, limits to this potential and there is always the risk of overstepping them. Equally, however, there is the risk of being too timid or too rigid about such limits, not utilizing, exploring, or testing the hidden potentialities of concepts. Freud's own aversion to technical terms and precise definitions of concepts undoubtedly has contributed to confusion in psychoanalytic theory and terminology. But he clearly wanted to keep his theories and concepts open to the winds of change while not condoning changes indiscriminately. In speaking of basic scientific concepts, he warns against prematurely confining them in definitions. In a well-known passage in his introductory remarks to "Instincts and Their Vicissitudes,"[8] he writes about this issue as follows:

> The true beginning of scientific activity consists . . . in describing phenomena and then in proceeding to group, classify and correlate them. Even at the stage of description it is not possible to avoid applying cer-

8. I quote this passage not only because of its immediate manifest content but also for its relevance to the broader problem of the interrelations between language and mental activity and the "thing" intended by it. I remark in passing that for Freud the "thing" tends to have the implicit meaning of "objective fact" (although he recognizes in principle the unknowableness of Kant's "thing in itself"), whereas in the view presented here the "thing" varies with the level or degree of differentiation of the mental activity that enters into an experience.

tain abstract ideas to the material in hand, ideas derived from somewhere or other but certainly not from the new observations alone. Such ideas—which will later become the basic concepts of the science— are still more indispensable as the material is further worked over. They must at first necessarily possess some degree of indefiniteness. . . . So long as they remain in this condition, we come to an understanding about their meaning [*Bedeutung*] by making repeated references to the material of observation from which they appear to have been derived, but upon which, in fact, they have been imposed[9] . . . everything depends on their not being arbitrarily chosen but determined by their having significant relations to the empirical material, relations that we seem to sense before we can clearly recognize and demonstrate them. It is only after more thorough investigation of the field of observation that we are able to formulate its basic scientific concepts with increased precision, and progressively so to modify them that they become serviceable and consistent over a wide area. Then, indeed, the time may have come to confine them in definitions. The advance of knowledge, however, does not tolerate any rigidity even in definitions. Physics furnishes an excellent illustration of the way in which even 'basic concepts' that have been established in the form of definitions are constantly being altered in their content. [p. 117]

9. The German text of the last sentence reads: "Solange sie sich in diesem Zustande befinden, verständigt man sich über ihre Bedeutung durch den wiederholten Hinweis auf das Erfahrungsmaterial, dem sie entnommen scheinen, das aber in Wirklichkeit ihnen unterworfen wird." A more precise translation would be: "So long as they remain in this condition, we arrive at an agreement about their meaning by repeated references to the material of observation from which they appear to have been derived, but which actually has been subjected to them." "Sich verständigen" means: to come to an agreement, a *mutual* understanding about something.

What psychoanalysis needs might not be a "new language" but a less inhibited, less pedantic and narrow understanding and interpretation of its present language, leading to elaborations and transformations of the meanings of concepts, theoretical formulations, or definitions—transformations that may or may not have been envisaged by Freud. Words, including concepts used in science, are, in their authentic function, living and enlivening entities. In their interactions with "things" to which they refer, they are informed with increased or transformed meaning as these things become better known, even as words and concepts inform things with increased and transformed meaning. This must be heard in the term *hypercathexis*, although Freud appeared to speak merely of some form of intensification or heightening of cathexis in terms of a quantitative energy influx. Words have a potential for development and change of meaning while remaining the same words, just as things have that potential while remaining "the same." Their potentials are realized to the extent to which they engage in live interplay with each other. Concepts tend to become dead issues by pedantic exegesis.

What I have said also applies to the definition of metapsychology itself, although I dislike the term and am looking for a better one. In other words, I do not wish to imply that there is no room for new concepts and terms and no point in eliminating inadequate ones. Nor do I imply that definitions and precise formulations of concepts are useless.[10]

I shall, all too briefly, attempt to reformulate the meaning of the terms *cathexis* and *primary and secondary process* and in this connection shall reconsider the concepts *preconscious* and *conscious* (see also my paper "Perspectives on

10. Discussions of psychoanalytic concepts and terms, outstanding for their thoroughness and sophisticated, flexible approach, are presented in *The Language of Psychoanalysis*, by Laplanche and Pontalis (1967).

Memory"). I begin with *cathexis,* especially in regard to object-cathexis and narcissistic cathexis. The notion of cathexis, as Freud used the term *Besetzung* and *besetzen* in his theoretical writings, implies preexistent entities— whether objects or intrapsychic presentations (or memory-traces)—that are infused or invested with instinctual energy. It assumes a ready-made external reality (objects) and a ready-made psychic apparatus, to which some instinctual charge is supplied. The entities so cathected would remain what they were before but would now be equipped with some charge or supercharge (*hypercathexis*). In my explication of hypercathexis I already tacitly changed this conception. In his later writings Freud arrived at a different understanding of the relations between ego (subject) and external reality, according to which they differentiate from and organize each other instead of being seen as accomplished facts *ab initio* (this is explicitly stated in the first chapter of *Civilization and its Discontents*). The understanding of perception as an interactive, not purely passive, process goes in the same direction. The implications for the concept of cathexis, however, were not spelled out.

In the light of such considerations and others that would lead us too far afield here, I propose to interpret *cathexis* as a concept for organizing activity (in contrast to what might somewhat facetiously be described as a fuel-injection notion). Applied to object-cathexis and narcissistic cathexis this means: object-cathexis is not the investment of an object with some energy charge, but an organizing mental act (instinctual in origin) that structures available material as an object—that is, as an entity differentiated and relatively distant from the organizing agent. Such a cathexis creates—and in subsequent, secondary cathecting activities re-creates and reorganizes—the object qua object. It is *objectifying* cathexis. Once objects are organized as objects in an initial cathecting act, they are then maintained or restructured in different ways by further objectifying cathexes. Narcissistic cathexis (in its metapsychological sense) is not investment of a preexisting ego or self with some energy charge, but a mental act (instinctual in origin) in which "available material" is not differentiated from the cathecting agent, not distanced in the cathecting act; the cathexis is *identificatory,* not objectifying. Narcissistic cathexis, then, contributes to the organization and reorganization of an ego or self, as object-cathexis contributes to the organization and reorganization of an object-world. The object character of an object may be dissolved, as it were, through narcissistic, identificatory, cathecting activity if an identification "with the object" takes place.

There are all kinds of gradations, intermediate states, and interminglings of these two cathexes. Winnicott's transitional objects (or "possessions") and Kohut's self-object would be examples of such. Insofar as primary process implies lack of differentiation (see below), narcissistic cathexis would be closely related to primary process, while object-cathexis—that is, objectifying cathexis—would be related to secondary process. These formulations are tentative and incomplete; significant modifications and qualifications are likely to be required.

According to this interpretation of cathexis, there is not a given structure—object or object-representation—that is invested with a charge of psychic energy. Instead, these very structures come into being, are maintained, and are restructured by virtue of objectifying cathexis. Similarly, such "psychic structures" as ego or superego come into being, are maintained, and are modified by virtue of narcissistic cathexis.[11] Winnicott (1967, p. 371) and Kohut

11. This view of narcissistic cathexis is in disagreement with Hartmann's definition of narcissism as cathexis of the self (a definition adopted by Kohut), for the reasons stated above. See Loewald (1973) for a brief discussion.

(1971, p. 26; p. 39, n. 1), I believe, think about cathexis along similar lines.

To turn now to *primary and secondary process,* primary process has been called primary because it is developmentally the first, the earliest form of mentation, and because it is seen as more primitive than secondary process. But the process is *primary* in a deeper sense insofar as it is unitary, nondifferentiating, nondiscriminating between various elements or components of a global event or experience. Thinking in terms of elements or components of an experience or act already bespeaks secondary-process thinking. In primary-process mentation, *oneness,* as against duality or multiplicity, is dominant. In secondary-process mentation, *duality* and multiplicity are dominant—that is, differentiation, division, a splitting-up of what was unitary, global, unstructured oneness. Earlier I spoke of the original uniform density conveyed in primary process, a density that may become reconstituted from secondary-process differentiation by regressive condensation as it occurs in repression. I also explained that the secondary process consists not simply in a splitting, dividing, discriminating—the word "diacritic" in Spitz's "diacritic perception" refers to the same phenomenon—but that in this same act the original wholeness is kept alive by an articulating integration that makes a textured totality out of a global one. What was homogeneous becomes a manifold whose elements are linked together. A weakening of these links, of this connectedness, can occur that may culminate in a virtual rupture, a fragmentation of experience and thought.

Developed language is a preeminent vehicle for articulating complex experiences or thought processes, for making explicit their elements and the mutual connections between these elements, for "scanning" experience and thought point by point, thus rendering present their immanent textured structure. Without language, or some other sensorimotor means or vehicle for articulating mentation, conditions are ripe for primary process. But language itself arises out of the homogeneous "thing-presentation" or primary-process experience. Therefore words and sentences, while bringing to the fore the textured linkedness in experience and thought, themselves become linked to concrete experience, inasmuch as secondary-process mentation differentiates vocables out of homogeneous experience as elements linked to it. I described how the mother's talking with her baby gives vocal accentuation to his experience that gradually becomes a separate but linked aspect of that experience.[12] Although in a derivative form, based on far more articulate modes of mentation to begin with, something similar takes place every time we first learn a word for a thing. In such learning, much of the time, the word is not simply added to the thing but the thing itself becomes first defined or delimited as an alive, circumscribed entity (hypercathexis). The emotional relationship to the person from whom the word is learned plays a significant, in fact crucial, part in how alive the link between thing and word turns out to be. Language, and any other mode of symbolization (visual representation, music, dance) in the course of its development may take on a life of its own, evolving its own laws in accordance with its particular sensorimotor possibilities and the limits set by them. But this "life of its own" nevertheless remains inperceptibly tied to and fed by the global experiences from which it

12. In language as it is used in religious services, there seems to be a tension toward such an early form of experiencing, by virtue of its sing-song quality and the fact that frequently words of an ancient language are used, incomprehensible or indistinct in their specific meanings to the congregation. The words, for the trusting, childlike congregation, not understood in their specific meanings, merge into the global religious experience.

has segregated, while at the same time giving them newly disclosed meaning.[13]

The primary form of mental acts is called unconscious, the secondary form, preconscious. I shall attempt to clarify the meaning of the word *conscious,* contained in these two basic terms of psychoanalytic theory, by going beyond the ordinary understanding of consciousness as conscious awareness. Although Freud briefly mentioned the possibility of unconscious perception,[14] he generally adhered to the notion that consciousness and perception are inextricably tied together. In his dominant thought, perception is a conscious, purely passive-receptive phenomenon (occurring in the system Pcpt./Cs.). Secondly, he understands consciousness itself as a perceptual phenomenon in the just-mentioned sense of *perception* (although he considers the possibility that consciousness involved further hypercathexis). Thirdly, he thinks of consciousness as conscious awareness.

I proposed earlier to think of the perceptual act as a psychical act "in which the continuum of memorial, reproductive activity interacts with novelty" (see p. 241). "Novelty" need not be material encountered in external sense-perception. In so-called inner perception the material would be internal. Nor does novelty, in the sense intended here, imply that what is encountered is brand-new

13. For a detailed and most perceptive and illuminating study of language from a developmental point of view, I wish to call attention again to Werner and Kaplan's book *Symbol Formation.* In one sense it can be described as a treatise on the relationship between "things" and "words" or their "presentations." A lengthy quotation (with discussion) from Helen Keller's autobiography beautifully illustrates and elaborates on the above remarks on the learning of words (pp. 110–12).

14. "It is a very remarkable thing that the *Ucs.* of one human being can react upon that of another, without passing through the *Cs.* This deserves closer investigation, especially with a view to finding out whether preconscious activity can be excluded as playing a part in it; but descriptively speaking, the fact is incontestable" (1915b, p. 194).

and has never been met before, but only that the interaction itself, the encounter, is new, takes place now ("new" and "now" are etymologically related). We should therefore correct our definition by saying: the perceptual act is an act in which a novel, present interaction takes place between the continuum of memorial activity and material *as differentiated from that activity* (in defining it thusly, we could not, strictly speaking, see identification as involving [diacritic] perception). Furthermore, I do not assume that a perceptual act is necessarily characterized by conscious awareness, nor that the word *conscious* a priori or only means "conscious awareness."

The word *conscious* derives from the Latin *conscius, conscire,* to know together. In secondary-process mentation—in contrast to primary-process mentation—the differentiation of uniform experience involves a knowing-together (as belonging together) of the now differentiating elements of that experience. The hypercathecting linking of the elements, in our case of thing-presentation and corresponding word-presentations, is a perceptual act, an act of *con-scire.* The linking is a knowing-together, but a *con-scire* that is not necessarily itself known in and by the linking activity; it may happen unbeknownst to the ego or self that is engaged in this *con-scire.* Freud has called that kind of linking mentation *pre-conscious.* Traditionally, what has been emphasized about preconscious mentation—and the prefix *pre-* suggests it—is its being a state preliminary and close to conscious awareness, but with the attributes of awareness lacking.[15]

If the word *conscious* is taken in the sense explained

---

15. Freud thought that conscious awareness involved the institution of a second "censorship between the *Pcs.* and the *Cs.,*" "that becoming conscious is no mere act of perception [perception understood here as passive-receptive], but is probably also a *hypercathexis,* a further advance in the psychical organization" (1915b, p. 194; Freud's italics).

above, the positive characteristic of "preconscious" mentation comes into relief—namely, that in contrast to dynamically unconscious mental processes, it is a differentiating-linking, a *con-scire.* Conscious awareness and
verbal expression of dynamically unconscious, primary-
process mentation is possible, as we know from psychotic
and certain other forms of verbal productions. Unconscious mental processes may be known to the ego, although the inner, preconscious *con-scire* is absent. Conscious awareness of psychic reality is not contingent on a
preliminary stage of preconscious elaboration of unconscious material. In order to stress the secondary-process
con-scire in "preconscious" mentation, and to distinguish
this radical meaning of "conscious" from the commonsense meaning of self-awareness, I propose to call secondary-process mentation *conscient* and to speak of conscient
instead of preconscious mental processes. Dynamically
unconscious mental processes (primary process) are nonconscient, but they may under certain circumstances be
known to the subject and verbalized in that nonconscient
mode of mentation.

It is to be noted that the distinction between identification and "object-choice" (libidinal object-cathexis) runs
parallel to that between unconscious and conscient mentation. These two distinctions refer to the same mental
development, the former seen from the instinctual-affective, the latter from the cognitive side. The dichotomy of
instinctual-affective and cognitive mental life, of course,
is itself a distinction arising in secondary-process mentation.

III

In the concluding part of this study I shall very briefly
consider that aspect of language which I shall call here its
magical-evocative function or quality. This aspect brings

us close again to primary process. It lets us see most clearly that there is no simple, one-to-one relationship between, on the one hand, primary process and thing-presentation, and, on the other, secondary process and word-presentations. Freud and other analysts, notably Ferenczi, have been well aware of this aspect of language. But psychoanalytic theory, to the limited extent to which it has dealt with language, has concerned itself mainly with its specific function in the development of discursive, conceptual, rational thought, consonant with Freud's valuation of scientific-rational thought as the highest form of human mentation. Partly because of this circumstance, and because of his having to embark on a fight against the prevailing equation of mind and consciousness, a distorting polarization of primary and secondary process was created. Freud recognized and combatted the cognitive-intellectualistic bias of the psychology and of the dominant trends in the philosophy of his formative years. But he was and remained firmly committed to a rationalistic-scientific *Weltanschauung*. One has only to read the last of his *New Introductory Lectures on Psycho-analysis* (1933) to be convinced of this.

When we think of the magical-evocational aspects of language we are concerned with the *power* of words. We are dealing then with words, not insofar as they refer to or are linked with things, but as embodying and summoning things and experiences, as bringing them to life. The relation of reference or signification, from this perspective, is merely a pale reflection, a faint echo, a highly derivative form of that original power of words to conjure up things. This power of words is intimately related to their being manifest physical, sensorimotor events. Poets and those concerned with words as the medium of poetry are keenly aware of this—to them—essential condition of words. The poet Mallarmé has said, "Approach-

ing the organism that is the repository of life, the word
with its vowels and diphthongs represents a kind of flesh"
(as quoted by Raymond). Raymond, in his book on modern French poetry (1947), speaks of the poetic word as
"an instrument of power. Its aim is to move, in the most
emphatic sense of the word, to shake the soul to its ultimate depths, to promote the birth and metamorphosis
of 'open' reveries, capable of operating freely and indefi-
nitely" (pp. 25–26). He quotes Mallarmé as saying that
" 'between the old methods of magic and the sorcery
which poetry will remain, there exists a secret parity' " (p.
26). The French poet and writer Paul Valéry, in his Oxford lecture, "Poetry and Abstract Thought," in referring
to a poetic line of Baudelaire's speaks of "the inestimable
value of a spell." He continues:

> the momentary being who made that line could not
> have done so had he been in a state where the form
> and the content occurred separately to his mind. On
> the contrary, he was in a special phase in the domain
> of his psychic existence, a phase in which the sound
> and the meaning of the word acquire or keep an
> equal importance—which is excluded from the habits
> of practical language, as from the needs of abstract
> language. The state in which the inseparability of
> sound and sense, in which the desire, the expecta-
> tion, the possibility of their intimate and indissoluble
> fusion are required and sought or given, and some-
> times anxiously awaited, is a comparatively rare state.
> It is rare, firstly because all the exigencies of life are
> against it; secondly because it is opposed to the crude
> simplifying and specializing of verbal notations. [p.
> 75]

At another point he speaks of "the miracles and prodigies
of ancient magic. It must not be forgotten that for cen-
turies poetry was used for purposes of enchantment.

Those who took part in these strange operations had to believe in the power of the word, and far more in the efficacy of its sound than in its significance" (p. 74).

Ferenczi, in his paper "On Obscene Words," writes: "An obscene word has a peculiar power of compelling the hearer to imagine the object it denotes, the sexual organ or function, *in substantial actuality* [*in dinglicher Wirklichkeit*]" (p. 137; Ferenczi's italics). He goes on to say that "obscene words have attributes which all words must have possessed in some early stage of psychical development" (p. 138). He describes how "abstract thought, thinking in words" develops out of such "imagining in substantial actuality," inasmuch as memory images (*Erinnerungsbilder*) get to "being represented merely by certain qualitative remains of these images, the speech-signs." He adds:

> it seems that speech-signs replacing images, i.e., words, retain for a considerable time a certain tendency to regression, which we can picture to ourselves in a gradually diminishing degree, until the capacity is attained for 'abstract' imagination and thought that is almost completely free from hallucinatory perceptual elements. [p. 139][16]

16. Ernest Jones, Ferenczi's translator, alternates in his translation of the German verb *vorstellen* and the nouns *Vorstellen* and *Vorstellung*. At one point he translates *Vorstellen* as "act of mental representation," at another point as "imagination." *Vorstellung* is translated as "image" in the passage above; but "image" also functions as a translation for *Bild*. In the *Standard Edition* of Freud's works, *Vorstellung* is usually rendered as "presentation" or "idea." The verb *vorstellen* is rendered by Jones as "imagine," whereas it usually is translated as "present" or "represent." The basic reason for this seeming confusion is that *Vorstellung* and *vorstellen* (literally, "that which is set before oneself" and "to set before oneself") is used in the more concrete sense of inner visual of auditory image (*Bild*), as well as in the more abstract sense rendered by "presentation," "representation," or "idea." Ferenczi describes the latter as *"abstraktes Vorstellen und Denken,"* which is "almost completely free from hallucinatory perceptual elements." Depending, then, on the degree of "abstraction" involved in *Vorstellung*, the sense of the word varies (in German, *Vorstellung* is also used in the sense of a stage performance, as an action set before an audience).

The magical, compelling power of words is not confined to forcing the listener to imagine the object "in substantial actuality." Language in its primordial form has the power or the significance of *action* for the *speaker*. Ferenczi, following Freud, speaks of the "original source of all speech in omitted action," adding that "on uttering an obscene joke we still have the definite feeling of initiating an act" (p. 141). In other words, the power of obscene and other primordial words may be such that in the experience of the utterer the act is not omitted but committed. Frequently the listener, too, experiences obscene jokes as sexual aggression. I mentioned earlier Freud's remark that primitive man treats "words in every sense as things" (1913, p. 56), and he points out that for primitive man, for our own children, and for certain neurotics and, to an extent, for ourselves as well, names are important parts or possessions of the person. The same is true for words that name things. The word as a name not only evokes or summons the thing, person, and so forth, rendering them present "in substantial actuality"; the word, as an action, also affects the "thing" it is addressed to because the word carries the "substantial actuality" (*dingliche Wirklichkeit*) of action.[17]

All of this is related to what I earlier pointed out about the original unity of thing and vocables, when the mother's flow of talking with the infant and, we may add, the growing child's own utterances are still undifferentiated or poorly differentiated ingredients of global experience. Words in their original or recovered power do not function then as signs or symbols for, as referring to, something other than themselves, but as being of the

17. *Ding* (in *dingliche Wirklichkeit*) must be understood in the same broad sense in which Freud uses *Sache* in *Sachvorstellung*. The German *Wirklichkeit* (actuality, reality), through its root word *wirken,* connotes concrete action or efficacy; it is related to the English "work."

same substance, the same actual efficacy as that which they name; they embody it in a specific sensorimotor medium. The sensorimotor elements of speech remain bodily ingredients of language, lending to words and sentences that aspect of concrete acts and entities which Ferenczi mentions. This aspect continues to dwell in language, although unattended to, even in its most abstract use, and in written and read language and "inner speech" as well.

I shall not discuss here the distinction between sign and symbol, despite its great importance for the understanding of language, nor the theory of symbolism.[18] Suffice it to say that the traditional, unduly narrow use of the symbol concept in psychoanalysis has more recently been criticized by analysts themselves, especially by those influenced by Melanie Klein. But Fenichel had already pointed out the difference between "archaic symbolism as a part of prelogical thinking" and the traditional psychoanalytic notion of symbolism as a "distortion by means of representing a repressed idea through a conscious symbol" (1945, p. 48). This distinction clearly relates to the "ambiguity" in the concept of primary process discussed by Gill (1967) (see above, p. 242).

In the course of the development of civilization, of the variegated ways in which language becomes both reduced and elevated to a vehicle for civilized human communication, expression of thoughts and feelings, and for abstract thought, the primordial power and concrete impact of language become attenuated and relatively neutralized, as the density of the primary process gives way

18. For an illuminating discussion of this distinction and its relevance to language as magic, see Werner and Kaplan (1963, pp. 35 ff., pp. 110 ff.). Regarding primitive mental life in general, see Heinz Werner's *Comparative Psychology of Mental Development* (1948). For discussions by psychoanalysts on symbolism, apart from Jones's well-known paper (1916), see, for example, Milner (1952), Rodrigué (1956), and Rycroft (1956).

to the discursiveness and articulation of secondary process. In the most creative forms of language, such as in its authentic religious use, in oratory, poetry, and dramatic art, the primordial power of language comes again to the fore. In great poetry and creative prose—in much of modern literature quite consciously—there is an interweaving of primary and secondary process by virtue of which language functions as a transitional mode encompassing both. We may say that language, being a vehicle for secondary-process or conscient mentation, being a medium of "hypercathexis" that creates higher organization, in its most genuine and autonomous function is a binding power. It ties together human beings and self and object world, and it binds abstract thought with the bodily concreteness and power of life. In the word, primary and secondary process are reconciled.

Let me conclude with some words of Paul Valéry. "Poetry is an attempt to represent or to restore, by articulate language, those things or that thing, which tears, cries, caresses, kisses, sighs, etc., try obscurely to express" (as quoted by Raymond, 1947, p. 156). Of the word in its essential function he says, "It enjoins upon us to come into being much more than it stimulates us to understand" (ibid., p. 26).

Dare I say that at propitious moments this may happen in a psychoanalytic hour?

REFERENCES

Fenichel, O. *The Psychoanalytic Theory of Neurosis.* New York: Norton, 1945.

Ferenczi, S. "On Obscene Words" (1911). In *Sex in Psychoanalysis: Contributions to Psychoanalysis.* Translated by E. Jones. New York: Robert Brunner, 1950.

Freud, S. *Standard Edition of the Complete Psychological Works.* London: Hogarth, 1955–64.

"Totem and Taboo" (1913), vol. 13.

"Instincts and Their Vicissitudes" (1915), vol. 14. (a)

"The Unconscious" (1915), vol. 14. (b)

"A Metapsychological Supplement to the Theory of Dreams" (1917), vol. 14.

"A Note upon the 'Mystic Writing-Pad' " (1925), vol. 19. (a)

"Negation" (1925), vol. 19. (b)

Civilization and its Discontents (1930), vol. 21.

New Introductory Lectures on Psycho-analysis (1933), vol. 22.

An Outline of Psycho-Analysis (1940), vol. 23.

Gill, M. "The Primary Process." *Psychological Issues* 5, no. 2/3. Monograph 18/19. New York: International Universities Press, 1967.

Jones, E. "The Theory of Symbolism" (1916). In *Papers on Psycho-analysis,* 5th ed. Baltimore: Williams & Wilkins, 1948.

Kohut, H. *The Analysis of the Self.* New York: International Universities Press, 1971.

Laplanche, J., and Pontalis, J.-B. *The Language of Psycho-analysis* (1967). Translated by D. Nicholson-Smith. New York: Norton, 1973.

Loewald, H. W. "On the Therapeutic Action of Psycho-analysis." *International Journal of Psycho-Analysis* 41(1960) : 16–33.

———. Book Review: *The Analysis of the Self,* by H. Kohut. *Psychoanalytic Quarterly* 42(1973) : 441–51.

———. "Perspectives on Memory." *Psychological Issues* 9, no. 4. Monograph 36. New York: International Universities Press, 1976.

Milner, M. "Aspects of Symbolism in Comprehension of the Not-Self." *International Journal of Psycho-Analysis* 33(1952) : 181–95.

Raymond, M. *From Baudelaire to Surrealism* (1947). Translated from the French. New York: Wittenborn, Schultz, 1950.

Rodrigué, E. "Notes on Symbolism." *International Journal of Psycho-Analysis* 37(1956) : 147–58.

Rycroft, C. "Symbolism and Its Relationship to the Primary and Secondary Process." *International Journal of Psycho-Analysis* 37(1956) : 137–46.

Spitz, R. *The First Year of Life*. New York: International Universities Press, 1965.

Valéry, P. "Poetry and Abstract Thought" (1939). In *The Art of Poetry*. Translated by D. Folliot. New York: Vintage Books, 1961. (*Collected Works of Paul Valéry*, vol. 7, Bollingen Foundation.)

Werner, H. *Comparative Psychology of Mental Development* (1948). New York: Science Editions, 1961.

Werner, H., and Kaplan, B. *Symbol Formation: An Organismic-Developmental Approach to Language and the Expression of Thought*. New York: Wiley, 1963.

Winnocott, D. "The Location of Cultural Experience." *International Journal of Psycho-Analysis* 48(1967) : 368–72.

7

The Significance of Jacques Lacan

STANLEY A. LEAVY

Jacques Lacan's ideas on psychoanalysis, of which he has been a practitioner and teacher for many years, have never been systematized by him. He has written voluminously, and his seminars over twenty years are in process of publication (Lacan, 1953–54, 1964, 1966, 1972–73). There are also in print studies that present his thoughts in more or less organized fashion (Palmier, 1972; Fages, 1971). Lacan looks on his work as essentially a rereading of Freud; unfortunately for the beginner, he prefers to state his ideas in a cryptic language more open to interpretation than to exposition.

Great and unpredictable shifts of emphasis are also the rule with him, to the peril of whoever would try to outline the development of his thought. It is perhaps just as well to bear in mind that his later views are not necessarily more valuable than his earlier ones—which are often clearer. For Lacan himself, Freud's greatest discoveries are his early ones, and we need only read Freud's preface to the later editions of *The Interpretation of Dreams* to remind ourselves that Freud stated this first. They have to do with dreams, jokes, parapraxias and slips, and neu-

A slightly different version of this paper appeared in the *Psychoanalytic Quarterly*, April 1977. It was also presented in a shorter version as part of a panel discussion on "Linguistics and the Unconscious," before the Boston and the Western New England Psychoanalytic societies in October 1975.

rotic symptoms. That is, they are his discoveries of what Lacan (who is addicted to recondite and complex puns) would call "lacunary phenomena," evidences of unspoken declarations to be read between the lines of manifest statements and actions. They open pathways to an unconscious discourse for which the speaker seeks utterance with the analyst's help.

I

"The unconscious is structured like a language" (Lacan, 1957, p. 103) is perhaps the most frequently pronounced dictum of Jacques Lacan and his school and can therefore serve as an introduction to an account of his ideas. Be it noted: (1) that the subject of that sentence is "the unconscious" in a strictly Freudian sense; (2) that the predicate goes "is structured like a language," not "*is* a language"; and (3) that the qualification "like a language" evokes the question, "According to which system of linguistics?" The danger of misinterpreting Lacan is, I think, even greater than usual when these considerations are neglected. For example, Lévi-Strauss, whose work has an important bearing on Lacan's, nevertheless often uses the word *unconscious* in quite a different sense from Freud's—namely, as the matrices that organize the rules of the social order rather than as a dynamic and personal system (Lévi-Strauss, 1967). Nor would it be correct to assert that the unconscious *is* a language, without careful qualifications to preserve the distinction between primary and secondary processes.

With regard to my third caveat, however, further discussion is called for, since "like a language" means something only in terms of the theoretical standards of what language is. Lacan certainly does not mean that the unconscious is like French or English or Tokharian. At the other, less naïve extreme, he does not mean that we can conceptualize the unconscious within the coordinates of all sorts of linguistic theories. Whether Chomsky's linguistics, for example, also reveals that the unconscious is structured like a language is a fascinating question, but of course outside Lacan's sphere (Edelson, 1972).

Lacan bases his understanding on the structural linguistics propounded by, among others, Saussure (1915) and Jakobson and Halle (1956). His most elementary concepts derive from Saussure: the relation between signifier and signified, the arbitrariness of the signifier, the distinction between language and speaking (*langue* and *parole*), and the communicative and therefore dialogical nature of language. The function in language of metaphor and metonymy, and of binary opposition, likewise are derived from Saussure, but in their contemporary versions in the work of Jakobson and the European structuralists. I shall later take up some implications of these linguistic dependencies.

Lacan is by no means the first analyst who asks us to focus on the psychoanalytic situation, but he stands out among theorists in returning all psychoanalytic concepts to this setting. In a sense, even his interest in language is subordinate to his interest in the psychoanalytic dialogue—or rather, he teaches the radical unity between the dialogue and language. We are able to make inferences about mind outside analysis—that is, compose our psychoanalytic psychology—because analysis serves as a model for all other forms of dialogue, real or imagined. From this point of view, it is not an exaggeration to say that the theory of psychoanalytic technique is the only metapsychology—although I do not think Lacan would put it quite that way.

Lacan's merciless attack on traditional (or "American") psychoanalysis as he sees it—and it is not easy to distinguish in this writer between theoretical criticism and ad

hominem polemic—is in general based on just this point
of view. He sees modern psychoanalysis as one-sidedly
derivative from Freud's longing for natural scientific ob-
jectivity, while ignoring Freud's less explicit allegiance to
problems of language and the centrality of the dialogue
(Lacan, 1956a, p. 47).

We can get to Lacan's meaning most directly, I believe,
by starting with the dream as our "road to the unconscious." In this instance we shall define as unconscious the
dream-thoughts that analytic method reveals to lie behind
the manifest dream and, in addition, the processes that
take place in the transformation of the thoughts into the
manifest dream as it is recalled and uttered. In so doing,
we come close to the categories of linguistic structures
that for Lacan are intrinsic to the unconscious.

Freud has stated as much indirectly—as Lacan shows—
when in *The Interpretation of Dreams* he counters the objection that the "real" dream undergoes alterations when
recollected and narrated (1900, vol. 5, p. 514). He states
that we get to the dream *only* within the framework of a
narrative, which means, looking at it from the linguistic
point of view, that the value of the dream is as the vector
of the word. Even the forgettings and doubtings that ac-
company the dream are parts of the message (or signifiers), and the point of any analysis is finally to discover
what the dreamer has to tell directly to the analyst.

Unconscious dream-thoughts are related to one another, according to Lacan, as "signifiers" are in language,
and the unconscious operations of the dream-work—condensation, displacement, and the consideration of representability—are equivalents of metaphor and metonymy
(1956a, p. 31). In language, according to Saussure, the
linguistic sign unites not a thing and a name, but a concept and a sound-image, which is the impression made by
the sound on our senses (1915, p. 99). It is physical, being

acoustic, but psychological as well. The concept is the signified, also mental in character and existing behind the
signifier. The words and expressions of language are always, of course, signifiers, and these are related to one
another through chains of equivalences or metaphors,
and of relations by contiguity, or metonymy.[1] The signified looms behind the signifier as its logical backing, but
it is abstracted from the world of meanings. For example,
naming a tree as such, one has in mind not only the real
object, the datum, but also the generic concept of trees.
To use the word in any concrete discourse is to evoke
many—maybe all—of the situations in which we have experience of trees, all the varieties of trees, and, most important for psychoanalysis, all of the metaphoric representations of trees—family trees, pulmonary trees,
trees-of-life, the Cross, phallic objects—all bound
together in chains of relative equivalence or contiguity
(Lacan, 1957, p. 112).

Dream-thoughts, like words as signifiers, exist only in
chains of meaning. Even in the dictionary there are no
one-to-one definitions (or very few), but rather there is
sufficient overlap that many words have to be looked up
to get even a fairly exhaustive definition of one of them;
and in the long run, of course, the process is circular. So
in concrete discourse—"speech"—any statement is an articulation of words having in themselves infinite contexts,
even for the speaker himself. What Freud called "overdetermination" is the constraint on these contexts imposed

1. Michel de Montaigne (1580) is worth quoting on this subject: "Oyez dire
Metonymie, Metaphore, Allegorie, et aultres tels noms de la grammaire, semble
il pas qu'en signifie quelque forme de langage rare et pellegrin? ce sont tiltres
qui touchent le babil de vostre chambriere." ["When you hear about metonymy,
metaphor, allegory and other such grammatical terms, don't they seem to mean
some rare and fancy kind of language? But really they apply to your chamber-
maid's chatter!"] *Essais*, vol. 2, book 1, chap. 51, "De la vanité des paroles"
(Paris: Garnier, 1925).

(synchronically) by the symbolic structure of his culture and (diachronically) by the intra- and interpersonal history of his symbols.

That which is true for words is also true for any other symbolic form. A picture, a sculpture, an image of any kind, exists as a conceptual representation permitted by arbitrary and conventional canons; even when it is a "likeness," it is such according to our standards of *like*ness, which are not universal either in space or time. It is perhaps easiest to see the comparison between words and dream-thoughts when we look at the "rebus" elements in dreams, which are pictorial, often punning, representations of verbal statements—that is, picture stories (Lacan, 1956a, p. 30). In these, the manifest dream is put together from signifiers that are unconsciously fitted to one another, maybe mostly metonymically—that is, deriving their meaning from the company they keep. But all of the ideas that the dream evokes, and their interconnections, are related as signifiers are related. In Freud's dream of the botanical monograph, for example, with its allusions to "cyclamen," to "Gärtner," to a "blooming" young woman, and to the "leaves" of the artichoke (Freud, vol. 4, 1900, pp. 169 ff.), the overlappings of meaning are exactly comparable to the functions of the signifier and are, indeed, metaphorical.

Like the signifier, too, dream-thoughts "float": they do not exist in a one-to-one relation with any particular signified element; indeed, this is the particular genius of the dream-work, that each element of the manifest dream is derived from more than one element of the latent thoughts, and, correspondingly, that each of the latent thoughts finds its way into more than one of the manifest elements. Such transformations of meaning are further comparable to metaphor—whereby a choice is made among words from a potential series of equivalents; and to metonymy—whereby the value of the signifier is transferred to a contiguous one, or to one of its parts (synecdoche). This condensation and displacement in the dream-work are analogous to, perhaps identical with, metaphor and metonymy as literary devices (Jakobson and Halle, 1956, p. 95).

The unconscious discovered in the analysis of dreams is the same unconscious of everyday psychopathology, of repression, and of symptom formation. Just as the meaning of a signifier in speech can be fully known only as the whole statement is made, so the meaning of the whole dream or symptom affects the meaning of any element in it. In this sense, any utterance or any dream is a network of signifiers organized by discoverable dominant signifiers. This has been put with rare clarity by Lacan:

> If what Freud discovered and rediscovers with a perpetually increasing sense of shock has a meaning, it is that the displacement of the signifier determines the subjects in their acts, in their destiny, in their refusals, in their blindnesses, in their end and in their fate, their innate gifts and social acquisitions notwithstanding, without regard for character or sex, and that, willingly or not, everything that might be considered the stuff of psychology, kit and caboodle, will follow the path of the signifier. [1956b, p.60]

Lacan thus states in linguistic terms the automaticity Freud attributed to the repetition compulsion that even overrides the pleasure principle: in each person's subjective existence is the set of meanings that he gives it; meanings are given initially by the symbolic order—a concept that must be elaborated further—and secondarily by the unique selections made by the individual and the variations that he performs on them in his development. The signifier insists on being heard. It is not just a linear series of variations, however, but as Lévi-Strauss pointed out in regard to the transformations of mythology, more like varying recurrences of musical themes in different staves of one orchestral score (Lacan, 1957, p. 112; Lévi-Strauss, 1967, p. 268).

I hope that all this may be loss esoteric if I illustrate with our most familiar theme, or signifier—namely, the oedipal theme. Here, if anywhere, the subject is constituted by the signifier, as Lacan would put it. The social structure intrudes itself on the individual subject's experiences through the existence of the family. The place of the child in the structure is preformed: to be a child and to have a mother and a father is the setting for the symbolic meaning of the oedipus complex. There is an identity between the status of each person of the triad and the signifier by which we designate it, each term being freighted with meaning that slowly but inexorably is revealed to the child's experience. The word, to be sure, is formed in the preconscious, but its metaphoric and metonymic bonds are forged in the unconscious and remain there, determinative of subsequent connections.

It is for this kind of reason (there are others) that Lacan summarily—even hilariously—dismisses animal observation and experimentation, and indeed all other studies of "behavior," as being totally irrelevant to psychoanalysis. It is simply impossible to conceive of the significations of animal actions, even when they involve exchanges analogous to human exchanges—courtship phenomena, let us say, or the social interactions of bees (1956a, pp. 36, 61). The human unconscious operates as it does, not because of conditioning, nor because of the responses it makes to the signs that interest ethologists, but because it interprets according to chains of signification which are organized in a symbolic order, of which language is a prototype. Signifiers, unlike signals, are not pure indicators of real objects; they always, as we have seen, refer to other signifiers, and in Lacan's words, "meaning is never capable of being sensed except in the uniqueness of the signification developed by the discourse" (1956a, p. 123). Think, for example, following my remarks about the oedipus complex, of a fundamental signifier like the word *father* and reflect on the impertinence of behavioristic or observational studies to the comprehension of unconscious meaning! Which is not to deny that such studies produce insights valuable elsewhere.

Symptoms, too, are signifiers (Lacan, 1966, p. 234). When they are not themselves verbal (but they may be) they are analyzable only to the extent that they can be used to set in motion the verbal associations[2] that shed increasing light on one another, and on the function of the symptom—which is its meaning. So, too, with defenses in the psychoanalytic sense, which, as students of rhetoric have demonstrated, fit neatly the descriptions of rhetorical tropes. I shall refrain from developing this topic here, except to state that for Lacan the process of repression corresponds with the substitution of one signifier for another signifier, the one substituted-for lapsing into the condition of a signified—that is, a metaphor (Laplanche and Leclaire, 1966). Again by way of oversimplified illustration, the repression of the signifier "father," as hated or loved object, is maintained by a substituted (countercathectic) signifier, "leader," "boss," or in the familiar discourse of our work, "analyst."

So far I have said little about the unconscious from the side of affect and desire. Certainly the unconscious cannot be conceptualized in an even remotely Freudian way without reference to desire, and Lacan has devoted his at-

2. The limitations of the word *associations* are evident, implying as the word does mere linear clusterings of signs, rather than networks of meaning.

tention to it on many occasions. With regard to affect, however—and it is worthwhile here to remind ourselves that Freud stressed the importance of placing affects in the conscious and not the unconscious system—Lacan has been charged with neglect, and his work called intellectualistic (Green, 1973, p. 37; Gear and Liendo, 1975, p. 21). I think that any acquaintance with his work should make it plain that he does not deny the existence of the feelings, despite his deliberate exaggerations of expression (1966, p. 799). The error he seems to show is in the tendency of traditional psychoanalysis to assert the primacy of the affects so as to point to feelings "behind" the signifiers (not only words), as if in so doing we designated the signified itself in the form of affects existing apart from the signifying chain. For example, even in speaking of a "nameless dread" as an unaccountable subjective state, we do name the dread and put it in a category, although a negative one; further analytic inspection leads to a set in which the surroundings of the feeling are a recognizable cluster of signifiers. Feeling, to be sure, is not the same as naming, but our feelings are assembled along networks of meaning, which, I think, is to say that they are "articulated."

Let us stop a moment. Lacan's theoretical position demands further elaboration, which does not depart from the linguistic mode of thought but includes a derivative of that mode—namely, the idea of the "symbolic order" more or less in the sense in which the term *symbolic* is used by Lévi-Strauss. That is, the whole system of signifiers is organized in advance of any individual's appearing on the scene. We are ushered into it by our acquisition of language, to be sure, but also by our introduction to all the other social forms, which, as Lévi-Strauss has tried to show, are themselves "structured like a language" (1967, pp. 67, 193). It is impossible to exaggerate the importance of this concept, since the transmission of all our modes of experience depends on the existence of the symbolic order. But it is by itself insufficient, since, in the first place, there is in addition to it an order of reality, the knowable world outside ourselves; and the preverbal world, to which Lacan has given the name "the imaginary order." He does not mean "illusory" by the word *imaginary*, but rather the organization of "images" in the Freudian sense, undisciplined by language, and by virtue of the modes of their appearance, essentially misrecognitions. The imaginary is nevertheless also a structure, standing in opposition to the fluctuating and fragmentary psychic world that precedes it. Lacan has for theoretical purposes persistently emphasized—sometimes as real event, sometimes only as model—the organizing effect of the infant's sudden and powerful awareness of himself in the mirror, by which he perceives himself as a controlling whole well before he is actually organized as a subjective unity (1968). It is the entry of the child into the symbolic order through language, however, that establishes his connection with the real world as well (1966, p. 704).

II

"The unconscious is the discourse of the Other" is a second of Lacan's gnomic pronouncements that serve as nodal points of his thought (1966, p. 549). First let it be said that Lacan sees in psychoanalysis a dialectical process, in which understanding is reached through a two-person discourse (leaving out of consideration the other persons "present" in intentional form in the minds of the two participants in the dialogue). But the concept "Other" has a shifting meaning for Lacan. It is sometimes justified as an equivalent of Freud's "ein anderer Schauplatz," "another scene," as the locus of the unconscious (1966, p. 548). But Lacan also means that (1) the unconscious talks about the other person (1966, p. 548); and (2) perhaps most idiosyncratically of all, the unconscious *originates* in the other person (1966, p. 9).

Again, I believe that this highly condensed idea is made more accessible when approached linguistically and psychoanalytically at the same time. We might start with the analytic proposition that all statements of the patient are addressed to the analyst at both conscious and unconscious levels. They are, in Jakobson's terms, among other things, "conative" and "phatic" (1958, p. 95)—that is, aimed at the hearer and seeking contact with the hearer. We attribute a transference value to the unconscious referents of all our patient's communications, although we do not heed them all equally. In this sense, the "discourse of the Other" means the "communications *about* the other" and is hardly news to the psychoanalyst.

The origin of the unconscious *in* the Other, however, is a genuinely original and rather startling concept. I believe that it may be paraphrased in the following way: As we have seen earlier, Lacan considers the unconscious to be "structured like language," and organized according to the plan of language—for example, with respect to the relation of the signifier to the signified. Since the language and the whole symbolic process are acquisitions that are taught to the child, it seems to follow that the unconscious as a symbolic content originates in that "other" who was its source. The startling, and perhaps valuable contribution of this idea is that it accounts for the "otherness" of the unconscious in a new way, and also underscores that the analyst's offering to his patient is the patient's own unconscious; or, as Lacan has characteristically put it, in human speech "the sender receives from the receiver his own message in reverse form" (1956b, p. 72). Repression takes place also because the "Other," the symbolic world, has provided alternative signifiers, the metaphors and metonymies which, in an older terminology, serve as countercathexes for the repressed.

It is in this analysis of intersubjectivity that Lacan also grounds his theory of desire. Whereas traditionally Freudian analysis derives desire directly from instinctual drive, from biological *need,* Lacan looks always to man's essentially dialectical situation. In some ways he is not too far from Melanie Klein and Ronald Fairbairn, with their emphasis on early object relations, although there are important differences. Desire is contextual, not isolated from the network of signifiers. As he puts it: "The phenomenology of analytic experience demonstrates the paradoxical character of desire, the deviations, wanderings, eccentricities, even scandals that distinguish it from need" (1966, p. 690). But what is most definitive of man's desire is that it is "the desire of the Other"[3] (1968, p. 75). That is, just as the unconscious discourse is to, about, and even from the person(s) addressed, so a person's desire is, in its essence, *to be desired;* in fact, the person's assurance of existing can only be gained through the Other's recognition of him/her.

III

One must hesitate before attempting to judge the "significance" of Lacan's work—although that seems to be the most appropriate word in considering this master of signification—on the basis of such a brief discussion of so

3. Lacan's own explanation for his use of the capital *A* in "Autre," for which I use the *O* of "Other," is as follows: "My reason for using a capital 'O' in stating that the unconscious is the discourse of the Other is to indicate the 'beyond' [l'au delà] wherein recognition of desire and the desire for recognition are joined" (1966, p. 524).

few representative ideas. Furthermore, I have tried to present them in exceedingly simplified form, which deprives them of the striking originality of their statement by Lacan. I have also omitted almost any reference to their philosophical origins. Nevertheless, even such an introductory essay, which I hope will lead others to explore Lacan's writings (if only as a psychoanalytic phenomenon), demands some justification.

Lacan has given us a lead toward the estimation of his significance in the epigraph that appears at the head of the French edition of his so-called "Discours de Rome." It is, he says, a quotation chosen in 1952 (it is not stated by whom it was chosen) as a motto for an Institute of Psychoanalysis:

> In particular it must not be forgotten that the separation into embryology, physiology, psychology, sociology, and clinical practice does not exist in nature, and that there is only one discipline: *neurobiology*, to which observation obliges us to add the epithet *human* in what concerns us. [1956a, p. xxiii]

It is typical of Lacan thus to nail to his masthead the motto of the party he most vehemently opposes, and then to demolish its presuppositions, for the greater part indirectly. Whatever else we shall come to assert about him, we shall, I believe, have to see in Lacan a pioneer on the psychoanalytic road that takes a direction antithetical to that proposed by this motto. Our science is *not* part of "neurobiology," and its future is not one of seeking ever closer coherence with biological science.

Paul Ricoeur has sufficiently summarized the arguments against classifying psychoanalysis as "observational" science (1970), and I shall not go over familiar ground in detail. The basis of the opposition between psychoanalysis and physical sciences rests in the nature of the data. These are publicly available and objective in physical science, private and subjective in psychoanalysis. We claim a very specialized kind of ascertainment of the psychic reality of another person through the establishment in our own minds of the ideas that are revealed in our patients' communications to us; and it is through this process, which is "intersubjective" (to which Ernst Kris and Abraham Kaplan also alluded, from a somewhat different point of view, in their paper "Aesthetic Ambiguity"), that we arrive at the inferences we interpret or, as I have said elsewhere, "translate" (Leavy, 1973) as the unconscious meaning of the patient's discourse. Nothing in all this is ever made physical and observable except in the form of sounds—and these sounds are arbitrary vehicles of meaning, so that the application to them of any kind of physical procedure whatever would never get us any closer to the message they convey. How, then, can we look to "neurobiology" to enlighten us? It is only a further obscuring of real differences to invoke here the undisputed psychosomatic unity: what is at stake is, rather, the recognition that we learn about that, too, only to the extent that we allow full freedom for the discovery of the meaning of symptoms, including physical symptoms, through the development of the discourse—through language.

Ricoeur (1970) has shown that Freud's system of energetics may be a necessary part of his metapsychological explanation, fully complementary to his interpretive or "hermeneutic" system; on the other hand, Ricoeur is the one who reminds us it is fatal to that system to subject it to the criteria of physical science. It looks not to the physical world of measurement and observation but to the inner world of meaning. Lacan has tried to reconstruct psychoanalytic theory without recourse to analogies perilously drawn from physical science. He leads us back

to where Freud started—to the "talking cure." Our kind
of science is founded in talk, not in tissues. We must look
to linguistics, semiology, rhetoric, for ways of organizing
our thought.

So much can be said with little reference to Lacan's
particular contributions toward a new theory of psychoanalysis. That he aims at a new theory is manifest, for all
his reference to Freud as the source of all his ideas—*his*
only because he has in effect sculpted them out of
Freud's conglomerate theory as Freud could not himself
do because he did not have the advantage of modern
linguistics. For it is, through and through, a linguistic
theory that Lacan proposes and, as we have seen, one
based on the work of Saussure. In fact, we may say that
Lacan's contributions stand or fall in their dependence on
Saussure—at least, as modified by the school of structural
linguistics he founded. To the extent that Chomsky, for
one, offers a different view of language from Saussure's,
it may be that Lacan's base of operations has been shaken
(Ricoeur, 1969; Edelson, 1975). I do not state this by way
of conviction, since it is more than probable that Saus-
surean and Chomskian linguistics are complementary
rather than opposed, but it is plain that a reconsideration
in which both theories are involved would substantially
alter a theory that calls on the signifier as its sole shibbo-
leth. Here, as elsewhere, it seems to me that Lacan's permanent importance resides in the thrust he has given to
psychoanalysis in a new direction—or as he would insist,
in a direction intended by Freud in the first place.

Nevertheless, it was a serious step to seem to identify
the unconscious with language, which is at first sight directly at variance with Freud's distinction, especially in
"The Unconscious" (1915, p. 201), between the presentation of the "thing" and the presentation of the "word."
Freud situated the latter in the preconscious, where it

exerts its function as signifier of the unconscious signified. It is in schizophrenia, according to Freud, that the
word undergoes the alteration of being treated as a thing-
presentation. Is this inconsistent with Lacan's view? Not, I
think, if we go back to the example I have given of the
transformations of the signifier: all of the metaphors that
appear in relationship with the dream-element (or any
other element in the speech of the patient or subject)
have partial overlappings of meaning and have evidently
been evoked through the work of the primary process.
That is to say, the metaphors for the (unconscious) signified themselves undergo the fate of the signified. I do
not think that we have to insert the word itself into the
unconscious; what we have to see, if Lacan is right, is that
the structural possibilities which constitute the subject's
unconscious experience—its "overdetermination"—are
identical with those that give rise to language.

I have alluded also to the objection to Lacan's treatment of affect. André Green, once one of his followers,
has devoted a book to the refutation of Lacan's position
on affect (Green, 1973), and here I shall only make a few
comments. Usually we differentiate between the unconscious representation and the drive with which it is
charged. Furthermore, we even consider this to be a theoretical position with a readily available empirical referent: the intensity with which ideas are entertained, for
one thing, and the apparent displaceability of that intensity. It is noteworthy, however, that Freud once commented that the "nucleus" of an affect is "the repetition
of some particular significant experience" (1916–17, p.
396). R. M. Loewenstein further reminds us that affects
have a discharge value "only while the memory-contents
are remembered, and this only in as much as they are
being told to the analyst" (1956, p. 462).

I cite these authorities only because their assertions

dovetail rather well with Lacan's view that affects, too, are "articulated" like language—which appears to me to mean that affects derive their meaning, too, from the signifiers—the "representations" of which they are a part. What may make this idea difficult is that we have grown accustomed to imagining affects as something like pools of fluid having an existence independent of mental representations, to which they may or may not adhere. For Lacan, the emergence in analysis of the signifier, or rather of the chain of signifiers ordered in metaphoric or metonymic linkages, is inseparable from the emergence of the affects. That there are problems in this conceptualization—just as there are in any other—is plain enough: it does not account easily for either displacement of affect, on the one hand, or for intellectualization, on the other.

Lacan's ideas about the unconscious are, as I have noted, intimately connected with his structuralist notions of the "symbolic order." Whereas the infant's first apprehensions of the world, "the real," are in terms of images that become organized around essentially false perceptions—"the imaginary"—he enters into the human experience only through the grasping of language. Lacan makes much of Freud's famous account of the child's *"fort-da"* experience (Lacan, 1956a, p. 83; Freud, 1920, pp. 14 ff.), in which the loss and reclaiming of the object are experienced repetitively through verbalization. In fact, the existence of language implies a loss and a restitution, the verbal symbol being a reclaimed object. But just as the original object, the "real" object, is lost to consciousness, so the words that signify it may follow in its path, each signifier being replaced by another, generally further and further away from the first.

What generates this process is desire. Lacan's differentiation of desire from biological need is a valuable contribution: much murky thinking can be avoided by recognizing that desire—ultimately for the lost object—is structured symbolically, and that its transformations are like those of any other symbolic transformation. Desire can be understood only as an aspect of subjectivity; to attempt to handle it even theoretically in terms of biology is to isolate it from its basis in experience. When, however, Lacan tries to posit desire as a metonymic process—apparently because metonymies achieve their status by their contiguities, through a displacing movement—we sense that Lacan himself is straining after consistency by borrowing analogies (1957).[4]

I cannot here discuss Lacan's technical innovations (1956a)—modifying the length of the analytic hour, among other things—which perhaps are not so capricious or manipulative as they sound. Nor shall I try to take up his important debt to the existential philosophy rooted in Hegel and Heidegger, although it is as fundamental to his thought as empiricist positivism is to Freud's. A final word, however, is owed to Lacan's feud with ego psychology. One must leave aside its political aspects, which are obvious enough from the record (Miel, 1966). More serious is Lacan's contention that beneath the preoccupation of ego pyschology with ego-functions so minutely anatomized, is an adaptational philosophy having as its

4. I do not think that it has hitherto been noticed that there are some affinities between Lacan's thought and that of two American psychoanalysts, Sullivan and Erikson. Sullivan's "interpersonal psychiatry" does not have a linguistic basis, but especially in his later work he seems to have applied "field theory" in ways that have a bearing on Lacan's understanding of intersubjectivity (Sullivan, 1953). Similarly, to the extent that Erikson's (1959) concept of "identity" means internalization of symbolic structures, it is also related to Lacan's view of the symbolic order. More recently, Schafer (1975), in his "psychoanalysis without psychodynamics," proposes a language of "action" for psychoanalysis, which, in a very different way from Lacan's, also would abolish the objectification and reification of experience that has pervaded psychoanalytic theory in the past.

goal the fitting of the mind to the accepted norms of the community—or at least to those of the analyst (1966, p. 425). The ego, for Lacan, is best understood as the organization of defenses; accordingly, it is anything but "autonomous," but rather is a distorting organization (1966, p. 335). Far from needing strengthening, the ego needs to be overcome. Here there may be mere terminological problems; but Lacan is not, once again, the only analyst to have seen in the later development of ego psychology a flight from the unconscious, on the one hand, and an exaggerated claim of psychoanalysis to be a general psychology, on the other.

It is this appeal to the unconscious, the "discourse of the other," that makes Lacan's writings and seminars, for all their self-indulgent obscurities, a summons back to psychoanalysis at its most demanding and its least pretentious. His original translation of Freud's famous aphorism is both odd and persuasive: "Wo es war soll Ich werden" becomes "Where *it* was, it is my duty that I come to be" (1966, p. 426). The unconscious is the realm of the subjective and the intersubjective; that which seems to be impersonal drive is revealed to be the person himself.

References

Edelson, M. "Language and Dreams: *The Interpretation of Dreams* Revisited." *Psychoanalytic Study of the Child* 27 (1972) : 203–82.
———. *Language and Interpretation in Psychoanalysis.* New Haven: Yale University Press, 1975.
Erikson, E. H. *Identity and the Life Cycle.* New York: International Universities Press, 1959.
Fages, J.-B. *Comprendre Jacques Lacan.* Toulouse: Privat, 1971.
Freud, S. *Standard Edition of the Complete Psychological Works.* London: Hogarth, 1953–63.
    The Interpretation of Dreams (1900), vols. 4, 5.

"The Unconscious" (1915), vol. 14.

Introductory Lectures on Psycho-Analysis (1916–17), vol. 16.

Beyond the Pleasure Principle (1920), vol. 18.

Gear, M. C., and Liendo, E. C. *Sémiologie psychanalytique.* Paris: Minuit, 1975.

Green, A. *Le discours vivant.* Paris: Presses Universitaires de France, 1973.

Jakobson, R. "Linguistics and Poetics" (1958). In R. T. and F. M. de George, eds., *The Structuralists: From Marx to Lévi-Strauss.* Garden City, N.Y.: Anchor, 1972.

Jakobson, R., and Halle, M. *Fundamentals of Language* (1956). 2d ed. The Hague: Mouton, 1971.

Kris, E., and Kaplan, A. "Aesthetic Ambiguity." In E. Kris, *Psychoanalytic Explorations in Art.* New York: International Universities Press, 1952.

Lacan, J. *Écrits.* Paris: Seuil, 1966. (This is the collection of Lacan's principal writings. Page references to this book in my text are to papers by Lacan that appeared at different dates. A partial translation is available: *Écrits, A Selection.* Translated by A. Sheridan. New York: Norton, 1977.)

———. *Le séminaire, livre i* (1953–54). Edited by J.-A. Miller. Paris: Seuil, 1975.

———. *Language of the Self: The Function of Language in Psychoanalysis* (1956a). Translated by A. Wilden. Baltimore: Johns Hopkins University Press, 1968.

———. "Seminar on 'The Purloined Letter' " (1956b), translated by J. Mehlman. In *French Freud: Structural Studies in Psychoanalysis, Yale French Studies* (1972), no. 48.

———. "The Insistence of the Letter in the Unconscious" (1957), translated by J. Miel. In J. Ehrmann, ed., *Structuralism.* Garden City, N.Y.: Anchor, 1970.

———. *Le séminaire, livre xi* (1964). Edited by J.-A. Miller. Paris: Seuil, 1973.

———. "The Mirror-phase as Formative of the Function of the I," translated by J. Roussel. *New Left Review* 51 (1968) : 71–77.

———. *Le séminaire, livre xx* (1972–73). Edited by J.-A. Miller. Paris: Seuil, 1975.

Laplanche, J., and Leclaire, S. "The Unconscious" (1966), translated by P. Coleman. In *French Freud: Structural Studies in Psychoanalysis, Yale French Studies* (1972), no. 48.

Leavy, S. A. "Psychoanalytic Interpretation." *Psychoanalytic Study of the Child* 28 (1973) : 305–30.

Lévi-Strauss, C. "The Effectiveness of Symbols" (1958). In *Structural Anthropology*. Garden City, N.Y.: Anchor, 1967. Also, in the same volume, "Linguistics and Anthropology."

Loewenstein, R. "Some Remarks on the Role of Speech in Psycho-analytic Technique." *International Journal of Psycho-Analysis* 37 (1956) : 460–68.

Miel, J. "Jacques Lacan and the Structure of the Unconscious" (1966). In J. Ehrmann, ed., *Structuralism*. Garden City, N.Y.: Anchor, 1970.

Palmier, J.-M. *Lacan: le symbolique et l'imaginaire*. Paris: Editions Universitaires, 1972.

Ricoeur, P. *Le conflit des interprétations*. Paris: Seuil, 1969. (*The Conflict of Interpretations*. Edited by D. Ihde, translated by K. McLaughlin et al. Evanston, Ill.: Northwestern University Press, 1974.)

———. *Freud and Philosophy*. New Haven: Yale University Press, 1970.

Saussure, de, F. *Cours de linguistique générale* (1915). Edited by T. de Mauro. Paris: Payot, 1972. (*Course in General Linguistics*. Edited by C. Bally and A. Sechehaye, translated by W. Baskin. New York: McGraw-Hill, 1966.)

Schafer, R. "Psychoanalysis without Psychodynamics." *International Journal of Psycho-Analysis* 56 (1975) : 41–56.

Sullivan, H. S. *Conceptions of Modern Psychiatry*. New York: Norton, 1953.

8

Image and Language in Psychoanalysis

PAUL RICOEUR

My goal in this essay is to appraise the attempts made by some recent theoreticians of psychoanalysis to reformulate psychoanalytic theory in terms of linguistic models borrowed either from structural linguistics or from transformational and generative linguistics. My line of argumentation will be as follows. In the first part I shall present the reasons favoring such a linguistic reinterpretation, principally by dwelling on analytic practice, and more generally speaking, on the analytic experience. At the same time, I shall try to explain why Freud's metapsychological theory lags behind his own practical work as regards the recognition of the semiotic dimension of psychoanalysis.

In the second part, beginning from the partial failure of such linguistic reformulations, I shall attempt to demonstrate that the universe of discourse appropriate to the analytic experience is not that of language but that of the image. As we shall see, this thesis is not purely and simply opposed to the linguistic one. Unfortunately, however, we do not yet possess an adequate theory of the image and the imagination to account for this discovery; more

Translated by David Pellauer. Paul Ricoeur's essay, written for this volume, was presented in October 1976 at the University of Chicago, as the first lecture in the series "Psychoanalytic Perspectives," sponsored by the University of Chicago Extension and the Chicago Institute for Psychoanalysis.

precisely, we lack a theory that would account for the semiotic aspects of the image that I shall bring to light. This explains why, in a day when linguistics has made considerable advances beyond the other human sciences, we should not have any recourse but to assign everything that presents a semiotic character to language. But by so doing we misunderstand—just as purely economic interpretations misunderstand, though in another way—the real discovery of psychoanalysis. That is, we overlook the level of semiotics that has to do with images and the imagination.

The second part, therefore, will not be a refutation of the first, to the extent that the case in favor of language is in fact a case in favor of the semiotic aspects of the analytic experience. Rather, it will be a question of reorienting the same arguments toward what I shall suggest we call a semiotics of the image and a theory of the imagination.

The case in favor of a linguistic reinterpretation of psychoanalytic theory proceeds first of all from reversing the relation between the metapsychology and what we may call in a general sense the analytic experience, if we gather together under this term what in Freud's own vocabulary are called the procedure of investigation and the method of treatment. I propose, therefore, to proceed by summarizing the arguments to be considered according to their decreasing degree of proximity to the analytic situation, the whole theory in a way constituting the metalanguage of psychoanalysis.

The Analytic Situation as a Speech Relation

First of all, the analytic situation itself may be characterized as a speech relation. The "treatment" is a talk-cure. And psychoanalysis continues to distinguish itself from every other therapeutic method by this veritable asceticism which it imposes on the analysand. He is placed in a situation where desire is forced to speak, to the exclusion of substitute satisfactions as well as every tendency to slip into acting out.

This simple starting point in analytic practice is heavy with theoretical consequences. What at first seems to be just a constraint inherent in the analytic technique conceals a theoretical requirement—namely, to include in the nomenclature of theoretical entities only those psychical realities that have an affinity for language. If the theory speaks of instincts or impulses, this will never be in terms of physiological phenomena, but only in terms of a meaning susceptible to being deciphered, translated, and interpreted. In other words, psychoanalysis only knows desire as what can be said.

Let us be clear on this point. It is in no way a question here of an amputation of human experience, which is thereby reduced to discourse. On the contrary, it is a question of an extension of the semiotic sphere as far as the obscure confines of mute desire antecedent to language, for psychoanalysis claims to rejoin such preverbal experience by passing through subsequent symbolic constructions that assure its enduring efficacy. We may even say here that psychoanalysis extends language beyond the logical plane of rational discourse to the alogical regions of life, and that in so doing it makes that part of us speak which is not so much dumb as it has been constrained to silence.

Next, the analytic situation makes desire speak to another person. It offers desire what Freud calls, in one of his technical texts, "a playground in which it [the patient's compulsion to repeat] is allowed to expand in almost complete freedom" (*S.E.,* 12 : 154). Now why does the analytic situation have this virtue of reorienting repetition toward remembrance? Because it offers desire a face-to-face relation in the process of transference. Not only does desire speak, but also it speaks to someone else, to the other person. This second starting point in analytic practice, too, does not lack theoretical implications. It reveals that from its beginning human desire is, to use Hegel's expression, the desire of desire, of the other person, and, finally, of recognition. This reference to something other than itself is constitutive of desire inasmuch as it is an erotic demand. The discovery of the Oedipus complex in Freud's self-analysis has no other signification: desire is structured as human desire when it enters into that transferable relation that brings into play two sexes and three persons, a prohibition, a death wish, a lost object, and so forth.

Hence, psychoanalytic theory is inadequate to the discovery made in psychoanalytic practice when it proposes a purely energetic definition of desire in terms of tension and discharge, and when it does not take intersubjectivity into account. And the theoretical model ignores language as well as the other person, since to speak is to address oneself to another person.

To conclude this discussion of the analytic situation, let me add that the analysand becomes capable of speaking about himself in speaking to the other person. Therefore, to speak of oneself in psychoanalysis is to move from an unintelligible story to an intelligible one. The analysand, after all, enters analysis not simply because he is suffering, but because he is troubled by symptoms, behaviors, and thoughts which do not make sense to him and which he cannot coordinate within a continuous and acceptable story. And the whole of analysis is only a reconstruction of contexts within which these symptoms, behaviors, and thoughts make sense. So by giving them, by means of the labor of speech, a referent framework wherein they become appropriate, psychoanalysis integrates them into a

history that may be recounted, and we may describe the
analytic process (with Marshall Edelson) as the "rejection
of immediate occasions or contexts . . . as sufficient
grounds for understanding such acts" and the substitution of "more remote or distant occasions and extended
contexts as these have been and are now symbolically
reconstructed (according to other norms) by the actor"
(Edelson, p. 55).

This labor of decontextualization and recontextualiza-
tion, principally with the help of "symbolizations he constructed as a child" (ibid.), implies that the analysand
must consider his experience in terms of texts and contexts—in short, that he enter into a semiotic reading of
his experience and that he raise his experience to the
rank of an acceptable and intelligible story or history.
Now this narrative structure of personal experience has
not received the recognition it merits in psychoanalytic
theory, even though a portion of analytic knowledge is
lodged within the case histories. This is true to such an
extent that an epistemologist such as Michael Sherwood
can claim that the epistemology of psychoanalysis must
begin with the case histories and the conditions of intelligibility of their narrative structure and then proceed
to the theory, which only furnishes explanatory segments
that are to be interpolated into an essentially narrative intelligibility (Sherwood, 1969). I will not pursue this epistemological aspect of the problem here, but I will retain
from the concept of a case history what it implies concerning the relations of language and the analytic experience. If Freud can write case histories it is because every
analytic experience takes place within a mode of discourse that may be called narrative. The analysand recounts his dreams and the episodes of his past. He recounts what he does not understand until he understands
what he recounts. Thus the whole of analytic experience is

crossed by that discursive modality which requires us to say that analysis is a narrative analysis or an analytic narration.

Let us now step back a bit from the analytic situation and introduce what Freud's writings call the investigatory procedure. By so doing, we only distance ourselves from the most formal aspects of the analytic relation, and we enter into the actual thickness of the analytic experience. What is more, we are only separating ourselves from the contemporary contexts of the pathological episodes in order to make the symbolic constellations emerge which at first are unknown to the analysand and which allow us to confirm the intelligibility of the troubles that he suffers.

Within this phase of interpretation and explanation, what counts in favor of a linguistic reformulation of the theory taken as a whole? Essentially, that analysis consists not just in listening to someone speak, but in listening to the analysand speak in an unusual manner, where he interprets his symptoms as another discourse, even as the discourse of someone else. This idea that the unconscious is structured like a language to the degree that it may be understood as another kind of discourse—an idea that finds its most monumental expression in the work of Jacques Lacan—constitutes the central thesis of what we are calling the linguistic reformulation of psychoanalysis.

Let us see to what extent Freud's written works may support such a reinterpretation.

Even before *The Interpretation of Dreams,* which will be the key document for my discussion, the *Studies on Hysteria* suggest for the first time a conception that we may call a semiotics of symptoms. In the "Preliminary Communication" of 1893, Freud establishes a symbolic connection between the determining cause and the hysterical symptom. Then he establishes a parallelism between this symbolic connection and the dream process. As the apparent content of the dream, the symbol counts as *X,* and its significative value consists in the indirect function of rememoration. Hence Freud speaks of "mnemonic symbols" (*S.E.,* 2 : 90–93) to indicate in an abbreviated fashion that the symptom, insofar as it is a symbol,[1] is the mnemonic substitute for a traumatic scene the memory of which has been repressed. The mnemonic symbols are the means by which the traumatism continues to exist in the distorted form of symptoms, and the semiotic nature of these mnemonic symptoms is confirmed by the analysis itself, to the extent that the symptom may be replaced by a discourse—a pain in the leg, for example, may be equivalent to a linguistic expression of the relation between the patient's desire and the paternal figure. Moreover, this transition from the symptom to the linguistic expression is often confirmed by the metaphorical values of words, where the symbolization of a psychical state by a corporeal expression is in a way brought to language after having been, in a way, buried in the body through hysteric conversion. Thus, do we not say when we feel insulted that it was like a slap in the face? Or when we are hopeless that we cannot take another step?

This possibility of translating a hysteric symptom into a metaphor—which Freud caught sight of very early—announces a universal feature of the semiotic universe which Freud traversed in every direction, namely, the indefinite substitutability of one class of signs for another. The dream will be the first link in these semiotic chains,

1. It is true that Freud does not continue to extend the term *symbol* in this direction, which is reserved for the cultural stereotypes revealed by "typical dreams." See below, pp. 317–18.

which I am going to consider next and along which it
may be exchanged for a symptom, a legendary theme, a
myth, a proverb, or a perversion.

That a dream should be a sort of text to interpret as
another discourse, or as the discourse of another person,
is attested to in multiple ways in *The Interpretation of
Dreams*. First of all, this presupposition is what confers
meaning on the very task that Freud sets himself in placing his undertaking under the title of interpretation
(*Deutung*) rather than explanation (*Erklärung*):

> The aim which I have set before myself is to show
> that dreams are capable of being interpreted [*einer
> Deutungfähig sind*]. . . . 'interpreting' a dream implies
> assigning a 'meaning' [*Sinn*] to it—that is, replacing
> [*ersetzen*] it by something which fits into [*sich . . . ein-
> fügt*] the chain of our mental acts as a link having a
> validity and importance equal to the rest. [*S.E.*,
> 4 : 96]

This kinship between the task of interpreting a dream
and that of interpreting a text is confirmed by the fact
that analysis takes place between the story of the dream
and another story which is to the first what a readable
text is to an unreadable rebus, or what a text in our maternal language is to a text in a foreign language.

The semiotic character of the dream is attested to a second time by what Freud designates as the dream-matter.
Indeed, he does not hesitate, to our astonishment, to
speak of dream-*thoughts*. Immediately after having said
that the dream is "the fulfilment of a wish" (p. 122), he
asks the question; "What alteration have the dream-
thoughts undergone before being changed into the manifest dream which we remember when we wake up?" (p.
122). It is easy to see why the latent content is called a

thought: when the dream has been interpreted as a
"wish-fulfilment" it becomes intelligible, because seeking
to attain a goal or to satisfy a desire is what we fully understand as the veritable axiom that governs our whole
comprehension of human action.[2] Consequently, to say
which desire the dream is the disguised accomplishment
of is to restitute the context within which it becomes intelligible. Therefore, inasmuch as it renders the dream
intelligible, desire is to be called the "dream-thought." It
constitutes, along with the distortions that complicate it,
the meaning of the dream:

> Dreams . . . are not meaningless, they are not ab-
> surd; they do not imply that one portion of our store
> of ideas is asleep while another portion is beginning
> to wake. On the contrary, they are psychical phe-
> nomena of complete validity [*Vollgültiger*]—fulfil-
> ments of wishes; they can be inserted [*einzureihen*]
> into the chain of intelligible [*aus verstandlichen*] waking
> mental acts; they are constructed by a highly compli-
> cated activity of the mind [*geistige*]. [*S.E.*, 4 : 122]

Freud also says at the end of chapter 6:

> Two separate functions may be distinguished in
> mental activity during the construction of a dream:
> the production of the dream-thoughts, and their
> transformation into the content of the dream. The
> dream-thoughts are entirely rational and are con-
> structed with an expenditure of all the psychical en-
> ergy of which we are capable. They have their place

2. Edelson quotes Freud, "it is self-evident that dreams must be wish-fulfil-
ments, since nothing but a wish can set our mental apparatus at work" (*S.E.*, 5 :
567), and comments: "This assumption in Freud's works, if we strain a bit, can
be viewed as an axiomatic postulate of a general theory of human action"
(Edelson, p. 46).

> among thought-processes that have not become con-
> scious—processes from which, after some modifica-
> tion, our conscious thoughts, too, arise. [*S.E.*, 5 : 506]

One could not put it any better. As regards its latent content, the dream-thought is homogeneous to all our
thoughts that come to language in the narrative consciousness that we draw from ourselves.

Certainly the same text warns us (and the note added
in 1925 [p. 506, n. 2] strengthens this warning) that the
problem of the dream is not that of the latent thoughts,
but that of the dream-work by which these unconscious
thoughts are transformed into the manifest content of
the dream. And this construction of the dream is "peculiar to dream-life and characteristic of it" (p. 507). So it is
here that a linguistic theory stands or falls. But at least it
is not presumptuous to emphasize that dreams "concern
themselves with attempts at solving the problems by
which our mental life is faced" (p. 507, n. added in 1925),
for it is this homogeneity between the unconscious and
the conscious that makes psychoanalysis itself possible, to
the extent that the latent dream-thoughts, because they
are thoughts, have a vocation for language.

Hence the semiotic character of the dream would be established on a solid foundation if it could be demonstrated that the dream-work itself brought into play processes that have their equivalents in the functioning of
language. But Freud seems to discourage this undertaking by forcefully asserting:

> The dream-work is not simply more careless, more
> irrational, more forgetful and more incomplete than
> waking thought; it is completely different from it
> qualitatively and for that reason not immediately
> comparable with it. It does not think, calculate or

judge in any way at all; it restricts itself to giving things a new form. [*S.E.*, 5 : 507]

The expression "dream-work" is there precisely to emphasize that it is a question of *mechanisms* whose description calls for a quasi-physical language: condensation is a kind of compression; displacement is a transference of intensity; and so forth.

No reader of Freud can escape the question of whether this language must be taken literally or be understood metaphorically. The linguistic reformulations of the theory are an attempt to interpret the energic language in the second sense. If the energic metaphors are inevitable, it is because the dream-work brings into play semiotic processes that have been desymbolized by the situation of repression. But these desymbolized processes are nevertheless semiotic processes. The proof is the very possibility of the work of analysis, which follows the reverse pathway of resymbolization and which unfolds entirely within the milieu of discourse. Thus, condensation recovers its semiotic status of being a form of abbreviation (laconism) when analysis is applied to it and brings to bear on different trains of thought the elements of the condensed representation. Freud's insistence on the expression "train of thought" confirms the fact that condensation is a condensation of thoughts, a case of overdetermination, so that "each of the elements of the dream's content turns out to have been 'overdetermined'—to have been represented in the dream-thoughts many times over" (*S.E.*, 4 : 283). Condensation, therefore, is one vicissitude of representation, not a physical mechanism.[3]

The elements retained in the abridged content constitute the nodal points toward which a large number of the

3. "Not only are the elements of a dream determined by the dream-thoughts many times over, but the individual dream-thoughts are represented in the dream by several elements" (*S.E.*, 4 : 284).

dream-thoughts converge. Hence, what are condensed are significations, not things. The case where a person assumes the function of a collective image is the clearest example. It suffices that the associative chains succeed in dismembering the dream figure among its initial elements, which bear names and are capable of precise description, for the condensation to be restituted to its semiotic status of the multiple overdetermination of an element common to several associative chains.

The linguistic reinterpretation of displacement at first glance appears more difficult, inasmuch as displacement is a transference of psychical intensity and because this transference of intensity immediately calls for an explanation of an economic type: to elude the censorship imposed by the resistance, an element far away from the affected interest—and therefore from the prohibited representation—receives the value that was originally placed on this representation. Therefore, it is in terms of a transference of cathexis that the displacement allows itself to be best expressed. And yet the displacement is not without a linguistic structure, as is attested by the reverse operation, which consists in reestablishing the distribution of elements as a function of a central point or a focal idea. The discourse of the waking state, too, consists of a hierarchy of topics, with dominant and secondary themes, relations of semantic distance or proximity, and so forth, in what we could call the logical space of discourse.

These remarks, backed by the numerous examples of dreams analyzed by Freud in *The Interpretation of Dreams,* constitute a good introduction to recent attempts to coordinate the linguistic aspect of the dream-work with the structures and processes that contemporary linguistics has brought to light. In so doing, the authors of these attempts at reformulation have given us not only original but also liberating work, especially with regard to the prejudices that even Freud himself remained trapped in concerning the functioning of language.

It seems true, for example, that Freud was caught up in the idea that language consists of a nomenclature of words understood as labels which arise from the mnemonic traces left by the things represented. What is more, he was seduced by evolutionary theories that derived the origin of language from the expression of primitive emotions. Thus, he thought that the return from the dream to a more primitive ontogenetic and phylogenetic stage would lead language back to an equally more primitive stage where the words would have antithetic significations reflecting the ambivalence of effects.[4]

Freud, it also seems, knew nothing of the idea of language conceived of as a group of signifiers defined by their differences within the interior of the system. Nor did he seem to know the distinction between signifier and signified which characterizes the linguistic sign, or of the resources of dissociation, linguistic shifts, and substitution which this double-edged constitution offers. Freud, who in the famous episode of the spool saw in what game of presence and absence the mastery of the lost object is constituted, did not have the semiotic theory to speak of this presence and absence.

He apparently did not recognize the universal polysemy of words in natural languages or the exploitation of this fact in poetry and in jokes; so Freud, the master of the psychoanalytic interpretation of the *Witz*, did not have an adequate linguistic model to account for it. Nor did he know of the covenant structure which the least exchange of speech represents, or of the symbolic order which each of us enters as soon as we speak and which

4. See "The Antithetical Meaning of Primal Words" (*S.E.*, 11 : 151–61).

has as its signifier this very covenant of speech. Nor, finally—and perhaps above all—did he recognize the rhetorical structures that govern the use of discourse in a situation.

I will insist only on this last point—the rhetorical resources of speech—because it is at this level that the progress of the science of language seems to reveal the
deepest affinity with the discovery made by psychoanalysis, which at the same time appears to be both in advance of its own linguistic theory and in search of a more
adequate one. From this point of view, one of the most
noteworthy contributions of linguistics to psychoanalytic
theory is certainly that of Roman Jakobson concerning
metaphor and metonymy. This great linguist has shown,
in effect, that the opposition expressed at the level of the
two classical figures of rhetoric—the trope by resemblance and the trope of contiguity—in reality runs
through every operation of language. Every linguistic
sign implies two modes of arrangement: combination or
selection. It is therefore possible to place all the phenomena that present aspects of either enchainment by contiguity or grouping together by similarity (every selection
being made within a sphere of resemblance) on two or-
thogonal axes of combination and selection. Then, to distinguish these two families of operations, one speaks of the
metonymic process and the metaphoric process. These
operations take place on every level—phonological, syntactic, and semantic—leading to an opposition between
personal styles, literary forms, plastic forms, and cinemat-
ographic forms. Jakobson also discerns this polarity in the
unconscious symbolic processes in dreams which have
been described by Freud. He suggests putting displacement (which would be metonymic) and condensation
(which would be synecdochic) on the side of contiguity,

and identification and all symbolism on the side of similarity.

Jacques Lacan, on the contrary, apportions these polarities differently, boldly identifying displacement with metonymy and condensation with metaphor. But these divergences are less important than the general attempt to break with the biologism and behaviorism attributed to post-Freudian psychoanalysis and to "return to Freud" by situating not only the analytic situation, but also the operations of the unconscious which the theory attempts to account for systematically, within the unique "field of speech and language."[5]

Having characterized the movement of the cure as the passage from empty speech—the empty speech of the analysand—to full speech—the "subject's assumption of his history inasmuch as it is constituted by speech addressed to the other person" (Lacan, p. 134)—Lacan does not hesitate in identifying the elaboration of the dream with its rhetoric:

> Ellipse and pleonasm, hyperbaton or syllepsis, regression, repetition, apposition—these are the syntactic displacements; metaphor, catachresis, autonomasy, allegory, metonymy, and synecdoche are the semantic condensations wherein Freud teaches us to read the intentions, be they ostentatious or demonstrative, dissimulative or persuasive, retortive or deductive, with which the subject modulates his oneric discourse.[6] [Lacan, p. 146]

5. Following the title of one of Lacan's important essays: "Fonction et champ de la parole et du langage en psychanalyse," in *Ecrits I*, pp. 111–209.
6. Concerning the symptom, Lacan says, "the symptom entirely resolves itself into an analysis of language because it is itself structured like a language and it is language whose speech must be realized" (p. 147).

The theory, consequently, in no way contradicts the concrete discovery of psychoanalytic practice, and we may say that "the unconscious is that part of concrete discourse insofar as it is transindividual which is not at the subject's disposition for reestablishing the continuity of his conscious discourse." Also: "The unconscious is that chapter of my history which is marked by a blank or occupied by a lie—the censored chapter. But the truth can be rediscovered; most times it is already inscribed somewhere also" (Lacan, p. 136).

As for analytic method: "Its means are those of speech insofar as it confers a meaning on the individual's functions; its domain is the domain of concrete discourse insofar as it is the transindividual reality of the subject; its operations are those of the history insofar as it constitutes the emergence of truth into reality" (Lacan, pp. 134–35).

What was said earlier in Freud's terms concerning the dream-thoughts now is supported by a global reinterpretation that there is thought wherever there is a symbolic organization. That part which is cut off from us is a slice of history which has already been interpreted:

> What we teach the subject is to recognize how his unconscious is his history, that is, we help him to complete the present historization of the facts which already have determined a certain number of historical turning points in his existence. But if they have had this role it is already as facts of history, that is, insofar as they are recognized in a certain sense or censured in a certain order. [Lacan, p. 139]

This concept of a primary historization permits the application of the laws of discourse and of symbolization over the full extent of the psychoanalytic domain. This does not mean that everything in man is discourse, but that everything in psychoanalysis is speech and language.

Authors, such as Marshall Edelson, who follow Noam
Chomsky rather than Saussure and Jakobson do not say
anything really different. They only differ as to the
linguistic model employed. Their claim is that there is
more affinity between a transformational and generative
linguistic model and the procedures of the unconscious
than is the case with a structural model. But their "Pro-
legomena to a Theory of Interpretation"[7] do not differ
when it comes to considerations regarding "Empty
Speech and Full Speech in the Realization of the Subject":[8] the analyst is shown as listening to and at work interpreting phenomena of a semiotic nature while the analysand is caught up with the symbolic constructions of his
childhood.

What is new is the definition of a "linguistic competence" required for the deciphering of the semiotic edifices. This competence is described as the internalization
of a group of rules for transformations which may be described within a theory of language and of symbolic systems.

If we bring this assertion to bear on the problem that
gives rise to our present discussion—namely, the possibility of furnishing a linguistic equivalent for what Freud
described as a dream-work—we immediately see what
may be seductive in borrowing a transformational model
from Chomsky. The linguist, in effect, runs into a problem homologous to that of the psychoanalyst: how to account for the surface structure of a sentence with its ambiguities in terms of its deep structure. Just as condensed
representation is the nodal point for several chains of
thought, "an ambiguous sentence has one surface struc-

7. The title of part 1 of Edelson's *Language and Interpretation in Psychoanalysis.*
8. Section 1 of Lacan's "Fonction et champ de la parole et du langage en
psychanalyse."

ture but as many different deep structures as it has senses" (Edelson, p. 76).

Thus, it seems wholly appropriate to bring to light in terms of transformational linguistics the operations by means of which the dream-thoughts are transformed into an apparent content. This will be the case principally when the interpretation is applied to deviant forms that the user of language has recourse to in order to engender significative representations. But each deviant form presupposes a system of rules whose violation appears as appropriate. And psychoanalytic interpretation is the interpretation par excellence of significant deviances, comparable to the forms of "linguistic audacity" which characterize a poem (G. N. Leech, in Edelson, p. 108).

I will stop my summary of the linguistic reformulations of the theoretical apparatus of psychoanalysis here. What has been said should be sufficient to give an idea of the direction taken by the search for a point of contact between linguistics and psychoanalysis.[9]

The Semiotic Dimension of the Image

The following reflections are centered on the notion of the image. They constitute just a partial critique of the linguistic reformulations of psychoanalytic theory, since I

9. The similarities between Lacan and Edelson, as I have indicated, are more important than their evident differences. For example, the role of resemblance in what Edelson calls a "presentation" (following Susanne Langer), and which he opposes to "representations," leads him to write: "The psychoanalyst's skill in interpreting a presentation depends upon his sensitivity to the possibilities of metaphor, his responsiveness to resemblance and his capacity to detect patterns, arrangements, and significant forms" (Edelson, p. 84). Then, using Katz's distinction between a "presupposition" (which is a part of the deep structure) and a "presumption" (which is something credited to the locutor by the auditor in a discourse situation), he remarks: "Here we are in the realm of what Katz terms *rhetoric*. The province of rhetoric is that meaning—which is other than the cognitive sense represented by the deep structure—conveyed by the choice of a particular surface structure" (p. 87). Obviously the latter remark is easily compared to Lacan's enumeration of the rhetorical figures brought into play by the unconscious.

will retain the crucial part of the preceding argumentation. I will, however, seek to reorient it in another direction. While the theses evoked above all conclude the linguistic character of the described phenomena from their semiotic character, I think it is mistaken to believe that everything semiotic is linguistic. At the same time, however, it is also an error to believe that the image does not arise from the semiotic order. It is this semiotic dimension of the image, therefore, that I will seek to explicate.

Unfortunately, the theories we have today hardly allow us to recognize this semiotic dimension, inasmuch as we remain the heirs of a tradition that sees the image as a residue of perception or as the trace of an impression. Consequently, lacking a theory appropriate to the image, psychoanalytic theory seems to be caught in the following disjunction: either it recognizes the function of the image in psychoanalysis but misunderstands the semiotic dimension of its field, or it recognizes this semiotic dimension but too quickly assimilates it to the realm of language.

My working hypothesis is that the universe of discourse appropriate to the psychoanalytic discovery is not so much a linguistic one as that of fantasy in general. To recognize this dimension of fantasy is both to require a theory appropriate to the image and to contribute to its establishment in the full recognition of its semantic dimension.

I will not take into account in my critique of the linguistic reformulations of psychoanalysis the reproach that is usually made against them—that they do not take into account the dynamic and economic aspects of unconscious phenomena, that they fail to say anything about the affects where the properly pulsional aspect of these phenomena is expressed nonlinguistically. I will suggest in concluding, however, that a theory of fantasy is perhaps more likely to account for the articulation of both the semiotic and the pulsional dimensions of psychoanalysis than is a linguistic theory. My critique, therefore, will stay within the limits set by the theoreticians of the linguistic approach.

I began by accepting that the analytic technique is one that makes language its field of action and the privileged instrument of its efficacy. The difficulty for me does not concern the discourse within which the analytic process unfolds, but that other discourse which is slowly confirmed through this type of discourse and which it has to explicate—I mean the discourse of the complexes enslaved in the unconscious.[10]

That these complexes should have an affinity for discourse, that they are sayable in principle, is not to be doubted. Therefore the analytic situation itself establishes a semiotic aspect. Moreover, that the phenomena thus brought to light are governed by relations of motivation that here take the place of what the natural sciences define as a causal relation, and that these relations are immediately constitutive of a history susceptible of being recounted, also is attested to by the narrative repetition that analysis produces. But none of this proves that what thus comes to language—or better, is brought to language—is or must *be* language. On the contrary, because the level of expression proper to the unconscious is not language, the work of interpretation is difficult and constitutes a veritable linguistic promotion.

1 THE IMAGE AS DREAM-WORK

Freud directly addressed himself to this problem in section C of the sixth chapter of *The Interpretation of Dreams*, entitled "Die Darstellungsmittel des Traums" (*G.W.*,

10. I borrow these terms from E. Benveniste's "Remarques sur la fonction du langage dans la découverte freudienne," in his *Problèmes de linguistic générale* (pp. 75–87).

2/3 : 315). The Standard Edition translates this as "The Means of Representation in Dreams." He begins with the fact that once the dream is interpreted, it presents numerous logical relations, including antithesis and contradiction, as well as conditions and consequences. In fact, every logical relation appears that finds appropriate expression in the syntax of our natural languages—if, because, identity, although, either/or, and so forth. Now it is not an accidental characteristic of dreams that they "have no means at their disposal for representing these logical representations between the dream-thoughts. For the most part dreams disregard all those conjunctions and it is only the substantive content [*den sachlichen Inhalt*] of the dream-thoughts that they take over and manipulate. The restoration of the connections which the dream-work has destroyed is a task which has to be performed by the interpretative process" (*S.E.*, 4 : 312). This incapacity of the dream to express logical relations is not a simple lack of the proper means. It is the counterpart of a positive feature which Freud calls "the psychical material [*psychisches Material*] out of which dreams are made" (ibid.). This psychical material, which may be compared with the plastic arts of painting and sculpture, is nothing other than the image, but the image constituted in its capacity to express or indicate plastically the dream ideas, as the term *Darstellung* (which originally signified *exhibitio*) conveys.[11] The dream-thoughts thus become (and are called) "dream-images."[12]

11. "But just as the art of painting eventually found a way of expressing, by means other than the floating labels, at least the *intention* of the words [*die Redeabsicht*] of the personages represented—affection, threats, warnings, and so on—so too there is a possible means by which dreams can take account of some of the logical relations between their dream-thoughts, by making an appropriate modification in the method of representation characteristic of dreams" (*S.E.*, 4 : 313–14). A long enumeration follows of the various processes by means of which the different logical relations are figured in the dream.

12. The *Standard Edition* translates *Bild* as either "image" or "picture," depending on the context (see, for example, 5 : 344, where both terms are used).

This exhibiting of the dream content in images, far from constituting a contingent feature of the dream-work, is in reality implied in the two major processes of condensation and displacement, for which we have attempted to give a linguistic and, more exactly, a semiotic interpretation. As section D of the same chapter—"Considerations of Representability [*Darstellbarkeit*]"—establishes, these two processes build on the ruins of the logical relations. Here Freud describes the heart of the "pictorial" (*bildlich*) expression:

> A thing that is pictorial [*das Bildliche*] is, from the point of view of a dream, a thing that is *capable of being represented* [*darstellungsfähig*]: it can be introduced into a situation in which abstract expressions offer the same kind of difficulties to representation in dreams as a politcal leading article in a newspaper would offer an illustrator. [*S.E.*, 5 : 339–40]

Here we are at the juncture of image and language, since on the one hand the creation of images consists in large part of a "visual representation" (p. 344) of the dream processes, and on the other hand of a "pictorial language" (p. 340) which has to do just with the concrete terms used. It is with regard to this, moreover, that Freud comments on the kinship between the dream and wit,[13] as he did earlier with regard to the rebus and as he will do again a few lines later with regard to hieroglyphics. The concept of representability, therefore, designates a work-

13. "In this way the whole domain of verbal wit is put at the disposal of the dream-work. There is no need to be astonished at the part played by words in dream-formation. Words, since they are the nodal points of numerous ideas, may be regarded as predestined to ambiguity; and the neuroses (e.g. in framing obsessions and phobias), no less than dreams, make unashamed use of the advantages thus offered by words for purposes of condensation and disguise. It is easy to show that dream-distortion, too, profits from displacement of expression" (5 : 340–41).

ing level where the kinship between condensation, displacement, and disguise is affirmed and which joins the figured aspects of language to the spatial and visual unfolding of a spectacle.

It is remarkable that condensation and displacement should be mentioned in the same context (see n. 13) with regard to words and visual images, as though these rhetorical figures and visual images belonged to the same realm of "representability." Yet the ancient rhetoricians had already noticed that a figured language is one that gives a contour or a visibility to discourse. Consequently, the problem is not so much that we find words in dreams and that the dream-work should be close to the "verbal wit" which governs jokes, but that language functions at a pictorial level which brings it into the neighborhood of the visual image and vice versa.

And it seems to me that we should interpret in the same fashion what in the next section Freud calls "representation by symbols" (pp. 350 ff.). As is well known, Freud reserves the term *symbol* for representations that have a certain fixity ("like the 'grammalogues' in shorthand," p. 351) and which belong to the oldest heritage of culture. This is why they are not limited to dreams but also may be found in folklore, popular myths, legends, linguistic idioms, popular wisdom, and current jokes. We may say that these symbols belong to the sphere of language if we mean by this not that they belong to the structure of a natural language or to individual speech, but to the things said, which by an effect of sedimentation are assimilated to the very code of the language and incorporated into speech. They thus become an integral part of what we call "language" in the broad sense of the term, which encompasses its structure, the dynamism of speech, and the heritage of symbolism.

But to recognize the linguistic character of symbolism—or what I would prefer to call its character of linguisticality, in order to emphasize that it is a question of a sedimented use of speech which mimics the anonymous character of language—constitutes only half the truth. The problem of psychoanalysis begins with the private use by the dreamer of this public treasury of symbols. And it is here that the symbol, first inscribed in language in the sense just mentioned, now inscribes itself in the image. Freud says this not only in his title, "Representation by Symbols" (where the instrumental character of the symbol in relation to the representation of the dream is made evident by the preposition *durch*), but also in the text: "Dreams make use of this symbolism for the disguised representation of their latent thoughts" (p. 352). It is a question, therefore, of "indirect methods of representation" (p. 351). In other words, the problem for interpretation is not the symbol's belonging to the verbal treasury of humanity, but its "pictorial" use by the dream. In this sense, the symbol is to be aligned with condensation, displacement, figured language, and the visual image—all processes arising from the same "considerations of representability."

Of course, if the psychoanalyst does not have a knowledge of symbols—that is, if he is not familiar with the verbal treasury of culture—the interpretation of the symbols in the dream is impossible. But it is their use in combination with other dream processes that allows them to be interpreted in a given situation. Thus, as Freud notices, they usually have more than one signification "and, as with Chinese script, the correct interpretation can only be arrived at on each occasion from the context" (p. 353). So the dream does not contain unadorned fragments of the cultural symbols. These are dramatized according to the need of the dream under consideration.[14]

14. This is why Freud warns us against any mechanical translation of symbols and against abandoning the associative technique of the dreamer in ques-

PAUL RICOEUR   317

When such symbols belonging to the whole of humanity organize a dream, we may speak not only of a representation by means of symbols, but also of a "typical
dream."[15] But this is through an abstraction from the individual history which makes singular use of such stereotypes. In reality, it is always about an individual dreamer
that we say it is he who puts together or exhibits the universal cultural motif. In this process of putting something
together, the realm of the image and its employment in
language is once again confirmed.[16]

I will conclude these remarks devoted to the image in
The Interpretation of Dreams by emphasizing one fundamental characteristic of the image that is implicit in the
whole analysis: *the image itself is not a content, but a process.*

---

tion. The translation of symbols must remain an auxiliary method (see p. 360).
It is easy to see why this is so, since to do otherwise would be to deny the
dream-work.

15. "It would be possible to mention a whole number of other 'typical'
dreams if we take the term to mean that the same manifest dream-content is
frequently to be found in the dreams of different dreamers" (p. 395).

16. As regards the place of the subject matter of "typical dreams" in *The Interpretation of Dreams,* it is noteworthy that Freud treats their content not in the
framework of the dream-work, but within the framework of the "material and
sources of dreams" (4 : 241 ff.), hence before the sixth chapter, on dream-
work. There Freud extensively presents the Oedipal dream in correlation with
Sophocles' drama (pp. 260 ff.). This confirms our thesis that the symbolism as
such belongs to the dream material and not yet to the dream-work. (Freud
even speaks of a primeval dream-material with regard to the points common to
the drama and the dream; see p. 263.) If the question of symbolism, and with it
that of the typical dream, occurs a second time (in chapter 6, section D), it is
from the point of view of the use of the symbolism, and not of its content. This
use rejoins the symbolism to the "means of representation," and therefore to
the problem of the image. That this distinction should be difficult to maintain
in practice is attested to amply by the rejected anticipations of 6D in 5D, and
the apologetic explanations of the section on typical dreams in chapter 5 (for
example, pp. 241–42). The section on symbolism in chapter 6 was not added
until 1914 and a part of the material from 5D was transferred to the new section. Thus, the division we are considering there between the content and the
use of symbols is in fact intentional and deliberate (see the editor's notes on pp.
xii and 242, n. 1).

That is why I call this section "The Image as Dream-Work." The image, in effect, is not distinct from the dream-work. It is the very process of transformation of the dream-thoughts into the manifest content. That is why Freud speaks of "considerations of representability." It is a process, like Kant's schema, which is a general procedure for obtaining an image for a concept.

It is this suggestion that I will pursue in the remainder of my essay, by seeking to discover other aspects of the process of putting the dream-thoughts and symbols into an image, as described in *The Interpretation of Dreams*.

2   THE IMAGE-FAMILY

Until now, my presentation has unfolded within the circle of the dream images. But the dream has made us constantly refer to other manifestations of the imaginary life: folklore, legends, myths, literary fictions, works of plastic art, and so forth. In what sense must we assign them to the same level of psychical operations? More specifically, are there any common features of this level of operation that might be characterized as what I have called elsewhere "a space of fantasy" (1976)?

The unity of this space is not easily recognized because of the diversity of situations where it occurs (waking and sleeping), the diversity of levels of its efficacy (from hallucinations to the work of art), and the diversity of its media (language, sensory images, plastic works inscribed on canvas or in stone, and so forth). Freud's vocabulary betrays this uncertainty. The term *Phantasieren,* for example—which we have not encountered to this point, having spoken so far only of the dream-images (*Traumbilder*)—oscillates between two uses.

The first and more narrow use applies to the symbolic constructions of early childhood, also called "primitive scenes," which are presented as true memories but which are largely fictive. It is this sense that Freud uses in section B of chapter 7, when he discusses "regression." Regression to the image is presented as a quasi-hallucinatory revivification of perceptual images[17] and a reemergence of the fantasies grafted onto infantile experience.[18] It is easy to see how the old psychology of the image as a revivification of a perceptive trace resists the psychoanalytic discovery of the constructed character of the fantasm. But it remains true that in these contexts the "fantasy" is closely bound to the scenario of the infantile scene.

But there is another use of the term *Phantasieren,* which is given in the title of the brief essay entitled "Der Dichter und das Phantasieren" (1908), badly translated as "Creative Writers and Day-Dreaming" (in *S.E.,* vol. 9). The term *Phantasieren* there is not assigned to real day-dreaming, but to the graduated scale of mental productions ranging from dream fantasms and neuroses at one extreme to poetic creations at the other, and passing through children's games, adults' day-dreams, heroic legends, and psychological novels. What unifies this field is, of course, the underlying common motivation— namely, the model of wish-fulfillment (*Wunscherfüllung*) furnished by the interpretation of dreams and analogically extended to these diverse mental productions. But this unity of motivation is not established unless we can identify the common mediation by means of the image and imagination which is comparable to the process of the dream-work. So we must now attempt to identify the noteworthy features of this imaginary mediation.

We already know the first one: it may be called the

17. *"In regression the fabric of the dream-thoughts is resolved into its raw material"* (5 : 543; Freud's italics).

18. "On this view a dream might be described as a *substitute for an infantile scene modified by being transferred onto a recent experience"* (p. 546; Freud's italics).

character of figurability, if we recall the "considerations of representability" in *The Interpretation of Dreams*. But the creation of a sensory image proper to the dream is not the only expression of this figurability. We have seen that figured language, common to dreams and jokes, is equally part of this figurability. Language, too, is figurable. And figurability also applies to plastic representation. Thus, for example, "The Moses of Michelangelo" (1914, *S.E.*, 13 : 211–36) presents the equivalent of a figured discourse in stone. This analysis, moreover, replaces the conflict incarnated in the stone by a discourse [19] and thus leads back from the stone figure to the text of the Book of Exodus, thereby revealing the fictive narrative common to both Scripture and the statue.

This last remark leads us to a second characteristic of the fantastic as such, which founds the analogy of its various incarnations. This is its character of being basically substitutable. Here the semiotic character of the image comes to the forefront. An image has the sign's capacity to stand for, to take the place of, or to replace something else. It is in this way that dreams are "typical." Not just, as we say, because they are common to several dreamers, but because their content is the structural invariant that allows a dream and a myth to stand for each other, as Freud discovered as early as the time of his self-analysis.[20] This movable structure allows Freud in his interpretation of dreams to move smoothly from a dream image to a proverb, a quotation from a poet, a joke, a colloquial expression, a myth. And this equivalence between such different expressions allows me to return to my previous suggestion that the image in its dynamic function has an obvious kinship with the Kantian schema, which is

19. "What we see before us is not the inception of a violent action but what remains of a movement that has already taken place" (13 : 229).
20. Letter to Fliess, October 15, 1897 (*S.E.*, 1 : 265).

not an "image" in the sense of a dead mental presence, but a procedure or method for providing images to concepts. In the same way, what we are calling the structural invariant is nothing other than the cross-reference from one variant to another, be it dream, symptom, myth, or tale. It is one of the functions of the dream-work to make this invariant work in the way proper to the situation of sleep—that is, in the condition of a lack of inhibition. And it is the function of the work of interpretation to follow the inverse route of that taken by the dream-work, both works being guided by the dynamics of the schematic image.

I should like now to introduce a third feature beyond those of figurability and substitutability, a feature that is more suggested by the reading of Freud's writings than explicitly stated by him. If we return to the ambiguity of the word *Phantasieren* in German—an ambiguity reflected in Freud's use of the term—is it not true that it belongs to the fantastic as such to display several levels and to oscillate among them? At the bottom of the scale we have the infantile fantasy, in which the image is caught in the regressive movement described in chapter 6, section B, of *The Interpretation of Dreams.* Here the image has quasi-hallucinatory features but at the same time presents the minimal factor of being a symbolic construction, what Lacan calls the primary historization of the child's experience. At the top of the scale, *Phantasieren* comes close to *Dichten.* It is, in one sense of this word, a fiction—in the sense of an invention embodied in stone or on canvas or in language. Whereas the "infantile scene is unable to bring about its own revival and has to be content with returning as a dream" (*S.E.,* 5 : 546), the fiction has the public existence of a work of art or of language.

This polarity of imagination is exemplified in one place in Freud's essay, "Leonardo da Vinci and a Memory of

his Childhood" (*S.E.*, 11 : 63–137). The captive mode of
Phantasieren finds expression in the fantasy of the vulture
opening the infant's mouth with its tail. This fantasy displays its substitutive value in a series of equivalent pictures ranging from the image of the maternal breast to
hieroglyphic writings and the mythical image of the phallic mother, or some infantile theory on sex, and the like.
The creative mode of *Phantasieren* finds expression in the
invention—in the strong sense of the word—of the different expressions of the famous Leonardesque smile.
Freud himself suggests "that in these figures Leonardo
has denied [*Verleuget*] the unhappiness of his erotic life
and has triumphed over it in his art [*und Kunstlisch über-
winden*]" (p. 118).

If I am correct in this interpretation of *Phantasieren,*
then Freud has summarized in this opposition between
mere fantasy and creative work the enigma of sublimation, which he did not think he had solved (cf. 11 : 136).
But in any case, we are able here to duplicate the economic scale from regression to sublimation with the scale
of *Phantasieren* and to display this scale within a unique
space of fantasy.[21]

21. In this essay I have made as little use as possible of Freud's metapsychology in order to let the psychoanalytic experience correct the theory.
Could we not say, nevertheless, that Freud was very well aware that language as
such was not the key issue in psychoanalysis and that, for that very reason, he
called *Vorstellung* the ideational "representatives" (*Repräsentant*) of the *Treib*? I
take this expression, borrowed from the German philosophical tradition, as
equivalent to what I have called the semiotic dimension, which is only partially
linguistic and fundamentally figurative, but nevertheless significative. For a discussion of Freud's use of *Vorstellung*, mainly in the metapsychological papers,
see my *Freud and Philosophy*, pp. 115–50, and "Psychoanalysis and the Work of
Art," pp. 19–21. A decisive question for metapsychology is whether the recognition of the privileged imaginative level of the processes described by Freud
does not make the articulation of the economic and the semiotic aspects of psychoanalysis intelligible, whereas a purely linguistic theory seems to make them
almost incomprehensible.

In conclusion, I want to emphasize once more that by underscoring the reference of psychoanalysis to this space of fantasy I do not intend to provide a refutation of the linguistic reformulations of psychoanalysis. What has to be preserved from them is the emphasis on the semiotic dimension of the expressions of the unconscious. Because we do not have a theory of imagination at our disposal that does justice to this semiotic dimension, it is natural that we tend to ascribe to language all that is semiotic. But what is specific in the psychoanalytic discovery is that language itself works at the pictorial level. This discovery is not only a call for an appropriate theory of the imagination, but a decisive contribution to it.

REFERENCES

Benveniste, E. *Problèmes de linguistic générale*. Paris: Gallimard, 1966.
Edelson, M. *Language and Interpretation in Psychoanalysis*. New Haven: Yale University Press, 1975.
Freud, S. *Standard Edition of the Complete Psychological Works*. London: Hogarth, 1953–66.
 "Extracts from the Fliess Papers" (1950 [1892–99]), vol. 1.
 Studies on Hysteria (1893–95) (with J. Breuer), vol. 2.
 The Interpretation of Dreams (1900–01), vols. 4, 5.
 "Creative Writers and Day-Dreaming" (1908), vol. 9.
 "Leonardo da Vinci and a Memory of His Childhood" (1910), vol. 11.
 "The Antithetical Meaning of Primal Words" (1910), vol. 11.
 "Remembering, Repeating and Working-through" (1914), vol. 12.
 "The Moses of Michelangelo" (1914), vol. 13.
Lacan, J. *Ecrits I*. Paris: Seuil, 1966.
Ricoeur, P. *Freud and Philosophy*. New Haven: Yale University Press, 1970.

————. "Psychoanalysis and the Work of Art." In J. H. Smith, ed., *Psychiatry and the Humanities*, vol. 1. New Haven: Yale University Press, 1976.

Sherwood, M. *The Logic of Explanation in Psychoanalysis*. New York: Academic Press, 1969.

9

Freudian Explanations and the Language of the Unconscious

Arthur C. Danto

> *Socrates:* Well, now, I wonder whether you would agree in my explanation of this phenomenon.
> *Protarchus:* What is your explanation?
> *Socrates:* I think that the soul at such times is like a book.
> *Protarchus:* How so?
> *Socrates:* Memory and perception meet, and they and their attendant feelings seem to me almost to write down words in the soul, and when the inscribing feeling writes truly, then true opinion[s] . . . come into our souls—but when the scribe within us writes falsely, the result is false.
>
> —Plato, *Philebus,* 38–39

> There is no element whatever of man's consciousness which has not something corresponding to it in the word; and the reason is obvious. It is, that the word or sign the man uses *is* the man himself. For, as the fact that every thought is a sign, taken in conjunction with the fact that life is a train of thought, proves that man is a sign. . . . Thus my language is the sum total of myself; for the man is the thought.
>
> —C. S. Peirce, *Collected Works,* 5 : 314

I

Freudian theory is sometimes treated as though it licenses a hermeneutical overlay on all our thought and conduct, none of which really and deeply means what we would suppose it does without benefit of that theory, and none of which is properly explained in the ways we would spontaneously explain it. It is as though Freud had discovered a system of 'signatures' on the basis of which we decipher conduct, read through to its final, ulterior signification, decode its surface meaning: whatever we do, and however fantastically various the modes of our behavior, the final meaning is everywhere and barrenly the same—so much so that one need hardly unriddle the signatures anymore, knowing in advance that the same dismal, fatal note sounds throughout—like the echo in the Marabar Caves.

Freud himself implied nothing quite so leveling or mechanical, and though certain everyday occurrences—slip-ups and errors, lapses of memory, and preeminently dreams—proved, according to his theory, to have a purpose in the economies of mental life scarcely appreciated before him, and even to be intentional enough to be explained through reasons rather than (mere) causes, Freud resisted treating all conduct as only symptomatical, as he resisted the dissolutive explanatory temptations of what he disparagingly spoke of as Pansexuality. I believe that if we examine the structures of psychoanalytical explanation, we shall find a deep argument less against Freud himself than against the insensitive generalization of his theories that aims at absorbing the whole of thought and conduct to a simple explanatory principle. It is an argument peculiarly against wholesale Freudianism itself, and not against absorbing the whole of conduct to some single explanatory principle, whatever may be the arguments available against that sort of reductionism.

Philosophers have sometimes resisted such reductions through mounting one or another version of what are termed Paradigm Case arguments: if one learns the meaning of a term T with reference to certain instances, then of those instances we cannot coherently with the meaning rules of our language deny that these instances are *T*. Freudianism, then, is accused of traducing these meaning rules and collapsing into nonsense, entailing the inapplicability of just those terms we know best how to employ and through which we describe what is closest to us as humans. But, the argument continues, we cannot intelligibly sacrifice these uses without in effect sacrificing the forms of human life we live. Or, it has been argued to whatever effect, Freud expanded immensely the denotation of such a term as "sexual" while holding its connotation constant, a simultaneous dilation and contraction in meaning under which the concept suffers semantical fracture, so much so that it no longer can be clear what the theory comes to. I have no great sympathy with this style of argument, or with the conceptual conservatism its use enfranchises, but I have no interest in pausing to harass the tattered regiments of common-usage philosophy.

My argument turns, rather, on certain features of *representation* that figure prominently in Freud's striking explanation of dreams and symptomologies. What I want to maintain is that representations could not have these features if they did not have those other features through which they cause thought and conduct in non-Freudian ways.[1] Roughly, my thesis has this form: it is impossible,

---

1. By causes in "non-Freudian ways," I have in mind cases in which something is at once a cause and also a reason for something else. For example, (1) I perform an action *a* because I believe that *b* will happen if *a* happens, and I mean for *b* to happen. Here the belief is my reason for doing *a*, and is arguably the cause of it as well; and (2) I believe that *p* because I believe that *q*, where believing *q* is my reason for believing *p*, and also arguably the cause of my doing so. By contrast, Freud cites any number of cases in *The Psychopathology of Everyday Life* in which one thinks that *s* because one thinks that *t*, but where in no sense is the latter a reason, but only a cause for the former. That reasons can be causes is classically argued by Donald Davidson in his "Actions, Reasons, and

much as it is impossible for every description to be metaphorical,[2] for every term to be a pun. And Freudian explanations involve, typically, a punning transformation of
terms, dreams, and symptoms, having as their roots plays
on words.

Let us consider a somewhat strange example of 'mental
causation' offered by G. E. M. Anscombe as preliminary
to our discussion: "A child saw a bit of red stuff on a turn
in a stairway and asked what it was. He thought his nurse
told him it was a bit of Satan and felt a dreadful fear of it.
(No doubt she said it was a bit of satin.) What he was
frightened of was the bit of stuff: the cause of his fright
was his nurse's remark" (1957, p. 16). The child was
afraid of something (ribbon, say) that does not ordinarily
elicit fear, and the etiology of the phobia enlists a factor
that, we shall see, is going to play a considerable role in
Freud's theory: an unwitting play on words. The child is
(rightly, in view of his religious education) afraid of
Satan. The nurse says what is on the stair is some satin: so
the child is afraid of what is on the stair—I assume a
parity of phonetic values between the two words that does
not quite carry over into Middle American speech. I can
imagine a child growing to adulthood with a curious,

Causes" (1963,p. 23). *How* they can be is elaborated in my "Action, Knowledge,
and Representation" (1976), which in its turn clarifies the analysis developed in
my *Analytical Philosophy of Action* (1974).

   2. This is true for quite trivial reasons—namely, the *concept* of metaphoric
presupposes the concept of literal usage—but there are far deeper reasons.
Josef Stern, a doctoral candidate at Columbia University, has made the clever
discovery that metaphors are intensional, or at least nonextensional. I cite this
fact without elaborating on it since I want it a matter of record that Stern has
made this breakthrough and is the first, to my knowledge, to have recognized
this crucial feature of metaphors, which puts an end to those wooly genialities
that "it is all a matter of degree." Stern's own work on the semantics of metaphor, from what I have seen of it, will pretty much render whatever has been
written on the subject, from Aristotle to Ricoeur and Goodman, happily obso-
lete.

mysterious fear of red satin, which his therapist will be
able to explain (and perhaps cure) only to the extent that
he can archeologize this early, forgotten episode: like
someone who finds himself unable to see Greece because
as a child he had a fastidious mother.

Using now a Saussurian distinction between the signifier (*signifiant*) and the signified (*signifié*)—between sign
(sound image) and meaning—we have, as it were, two
phonetically indiscriminable signs with quite discrimi-
nable meanings: and what has happened is that the child
has effected an interchange of signifieds, in consequence
of which his subsequent behavior is manifestly weird.
This sort of interchange presupposes properties of representations—in this instance associated phonetic values—
distinct from their meanings, inseparable from their representational properties. Then what I want to claim is that
signs (representations) can be causal through both sorts
of properties, so that there are two distinct ways in which
they may enter explanations, much as there are two distinct ways in which they enter communication. In Freudian explanations, they are, as in Anscombe's example,
causal through confusions of meaning of the sorts exemplified in puns. And confusions of meaning of this
order are not possible unless signs have fixed meanings to
confuse. But the distinction is crucial, and there is a difference in logic that we are constrained to mark depending upon which of the two ways in which a sign in fact occurs. Let me illustrate this by commenting on a famous
pun.

Grice, to bring out a point in his discussions of conver-
sational implicature, cites the dispatch sent by a British
general upon his conquest of Sind: *"Peccavi."* [3] This, as

3. This comes up but only en passant, in his William James Lectures (Harvard, 1971), which to my knowledge have never been published, and in my
belief never will be (alas!). I read them in a bootleg version, barely legible.

Latinists appreciate, translates into the English sentence
"I have sinned," which then admits the punning "I have
Sind"—a turn of wit that would have been impossible
with the latter-day name of approximately the same terri-
tory, Pakistan. The general, as it happens, was Sir Charles
Napier,[4] and he was not just announcing his victory in a
remarkably arch way; he also was saying that he had, *literally,* sinned in winning, that his means were morally rep-
robate, and indeed they were—as anyone who reads
those pages in the British conquest of India recognizes.
There was, in fact, a major debate in England over the
rightness of his conduct of his campaign. My concerns
here remain logical rather than moral, however; I wish to
comment upon the overdetermination of his message as a
linguistic specimen.

For one thing, we lose the overdetermination if we
translate the message into any language but English—for
example, *ho peccato, Ich habe gesündigt, j'ai péché,* all lose the
sounds that make the pun possible. And it is the sounds in
particular that I am thinking of as properties of the signifier in abstraction of the signified. Translation is a particularly good test of whether such features of signifiers
play a significant role in the content of any given message. Thus, it is a fair assumption that translations must
be truth-preserving: that *S'* cannot be a good translation
of *S* if *S* and *S'* differ in truth value. For example, "Paris
has five letters" obviously refers to the word rather than
to the city. If we translate the statement into Italian this
way, "Parigi ha cinque lettere," we get something obviously false. So it would only be a matter of luck that
"Paris hat funf Buchstaben" comes out right. Phrases
whose semantics involve reference to signs as *significant*
are made true or false on the basis of properties of these

4. I owe the historical precision to my friend and colleague, the noted In-
dianist Ainslie Embree.

as entities—not on the basis of properties of their *sig-nifications* or their normal referenda. And it is these language-locked features of signs that play the central role in much of psychoanalytical explanation. These are, as it were, textual features that are lost or sacrificed when the texts are translated, and which, because they are *entities* as much as cities or stones, are untranslatable in this dimension of their being; it is only in their status as significant that we can translate them by finding equivalent signs having the same meaning.

Let me, before proceeding to our structures, cite two examples, both from French psychoanalysts who are especially sensitive to these factors, which turn on essentially untranslatable features of signs that nevertheless play an important part in the analysis of conduct. These examples, if they are sound, imply something crucial about psychoanalysis as well as about us: our conduct is deeply involved in these features of our own language, so much so that it would not be possible, one feels, to psychoanalyze a person whose language one did not know— say, by using a translator.[5] The wider implications of this I shall defer until later in the paper.

5. In a footnote added in 1909, Freud cites an observation by Dr. Alfred Robitsek, that "the oriental 'dream-books' (of which ours are wretched imitations) base the greater number of their interpretations of dream-elements upon similarity of sounds and resemblance between words. The fact that these connections inevitably disappear in translation accounts for the unintelligibility of the renderings in our own popular dream-books." He goes on to observe that "Indeed, dreams are so closely related to linguistic expression that Ferenczi has truly remarked that every tongue has its own dream-language. It is impossible as a rule to translate a dream into a foreign language, and this is equally true, I fancy, of a book such as the present one" (Freud, 1900, p. 99 n.). Whether in charity or out of some human—all too human—impulse, Freud added the comical observation in 1930 that "Dr. A. A. Brill . . . and others after him, have succeeded in translating *The Interpretation of Dreams*." This footnote, to which my attention has been drawn by my student John Rajkman, supporting as it does the *logical* analysis of my text, must raise a fresh question about reading Freud in a language other than the one in which he wrote.

The first example comes from Jacques Lacan. It is
always difficult to know when he is being serious, as he is
a profoundly frivolous writer, but he draws the example itself from a study by Freud of fetishism, which gives it a
measure of validity. Nevertheless, Lacan's own sensibil-
ities make him alive to features in the example that might
have been utterly lost to someone who thought merely in
the explanatory frameworks of street-corner psychotherapy. Here, then, is a man who can achieve sexual satisfaction only when something is shining on his partner's
nose—a *Glanz auf der Nase*. Let me quote Lacan's gloss:

> Analysis showed that his early, English-speaking
> years had seen the displacement of the burning curi-
> osity which he felt for the phallus of his mother, that
> is for that eminent failure-to-be the privileged sig-
> nification of which Freud revealed to us, into a *glance
> at the nose* in the forgotten language of his childhood,
> rather than a *shine on the nose*. [1970, p. 131]

Here the transformation from *glance at the nose* to *Glanz
auf der Nase* contains two elements it is important to distinguish. The nose may indeed be a visual metaphor for
the penis. It is explicitly so treated in one of Goya's *Capri-
chos—El Vergonzozo*—and Goya writes in his sardonic ac-
companying commentary: "It would be a good thing if
those with such obscene faces were to hide them in their
pants." And perhaps "the nose" is an infantile usage for
what certainly at the time could not have been designated
by its right name with propriety. But, and this is the
point, the nose has the appropriate shape to function in
almost a universal lexicon as a substitute symbol for the
penis.

Freud, at times in *The Interpretation of Dreams,* supposes
that there might almost be a universal lexicon of such
symbolic equivalents: "All elongated objects . . . sticks,

tree-trunks and umbrellas . . . all sharp weapons, such as knives, daggers, and pikes" represent the male member. "Boxes, cases, chests, cupboards and ovens" correspond to the female organ, also cavities, "ships, and vessels of all kinds." "Small animals and vermin represent small children" (1900, pp. 354–57). Freud is perhaps insufficiently sensitive to cultural parochialisms, which in some measure restrict the universal obviousness of some of these symbols, but in any case, the connection between the English *glance* and the German *Glanz* (and note that the English word has to be spoken in a British accent to get the phonetic equivalence) is not at all of this order of equivalence: it is a substitution that goes through only at the level of sound, and is so bound up with the physical qualities of spoken language that to destroy Freud's explanation it would suffice to show that the person involved had never known English, even if he indeed had had the more typical Freudian curiosity alluded to.

Let me bring the difference out this way: There is a painting by Titian of *Venus with the Lute Player*. Venus is holding a flute, and it is disgustingly easy to give this a "Freudian interpretation." It could be given, moreover, by anyone who knows the game of "elongated objects." In the corner lies a *viol d'amore*. The term "viol" carries implications, at the phonetic level, of rape. (Think of the condensation in *Finnegans Wake*, where Joyce writes, almost at the beginning, of "Sir Tristram, violer d'amores. . . .") Did Titian intend this connotation of sexual violation? I have absolutely no idea, but my point is less one in iconography than psycholinguistics: unlike the flute, the viola can be read as *that* sort of symbol only by someone in whose language there is a phonetic parity between the two pertinent senses of *viol.*

My second illustration comes from the well-known paper on the unconscious by Jean Laplanche and Serge

Leclaire. Much of it turns on the analysis of a dream, in which a girl, Liliane, appears. I chose to discuss a dream since my first example concerned a symptom. The dreamer and the girl are in a forest, and at a certain point a unicorn crosses their path and "we walk, all three of us, toward a clearing that we suppose is below" (p. 48). With the substance of the dream analysis I shall not be concerned, but I want to remark on this: The French word for unicorn is *licorne,* and as the analysis proceeds, the first syllable, which is morphemically indiscernible from the French word for bed (*lit*), becomes important. It also appears in the name Lili, which echoes also the infantine word for milk (*lolo*), and a complex content is gradually found in the dream through these echoes. I have no idea whether their analysis is in fact sound. All I wish to say is that it is based not upon any properties of unicorns as such, but on the *word*—in French—for unicorn. And furthermore, that an American, having just the same dream, could not have it represent what it does in French: there is no phonetic echo between "uni-" and "bed"—much less "Lili" and "milk."

To be sure, the single protruding horn can have, in virtue of Freud's glossary, a phallic significance transcending language: it is not an accidental application of a theory of sympathetic resemblances that the Chinese should have regarded pulverized rhinoceros horn as an aphrodisiac. If we translate the dream, we lose its meaning utterly. Part of the meaning of the dream is given by features of the description of it in which words are mentioned rather than used. It is the *word* "licorne" *as a word* that carries the symbolic charge; and it is just these sounds that do not carry over, here or elsewhere, into a translation. The same bedeviling properties haunt the psychoanalyst as haunt the translator of a poem, whose meaning resides in part in the acoustic or graphic identity of the words it is composed of, and not merely in what these words might mean, which can, in principle, simply enough be transferred to verbal equivalents in another language. The translation of a poem has to be more than a translation: it has to be a reconstruction preserving the music of the sounds, so far as this is possible. We dream in our own languages in such a way that only someone who knows the language can unriddle the dream. And this, I think, goes a certain distance toward illuminating the claim advanced in the epigraphs to this paper—that we are built as a text is built. "We are such stuff as dreams are made on," if we see Shakespeare's line through Freudian lenses.

II

I want now to discuss for a moment some questions about the unconscious—the *Ucs.* system, as Freud designates it. I think a good beginning in the philosophical analysis of unconscious beliefs has been made by Arthur Collins in his 1969 paper "Unconscious Beliefs," though I think it does not go as far as it ought in explaining how unconscious beliefs are possible.

Begin by considering a well-known asymmetry between the avowal and the ascription of belief: I cannot say that I believe that p, but p is false, but I can without tension say that *you* believe that p, but p is false. Imagine that a therapist ascribes to me the belief that competition is dangerous; *he* need not believe that competition is dangerous in order to say that *I* do. Suppose he ascribes this belief to me on the basis of a great deal of evidence—namely, on the basis of my avoiding competitive situations, or failing whenever I am in them though it is plain enough that I could have succeeded instead; this might be the case, for instance, if I went to a therapist with a complaint of impotence and there was no physiological basis for my failure to secure erection. But I could also fail examinations of all sorts, and just the ordinary Tests of Life—getting a decent job, finding a romantic partner, and so forth. The therapist acquaints me with this evidence. I accept his explanation: it makes sense of a great deal of my conduct. To be sure, I do not consciously believe that competition is dangerous *as such*. But I do—I may say—believe it unconsciously. There is no contradiction here of the sort that affects "I believe that *p*, but *p* is false," a contradiction (of whatever sort) that we now see implies a presumption of consciousness. So "I believe that *p* (unconsciously), but *p* is false" is a possible utterance. The upshot, then, is this: a belief of mine is unconscious if (1) I can believe it is false while knowing it to be mine, and (2) I come to know it is my belief on the basis of the same sort of evidence upon which I know what your beliefs are.

In Collins's view, the *Ucs.* system is, in effect, an Other Mind. Needless to say, none of this has to imply, even if true, that the knowledge of the truth will set me free: knowledge need not entail cure. But I would like to shelve therapeutic considerations completely, and just stick to the philosophical points. And admirable as Collins's analysis is, I think one point in it that is overlooked is the *peculiarity* of unconscious beliefs. He has addressed himself only to certain epistemological disparities and parities; he maintains that none of our ordinary beliefs can be unconsciously held and has overlooked the possibility that "competition is dangerous" could be a perfectly ordinary belief. And is the difference between conscious beliefs and unconscious beliefs merely the difference between conscious and unconscious? Note that this would make the patient's conduct altogether rational in the sense that doing what he does would be exactly right *if he held the belief to be true:* it would be paradigmatic of rational conduct. Of course, he may fail to satisfy a test of rationality in that he believes p and also does not believe it; but as I indicated, this inconsistency is exactly muted if we qualify the belief ascriptions as conscious and unconscious, just as there is no incoherence in "I believe that p, and you don't." After all, Collins's view is more or less that the unconscious is an Other Mind.

A degree of progress has been made on the matter by Peter Alexander (1963), who has argued brilliantly that a condition for a belief as an unconscious reason for conduct is that it *would not be a reason if it were conscious.* And this suggests a stronger criterion than any we have so far encountered, for after all, it is wholly reasonable to assume that the beliefs of Other Minds at least are conscious to them—*they* must believe them true if they believe them at all; and all Collins has furnished us with in distinguishing consciousness from unconsciousness is this difference between self-knowledge and other-knowledge. It is only complicating psychology to say that our unconscious is an Other Mind to us.

As indicated above, Collins says that none of our ordinary beliefs can be unconsciously held. But what is the criterion of ordinariness or normality? At least a beginning is made in saying that a belief is *unordinary* if it would not be given as a reason for the action *it in fact would explain* if it were conscious: it is not a reason that the agent would, or perhaps could, sensibly give for what he does. And the difficulty, in a way, with Collins's example is that one could very easily cite as a reason for one's conduct that one believed competition was dangerous.

Let us consider, then, Alexander's example of a man lunging at lampposts with his umbrella. Perhaps, like Collins's imaginary example, this is not intended to be taken with clinical exactitude as a routine symptom. Seeing someone behaving that way we might rationalize his conduct by supposing him to be practicing fencing moves, or trying to unstick his umbrella, or, ineffectually, trying to impale fireflies. These would all be rational enough, but the truth is that it is to be explained through his oedipus complex: I want to kill my father, who is my rival for my mother's love, but since I cannot admit either the incestuous wish nor the parricidal one to myself—indeed, am not conscious of it—I find some substitute way of gratifying my wish, in this instance lunging away at lampposts. And "I want to kill my father" could not be offered as a reason for lunging at lampposts unless I espoused some special magical theory and believed my behavior was a means to that, which is unlikely. The normal pattern of explanation in the case of action is this: I do a because I want b to happen, from which it is plausible to suppose that I also believe a to be a good means to b, or at least not inconsistent with the production of b.

Imagine I see a man posting a letter. The very use of the word *posting* implies that he intends the letter to arrive at a destination and regards putting it in a mailbox as a good way to ensure that that happens. If I see a man putting a letter deliberately in a trash can, so deliberately as to rule out the possibility that he is throwing it away, it is reasonable, especially if the letter has an unfranked stamp, to ascribe an error to him: Quixote-like, he has mistaken a trash can for a mailbox; or is just absent-minded. But suppose he says no, he has no confidence in the postal system, or he has more confidence in the department of sanitation than in the postal service and believes that his action is a means to having his letter arrive at its intended destination. Then, apart from my wondering why he has bothered to put a stamp on the letter, I can regard his behavior as rational; it is just his beliefs that are devious or false. But in any case, R counts as a reason for b only if the bridging beliefs can be attributed to a person. And the question is: Can they be so attributed in Alexander's case?

I think that what Alexander brings out is that we do not suppose the lunger *unconsciously* to hold the bridging belief that is required to rationalize his conduct. Or we do so only if we adhere to the universal applicability of the model just sketched, and resort to the unconscious system in order to assure that it applies in every instance, whereas it is not plain that this is the case here. If it were, the behavior would be rational enough. As is more plausible, the bridging belief is not even unconsciously held. "The behavior," writes Alexander," does not seem to be related to the alleged reasons in the way in which ordinary behavior is related to ordinary good reasons for it." But then he does not tell us how it is related to its reasons, only suggesting, in the manner of Paradigm Case argumentation, that we cannot call neurotic behavior rational without changing the meaning either of "good reason" or "rational" in some unhelpful way.[6]

Nevertheless, Alexander does, through his examples, suggest a partial analysis of irrational behavior, which after all is what we are after: b is an irrational piece of conduct if R is m's reason for b but m does not hold the necessary bridging beliefs. And the question then to be asked is this: If he does not hold the requisite beliefs, in what sense does he *have* a reason for this conduct? In what way can R *be* a reason and yet not connect in any way through his own system of beliefs with what it is allegedly to explain? Unless we have an answer to this, we still have no very clear picture of irrational behavior. My

6. To be fair, Alexander's polemic is against those who regard all action as rational *from the point of view of the agent,* so the question is not *whether* it is rational, only whether the reasons are always "reasonable" from *our* point of view. Alexander is saying, in effect, that there is something wrong in calling every action rational in this extended sense; and there, I think, he is right.

claim is that Freud gives us such an answer, and indeed, we have already established the way in which this answer works. To this I now turn.

III

It is widely appreciated that Freud believed that dreams, as well as symptoms, were fulfillments of unconscious wishes, wishes that, though active enough to continue to cause conduct of a highly symbolical order, were not available to the person whose wishes they were: they were not so much forgotten as repressed, the wishes themselves being so forbidden or threatening that their owner could not admit to having them. In dreams especially, it is important to distinguish the *manifest dream content,* which is in some measure epiphenomenal, from the latent dream thought, itself housed in the unconscious, which stands to it in a causal relation and also in one further, more semantical relationship, which I would like to spell out.

Let the unconscious element be $W(p)$—the wish-that-p-be-the-case. Let the manifest element be $W(p^*)$—the wish-that-p-be-represented-as-fulfilled. But matters are not so simple as, say, wanting a glass of water and dreaming that one in fact has a glass of water: p itself undergoes a transformation as it passes the barrier from unconscious to conscious, and in fact this transformation is all that concerns me now. In *some* way, it is a very heavily disguised form of p, since there is no direct way that p can come to consciousness: Freud supposes it would be too painful, and indeed, that one would wake up, one function of dreams being to preserve sleep while allowing the repressed wish to rise transfigured to consciousness. Let the transfiguration of p be p^*. Freud at one point thought p^* might plausibly be a translation of p, the unconscious and conscious systems standing to one another as two languages do. He then abandoned this theory in *The Interpretation of Dreams* in favor of another one, which retains just the sorts of properties of representations I have been discussing. In the following excerpt, he now supposes that *p** is a rebus on *p:*

> The dream-thoughts and the dream-content are presented to us like two versions of the same subject-matter in two different languages. Or, more properly, the dream-content seems like another transcript of the dream-thoughts into another mode of expression, whose characters and syntactic laws it is our business to discover. . . . The dream-content . . . is expressed as it were in a pictographic script, the characters of which have to be transposed individually into the language of the dream-thoughts. If we attempted to read these characters according to their pictorial value instead of according to their symbolic relation, we should clearly be led into error. . . . A dream is a picture-puzzle of this sort and our predecessors in the field of dream-interpretation have made the mistake of treating the rebus as a pictorial composition: and as such it has seemed to them nonsensical and worthless. [1900, pp. 277–78]

A rebus is a very elementary sort of puzzle, in which the 'solution' is a sentence, the words of which are sounded in such a way as to generate homonyms that can be given pictorial representation—as "pick" in "take your pick" has the homonym of "pick" as in "pick and shovel" and can thus be represented via a picture of one. We solve the rebus by pronouncing the words that go with the individual pictures, replacing these with homonyms, and getting a spoken sentence that makes sense—the solution of the rebus. Usually, the pictures have nothing to do with one another; indeed, the row of pictograms is nonsense in the typical rebus.

Let me give some examples of rebuses. On the cornice of the house of Jacques Coeur in Bourg are alternate cockle shells and hearts. The French word for heart is *coeur,* his last name. The shell symbolizes the *coquille de St. Jacques,* the emblem of the pilgrims. So Jacques Coeur. In the tympanum of St. Domenic's in Rome is a spotted dog where some prominent religious figure might be expected. This is one of the *domini cani*—the 'dogs of God'—which, of course, is a rebus for *dominicani,* the Dominican Order, for whose leader the church is named. An Italian printer celebrates his fiancée, Caterina, by showing a broken chain on which is superimposed a King. The chain is *catena,* king is *re:* hence *cate-re-na.*[7] The two pieces of the chain correspond to the broken word. The fish is a symbol of Christ, but again, through a rebus: the word *icthos*—Greek for fish—in fact is an acronym for Jesus Christ the Son of God, Savior (Ieusous Christos Theou Hyios, Soter). And so on. Duchamp's L.H.O.O.Q. is a good French rebus, yielding a mild obscenity when the letters are pronounced in French, but not in English. What is important to notice is that none of the *Bilderrätsel* show anything that tells us very much about what the phonetically equivalent solution describes: What have dogs to do with Dominicans, or fish with Christ?

> Suppose I have a picture-puzzle, a rebus, in front of me. It depicts a house with a boat on its roof, a single letter of the alphabet, the figure of a running man whose head has been conjured away, and so on. Now I might be misled into raising objections and declar-

ing that the picture as a whole and its component
parts are nonsensical. A boat has no business to be on
the roof of a house, and a headless man cannot run.
Moreover, the man is bigger than the house; and if
the whole picture is intended to represent a land-
scape, letters . . . are out of place in it. . . . But obviously we can only form a proper judgement of the
rebus if we put aside criticisms such as these . . .
[and] try to replace each separate element by a syllable or a word. [Freud, 1900, pp. 277–78]

It is crucial that the solution of a rebus does not translate. A French rebus shows a man holding in his hand a
large green letter *I—un grand I vert*—which gives as part
of the solution *un grand hiver*—"a long winter," to which
the English description "a big green I" has no phonetic
tie whatever. Lose the language and you lose the possibility of resolving a puzzle of this sort. Think of this invita-
tion, $\frac{P}{20}$ a $\frac{6}{100}$, alleged to have been sent Voltaire by
Frederick the Great.[8] It is indecipherable save in French.
Well, whatever the case, the dream-content stands to the
dream-thought as a rebus stands to its solution. And
much the same is true of symptoms, though with this difference: the symptom is an action whose *description* must
be found, for we will see that the description, again,
stands to the unconscious wish in this rebuslike relationship. I want now to illustrate this with some examples
from the literature.

First, we begin with the famous case of the Rat Man
(1909) (a Holmesian title), a profoundly disturbed and
unfortunate man whom Freud analyzed. At one point the
Rat Man began a peculiar regime. It occurred to him that

8. Voltaire's accepting note was simply "Ga," which riddles out to "*G grand, a
petit*" and hence to "J'ai grand appetit," to which "Big G, small a" has no connection whatever.

he was too fat, and he began to get up from meals and engage in quite strenuous exercises. This was obsessional behavior, though he was able to give a perfectly good reason for doing it—and his own description of his behavior is critical—he was too thick (German =*dick*), and it was this being "thick" that he described himself as trying to change. The fact, I suppose, is that he was not all *that* "dick"—that is, not so thick as to merit that much exercise. Some line had been crossed, as in the case of the compulsive handwasher, for whom the ordinarily perfectly good reason "in order to be clean" seems no longer to be commensurate with the conduct.

In any case, there was something neurotic about the Rat Man's behavior, and what analysis brought out is the following: his belovèd had an English suitor, the Rat Man's rival, whose name was Dick. So in getting rid of *dick* (=thickness), he was in some way getting rid of Dick. It is plain that he had not selected a very efficient way of doing this, and also that he did not consciously believe that that was what he was doing; indeed, it would be absurd to attribute to him even the unconscious belief that in ridding himself of a thick waistline, he was doing his rival in, or the practical syllogism, "I want to get rid of my rival, and reducing my waistline is a good means of doing that. Jogging is said to reduce waistlines: so, I'll jog." Were the matter as simple as that, we would have only a wayward premise to rectify, and instruction in the technology of rival-riddance would take care of the Rat Man's therapeutic needs: what he would be lacking would be common sense or practical intelligence. (Of course, the matter would be different had his lady-love told him that the reason she preferred Dick to him was that he, the Rat Man, was too fat. Then, indeed, his conduct would be rational and even reasonable. But that is not the lethal sense of "getting rid of Dick" that festered in the Rat

Man's unconscious.) The point is that he had no such belief as the practical syllogism requires. Nevertheless, *getting rid of Dick* (the rival) was his (real) reason for running. It is not even a *bad* reason for that, being too insane. And this, I think, is what Alexander has sensed. Speaking of one of the lapses Freud discusses, he writes:

> The woman who read 'storks' for 'stocks' does not appear, by so doing, to have furthered either the end of obtaining children or of concealing from herself her own unhappiness, and it is doubtful that she or others could have seen the behavior as achieving anything except with the help of Freud's theory. . . . In general, similar things can be said about Freud's explanations of neurotic symptoms. If I am said to *x* for unconscious reason *y*, it is nearly always the case that *y* is not the sort of thing which we would normally consider a good reason for *x*. [p. 339]

What is missing in this somewhat grudging account, which I believe is true as far as it goes, is the connection between the unconscious reason and the given one: they are related homonymically, as rebus to resolution.

Second, Merleau-Ponty (whose wife was a psychoanalyst) gives this case en passant (1962, p. 160). A young girl was forbidden by her mother to see her lover any more. The girl stopped eating not long afterward, and settled into *anorexia nervosa,* a quite distressing eating disorder. Crude analysis suggests something like this: by ceasing to eat, she was trying to put pressure on her mother, or even to punish her mother, in a situation in which she herself had almost no other form of control over her life. The fact is, no one wants anyone to stop eating, certainly not one's daughter, and by doing what she (the girl) knew no one wanted her to do, she was asserting her autonomy and bringing her mother to her knees. So considered, her

conduct was rational enough, though extreme, and therapy ought, then, to consist in finding some substitute way
of achieving the same ends—or at least in showing her
the suicidal consequences of protracted anorexia. Those
with any experience in such disorders appreciate how
ineffective such "therapy" is: the patients in some way
cannot help themselves. In this instance, what analysis
evidently revealed was the following. The girl obviously
resented her mother's interdiction and said to herself that
she would not accept it. The actual *form* of the thought
was: "I won't swallow that." *Avaler,* like "swallow" in English, has this metaphorical sense. And not swallowing is
what she proceeded to do, though her reason was to re-
sist her mother's demand. Once more, we find this trivial
phonetic connection between unconscious and conscious
reasons.

On the basis, then, of these examples, and many more
which could be cited, let us briefly sketch the structure of
psychoanalytical explanations. Let R be m's reason for a
piece of conduct (or any appropriate explanandum) that
we call a. R is in the unconscious system, and the fact is
that m has no bridging belief of the sort logically required
by a practical syllogism, according to which R would be a
good reason for a. And R^* *is* a good reason for a, but in
fact it is not the explanation of m's doing a at all. The explanation is through R. But R^* has replaced R, and is
able to do so through the fact that the phonetic values of
R and R^* are *close if not perfect* (as *stork* is merely close to
stock).

Let me clarify this by drawing the contrast between it
and an ordinary or rational explanation, where a is an action and R the reason for the action. In the normal case,
two relationships hold between R and a: R explains (say,
causes) a and a satisfies R. These relations are divided in
the psychoanalytical case: here let R^* be the transform of

R. Then the difficulty is that *R* explains *a,* but unfortunately, *a* doesn't satisfy *R.* Rather, it is seen as satisfying *R*,* which unfortunately does not really explain *a.* The usual reason-action connections are divided between the two forms of the reason, and inevitably, in consequence, the behavior is at once frustrating and puzzling: puzzling because it is not recognized as fulfilling what is its real reason, and because it is only apparently explained by the reason the victim accepts. The person in question is typically disturbed by the conduct, wishes he or she could stop, and so forth: *something* brings him or her to the therapist. As before, I am not concerned with the therapy: all I am saying is that if Freud is right, we must find a reason in the unconscious, a reason that in fact is never and can never be recognized as satisfying the conduct it explains, since that conduct is understood merely as satisfying the rebus-related but wholly irrelevant reason the patient might spontaneously accept or offer. The symptom is like a puzzle that has to be solved. It expresses a thought the patient cannot admit he has. More important for our purposes, the case of the anorexic offers a paradigm of irrational conduct, since it exactly satisfies the conditions we have specified. Obviously, I am in no position to offer any general account of anorexia.

Third, the Rat Man and the anorexic are victims of a truth that is hidden from them, which explains the therapeutic optimism that when the truth is revealed the symptoms will dissipate. Neither of these neurotics is deluded or deceived as such; they are only mistaken as to the real reasons for their conduct. And this is due to a mistake of a more philosophical order, because each applies to irrational conduct a structure of explanation that applies to rational action. The plausible reasons they give for what they do amount to rationalizations of their behavior—in the instance of the Rat Man, for example, that he is "too fat." Thus, they regiment to the structures of practical reason behavior that answers to another sort of model. And so long as they persist in misapplying this model, their conduct will never, because it *can* never, if Freud is right, receive a correct account.

Symptoms, as we have seen, have something in common with at least that order of dream that disguises unfulfilled and repressed wishes, with perhaps this difference. The neurotic is right about what he is doing, at least under *some* description—for example, the Rat Man knows that he is running. He is mistaken only in the description of his conduct under which it can truly be explained. But dreamers are deceived into believing that something is happening which is not, and so are deceived about its causes and explanations. My dog, when he dreams, as apparently he does, of chasing squirrels in Riverside Park, believes not only that he is chasing squirrels but that their presence explains his conduct, if I may be permitted to assign him this degree of ratiocination. And as there are neither squirrels nor chase, nothing of what he believes he is explaining is there to be explained at all. What requires explanation is why he is dreaming and what; and caught up as he is in the dream, he is not aware that what he is caught up in is a dream, and misses the explanandum completely. So he is twice deceived, first in believing in the ultimate reality of his experience, and then in its explanation—like someone who believes that the presence of the palm trees in what he does not know is a mirage is to be accounted for by the presence of water.

Dreams are not, of course, disorders calling for cure, but there are cases intermediate between neurosis and dream, where the symptoms arise from the unconscious but the victim is also deluded, as we all may be said to be in dreams: and this, to a degree, must characterize psychosis. I want to mention as a concluding illustration a case of schizophrenia cited by Freud toward the end of his great paper on the unconscious (1915). Here he cites some findings brought to his attention by his brilliant, ill-starred disciple Victor Tausk. A girl, after a quarrel with her lover, came to him with this complaint: *"her eyes were not right, they were twisted"* (p. 198; Freud's italics). As it happens, the German word for deceiver is *Augen-verdreher*—eye-twister—and the girl went on to say "he had twisted her eyes; now . . . they were not her eyes any more" (p. 198). Freud cites this in illustration of "the meaning and the genesis of schizophrenic word-forma-tion" (p. 198). Again, the girl complained that her lover had *"given a false impression of his position"* (p. 198; Freud's italics) (in German *sich verstellen,* meaning to feign, or disguise oneself); and now *she herself had changed her posi-tion (Verstellen* = to change the place of)—she claimed that in church she had felt a strange jerk and had to *change her position.*

A *hysteric,* Freud writes, instead of claiming his eyes were twisted, would have rolled them, and wondered why; instead of claiming his position had changed be-cause of a jerk, he would actually have *manifested jerky be-havior.* "In schizophrenia," Freud writes, *"words* are sub-jected to the same process as that which makes the dream-images out of latent dream-thoughts—to what we have called the primary psychical process. They undergo condensation, and by means of displacement transfer their cathexes to one another in their entirety" (p. 199). And finally, in explaining the strangeness of the symptom in schizophrenia, he says it derives from "the predomi-nance of what has to do with words over what has to do with things. . . . What has dictated the substitution is not the resemblance between the things denoted but the sameness of the words used to express them" (pp.

200–01). The schizophrenics "find themselves obliged to be content with words instead of things" (p. 204).

IV

"To interpret the unconscious as Freud did," Lacan writes (1970, p. 130), "one would have to be as he was, an encyclopedia of the arts and muses, as well as an assiduous reader of *Fliegende Blätter*.[9] And the task is made no easier by the fact that we are at the mercy of a thread woven with allusions, quotations, puns and equivocations. And is that our profession; to be antidotes to trifles?" "And yet," Lacan concludes, "that is what we psychoanalysts must resign ourselves to. The unconscious is neither primordial nor instinctual; what it knows about the elementary is no more than the elements of the signifier" (p. 130).

Just here, I think, we can perceive a curious blindness in Freud himself, as the very use of the expression *primary process* connotes—as though he were blocked from appreciating the import of his discoveries by a kind of romanticism, as though the unconscious itself were somehow primitive and savage. In fact, the primary process involves conduct on the surfaces of language of an almost exquisitely, ultracivilized order—the sort of conduct that goes into the most mannered of literary productions, anagrams and acrostics and self-referentiality, where letter becomes substance, and the enterprises pursued merely virtuoso, like elaborate palindromes. Even in his late writ-

9. In *Art and Illusion,* Ernst Gombrich has shown that the celebrated duck-rabbit of Wittgenstein made its first appearance in *Fliegenden Blätter,* thence making its way, as Gombrich remarks, to the philosophical seminar (p. 5). Given the influence of Freud and Wittgenstein, the pages of *Fliegenden Blätter* must be regarded as one of the fountains of contemporary thought. I am collecting anecdotes regarding the way in which it penetrated Freud's own idiom, professional and personal.

ings, with a lifetime of accumulated evidence behind him, Freud was unable to perceive this.

The Ego and the Id—the "last of Freud's major theoretical works" (editor's preface)—appeared in 1923. Here Freud writes: "the real difference between a *Ucs.* and a *Pcs.* idea (thought) consists in this: that the former is carried out on some material which remains unknown, whereas the latter (the *Pcs.*) is in addition brought into connection with word-presentations" (p. 20). He then asks the question of how something goes from the unconscious to the preconscious (or for that matter, the conscious), "How does a thing become conscious?" and answers, "Through becoming connected with the word-presentations corresponding to it." A "material which remains unknown" indeed: when it has to be an almost logical truth that if the connection between dream-content and dream-thought, symptom and wish, is to be as I have described it, the unconscious itself must be made of the same stuff consciousness is—namely, *words.* After all, what is in the dynamically repressed is there by *repression,* and what is repressed today was once conscious, and connected then with "word-presentations," if that indeed is the criterion of consciousness. The dynamically repressed, whatever its relation to the id, is not the id. "How could a psychoanalyst of today not realize," Lacan asks rhetorically near the beginning of his essay (p. 103), "that his realm of truth in fact is the word, when his whole experience must find in the word alone its instrument, its framework, its material, and even the static of its uncertainties?"

I am in no position, of course, to vouch for the accuracy of Freud's accounts. I am only interested in drawing attention to what must be the fabric of the mind if these accounts are in fact true—namely, that it is a fabric woven of language, and must be so in the *normal* case if Freud's characterization of the *abnormal* cases has the slightest basis in fact. For the abnormal cases all enshrine a fallacy, broadly speaking, of *quaternio terminorum,* and a consequent substitution of words for things; and, indeed, it is in exactly these terms that we may characterize irrational thought and conduct. But then, as I have argued, there can be confusion of meaning only if there can be clarity of meaning, and only if the vehicles of confusion exchange their identities like twins in an ancient dramatic form and appear henceforward *en travestie.* Not every phenomenon can be a Freudian one, not every explanation a Freudian explanation. But to the degree that it admits *those sorts of vagaries,* we get a glimpse of what the structure of mind and thought must in the normal case be. We are all of us, in our normal conduct, words made flesh.

REFERENCES

Alexander, P. "Rational Behavior and Pyschoanalytical Explanation." *Mind* 71 (1963) : 324–41.

Anscombe, G. E. M. *Intention.* Oxford: Blackwell, 1957.

Collins, A. "Unconscious Beliefs." *Journal of Philosophy* 56 (1969) : 667–80.

Danto, A. *Analytical Philosophy of Action.* Cambridge; Cambridge University Press, 1974.

———. "Action, Knowledge, and Representation." In M. Brand and D. Walton, eds., *Action Theory.* Amsterdam: D. Reidel, 1976.

Davidson, D. "Actions, Reasons, and Causes." *Journal of Philosophy* 60 (1963) : 685–700.

Freud, S. *Standard Edition of the Complete Psychological Works.* London: Hogarth, 1953–61:
   The Interpretation of Dreams (1900), vols. 4, 5.

"Notes upon a Case of Obsessional Neurosis" (1909), vol.
10.

"The Unconscious" (1915), vol. 14.

The Ego and the Id (1923), vol. 19.

Gombrich, E. *Art and Illusion.* Princeton: Princeton University Press, 1960.

Lacan, J. "The Insistence of the Letter in the Unconscious." In J. Ehrman, ed., *Structuralism.* New York: Anchor Books, 1970.

Laplanche, J., and Leclaire, S. "The Unconscious" (1966), translated by P. Coleman. In *French Freud: Structural Studies in Psychoanalysis, Yale French Studies* (1972), no. 48.

Merleau-Ponty, M. *The Phenomenology of Perception.* New York: Humanities Press, 1962.

Schenck, E.-M. *Das Bilderrätsel.* Hildesheim: Olms, 1973.

10

On Overdetermination

BONNIE E. LITOWITZ

This paper is about overdetermination, a term first used by Freud in 1891 and found extensively in the psychoanalytic literature and elsewhere. Freud's work on overdetermination essentially centers on two issues: (1) information in memory is organized in three specific ways; and (2) the pathways to consciousness of, for example, dreams, symptoms, parapraxes, are multiple. In this paper, I attempt to demonstrate the interdependency of (1) and (2): how information is organized will determine the nature of the pathways through it; and, inversely, the possible pathways through the information will be influenced by the very structure of that information. Furthermore, I suggest that the science of linguistics has existing formal rules of sufficient power to capture and potentially formalize the Freudian concept of overdetermination.

The choice of linguistic rules is not arbitrary but, I feel, appropriate, inasmuch as both psychoanalysis and linguistics are concerned with the content and expression of meanings. Language is also the major medium of psychoanalysis, and recognition of these facts has caused an increasing interest in language and linguistics recently. Some authors—for example, Edelson (1972, 1975)—compare the deepest level of linguistic meaning (deep structure) to the unconscious; and movement from deeper to

surface levels is seen as comparable, that is, transformations in language and the dream-work in dreams. The
discovery by Chomsky of two different levels within language (the deep and the surface structure) virtually gave
to linguistics what Freud had given to psychology, that is,
the level of the unconscious. This new distinction of levels, however, is more significant for linguistics than for
psychoanalysis (which already had a level of the unconscious). In contrast, here I focus on what I believe to be
the most powerful advance in linguistic theory and an advance of potential significance for psychoanalysis, that
there are two different kinds of rules available: the
phrase structure and the transformational.

As we shall come to see, only the transformational rules
are powerful enough to formalize Freud's third type of
organization of mnemic information, the type he claimed
was truly "dynamic" (the most difficult to describe but the
most important). It is this type of organization, combined
with the earlier two "morphological" types, which allows
for the creativity and generative capacity of the psychic
apparatus. In the same way, the transformational rules,
combined with the more "static," "morphological" phrase
structure rules, provide the generative capacity in language.

I have tried not to be reductionistic, reducing a psychoanalytic concept into linguistic terminology. Rather, I
have attempted the opposite—not a reduction, but a
statement of an isomorphism of the psychoanalytic and
linguistic systems that would ultimately make it possible
to see language and symptoms/dreams/parapraxes as two
subsystems of a larger system, the psychical, whose "acts
and structures are invariably overdetermined" (Freud,
1913, p. 100; my italics).

I have described what linguistic theory can provide.
Psychoanalytic theory, on the other hand, can provide the
motivational theory gained from viewing all symbolic be-

havior in a depth that linguists usually lack and that has
allowed language to be treated atomistically, even structurally, but not systemically. I believe the examination of
overdetermination that follows can benefit both linguistic
and psychoanalytic theories.[1]

In order to show the isomorphism of these two systems,
I shall borrow a few concepts from general systems and
information theories that prove useful: from general systems theory, equi/multi-finality; from information theory,
redundancy. As von Bertalanffy has said, systems theory
does not seek to reduce elements of all fields into the terminology of one field, but rather to enable models useful
in one field to be used in others, that is, to establish "a
formal correspondence" (1968, p. 85).

Origins of Overdetermination

We are told by the editors of the *Standard Edition* of
Freud that the term "overdetermined" first appeared in
the Freudian literature in *Studies on Hysteria* (1893–95). In
writing on a case of hysteria, Freud noted that: "Almost
invariably when I have investigated the determinants of
such conditions what I have come upon has not been a
single traumatic cause but a group of similar ones"
(1893–95, p. 173). This grouping consisted of memories
related by subject matter and forming a "mnemic symbol
. . . which applied to the whole group of memories"
(ibid.). In a later section of the *Studies on Hysteria,* Freud's
coauthor, Breuer, refers to the "convergence of several
factors" in the etiology of the hysterical symptom: "Such
symptoms are invariably 'overdetermined,' to use Freud's
expression" (p. 212).[2]

1. Sherwood (1969, p. 32) has said that Freud offers genetic and functional
explanations, whereas this paper attempts an explanation in terms of "significance."
2. This is the first published use of the German term "Überdeterminiert."
Freud's first use of the term follows on p. 263. An alternate term, "Überbe-

In the same work, Freud reemphasizes many times over that this overdetermination is the "principal feature in the aetiology of the neuroses" (p. 263). He outlines a definition of what he means by the overdetermination of the genesis of a neurosis.

A typical case might include a traumatic incident which seems to have been forgotten. However, it is actually present in memory, though unavailable—that is, "not at the ego's disposal" (p. 287). It is "stored up in the memory"; "in correct and proper order. . . . the correct connections between the separate ideas and between them and the non-pathogenic ones, which are frequently remembered, are in existence" (p. 287). At some point the nervous system becomes overloaded: *"whether a neurotic illness occurs at all depends on the total load upon the nervous system (in proportion to its capacity to carry the load)"* (1895, p. 131; Freud's italics). A neurotic symptom appears, though in what "FORM" depends upon what "QUALITATIVE" factors of the memories are present in the same way that the overloading depends upon "QUANTITATIVE" factors (ibid.).

> The patient and those about him attribute the hysterical symptom only to the last cause, though that cause has as a rule merely brought to light something that had already been almost accomplished by other traumas. [1893–95, pp. 212–13]

Between the original traumatic event and the presenting of a neurotic symptom, events and memories develop around the original event which cause the symptom to occur (emerge). These multiple but related traumas allow Freud to say that the symptom is overdetermined. In fact,

stimmt," appears on p. 290. The reader is referred to the index of the *Standard Edition*, vol. 24, pp. 339–40, for references to "overdetermination" and to these additional references: 15 : 228–33, 173–74; 5 : 569.

Freud has demanded that all symptoms must have more than one cause (1900, p. 569).

> As you already see, psycho-analysts are marked by a particularly strict belief in the determination of mental life. For them there is nothing trivial, nothing arbitrary or haphazard. They expect in every case to find sufficient motives where, as a rule, no such expectation is raised. Indeed, they are prepared to find *several* motives for one and the same mental occurrence, whereas what seems to be our innate craving for causality declares itself satisfied with a *single* psychical cause. [1910, p. 38; Freud's italics]

Given that "psychical acts and structures are invariably overdetermined" (1913, p. 100), the questions arise: exactly by which causes (nonarbitrary/nonhaphazard/nontrivial), and how are these causes related?

Freud was influenced by Wundt's principle of the complication of causes (see Freud, 1901, pp. 60–61, 61 n. 1). He often spoke of the "convergence" of causative factors (1893–95, p. 263), "a confluence of several sources" (1900, p. 480), and the "combination of several factors . . . aroused from various directions simultaneously" (1896, p. 216). These determinants cluster in a pattern around the symptom "like the grain of sand around which an oyster forms its pearl" (1905, vol. 7, p. 83).

Why one particular pattern and not another? The answer to this question, a variant of the above question, lies in the possible structures of organization. There are three types of such patterning (1893–95, pp. 288–89; the order has been changed from the original):

1. Groupings by a shared quality/property
2. Groupings by linear chronology
3. Groupings by logical arrangements

First, memories of events can be related by time or
space similar to syncretic groups/heaps/complexes
(Vygotsky, 1962, p. 60; or Piaget, 1955, pp. 144–56).
For example:

> The first and no doubt the most important of these
> reasons was that the pain was present in her con-
> sciousness at about the same time as the excitations.
> In the second place, it was connected, or could be
> connected, along a number of lines with the ideas in
> her mind at the time. [Freud, 1893–95, p. 175]

They happened at the same time or in the same place
as the traumatic event and cluster around it as the nucleus. These are "themes. . . . stratified concentrically
round the pathogenic nucleus" (1893–95, pp. 288–89).
They contain some element in common with the nucleus,
either by association of topic or property (the common
semantic field [see Luria and Vinogradova, 1959] and the
usual taxonomic/attributive associative linking). However,
Freud includes the more primitive syncretic linking of
shared time or space along with the usual higher type of
logical groupings (cf.: taxonomic/attributive associations
to genus/species dictionary definitions), correctly perceiving their similarity.

The second arrangement is by chronological sequence.
This use of time is not to be confused with the synchronic
use in the first arrangements (that is, syncretic groupings). This use of time is the strictly diachronic. Freud repeatedly refers to "series of several provoking causes"
(1893–95, p. 212), "*successions* of *partial* traumas" and
"*concatenations* of pathogenic trains of thought" (1893–95,
pp. 287–88; Freud's italics). He speaks of a "succession of
meanings" for a dream, which "may be superimposed on
one another, the bottom one being the fulfilment of a

wish dating from earliest childhood" (1900, p. 219 and n. 1).

This layering represents chronologically ordered memories on a theme "arranged in linear sequences (like a file of documents, a packet, etc.)" (1893–95, pp. 288–89). In a true diachronic sequence of this type, new material will affect old material and change will occur. Just so, Freud tells us that "In the course of years a symptom can change its meaning or its chief meaning, or the leading role can pass from one meaning to another" (1905, vol. 7, p. 53).

The third kind of arrangement of determinants around a symptom nucleus is neither by association of a property or quality nor by a simple linear chronology. It is

> an irregular and twisting path, different in every case. . . . indicated by a broken line which would pass along the most roundabout paths from the surface to the deepest layers and back, and yet would in general advance from the periphery to the central nucleus, touching at every immediate halting-place— a line resembling the zig-zag line in the solution of a Knight's Move problem, which cuts across the squares in the diagram of the chess-board. [1893–95, p. 289]

Therefore, to continue the file-cabinet metaphor, there is not only chronologically ordered material in each file— each file in turn listing a particular theme—but also some form of "cross-filing system."[3] Or, to continue the chess

3. See Litowitz (1975) on some examples of associations/memories, especially relating to dreams, in "cross-filing" metaphor. (Cf. Chomsky, 1965, p. 79: "The difficulty is that this subcategorization [of the lexicon] is typically not strictly hierarchic, but involves, rather, cross classification.")

metaphor, not only the "rank and file" but also the particular movements of the different pieces across the chessboard. To file material or to play chess, it is necessary to possess all three types of information about the system. The first two types alone would be static, "morphological," but the third is "dynamic," "the most important, but the . . . least easy to make any general statement" about (1893–95, p. 289).

Concerning this third type of arrangement, Freud goes on to say:

> The logical chain corresponds not only to a zig-zag, twisted line, but rather to a ramifying system of lines and more particularly to a converging one. It contains nodal points at which two or more threads meet and thereafter proceed as one; and as a rule several threads which run independently, or which are connected at various points by side-paths, debouch into the nucleus. [1893–95, p. 290][4]

Unfortunately, Freud does not pick up this particular thread in his later writings and bring more specificity to what was stated in 1893–95.

He consistently upholds the principle of multiple causality as "a complication of motives," the "accumulation and conjunction of mental activities" (1905, vol. 7, p. 60), using it as a guide in deciding how deeply to delve into material (for example, he is not willing to stop at the Boltraffio solution to the Signorelli-Botticelli puzzle, 1898, p. 294). However, he never directly returns to the various patterns of determinations.

Nevertheless, from later material we can glean some of his further ideas on the nature of overdetermination. Of

---

4. "To put this in other words, it is very remarkable how often a symptom is determined in several ways, is 'overdetermined' " (1893–95, p. 290; "Überbestimmt").

the minimum two determinants, one must arise "from each of the systems involved in the conflict" (1900, p. 569). In the case of dreams, the number of determinants is limitless and can proceed in a one-to-many relation (for example, a single dream-thought is represented by more than one dream-element) or in a many-to-one relation (for example, "each element of the dream to several dream-thoughts"—1900, p. 653).[5] These "threads of association do not simply converge from the dream-thoughts to the dream-content, they cross and interweave with each other many times over in the course of their journey" (1900, p. 653). Nor need the connecting elements be closely related; they can, rather, "belong to the most widely separated regions of the fabric of those [dream-] thoughts" (1900, p. 652).

Freud offers many actual examples of overdetermination of both symptoms (1905, vol. 7, pp. 91–93, 96, 98) and dreams (1900, pp. 417, 452). I shall examine only one example: the analysis of his comparison of three types of condensation forming the visual image of faces in dreams. In one case, Irma in the Irma Dream (1900, p. 107), many female figures merge into one woman's actual face; in another case, Dr. M of the Irma Dream (ibid.), the several parts of different faces form a composite image; in still another case, the uncle with the yellow beard of an unnamed dream (1900, p. 137), superimposed images form one whole in the manner of the Galton familial photographs.[6] These three types of montages represent three different part-to-whole relations. In the first, the whole represents several parts—a synecdochic relationship. In the second, the whole is equal to the sum

5. See also 1900, pp. 283–84, using comparative analogies of an electorate choosing parliamentary representatives versus election by "scrutin de liste."
6. Galton photographed several family faces on the same plate, thus revealing the common (and disparate) features (1900, p. 139).

of its parts—a combinatory or additive relationship. In the third, the whole equals each part or is a class type distilled from the multiple individual tokens—holotypic or hyponymic.

Notice that all these variants can be called metaphorical, giving credence to the widely held belief that dreams, and especially condensation, are metaphorical. As many authors have seen (Werner, et al., 1975; Rubinstein, 1972; Wilden, 1972), however, metaphor simply signifies a metarelation of similarity in one aspect, for example, a shared quality or property. The discussion here of the relations should show that merely to say the relation is metaphoric obscures the deeper and more meaningful variety of part-to-whole relations possible. (That is to say, that the woman figures share their patienthood, the men, their doctorhood or their pied hirsuteness.) Nor is it accurate to associate metaphor exclusively with dreams in the same manner as metonymy is associated with schizophrenia. For although the above examples of condensation are generally metaphoric, the first is specifically synecdochic, that is, metonymic, and the other part of the dream-work, displacement, is considered metonymic (Jakobson, 1956, p. 81). Therefore, both types of relations are operating in the dream formation (and in symptom formation) as metarelations, just as they are in language and all symbolic activities.[7]

These three examples of symbol formation are descriptions of kinds of relations used in nuclei formation.[8] Material within memory clusters is organized by these relations. The examples of the images from dreams illustrate three possible representations of this already-clustered

7. See Wilden, 1972, pp. 50–56, on the interchange of these two relations with examples, especially of Signorelli-Botticelli.

8. See Litowitz (1975) on the importance of relations in the organization of memories to the understanding of the semantics of language and dreams.

material. It is possible that Freud meant the third type of arrangement (that is, the logical, above) to be precisely this kind of internal relation (namely, part-whole, synecdoche) which forms the nuclei in different ways. Or possibly these images exemplify only the morphological nature of the nuclei as described in the first two types of arrangements, and not the dynamic transformation into infinite and novel variations as in the third type of organization.

Of the two types of activity present in the dream-work, condensation and displacement, both are mentioned as exemplifying overdetermination (for example, 1900, pp. 652, 307). However, Freud also states:

> The question of the interplay of these factors—of displacement, condensation and overdetermination—in the construction of dreams, and the question which is a dominant factor and which a subordinate one—all of this we shall leave aside for later investigation. [1900, p. 308]

It never becomes any more explicitly clear what the relationship is except that the examples seem to support the view that the processes of condensation and of displacement are evidence of the principle of overdetermination.

There are two conditions of dream-thought elements that enable them to become part of the dream: (1) "they must be overdetermined" (1900, p. 309 n. 3); and (2) *"they must excape the censorship imposed by resistance"* (1900, p. 308; Freud's italics). We can say, then, that (1) several elements must combine (in one of the three ways suggested) and (2) there is a goal in their combination. That is, the function of the combination of elements Freud had been considering in hysteria is the formation of a symptom. In dreams, the function of overdetermination is to escape censorship.[9] Taken together with Freud's statements concerning the two systems (that is, the Ucs. and Cs.) that must combine (1900, p. 569), we see that overdetermination can also signify—besides the combination of elements—the goal of such a combination, for example, the crossing from one system into another.

> The newly-created common elements of condensation enter the manifest content of the dream as representatives of the dream-thoughts, so that an element in the dream corresponds to a nodal point or junction in the dream-thoughts, and, as compared with these latter, must quite generally be described as "overdetermined.' [1905, vol. 8, p. 163]

Again, in describing the central character of Jensen's *Gradiva:*

> Thus in the very first products of Hanold's delusional phantasies and actions we already find a double set of determinants, a derivation from two different sources. . . . One of them . . . was conscious to him. . . . the other arose from the repressed childhood memories. . . . One might be described as lying on the surface and covering the other. . . . the unconscious determinants could not effect anything that did not simultaneously satisfy the conscious, scientific ones. . . . [These are] products of compromise between the two mental currents. [1907, pp. 51–52]

Such a notion of transformation of material between systems of the mind might seem to depend wholly upon

9. Freud called displacement "the most powerful instrument of the dream-censorship" (1916, p. 233). In contrast, condensation is not "an effect of the dream-censorship," but "traceable rather to some mechanical or economic factor" (1916, p. 173). Nevertheless, the function of both is to enable material to escape the censorship.

the concepts of censorship and resistance, as Freud undoubtedly intended. For indeed, if no such mechanisms were preventing the transfer of material from Ucs. to Cs., why would it not be able to come directly, untransformed, across the intersystemic border?[10]

If we accept that Freud is correct in saying, "It is obvious . . . that multiple determination must make it easier for an element to force its way into the dream-content" (1900, p. 295), then we can reinterpret "easier" in communicational terms. In other words, the more redundant an element is, the easier its transmission (communication) will be. Ideally, one should strike a balance between redundant and distinctive aspects of the elements so that a maximum amount of information will be passed with maximum ease. Freud's earlier notion of "overloading the nervous system" can similarly be translated into communication terminology without recourse to opposing forces such as repression or censorship.

The translation into communicational terms combines the senses of functional load—that is, a ratio of efficient transmission of information—and the interrelatedness of variables. In other words, it combines the fact that there is an optimal ratio of information : redundancy in a given channel with the fact that some variables/elements may seem insignificant at one point but can change to become significant at another (cf. reaching a threshold of tolerance or "step-function" in Buckley, 1967, p. 67). Also, a variable/element may seem insignificant but may actually be serving a delaying function in relation to other elements (cf. "buffer mechanism," ibid.). These are other aspects of diachronicity that must be included in any un-

10. At one point, Freud refers to smuggling across borders and to the "frontier-control commissions" in a pun on this subject (1916, p. 234). Compare with Wilden (1972, p. 328), who uses the same frontier metaphor from a cybernetic perspective, emphasizing the no-man's land between borders.

derstanding of Freud's statement concerning the changes among the possible meanings of a symptom (1905, vol. 7, p. 53). I will deal with the interrelatedness of elements, especially in terms of ordering (cf. "primacy" in Buckley, p. 67), below. At this point I simply wish to show that what Freud described can be explained as the natural functioning of complex open systems and need not necessarily rely on concepts of opposing forces such as repression and/or censorship.

In spite of the fact that Freud insists that the dream is not intended for communication (1916, p. 231)—unlike language, whose aim is to be communicated and understood—his life's work has established that the dream is communication and is understandable. We must leave the intention of the dreamer to one side, in the same way that linguists put aside the intention of the speaker or hearer. The speaker's intention may be to provoke/soothe/convince/inform; nevertheless he communicates and what he says can be understood. The real difference, in terms of communicaton, between dream-as-communication and language-as-communication lies in the structure of the two. Dreams do not have to be socially conscious in their construction; that is, there need not be a surface subject, an agreement about topics, a set order of subject and predicate (or topic and comment), and so forth.[11] Dreams are communication between the system Ucs. and the system Cs., as language is communication between the speaker as metasystem and the hearer as metasystem (of which the other systems are parts). In short, though dreams are idiosyncratic, yet they are communication of the same kind, if not the same level.[12]

11. For a discussion on this point, see Litowitz (1975).

12. Note that Freud claimed that not only "psychical acts," but also "structures" are overdetermined (1913, p. 100)—that is, not just the product but the processes as well.

Therefore, summarizing Freud's original idea of over-determination, we can say: (a) psychical events must have more than one determinant; (b) these determinants (causative factors) must be related in at least one, but maybe more, specific ways; (c) they are related by themes (subject matter or shared quality), by chronological order (superimposed layers), by logical schema (respectively, concentric pattern, linear pattern, zig-zag pattern on one level or through several levels).

Furthermore, this organization of mental activities (overdetermination) serves not only the function of the formation of the neurotic symptom but also the structure of dream formation and other "normal" functioning. For in moving from the traumatic memory to the hysterical symptom, from the wish-fulfillment of the dream-thought to the content of the dream, from the unconscious to the conscious, some rules of transformation must be used. The most general term for the variety of rules possible seems to be "overdetermination." Inasmuch as this term also implies a kind of causality that scientists seek in determining what lies behind surface phenomena—whether neurotic symptom, a sentence, or the exchange of women by cross-cousins—it serves a double purpose.[13]

Uses of Overdetermination: Compendia of Psychoanalytic Terms

It would be a Sisyphean labor to trace all references to overdetermination in the psychoanalytic literature subsequent to Freud's introduction of the term. I will, rather, take various psychoanalytic glossary and dictionary definitions for comparison. Since these compendia of definitions are written by and for, and presumably are used by,

13. One might even say that as a term it is "overdetermined."

those working with psychoanalytic terminology, I am assuming they represent a very general conception of the term "overdetermination." As with any dictionary listing, the entry represents a normative denotation around which individual connotative variants will cluster. I am interested in how closely these entries approximate the observations I have made from the Freudian texts.[14]

Of the four compendia I consulted, Fodor and Gaynor (1969) did not list the term "overdetermination" nor the often-associated term "multidetermination." The three others, Moore and Fine (1968), Rycroft (1968), and Laplanche and Pontalis (1972) all had entries for overdetermination.

Moore and Fine (p. 69) equate overdetermination with "causality" or "production" of symptoms or "any element of psychic life." This element *"may* be determined simultaneously" by conscious and nonconscious ("transference feelings," "drive derivatives," "defensive operations of the ego, etc.") meanings (my italics). Moore and Fine reiterate the above statement concerning multiple causation, mentioning dreams and symptoms, determined by " 'intersecting' lines of latent thought content" and layers of meaning. This is followed by a statement that the term originates from geometry, where two intersecting lines determine a point and three overdetermine that point. As the analogy between geometry and psychoanalytic usage is not exact, Moore and Fine think multidetermination is a preferable term. One cannot help but feel that Moore and Fine have been captured in the metaphorical net of Freud's straight, broken, and zig-zag lines.

Slightly truer to the Freudian origins but too general and too highly compressed is Rycroft's entry (p. 110).

14. Though some authors distinguish Freud's word from his "thought" (for example, Sherwood, 1969, p. 181), I have confined myself to his word alone.

Rycroft states that a "symptom, dream-image, or any other item of behaviour" is overdetermined if: (1) it has more than one meaning, *or* (2) expresses drives and conflicts from more than one "level or aspect of the personality," *or,* "preferably," (3) if several convergent tendencies end in a " 'final common pathway' " or if (4) "various stages of development are superimposed on one another in layers."

Rycroft touches upon several points that Freud has characterized as being not only important to but indeed defining for psychic activities. They have multiple meanings (1 above) because they are representative of the various levels of the mind (2 above, though Rycroft assumes the reader knows the mental systems and the repressive/censoring borders between them); and because these meanings have been accumulated through time (4 above). Furthermore, these multiple meanings are represented in lessened form—that is, there is a constriction to a "common pathway" (3 above). Notice, however, that the organization of meanings, in nuclei/clusters, by themes, and so forth, is not mentioned, nor is the dynamic organization, the "most important" arrangement. The overgeneralization in Rycroft's entry is enhanced by his use of *or.* Even if it is inclusive disjunction, it makes it appear that any one of the requirements can suffice to define overdetermination. Actually, all are included by Freud (plus other complexities); and "meaning" 1 really implies the rest (2, 3, 4).

In the last compendium, Laplanche and Pontalis's, the role of language and its function in psychoanalysis is highlighted. Titled *The Language of Psychoanalysis (Vocabulaire de la Psychanalyse)*, it is often referred to by the French Structuralist school (for example, Lacan, 1956) and other Structuralists for whom language is important (for example, Wilden, 1972). Also, it is the only one of the compendia that cites the original Freudian texts (and the *Gesammelte Werke,* 1942, as well), though not exhaustively.

The "plurality of determining factors" in the "formations of the unconscious (symptoms, dreams, etc.)" is the main definition (pp. 292–93). Two interpretations of this "plurality" are given: (a) multiple causes are necessary, or (b) "multiplicity of unconscious elements which may be organized in different meaningful sequences, each having its own specific coherence at a particular level of interpretation." Laplanche and Pontalis feel that the second is the more generally accepted of the two interpretations. They then go on to integrate the two interpretations, mentioning both the *Studies on Hysteria* and the evidence from dreams. They alone point out that "the chain of associations which links the symptom to the 'pathogenic nucleus' is here said to constitute 'a ramifying system of lines and mɔre particularly . . . a converging one.'" They mention condensation in dreams but not displacement, nor Freud's relating of these terms to overdetermination. They do, however, point out that the source of meanings arises from two different psychical systems and consists of a compromise.

Though Laplanche and Pontalis do not mention the third type of arrangement that Freud had said was so important, they do speak of the nucleus. However, they alone stress the fact that "the phenomenon with which we are concerned is a *result.*" In a discussion of levels, inherent in all comments on systems, it is important to stress that these levels form a hierarchy that has directionality. The unconscious level only appears in the manifestations of the conscious levels. Overdetermination is the *resulting* symptom or dream or behavioral event. It describes the nature of the resultants in ascribing to them a history of derivation that is *not* one of direct linear, one-to-one causation. This point is an important addition made by Laplanche and Pontalis—an observation distilled from the Freudian texts. How is it that it is made only here?

I think the answer lies in the importance of language to these writers. For in language we are accustomed to ambiguity, to multiple derivations, to hierarchical levels.

As we have come to expect, Freud anticipates our thought once again here. He comments on the ambiguity of speeches in *Gradiva* as "nothing other than a counterpart to the twofold determination of symptoms, in so far as speeches are themselves symptoms, and, like them, arise from compromises between the conscious and the unconscious. It is simply that this double origin is more easily noticed in speeches than, for instance, in actions. And when, as is often made possible by the malleable nature of the material of speech, each of the two intentions lying behind the speech can be successfully expressed in the same turn of words, we have before us what we call an 'ambiguity' " (1907, p. 85; cf. 1916, p. 229).

Freud had been interested in language, often using a graphic metaphor (see Wilden, 1972, pp. 43–46) and comparisons from ancient languages (1916, p. 229) and pictographic languages (for example, hieroglyphics, 1900, p. 321; rebuses, 1900, p. 277). In warning against the use of overdetermination as permission to interpret a symptom or the like in an infinite number of ways, Freud uses the analogy of some ancient languages where seemingly infinitely varied interpretations are actually narrowed down to the proper one by context, intonation, gestures, and so forth (1916, pp. 228–33).

Jacques Lacan (1956) has been most instrumental recently in restoring the relationship of language to psychoanalytic theory, which Lacan feels Freud intended and which is now possible through advances in linguistics. Laplanche and Pontalis make this point, reemphasizing Lacan's oft-stated dictum: the symptom is structured like a language (Lacan, 1956, p. 32).[15]

In summary, first, we can see that these general definitions do not include all the material available in the Freudian original. And, secondly, in anticipating the next sections, we can use them to explore three topics that they raise: the relationship of overdetermination to causality and of causality to equi/multifinality; the relationship of overdetermination to redundancy; the relationship of overdetermination to language.[16]

Overdetermination qua Equi/Multifinality

Why should one think that overdetermination is related to equi/multifinality? First of all, some authors, such as Wilden (1972, p. 34) explicitly equate the two terms. Secondly, we have been speaking about causality as the main aspect of overdetermination—that is, what *causes* the resultant symptom, dream-image, and so forth. The questions we have been raising take causality as given, asking: what kind of causality, and, is there more to overdetermination than just the notion of multiple causality? However, human psychic/biological activities are considered open systems; whereas causality is a concept of closed systems, equifinality is a concept of open systems.[17] Von Bertalanffy has stated this distinction as follows:

> In a closed system, the final state is unequivocally determined by the initial conditions . . . this is not so in open systems. Here, the same final state may be

15. Cf. "the unconscious is structured like a language" (Lacan, 1956, quoted in Wilden, 1972, p. 15). Also see Wilden (1972, p. 44): "The symptom . . . is a PARAPHRASE (*Umschrift*)."

16. See note 28 for a brief description of what minimally defines language herein.

17. See Wilden on Althauser's confusion of this point in trying to transpose "overdetermination (from Freud; via Lacan) into Marxism as a causal conception" (1972, p. 336).

reached from different initial conditions and in different ways. [1968, p. 40; also see pp. 132–34]

In fact, von Bertalanffy defines open systems as being equifinal and as obeying the second principle of thermodynamics, that is, the entropy principle.

The change of entropy in closed systems is always positive; order is continually destroyed. In open systems, however, we have not only production of entropy due to irreversible processes, but also import of entropy which may well be negative. [p. 41]

Open systems, then, tend toward increased order and organization, not less. We shall return to the entropy principle later when we consider the relationship of overdetermination to redundancy.

Therefore, simple linear causality that looks back to an initial cause is not adequate to our needs. Equifinality, which looks forward toward the *result*, which has " 'teleological' final-value" (von Bertalanffy, p. 77), is what we need in describing the kind of causality embodied in overdetermination. However, von Bertalanffy points out that equifinality is "but merely a sometimes useful formulation of a fact which can be expressed in terms of causality" (ibid.). Then, equifinality is a kind of causality; but what kind?

Von Bertalanffy distinguishes two main types of finality: static and dynamic. Static finality means "that an arrangement seems to be useful for a certain 'purpose' " (p. 77). Dynamic finality, on the other hand, means "a directiveness of processes" (p. 78), for example: (*a*) "direction of events towards a final state which can be expressed as if the present behavior were dependent on the final state"; (*b*) "directiveness based upon structure, meaning that an arrangement of structures leads the process in such way that a certain result is achieved"; (c) equifinality, "that the same final state can be reached from different initial conditions and in different ways";[18] (d) "true finality or purposiveness, meaning that the actual behavior is determined by the foresight of the goal" (pp. 78–79)—not necessarily conscious.

All these notions are present in Freud's use of the concept of overdetermination. However, this does not mean that we can reduce overdetermination to mere causality, or even to a variant of causality—finality. Sherwood (1969), wishing to dismiss overdetermination as suspect in creating a separate domain thesis that would separate psychoanalytic theory from the natural sciences, suggests that "the concept of overdetermination, far from being an essential feature of the psychoanalytic approach, is one that might well be dropped entirely without loss. It is constantly open to misinterpretation" (p. 184).[19] He gives as Freud's definition of overdetermination: "the causes of behavior were *both* complex (overdetermined) and multiple (in the sense of there being alternate sets of sufficient conditions)" (p. 181). As we have seen, this is inadequate to define Freud's concept. Nor is Sherwood's example of motivation for "Dr. Jones' interest in surgery" (p. 183) very clear. He says: Dr. Jones may be motivated by (1) either love of humanity or sadistic love of inflicting injury; (2) by both together; (3) by both together because

18. Note here that equifinality and multifinality are being treated interchangeably but that actually this definition is of multifinality, with equifinality representing more the "convergent path" notion of Freud's. (See below in text.)

19. Robert Wälder (1936) presents a similar position, claiming that overdetermination would not stand up in the natural sciences or mathematics, and wishing to replace it with the concept of multiple function (p. 51). Multiple function relies upon the *Ego and the Id* model, utilizing character, identifications, superego/ego/id distinctions. In this model, the ego's function is to adapt to reality, and thus Wälder emphasizes multiple solutions to problems.

love of humanity alone (conscious) would not be sufficient without the unconscious factor of sadism. It would seem that 3 is a special case of 2 and that 2 (and 3) would be absolutely necessary to fulfill Freud's requirement since, as we have seen, there *must* be at least two determinants and different psychic systems must be represented in the resulting compromise. Of course, Sherwood has mentioned nothing about the organization on the different (systemic) levels. Thus, as he describes overdetermination it is not very important, but as Freud used it throughout his writings, it is of primary importance: it defines structure on different levels as well as movement between levels.

Overdetermination qua Redundancy

Wilden has pointed out that while overdetermination embodies the notion of equi/multifinality (1972, pp. 34, 38, 203, 322–23),[20] it is also linked to the concept of redundancy in information theory (pp. 35, 38). This is a necessary point to be made since in this way we see the importance of overdetermination to the functioning of open systems—defined by equifinality *and* the entropy principle, a feature of which is redundancy. Wilden relates these two features of the open system to Freud:

More in keeping with contemporary concern for systems and structures than the later Freud's 'ego psychology,' is his early model of primary and secondary

20. Following von Bertalanffy, Wilden differentiates equi/multifinality from causality (1972, p. 43) as distinguishing open and closed systems respectively. Closed systems are determined causally but open systems are *over*determined, that is, allowing of ambiguity. I have tried to show, following von Bertalanffy, that finality is a forward-looking (goal-seeking) causality of the open system. As Wilden observes, there is no traditional classical causality (of entities) in an open ("relational") system, but it is also true that "it seems we cannot do without a terminology of 'because' " (p. 39). Equi/multifinality represents a compromise between these two needs.

processes. More significant than his determinism is
his theory of the 'overdetermination' of the symptom
or the dream, which is a concept akin to redundancy
in information theory and to equifinality in gestalt-
ism and biology. [p. 5][21]

Quoting from Freud's *On Aphasia* (1891, p. 74), which he
says is the earliest mention of the term (prior to the *Standard Edition* editors' claims, used above), Wilden relates
overdetermination to the concept of redundancy.

The safeguards of our speech against breakdown
thus appear overdetermined, and it can easily stand
the loss of one or the other element. [Quoted in Wilden, p. 35]

Any system that is complex and that transmits information—namely, communicates—must necessarily contain
redundance. One assumes, in psychology, that the channel is noisy and also "part of the psychic system is actively
opposing the transmission of the message" (Wilden, p.
37). As I have mentioned above, Freud's "ease" of elements appearing in the dream-content (1900, p. 295) can
be translated into redundancy without the necessity of
tying redundancy to the concepts of censorship and/or
repression. Redundancy is an aspect of the organization
of information. It has survival value for the individual in
that it makes storage and transmission of information
more efficient (easier and surer).

In any nonrandom system, material is both organized
and meaningful. If material is not random, it exhibits a
probability of occurrence. Its meaningfulness is reflected
inversely to this probability of occurrence (that is, low
probability = high meaningfulness; and high probability =

21. See Litowitz (1975, p. 92) for relation of primary/secondary process to
semantic organization.

low meaningfulness). However, probability of occurrence can only make sense if one knows what to expect. That is, one must already know the total field to know how probable is an occurrence of X in that field. Or to put it a different way: if information is a choice between alternatives, one must know the alternatives from which one chooses. Therefore, information represents a relation between what is already present and what may occur. The efficient transmission of information depends upon the spacing out of highly significant (that is, highly improbable) material so that the energy necessary to process significant information will be available. If every element in a message is significant, it will require tremendous energy to understand it, and the loss of even one element, through noise or other exigencies beyond one's control, will endanger the whole. Therefore, redundancy allows some of the messge to be lost or to be so easy that no energy is needed to process it.[22]

It is efficient to have a proper balance of significant/redundant elements to ensure passage of information. Syntax in language is just such a redundant organization of material. For example: it is usually not necessary to wonder what the subject of a sentence is; since you usually know what it is (usually the first noun-phrase), you are freed to deal with the semantics of it. Syntactic organization is evident on all levels of language. For example: third-person singular is marked in English on both subject noun (e.g., *boy* + Ø) or prounoun (e.g., *he*) and on the verb in the present tense (e.g., *hit* + *s*); the feature of singularity is optionally further marked by the articles *a*/*the*. This is so in spite of the fact that the word-

22. Since this paper is not on semantic meaning, I have not separated meaningfulness and significance. See Litowitz (1975, p. 172) or Lyons (1966, p. 299). Also note that in terms of energy consumption, replication media such as TV are "easier" than coded media such as printed matter (see Mead, 1964, p. 283).

order would sufficiently mark *boy* as the subject of *hit* since word-order is stronger in English than the inflectional system (such as the ending *s* on *hits*). This syntactic redundancy of concord and agreement has no significance except to free one from worrying about which word is the subject of the verb.[23]

In this regard, Wilden can say that "redundancy is . . . a function of syntax" (p. 234). Though this statement is misleading unless syntax is very broadly understood to mean organization of elements (that is, symbols, signs) and not narrowly as merely a linear grammatical rule, for example, S→NP + VP. It is true, in the largest sense, that since information depends upon a choice among alternatives, those elements that do not represent a choice are redundant. These predictable elements are capable of being supplied by rules in a system and thus can be seen as 'syntactic.'

In a complex, highly contextual system consisting of shared information, redundancy will be greater than in a simple, acontextual, nonshared system (Wilden, pp. 374, 233, 234). A language is such a complex sytem (as is a human being).

Wilden has correctly seen in overdetermination the two concepts of equi/multifinality and redundancy, which he relates as follows:

> Overdetermination is a communicational concept, sometimes akin to redundancy in information theory. [p. 446]

> So long as the parameters of the system exhibit redundancy, there will be equifinality or multifinality, and this rule applies, not only to language, but to any information-processing system whatsoever. [p. 38]

23. See also text below as an example of "displacement" in language.

However, from the perspective of this paper, which is to reintegrate overdetermination as Freud used it, it is necessary, but not sufficient, to illustrate that overdetermination is a vital term for the exploration of open systems, embodying the concepts of equi-multifinality and redundancy. We must further heed the warnings that Freud gave in reference to allowing just any interpretation (1916, p. 228). If all roads lead to Rome (equifinality) or if "all rivers lead somewhere safe to sea" (Swinburne; multifinality) and if ideas cluster around a nucleus "like the grain of sand around which an oyster forms its pearl" (Freud, 1905, vol. 7, p. 83), how can we map these pathways and model this structure to reflect, as Freud originally claimed, the nature of these types of organization?

Application of Overdetermination: Symbols and Rules [24]

Even though Freud warned against seeking "fixed rules" to transcribe the dream-thoughts, he was arguing more against what have become the pitfalls of machine translation—that is, "word-for-word or a sign-for-sign translation," or some arbitrary rule that, say, deletes every third element or makes a constant substitution, or "representative selection" (1916, p. 173). These kinds of general translations have failed for the very reason Freud had suggested: the process involved "is something different and far more complicated" (ibid.).

This does not mean that rules, as expressions of organization or order, should be suspect. One knows from linguistics that rules can represent structure, especially those redundant aspects that we have here loosely called syntax.

24. I am here exploiting a distinction that Wilks has uncovered in the original German of Wittgenstein's *Philosophical Investigations,* obscured in the English word *use.* That is the difference between *Anwendung* = static use, and *Anwendung (Applikation)* = application (1972, p. 90).

We proceed from a view of mental activity as a leveled metasystem. This metasystem contains two systems: the conscious and the unconscious. As Wilden has observed: "the superstructure and the base, like consciousness and the unconscious, or the signifier and the signified, are of different logical types" (p. 142). And furthermore, the unconscious is a set of rules (pp. 237–38, also see p. 15), which must necessarily be of "a higher logical type than that which it governs" (p. 238). The higher the logical type of rule, the more abstract it will be. The less abstract manifest phenomena must be organized at their own level *as well as* governed by rules of a higher—more abstract—level of logical typing (pp. 238–39).

Then, when we speak here of symbols and rules we are speaking of symbol formation on a given level and also of movement between levels.

As for symbol formation, we have seen above that Freud described several forms of associational networks to illustrate these patterns: groupings by shared quality or property, including time and space (syncretism) and shared theme;[25] and groupings of linear chronology. Elsewhere he has spoken of the grooving of neural networks (similar to "overloading" the nervous system) to imply a patterning by frequency and/or intensity. I have illustrated elsewhere the necessity of stating relations in connecting semantic entities (Litowitz, 1975, 1978), whereby semantic networks would be organized by virtue of these very relations—for example, organization by themes is a taxonomic relation, that by attribute or property is a modification relation, and so forth—and whereby mental productions (for example, dreams) can vary the relations between elements. (See above example of the various faces in dreams and note that Freud called con-

25. Cf. extensional/intentional.

densation "mechanical or economic" [1916, p. 173], that
is, syntactic/redundant.)[26]

The first two types of overdetermination are of this
type—exactly morphological, as Freud claimed. I must insist, however, that morphological does not mean static
like a paradigm; even here a dynamic organization exists.
To merely see the 'nodal-point' of the dream as condensation of, for example, a face, "like a railroad switch"
(Wilden, p. 46), is to fail semantically (see Werner, 1972,
p.278). The railroad switch or concentric circle metaphors are still linear and cannot accommodate nested or
embedded relations. Therefore, these remain Markovian
(cf. Weinreich on the necessity of linking and nesting as
metarelations, 1963, pp. 163–67, 199 n. 33).

The last type of overdetermination, however, and the
movement between systems can only be expressed by a
variety of rules. As the metaphor of chess (the knight's
puzzle) suggests, the third type of Freud's arrangements
is a movement from some point toward some end—that
is, equifinality (Wilden, p. 340, also p. 316). We can define equifinality as the process by which an end or final
state may be accomplished by a variety of pathways
and/or from a variety of origins. See figure 1.

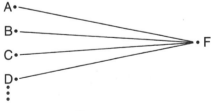

Figure 1

26. Neither Freud nor Jones was able to "understand that 'symbols' are messages" (Wilden, p. 34) and that messages become part of the code (and vice
versa) (p. 269).

And multifinality may be distinguished from the above as its inverse: "Similar initial conditions and/or routing by different paths, may lead to dissimilar end states" (Wilden, p. 323). See figure 2.

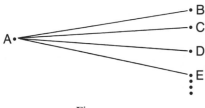

Figure 2

However, notice that neither diagram expresses the modalities of the definitions that are expressions of the relations holding between: points A, B, C, D and routes AF, BF, CF, DF in figure 1; points B, C, D, E and routes AB, AC, AD, AE in figure 2. These figures indicate that rather than simple causality, we have here a complex, multiple type of relation. On the level of the symbol, this would be comparable to saying that we have a complex symbol, that is, one composed of various features (cf. Chomsky's complex category symbol, 1965, pp. 82–84). Again, however, what is missing in such a conceptualization of the symbol is an indication of the relations. A symbol is not overdetermined because it is complex and complex because it consists of multiple parts. Rather, the overdetermination consists in a complexity that is the multiple elements related to each other, to the repertoire of symbols, and to the structure (syntax, code, and so forth).

Let us use only equifinality as an example, assuming that the same kinds of statements could be made for mul tifinality. If we express the relations in the definition, we could restate figure 1 as figure 3.

$$(A) \quad (B) \quad (C) \quad (D) \Rightarrow F$$

Figure 3

Figure 3 embodies the notions of concatenation (or series or successions or accumulation and conjunction or confluence) which are not specified in the definition.[27] Furthermore, any or all initial elements may be expanded from such a simple context-free rule, for example, $A \Rightarrow F$, $A + B \Rightarrow F$, $A + B + C \Rightarrow F$, $A + C \Rightarrow F$, and so forth. However, Freud had said that at least two elements were necessary and, further, that these must represent an element from the two systems (1900, p. 569). Therefore, a new element is added—context. Context-*free* (phrase structure) rules must be replaced by context-*sensitive* (phrase structure) rules.

$$\begin{pmatrix} A \\ B \end{pmatrix} + \begin{pmatrix} C \\ D \end{pmatrix} \Rightarrow F \qquad \begin{Bmatrix} A \\ B \end{Bmatrix} + \begin{Bmatrix} C \\ D \end{Bmatrix} \Rightarrow F$$

Figure 4   Figure 5

Figure 4 represents, as possible equations, $A + C \Rightarrow F$, $A + D \Rightarrow F$, $B + C \Rightarrow F$, $B + D \Rightarrow F$. Figure 5 represents, as possible equations, $A + C \Rightarrow F$, $B + D \Rightarrow F$.

Figures 3, 4, and 5 illustrate the relationship of redundancy to equifinality in that the equipotentiality of arriving at F is expressed in the rule itself (the syntax). However, another form of the principle of redundancy is

27. Concatenations are seen here as linking relations or simple additions, following Freud's *"in addition"* (1900, p.505; cf. Wilden, p. 38). First, other relations are possible, for example, deletion. Secondly, the simple linking *and* of natural language obscures several complex relations: symmetrical combinations of the same class ("Jane and Jerry ran and played"); asymmetrical combinations of propositional elements that are temporally connected ("He folded his napkin and [then] rose to leave"); asymmetrical combinations of propositions that are causally connected ("He missed the bus and [consequently] was late for work").

expressed in relationships among the elements. For example, in figure 5, if A is chosen, C must follow (or if B is chosen, D is obligatory) to reach F. In other words, A implies C in the context of F, and B implies D in the context of F.

It has been considered axiomatic in linguistics that elements not optionally chosen—that is, obligatorily systemic—are redundant (see, for example, Martinet, 1962). However, in more complex systems, elements are themselves complex and are composed of redundant and significant elements/features which are interrelated with each other (for example, phonemic features; see Jakobson, Fant, and Halle, 1951). These features belong to a class that defines the elements, and the elements themselves belong to a class . . . and so forth; for example, features define /p/, which belongs to "stop" class of phonemes, which belongs to "consonant" class . . . and so forth.

As we have seen, part of the sensitivity to context may be called immediate "neighborhood" context—that is, on the same level, such as A, C, F in figure 5. But we must also account for the source of elements from two different systems. Therefore, in figure 5, A, B could represent the class Cs. and C, D could represent the class Ucs., that is {A, B, . . }$_{cs}$, and {C, D, . . .}$_{ucs}$. Semantic analyses have shown this kind of componential analysis to be too simplistic to deal adequately with human meaning systems.

Therefore, we need a new type of rule which is sensitive to context and can deal with complex category symbols. It must operate on these symbols to delete, substitute, or permute them—as complex symbols or as componential groups of features or even on a single feature of the symbol. But this is not all. We also need a rule to correspond to Freud's warning that "the threads of association do not simply converge . . . they cross and interweave with each other many times over" (1900, p. 653). Such a type of rule must express these "roundabout paths from the surface to the deepest layers and back" (1893–95, p. 289). It must also express displacement, a process whereby "a latent element is replaced not by a component part of itself but by something more remote" and whereby "the psychical accent is shifted from an important element on to another" (1916, pp. 173–74).

Such a rule is the transformational rule from generative grammars.[28] An example of this type of rule is given in figure 6.

$$X - _{N_1} [N - _{S_2} [X - (P)_{P_1} - N - X_{S_2}]_{N_1}] - X$$

Structural Description	1	2	3	4	5	6	7
Structural Change	1	2	$\begin{Bmatrix} 4 \\ \emptyset \end{Bmatrix}$	$\begin{bmatrix} 5 \\ +p_i \\ +w_j \end{bmatrix}$	3	$\begin{Bmatrix} \emptyset \\ 4 \end{Bmatrix}$	6 7

$\Rightarrow$

Conditions: (1) rule is obligatory when S.D. is met
(2) X = unspecified structure
(3) $X \neq N_i [N_j, S]$
(4) 2 = 5

Figure 6

28. This type of rule is not unique to linguistics. See Wilks (1972, p. 47) for discussion of similarity in logical syntax concerning "well-formed formulae" and rules of transformation (also, Chomsky, 1957, p. 22 n.).

The theory of language competence that applies here includes at least two levels—a surface level, manifested by the speech utterances, and a deeper level that is more abstract and closer to "semantics." These levels are connected by rules of varying types, but two main types are important: phrase-structure rules and transformational rules. The elements connected, combined, substituted, deleted, permuted, or embedded (nested) by these rules are complex symbols (cf. category symbols, Chomsky, 1965, p. 82). However, the complexity of the symbols, whether semantic or syntactic, is structured in an organized manner, according to principles of the theory (see, for syntactic, Chomsky, 1965; for

Transformations are equations that represent the
change-potentials of relations among elements. Transformations expand the immediate neighborhood context of
left-right linearity in the simpler type rule (that is, con-
text-free/sensitive phrase structure rules). Transformations utilize variable reference of a high degree of
power—being able to "look backwards or forwards" to
different levels of derivation. Transformations can be ordered either intrinsically (for example, if the output of
rule T_5 is the input of rule T_6, then rule T_5 must precede
rule T_6) or extrinsically (by a metastatement). Therefore,
transformations order elements within levels as well as
between levels (the ordering of the rules themselves). Another type of ordering is the placement of conditions on
the rules, such as "obligatory" or "optional." Obligatory
rules must operate, but optional rules can produce style
changes and other variations. Furthermore, there are
some rules that are optional unless a precondition is met
that renders them obligatory; thus, there is a structural
interdependence among the rules, just as there is among
significant and redundant elements.[29]

The most important feature of transformations is that
they operate in these ways while preserving a derivational

semantic, Litowitz, 1975). It is not important whether there is a distinct level of
deep structure (a hotly contested point between some variants of transformational grammar). The other-than-manifest level is necessary in any hierarchical
arrangement. Each level is characterized by its structure or organization (particular to that specific level) but it must be isomorphic enough to other levels to
guarantee the possibility of derivation.

For examples of transformational generative grammars, see Chomsky (1957
and 1965); Stockwell, Schachter, and Partee (1973, including bibliography).

29. Note that the transformations acquired by children are like all other
structural operations that are acquired in that they increase organizing ability
(see Piagetian operations, Piaget and Inhelder, 1969). Children progress from
nontransformational context-free grammars, to nontransformational context-
sensitive grammars, to series of transformational grammars of increasing complexity, until the goal of adult grammar is reached.

history. In other words, though their presence enables
the infinite novelty and variety of the end result, through
them one can retrace the derivation to a deeper level that
was the original source or base of the variations. Though
this base may be a "plentitude of meaning" (Lacan,
quoted in Wilden, p. 446), that does not preclude the
possibility that it too can be represented by a set of relations. In fact, this would necessarily be so. In this context,
then, it makes sense to speak of the symptom or dream as
paraphrase (Wilden), the unconscious as a language
(Lacan), and the Cs. as a transcription (= transformation)
of the Ucs. (Freud).

Though "the end result is independent of the route
taken" (Wilden, p. 323), in that linguistically it is a sentence and psychically it is a symptom or a dream-image,
the notion of transformation can illuminate the variety of
pathways to that end result and the interrelatedness of
the pathways. And only a transformational rule can preserve the deeper unified source while distributing discon-
tinuous elements—for example, auxiliaries and tenses in
natural language (or see example above, third-person singular) or displacement in psychical activity (Freud, 1900,
pp. 305–09).

Therefore, it is apparent that only a transformational
type of rule has the power to answer "The question of *the
interplay* . . . of displacement, condensation and overdetermination . . . and the question which is a dominant
factor and which a subordinate one" (Freud, 1900, p.
308; my italics).

Change

It would be remiss to close this section on the relationship of overdetermination to language without speaking of change. As I have mentioned above, there can be
no real notion of change in a static structure, where all

variables have equal valence. To have change within a
system, elements must be organized in multifarious relations to each other: some significant or distinctive; others
redundant or catalytic, that is, significant only in combination; and so forth (cf. Buckley, 1967, p. 67). As we
have seen, the ordering of transformations in linguistics
provides an excellent example. It is among the redundant
elements that change, including random errors, can
occur productively. If all elements were necessary to
transmit a message or if there were only one pathway to a
goal, there could be no change. The system would be
static and merely reproduce itself endlessly or die out.
The statements that Freud has made concerning the
shifts in meaning (1905, vol. 7, p. 53) and multiple
pathways (passim) could not describe a closed system in
which all variables were of equal primacy or where causality was simply linear.

The simplicity and discreteness of the phonological example make it still the best available: A phoneme is a
combination of distinctive (= significant) and redundant
features; variation occurs among the redundant features
(for example, contextual variants or random/"free"
variants); change occurs among these variations, and this
change can even ultimately alter the total system, even
shifting the distinctive features, since in the end these,
too, are not significant in a reified sense but are only
defined by their (transient) interrelatedness within the
(evolving) system. Jakobson and Halle (1956) have stated
these ideas as follows:

—The auxiliary role of redundancies must not be
underestimated. Circumstances may even cause
them to substitute for distinctive features. [p. 9]
—A distinctive feature is a relational property. [p.
14]

—Thus synchronic analysis must encompass linguistic changes, and, *vice versa*, linguistic changes may be comprehended only in the light of synchronic analysis. [p. 51]

Otherwise, as is so often the case, structural change is simply defined a posteriori by contrasting two synchronic descriptions and allowing the difference in the structures to attest to the presence of change. Jakobson and Halle were able to show the potentiality for change in the seeds of variation within the structure itself in the form of redundancy. Thus, the paradox exists that redundancy ensures constancy of communication *and* also change, both equally necessary to adaption and to survival of the system.

In this sense, then, one can say that by virtue of the redundancy of its organization, its symbol formation, its rules of transformation, and the equifinality of its result, the system is overdetermined.[30]

REFERENCES

Buckley, W. *Sociology and Modern Systems Theory.* Englewood Cliffs, N.J.: Prentice Hall, 1967.
Chomsky, N. *Syntactic Structures.* The Hague: Mouton, 1957.
———. *Aspects of the Theory of Syntax.* Cambridge, Mass.: MIT Press, 1965.
Edelson, M. "Language and Dreams: *The Interpretation of Dreams* Revisited." *Psychoanalytic Study of the Child* 27 (1972) : 203–82.
———. *Language and Interpretation in Psychoanalysis.* New Haven: Yale University Press, 1975.

30. I have artificially separated symbols and rules for discussion. It should be obvious that the paradigmatic/syntagmatic or metaphoric/metonymic (Wilden, p. 58) or associative/syntactic are never separated. Symbols are syntactically related internally and externally as syntax is related paradigmatically.

Fodor, N., and Gaynor, F., eds. *Freud: Dictionary of Psychoanalysis*. New York: Greenwood Press, 1969.
Freud, S. *On Aphasia* (1891). London: Imago, 1953.
———. *Standard Edition of the Complete Psychological Works*. London: Hogarth, 1953–74.
    [With J. Breuer] *Studies on Hysteria* (1893–95), vol. 2.
    "A Reply to Criticisms of my Paper on Anxiety Neurosis (1895)," vol. 3.
    "The Aetiology of Hysteria" (1896), vol. 3.
    "The Psychical Mechanism of Forgetfulness" (1898), vol. 3.
    The Interpretation of Dreams (1900), vols. 4–5.
    The Psychopathology of Everyday Life (1901), vol. 6.
    "Fragment of an Analysis of a Case of Hysteria" (1905), vol. 7.
    Jokes and their Relation to the Unconscious (1905), vol. 8.
    "Delusions and Dreams in Jensen's *Gradiva*" (1907), vol. 9.
    "Five Lectures on Psycho-Analysis" (1910), vol. 11.
    Totem and Taboo (1913), vol. 13.
    Introductory Lectures on Psycho-Analysis (1916), vol. 15.
    "Dreams and Telepathy" (1922), vol. 18.
    Indexes and Bibliographies, vol. 24.
———. *Gesammelte Werke*. London: Imago, 1942.
Jakobson, R. "Two Aspects of Language and Two Types of Aphasic Disturbances." In R. Jakobson and M. Halle, eds., *Fundamentals of Language*. The Hague: Mouton, 1956.
Jakobson, R.; Fant, C.; and Halle, M. *Preliminaries to Speech Analysis: The Distinctive Features and Their Correlates*. Cambridge, Mass.: MIT Press, 1951.
Jakobson, R., and Halle, M. *Fundamentals of Language*. The Hague: Mouton, 1956.
Lacan, J. *Language of the Self: The Function of Language in Psychoanalysis* (1956). Translated by A. Wilden. Baltimore: Johns Hopkins University Press, 1968.
Laplanche, J., and Pontalis, J.-B. *The Language of Psycho-Analysis*. London: Hogarth, 1972. (*Vocabulaire de la Psychanalyse*. Paris: Presses Universitaires, 1967.)
Litowitz, B. "The Structure of Semantic Networks." Un-

published Ph.D. dissertation. Parts appear in "Language: Waking and Sleeping." *Psychoanalysis and Contemporary Science* 4 (1975) : 291–330.

———. "Individual and Shared Meanings." *Papers in Linguistics.* Edmonton, Canada: Linguistic Research, Inc., 1978.

Luria, A. R., and Vinogradova, O. "An Objective Investigation of the Dynamics of Semantic Systems." *British Journal of Psychology* 50, no. 2 (1959) : 89–105.

Lyons, J. "Firth's Theory of 'Meaning.' " In C. E. Bazell, J. C. Catford, M. A. K. Halliday, and R. H. Robins, eds., *In Memory of J. R. Firth.* London: Longmans, Green, 1966.

Martinet, A. *A Functional View of Language.* Oxford: Oxford University Press, Clarendon Press, 1962.

Mead, M. "Vicissitudes of the Study of the Total Communication Process." In T. A. Sebeok, A. S. Hayes, and M. C. Bateson, eds., *Approaches to Semiotics.* The Hague: Mouton, 1964.

Moore, B. E., and Fine, B. D., eds. *A Glossary of Psychoanalytic Terms and Concepts.* New York: American Psychoanalytic Association, 1968.

Piaget, J. *The Language and Thought of the Child.* New York: World Publishing, Meridian Books, 1955.

Piaget, J., and Inhelder, B. *The Psychology of the Child.* New York: Basic Books, 1969.

Rubinstein, B. "On Metaphor and Related Phenomena." *Psychoanalysis and Contemporary Science* 1 (1972) : 70–108.

Rycroft, C. *A Critical Dictionary of Psychoanalysis.* London: Thomas Nelson, 1968.

Sherwood, M. *The Logic of Explanation in Psychoanalysis.* New York: Academic Press, 1969.

Stockwell, R.; Schachter, P.; and Partee, B. *The Major Syntactic Structures of English.* New York: Holt, Rinehart & Winston, 1973.

von Bertalanffy, L. *General System Theory.* New York: George Braziller, 1968.

Vygotsky, L. *Thought and Language.* Cambridge, Mass.: MIT Press, 1962.

Wälder, R. "The Principle of Multiple Function: Observations on Over-Determination." *Psychoanalytic Quarterly* 5 (1936) : 45–62.

Weinreich, U. "On the Semantic Structure of Language." In J. Greenberg, ed., *Universals of Language.* Cambridge, Mass.: MIT Press, 1963.

Werner, O. "Ethnoscience 1972." *Annual Review of Anthropology* 1 (1972) : 271–308.

Werner, O.; Levis-Matichek, G.; Evans, M.; and Litowitz, B. "An Ethnoscience View of Schizophrenic Speech." In M. Sanches and B. G. Blount, eds., *Sociocultural Dimensions of Language Use.* New York: Academic Press, 1975.

Wilden, A. *System and Structure.* London: Tavistock Publications, 1972.

Wilks, Y. A. *Grammar, Meaning and the Machine Analysis of Language.* London: Routledge & Kegan Paul, 1972.

Index

Date Due

APR 27 1981